Coastal Ships & Ferries

Coastal Ships & Ferries

Stolt Avocet

David Hornsby

Ian Allan PUBLISHING

Contents

First published 1964
This edition 1999

ISBN 0 7110 2649 1

Published by Ian Allan Publishing

An imprint of Ian Allan Publishing Ltd, Terminal House, Shepperton, Surrey TW17 8AS

Printed by Ian Allan Printing Ltd, Riverdene Business Park, Hersham, Surrey KT12 4RG

Code 9907/B2

Front Cover: **Irish Ferries** Isle of Inishmore. *J. Krayenbosch*

Back Cover: **Anchor Line PLC (George Gibson & Co. Ltd)** Ettrick. *J. Krayenbosch*

Half title: **Forde Reederei Seetouristik** Wappen von Hamburg. *J. Krayenbosch*

Title Page: **Stolt-Nielsens Rederi A/S** Stolt Avocet. *J. Krayenbosch*

Below: **Brittany Ferries (Truckline Ferries)** Coutances. *M. D. J. Lennon*

Below right: **Mercandia Linierne I/S** Mercandia I. *M. D. J. Lennon*

Preface

After an interval of more than a decade, it is a pleasure to reintroduce *Coastal Ships* to once again chronicle the short-sea fleets operating or owned in northern Europe, as a companion volume to the well established *Ocean Ships*.

Compared with earlier editions of *Coastal Ships*, both the title and contents have been slightly altered to reflect the current shipping scene. The choice of coastal vessels, rather than traditional coasters, will undoubtedly rekindle the long-standing discussion amongst enthusiasts as to what constitutes a 'coaster', a debate which has been accentuated in recent years by the gradual decline of the traditional northern European coaster and of the Captain/owner system.

The days of 'paragraph' coasters built to tonnage or length limits have all but disappeared and many traditional coastal shipping owners are now buildings vessels in the 5-10,000 deadweight range and even larger. Nor is it a simple task to define a coaster, particularly when many small vessels trade on world-wide routes or are chartered to another hemisphere, whilst modern vessels - larger than deep-sea cargo liners of only a generation ago - operate on short-sea routes to the Baltic, across the North Sea or from northern Europe into the Mediterranean.

The section on ferries is less controversial, listing not only the major international passenger ferries and services, but also many of the roll-on and freight services operating between defined ports on a regular schedule. Details of some local ferry routes employing vessels over 1,000 gross tons are also included, together with some of the larger fast ferries which are becoming increasingly common in some areas.

The preparation of this book, in such a relatively short time scale, is a major exercise which requires extensive research and the cross-referencing of many conflicting sources of information. I would like to express particular thanks to friends in the World Ship Society for their help, suggestions and comments, to those shipping companies who responded to my requests for information and to the photographers, particularly Mike Lennon and Hans Krayenbosch, who provided such a wide range of excellent material at relatively short notice.

This book, like all my previous editions of *Ocean Ships*, could not have been achieved without the support and tolerance of my wife, who is 'deserted' for so many evenings and weekends, while I yet again rearrange more information on the PC. Thank you for being so understanding of my enthusiasm, which one day may extend to the redecoration and gardening.

David Hornsby
Southampton, England
June 1999

Glossary

The companies in each section are listed in alphabetical order under the main owner or management company name, followed by the country of origin. Individual ship-owning companies are not given, but subsidiary fleets are separately listed in many cases. Other variations in ownership, joint ownership or management are generally covered by footnotes. Funnel and hull colours are given for some of the principal companies or managers, although these may vary when a vessel is operating on a particular service, or on charter to another operator. Many managed vessels are owned by one-ship companies or owner/captains, each with their own colour scheme which are too numerous to list.

Name   Registered name (variation in translation also shown)

Almost all vessels in the Ferry Section are either twin or multi-screw propulsion, the main exceptions being freight ferries. All vessels in the Cargo Section are single screw motor ships, unless indicated after the vessels name, as follows:

2	number of screws, if more than one
me	diesel with electric drive
gt	gas turbine
wj	water jet

Flag

Ant	Netherlands Antilles	Esp	Spain	Khm	Cambodia	Pol	Poland
Atf	Kerguelen Islands	Est	Estonia	Lbn	Lebanon	Prt	Portugal
Atg	Antigua and Barbuda	Fin	Finland	Lbr	Liberia	Rom	Romania
Aut	Austria	Fra	France	Ltu	Lithuania	Rus	Russia
Bel	Belgium	Fro	Faroe Islands	Lux	Luxembourg	Sgp	Singapore
Bhs	Bahamas	Gbr	United Kingdom	Lva	Latvia	Swe	Sweden
Blz	Belize	Gib	Gibralter	Mhl	Marshall Islands	Ton	Tonga
Bmu	Bermuda	Gnq	Equatorial Guinea	Mlt	Malta	Tuv	Tuvalu
Brb	Barbados	Hkg	Hong Kong	Mmr	Myanma (Burma)	Ukr	Ukraine
Che	Switzerland	Hnd	Honduras	Nis	Norwegian International	Vct	St. Vincent & Grenadines
Cym	Cayman Islands	Hrv	Croatia	Nld	Netherlands	Vut	Vanuatu
Cyp	Cyprus	Iom	Isle of Man (British)	Nor	Norway		
Deu	Germany	Irl	Irish Republic	Pan	Panama		
Dis	Danish International	Isl	Iceland	Phl	Philippines		
Dnk	Denmark	Ita	Italy	Pmd	Madeira		

Year	year of completion — not necessarily of launching or commissioning
GRT	gross registered tonnage — volume of hull and enclosed space (one ton equals 100 cu. ft.)
DWT	deadweight tonnes — maximum weight of cargo, stores, fuel etc. (one tonne (1000 kg) equals 0.984 ton)
LOA	overall length (metres); (- -) length between perpendiculars
Bm	overall breadth (metres)
Draft	maximum laden draft (metres)
Kts	service speed in normal weather and at normal draught -- one knot equals 6,050ft per hour or 1.146 miles per hour
Type	general description of type of vessel

	B	bulk carrier	Dss	dredger - sand suction	Ro	roll-on, roll-off cargo
	C	cargo - dry general	Lpg	liquefied petroleum gas carrier	T	tanker
	CC	fully cellular container	Lv	livestock carrier	V	vehicle carrier
	Ce	cement carrier	R	refrigerated cargo		

Supplementary information

	a	asphalt/bitumen	hl	heavy lift capacity	s	slurry tanks
	bg	barge carrier (semi-submersible)	n	nuclear fuel carrier	t	oil tanks
	c	some container capacity, but not fully cellular	p	pallet/paper/newsprint (often with side loading)	u	self-undischarging
	ch	chemical	pr	pollution recovery	w	wine

Remarks:

ex:	previous names followed by year of change to subsequent name
l/d	name given when laid down
l/a	name at launch or prior to delivery
len	year lengthened
widen	year widened
deep	year deepened or superstructure heightened
rblt	year rebuilt
conv	year converted from type indicated

Additional information in Ferry Section

Pass	maximum number of passengers in lower and upper berthes
Car	number of cars carried (approximate figure depending on size and mix with goods vehicles - see below)
HGV	number of lorries/trailers or rail wagons carried (approximate figure depending on mix)
Type	general description of type of vessel

F	Freight ferry, sometimes with driver accommodation		H	Hovercraft
P	Passenger ferry		M	High-speed monohull
R	Train ferry		T	High-speed multi-hull

secondary

r	rail traffic facilities		h	Bazan 'Alhambra' type
i	InCat		f	Fincantieri MDV1200 type
j	Kvaerner-Fjellstrand 'JumboCat' type.		k	Mjellem & Karlsen type
a	Austral type		d	Danyard 'SeaJet 250' type
e	Auto Express 82 type		s	Finnyards 'HSS' type

Elite-Shipping A/S Arktis Meridian. *J. Krayenbosch*

Disclaimer

Every effort has been made to ensure that information is correct, but the publishers, the shipping companies and the Author accept no liability for any loss or damage caused by any error, inaccuracy or omission in the information published in this edition of *Coastal Ships and Ferries*.

Commodore Ferries (CI) Ltd (Condor Ferries) Condor Express *M. D. J. Lennon*

K/S Difko (Mols-Linien A/S) Mette Mols *M. D. J. Lennon*

PART ONE

Ferries

Name	Flag	Year	GRT	loa	bm	kts	pass	car	HGV	Type	Former Names

Anedin-Linjen — Sweden

Funnel:	Blue with white 'clouds', black top.										
Hull:	White with 'Anedin-Linjen'.										
Routes:	Mariehamn - Stockholm.										

Name	Flag	Year	GRT	loa	bm	kts	pass	car	HGV	Type	Former Names
Baltic Star *	Pan	1953	3,564	93	14	-	1287	-	-	P	ex Minisea-78, Bore Nord-77, Birger Jarl-73

* owned by Scandinavian Marine Services Ltd., UK.

Argo-Mann Ferry Service GmbH — Germany

Funnel:	Cream with white 'E' on broad blue band.
Hull:	Green with yellow 'ArgoMann', red boot-topping.
Routes:	Harwich - Cuxhaven - Tallinn - Turku - Bremerhaven.

Name	Flag	Year	GRT	loa	bm	kts	pass	car	HGV	Type	Former Names
Estraden *	Fin	1999	18,205	163	25	19	12	-	160	F	
Garden *	Fin	1977	10,762	151	19	18	4	1000	-	F	ex Liro Sun-93, Bore Sun-92

Owned by Argo Reederei and Mann & Son Holdings, UK.
* on charter Rederi AB Engship, Finland.

Birka Line AB — Finland

Funnel:	White with separated black, blue, yellow and red angles stripes.
Hull:	White.
Routes:	Mariehamn - Stockholm.

Name	Flag	Year	GRT	loa	bm	kts	pass	car	HGV	Type	Former Names
Birka Princess	Fin	1986	21,484	141	25	18	1100	80	0	P	

Bornholms Trafikken — Denmark

Funnel:	Black with white band on broad red band.
Hull:	White with 'Bornholms Trafikken'.
Routes:	Ronne - Copenhagen; Ronne - Ystad; Ronne - Mukran; Ronne - Swinoujscie (from summer 1999).

Name	Flag	Year	GRT	loa	bm	kts	pass	car	HGV	Type	Former Names
Jens Kofoed	Dmk	1979	12,131	121	22	17	1500	270	30	P	
Peder Olsen	Dmk	1974	8,586	119	19	21	1150	284	50	P	ex Prince-91, Wasa Prince-91, The Viking-89, Kalle III-83, l/a Kattegat II
Povl Anker	Dmk	1978	12,131	121	22	17	1500	270	30	P	

Brittany Ferries — France

Funnel:	White with blue over orange bands, interrupted by similar 'flag'.
Hull:	White with blue above orange bands.
Routes:	Roscoff - Plymouth; Caen - Portsmouth; St. Malo - Portsmouth; Plymouth - Santander; Portsmouth - Santander.

Name	Flag	Year	GRT	loa	bm	kts	pass	car	HGV	Type	Former Names
Barfleur	Fra	1992	20,133	158	23	19	1212	304	66	P	
Bretagne	Fra	1989	24,534	151	19	19	2056	580	-	P	
Duc De Normandie	Fra	1978	9,677	131	23	21	1500	354	78	P	ex Prinses Beatrix-86
Normandie	Fra	1992	27,541	161	26	20	2120	680	-	P	
Quiberon	Fra	1975	8,314	129	21	22	1140	250	30	P	ex Nils Dacke-82
Val De Loire	Fra	1987	31,395	161	28	20	2280	570	-	P	ex Nils Holgersson-93

Truckline Ferries

Funnel:	White with yellow flag having black/white disc interupting white line.
Hull:	Black with yellow 'Truckline' interrupting broad yellow band.
Routes:	Cherbourg - Poole.

Name	Flag	Year	GRT	loa	bm	kts	pass	car	HGV	Type	Former Names
Coutances	Fra	1978	6,507	126	18	18	12	0	171	F	(len-86)
Normandie Shipper	Fra	1973	4,078	142	19	18	0	-	-	F	ex Kirk Shipper-89, Stena Shipper-88, Caribe Express-88, Speedlink Vanguard-87, Stena Shipper-80, Alpha Express-80, Union Wellington-77, l/a Stena Shipper (len-77)

See also vessel on charter to Falcon Distribution Group.

Bornholms Trafikken Povl Anker. *M. D. J. Lennon*

Brittany Ferries Val De Loire. *M. D. J. Lennon*

Caledonian MacBrayne Ltd.

UK

Funnel:	Red with red lion rampant on yellow disc, black top.
Hull:	Black with white 'Caledonian MacBrayne', red boot-topping.
Routes:	Ardrossan - Brodick; Gourock - Dunoon; Kennacraig - Islay - Colonsay;
	Mallaig - Syke; Mallaig - Barra - South Uist; Oban - Barra - South Uist;
	Oban - Colonsay; Oban - Mull - Coll - Tiree; Bute - Largs; Arran; Ullapool - Lewis;
	Skye - Harris; Wemyss Bay - Bute; * Ballycastle - Cambeltown.

Name	Flag	Year	GRT	loa	bm	kts	pass	car	HGV	Type	Former Names
Caledonian Isles	Gbr	1993	5,221	94	16	15	1000	110	0	P	
Clansman	Gbr	1998	5,400	101	17	16	634	90	-	P	
Hebridean Isles	Gbr	1985	3,040	85	16	15	510	-	10	P	
Isle of Arran	Gbr	1984	3,296	85	16	15	800	80	0	P	
Isle of Lewis	Gbr	1995	6,753	101	19	18	968	122	0	P	
Isle of Mull	Gbr	1988	4,719	90	16	15	1000	33	10	P	
Lord of The Isles	Gbr	1989	3,504	85	16	16	536	60	0	P	
Pioneer	Gbr	1974	1,088	67	14	16	356	28	7	P	

Numerous smaller vessels.

Cenargo Ltd.

UK

Merchant Ferries

Funnel:	White with blue 'MF'.
Hull:	Blue with blue 'MERCHANT FERRIES' on white superstructure.
Routes:	Heysham - Dublin; Liverpool - Dublin.

Name	Flag	Year	GRT	loa	bm	kts	pass	car	HGV	Type	Former Names
Brave Merchant	Iom	1998	22,046	180	25	24	252	-	155	F	
Dawn Merchant	Iom	1998	22,046	180	25	24	252	-	155	F	
Merchant Bravery	Bhs	1978	9,368	135	22	17	6	56	106	F	ex Jolly Giallo-93, Norwegian Crusader-82, Jolly Giallo-82, Norwegian Crusader-80, I/a Stevi
Merchant Brilliant	Bhs	1979	9,368	133	22	17	6	56	106	F	ex Jolly Bruno-93, Norwegian Challenger-82
Merchant Venture *	Iom	1979	6,056	119	20	17	12	34	55	F	ex Merchant Isle-87, Argentea-87, Med Adriatica-85, Farman-82 (deep-88)
Saga Moon	Gib	1984	7,746	135	18	15	12	50	72	F	ex Lidartindur-86 (len-95)

Two further newbuildings due from Spanish builders in 1999 and 2000.

Belfast Freight Ferries

Funnel:	Blue with blue 'S' on white waving flag.
Hull:	Blue with white 'BELFAST FREIGHT FERRIES'.
Routes:	Heysham - Belfast.

Name	Flag	Year	GRT	loa	bm	kts	pass	car	HGV	Type	Former Names
Merle	Bhs	1985	9,088	120	21	14	12	49	94	F	ex Sally Euroroute-96, Bazias 3-93, Balder Sten-85
River Lune	Bhs	1983	7,765	121	21	18	12	49	94	F	ex Stena Topper-93, Salar-93, Stena Topper-89, Bazias 7-89, Balder Vik-86
Spheroid	Iom	1971	7,171	124	19	19	12	0	52	F	ex Niekirk-87, Roro Trader-85, Starmark-81 (len-90)

Cobelfret NV

Belgium

Funnel:	Yellow with red 'C' on white diamond on blue band.
Hull:	Light grey with blue 'cobelfret ferries', red boot-topping.
Routes:	Zeebrugge - Purfleet; Zeebrugge - Immingham.

Name	Flag	Year	GRT	loa	bm	kts	pass	car	HGV	Type	Former Names
Amandine	Gbr	1977	14,715	173	22	15	12	-	150	F	exVega-98, Bruarfoss-96, Persia-88, Merzario Persia-86
Belvaux	Lux	1979	6,832	117	19	14	12	520	150	F	
Clementine	Lux	1997	23,986	162	26	17	0	654	156	F	
Cymbeline	Pa	1992	11,866	147	21	17	0	400	160	F	
Eglantine	Pan	1990	10,035	147	21	14	10	790	120	F	
Loverval	Lux	1978	10,931	161	18	17	12	150	112	F	ex Matina-85, Vallmo-83
Rodona **	Swe	1980	6,568	136	17	14	6	300	82	F	ex Balder Dona-84

Cobelfret NV Belvaux. *M. Beckett*

Color Line AS Peter Wessel. *J. Krayenbosch*

Name	Flag	Year	GRT	loa	bm	kts	pass	car	HGV	Type	Former Names
Symphorine	Pa	1988	10,030	147	21	14	0	350	125	F	
Sapphire **	Swe	1980	6,568	136	17	14	6	300	82	F	ex Azua-87, Rovinga-85, Balder Vinga-84 (len-82)
Sea Crusader *	Gbr	1996	23,986	162	26	17	0	654	157	F	ex Celestine-96
Undine	Lux	1991	11,854	147	21	15	10	760	130	F	
Valentine	Gbr	1999	23,987	162	26	17	0	654	157	F	

Managed by EuroShip Services subsidiary
* on charter to British government or ** owned by Engstrom Shipping AB, Sweden.

Color Line AS   Norway

Funnel:	White with small blue over green, yellow and red waves inside large blue 'C'.
Hull:	Blue with white 'Color Line' and multi-coloured vessels name on white superstructure; fast ferries - white with 'ColorLineExpress'.
Routes:	Frederikshavn - Larvik; Frederikshavn - Moss; Hirtshals - Kristiansand; Hirtshals - Moss; Hirtshals - Oslo; Skagen - Larvik; Oslo - Kiel.

Name	Flag	Year	GRT	loa	bm	kts	pass	car	HGV	Type	Former Names
Christian IV	Nor	1982	21,699	153	24	20	2000	550	110	P	ex Bayard-90, Olau Hollandia-90
Color Festival	Nor	1985	34,417	168	28	22	2000	440	88	P	ex Silja Karneval-94, Svea-92
Kronprins Harald	Nor	1987	31,914	166	28	22	1481	700	100	P	
Pegasus II *	Ita	1997	4,000	95	16	36	600	173	0	Mh	
Peter Wessel	Nor	1981	29,706	168	25	19	2200	650	42	P	ex Wasa Star-84
Prinsesse Ragnhild	Nor	1981	35,438	202	24	21	1875	745	53	P	(len-92)
Silvia Ana L *	Bhs	1996	7,895	125	19	38	1250	238	12	Mh	
Skagen	Nor	1975	12,333	130	20	19	1238	400	22	P	ex Borgen-90 (len-82)

Owned by B. Skaugen Shipping Group.
* on seasonal charter.

Scandi Line, Norway

Funnel:	White with blue 'S' and red wave, black top.
Hull:	White with blue 'Scandi Line' and broad red band on top of blue boot-topping.
Routes:	Sandefjord - Stromstad;

Name	Flag	Year	GRT	loa	bm	kts	pass	car	HGV	Type	Former Names
Bohus	Nor	1971	8,772	123	20	20	1400	250	40	P	ex Lion Princess-94, Europafarjan II-87, Europafarjan-85, Prinsessan Desiree-83
Sandefjord	Nor	1965	5,678	100	18	18	1205	200	32	P	ex Fenno Star-92, Scandinavia-90, Terje Vigen-86, Viking III-82

Commodore Ferries (CI) Ltd.   UK

Funnel:	Blue with gold lion symbol.
Hull:	Blue with white ' Commodore', grey boot-topping.
Routes:	Portsmouth - Channel Islands.

Name	Flag	Year	GRT	loa	bm	kts	pass	car	HGV	Type	Former Names
Commodore Clipper	Bhs	1999	12,500	125	23	19	480	200	105	P	
Commodore Goodwill *	Bhs	1996	11,166	126	21	18	12	0	94	F	
Island Commodore *	Bhs	1995	11,166	126	21	18	12	0	95	F	

* on charter from Goliat Shipping AS (Nils Hugo Sand), Norway.

Condor Ferries

Funnel:	White.
Hull:	White with blue/red 'CONDOR' or 'CONDOR Ferries', red and blue bands above blue boot-topping.
Routes:	Jersey - St. Malo; Poole - Jersey - St. Malo; Poole - Guernsey - Jersey; Jersey - Sark;

Name	Flag	Year	GRT	loa	bm	kts	pass	car	HGV	Type	Former Names
Condor 10 *	Sgp	1993	3,241	74	26	38	574	90	-	Ti	
Condor Express	Sgp	1996	5,005	87	26	39	776	200	-	Ti	
Condor Vitesse	Sgp	1997	5,005	87	26	39	776	200	-	Ti	ex InCat 044-98
Havelet	Bhs	1977	6,918	110	17	16	500	205	40	P	ex Cornouailles-89

Also smaller Condor 8 (1988/ 387 grt 300 px), Condor 9 (1990/752 grt 450 px) and Condor France (1993/585 grt 350 px)
* owned by and currently operating in New Zealand waters.

Color Line AS Silvia Ana L. *J. Krayenbosch*

Color Line AS (Scandi Line) Bohus. *M. D. J. Lennon*

DFDS A/S Denmark
DFDS Seaways

Funnel: White with three diagonal blue stripes and white Maltese cross on dark blue disc.
Hull: White with 'DFDS SEAWAYS' and three diagonal blue stripes, blue boot-topping.
Routes: Copenhagen - Oslo; Helsingborg - Oslo; Esbjerg - Harwich; Hamburg - Harwich;
               Gothenburg - Kristiansand - Newcastle; Amsterdam - Newcastle;
               Hamburg - Newcastle (summer).

Name	Flag	Year	GRT	loa	bm	kts	pass	car	HGV	Type	Former Names
Admiral of Scandinavia	Bhs	1976	18,888	156	24	21	1135	404	45	P	ex Hamburg-97, Kronprins Harald-87
Crown of Scandinavia	Dis	1994	35,498	169	28	18	2136	400	80	P	I/a Thomas Mann
Dana Anglia	Dmk	1978	19,321	153	24	21	1370	470	0	P	
King of Scandinavia	Dis	1974	13,336	152	20	18	1040	320	0	P	ex Venus-94, Scandinavica-90, Tarak L-89, Scandinavica-89, Stena Scandinavica-89, Prinsessan Birgitta-82
Prince of Scandinavia	Dis	1975	21,545	182	24	24	1692	375	70	P	ex Tor Britannia-91, Scandinavian Star-82, Tor Britannia-81
Princess of Scandinavia	Dis	1976	21,545	182	24	26	1704	375	70	P	ex Tor Scandinavia-91, World Wide Expo-83, Tor Scandinavia-82
Queen of Scandinavia	Dmk	1981	33,575	166	29	20	1900	450	86	P	ex Finlandia-90

DFDS Transport & DFDS Baltic Line

Funnel: Blue with white Maltese cross inside white ring.
Hull: Blue with white 'DFDS' or DFDS TRANSPORT', red boot-topping.
Routes: Copenhagen - Klaipeda; Fredericia - Klaipeda; Kiel - Klaipeda;
               Esbjerg - Immingham (DFDS North Sea Line); Cuxhaven - Immingham(Elbe-Humber RoLine);
               Esbjerg - Harwich.

Name	Flag	Year	GRT	loa	bm	kts	pass	car	HGV	Type	Former Names
Dana Cimbria	Dis	1986	12,189	145	22	17	12	-	150	F	I/a Mercandian Express II
Dana Corona *	Nis	1972	12,110	138	22	18	12	-	-	F	ex Seahorse-92, Finnrover-88, Jalina-87, Kotka Lily-85, Nedlloyd Rockanje-83, Rheinfels-77, Antares-75
Dana Futura	Ita	1996	18,469	183	25	19	12	0	156	F	
Dana Hafnia	Dis	1979	11,125	161	18	16	12	542	121	F	ex Nordborg-94, Belinda-88, Linne-85
Dana Maxima	Dis	1978	17,068	173	21	17	12	-	183	F	(len-95)
Dana Minerva	Dis	1978	21,213	183	24	18	-	-	171	F	ex Boracay-98, Karawa-87, Saudi Express-86, Jolly Avorio-86, Saudi Express-83, Bandar Abbas Express-80

* on charter from Goliat Shipping AS (Nils Hugo Sand), Norway.

DFDS Tor Line

Funnel: Blue with white Maltese cross inside white ring.
Hull: Blue with white 'DFDS TOR LINE', red boot-topping.
Routes: Gothenburg - Immingham or Harwich (AngloBridge route);
               Gothenburg - Ghent (EuroBridge route); Rotterdam - Immingham (ShortBridge route);
               Oslo - Larvik - Frederikstad - Kristiansand - Fexixstowe - Rotterdam;
               Oslo - Heroya - Kristiansand - Immingham - Zeebrugge.

Name	Flag	Year	GRT	loa	bm	kts	pass	car	HGV	Type	Former Names
Tor Anglia	Swe	1977	17,492	172	22	15	12	-	196	F	ex African Gateway-87, Nordic Wasa-87, Tana-83, Merzario Gallia-81 (len 79 & 89)
Tor Belgia	Swe	1978	21,491	193	25	16	12	200	186	F	ex Tor Britannia-99, Maersk Kent-92, Kamina-90, Ville du Havre-87, Foss Havre-81, Ville du Havre-78
Tor Caledonia	Dis	1976	14,424	189	21	15	12	-	160	F	ex Galloway-85, Gothic Wasa-85, Tor Caledonia-84 (len-90)

DFDS A/S Admiral of Scandinavia. *J. Krayenbosch*

DFDS A/S Dana Cimbria. *M. D. J. Lennon*

Name	Flag	Year	GRT	loa	bm	kts	pass	car	HGV	Type	Former Names
Tor Dania	Dis	1978	21,850	194	25	19	12	-	207	F	ex Brit Dania-93, Tor Dania-93, Maersk Essex-92, Dana Hafnia-89, Railo-88, G and C Express-88, Ville de Dunkerque-86, Foss Dunkerque-81, Ville de Dunkerque-79 (len-95)
Tor Flandria †	Swe	1981	33,652	194	28	19	-	-	1050	F	ex Stena Partner-98, American Falcon-98, Zenit Clipper-86, Finnclipper-83
Tor Gothia	Swe	1971	12,259	163	21	16	12	-	120	F	(len-77)
Tor Hollandia	Swe	1973	12,254	163	21	16	12	-	120	F	ex Tor Dan-93, Tor Dania-92, Bandar Abbas Express-78, Tor Dania-75 (len-77)
Tor Humbria	Nis	1978	20,165	183	24	18	-	-	-	F	ex Borac-99, Finneagle-87, Fosseagle-85, Abuja Express-83, Emirates Express-81
Tor Norvegia	Nis	1975	12,494	168	21	18	-	-	-	F	ex Balduin-99 (len-80)
Tor Scandia	Swe	1981	33,652	194	28	19	-	-	1050	F	ex Stena Porter-98, American Condor-98, Zenit Express-84, Kuwait Express-83
Tor Selandia	Dis	1999	24,196	198	26	21	12	-	200	F	
Tor Suecia	Swe	1999	24,000	198	26	23	-	-	200	F	
Tor ???????	???	1999	21,700	198	26	23	-	-	200	F	

* on charter from B&N Rederi and † on 5 year bareboat charter from Stena Group.

K/S Difko
Mols-Linien A/S

Denmark

Funnel:	White with yellow 'ML' symbol over blue diamond.
Hull:	White with blue 'Mols-Linien' above narrow blue band.
Routes:	Ebeltoft-Sjaellands Odde.

Name	Flag	Year	GRT	loa	bm	kts	pass	car	HGV	Type
Mai Mols	Dmk	1996	3,971	76	23	43	450	120	-	Ts
Maren Mols	Dmk	1996	14,221	136	25	19	600	344	100	P
Mette Mols	Dmk	1996	14,221	136	25	19	600	344	100	P
Mie Mols	Dmk	1996	3,971	78	23	43	450	120	-	Ts

Scandlines have acquired a 40% share in the company; see also entry under Scandlines AG (Cat-Link A/S).

Vognmandsruten

Funnel:	Black stovepipes only.
Hull:	Red with red 'sun' symbol on white superstructure.
Routes:	Rodby - Puttgarden.

Name	Flag	Year	GRT	loa	bm	kts	pass	car	HGV	Type	Former Names
Difko Fyn	Dmk	1989	4,101	96	17	12	253	36	30	P	ex Superflex Echo-95
Difko Korsor	Dmk	1988	4,101	96	17	14	253	36	30	P	ex Superflex Charlie-90
Difko Nyborg	Dmk	1987	4,101	95	17	14	253	36	30	P	ex Superflex Alpha-90
Difko Storebaelt	Dmk	1989	4,296	96	17	14	300	85	16	P	ex Superflex Delta-90

Operated as joint venture with Stena Line q.v.

EckeroLine

Finland

Funnel:	White with yellow 'E' on blue disc, blue top.
Hull:	White with blue 'ECKERO LINE' and 'E' symbol interupting blue above yellow bands, blue boot-topping.
Routes:	Eckero - Grisslehamn; Tallinn - Helsinki.

Name	Flag	Year	GRT	loa	bm	kts	pass	car	HGV	Type	Former Names
Alandia	Fin	1972	6,754	109	17	18	1200	260	71	P	ex Botnia Express-92, Diana-79
Apollo *	Fin	1970	6,480	109	17	20	870	250	34	P	ex Corbiere-94, Linda-92, Corbiere-91, Benodet-85, Gelting Nord-84, Olau Kent-80, Apollo-76
Nordlandia	Swe	1981	21,473	153	24	21	1600	55	65	P	ex Nord Gotlandia-98, Olau Hollandia-89
Roslagen	Fin	1972	6,652	109	17	18	1200	265	23	P	ex Wasa Express-88, Viking 3-84, Wasa Express-83, Viking 3-76

* currently laid up.

K/S Difko (Mols-Linien A/S) Mai Mols. *M. D. J. Lennon*

EckeroLine Roslagen. *M. D. J. Lennon*

Name	Flag	Year	GRT	loa	bm	kts	pass	car	HGV	Type	Former Names

Eidsiva Rederi ASA
Easy Line
Norway

Funnel: Silver and black stovepipes only.
Hull: Red with red 'easy line' interrupting red band.
Routes: Rodby - Puttdarden; Gedser - Rostock.

| Anja #11 | Dmk | 1989 | 4,101 | 96 | 15 | 12 | 253 | 36 | 30 | P | ex Mercandia I-98, l/a Superflex Kilo |

Emeraude Lines SA
France

Hull: White with red 'EMERAUDE Line'
Routes: St. Malo - Sark - Jersey - Guernsey; Granville - Jersey (summer); Carteret - Jersey (summer);

| Solidor 3 | Fra | 1996 | 2,068 | 60 | 17 | 33 | 427 | 52 | 0 | Tj | |
| Solidor 4 | Fra | 1987 | 1,060 | 49 | 14 | 31 | 420 | 40 | - | T | ex Elba Express-99, Madikera-95, Anne Lise-93, |

Also 28-knot catamarans Trident 5 *(1974 /211 g. 200px) and* Trident 7 *(1979/210 g. 191px)*

Estonian Shipping
EstLine AB
Estonia

Funnel: Pale grey with narrow yellow, blue, black and white vertical bands (national colours) on lower part.
Hull: Blue with white 'TALLINN-STOCKHOLM', red boot-topping.
Routes: Tallinn - Stockholm.

Baltic Kristina	Est	1973	12,281	128	22	22	1200	344	-	P	ex Westward Pride-97, Anastasia V-97, Ilyich-96, Stena Baltica-83, Skandia-83, Bore I-80
Regina Baltica	Est	1980	18,345	145	26	21	2000	540	-	P	ex Anna K-96, Anna Karenina-96, Baltika-91, Braemar-91, Viking Song-85
Transbaltica	Est	1971	6,136	118	16	14		-	-	F	ex Sea Clipper-98, Commodore Clipper-96, Euro Nor-91, Misida-90, Normandia-86, Juno-79

ESC EuroLine AB
Routes: Tallinn - Stockholm;

| Transestonia | Est | 1972 | 6,040 | 118 | 16 | 15 | 12 | - | - | F | ex Farona-90, Largo-89, Larona-87, Arona-86 |

Euroseabridge Fahrdienst GmbH
Germany

Funnel: Yellow.
Hull: White with black 'EUROSEABRIDGE', red boot-topping.
Routes: Rostock - Trelloborg; Mukran - Klaipeda; Rostock - Liepaja.

Gleichberg	Lbr	1982	10,243	139	24	14	12	520	-	F	ex City of Dublin-94, Gleichberg-91
Greifwald	Lbr	1988	24,084	191	28	16	96	-	48	Fr	
Kahleberg	Deu	1983	10,271	140	21	14	75	-	45	F	
Petersburg	Deu	1986	25,353	191	28	16	140	-	-	Fr	ex Mukran-95

all managed by Reederei F. Laeisz Gmbh
Service 50% owned by Scandlines A/S, Denmark q.v.

Falcon Distribution Group
UK

Funnel: Red with black bird symbol.
Hull: Blue with red boot-topping.
Routes: Folkestone - Boulogne.

| Picasso * | Cym | 1977 | 5,669 | 115 | 18 | 17 | 12 | - | 64 | F | ex Poker-95, Beaverdale-91, Wuppertal-87, Canaima-79, Wuppertal-78 |
| Purbeck ** | Bhs | 1978 | 6,507 | 126 | 18 | 21 | 58 | 45 | 53 | F | (len-86) |

* on charter from Sea Containers or ** from Channel Island Ferries Ltd (Brittany Ferries)

Eidsiva Rederi ASA (Easy Line) Anja #11. *M. D. J. Lennon*

Estonian Shipping (Euroseabridge Fahrdienst GmbH) Gleichberg . *M. D. J. Lennon*

Name	Flag	Year	GRT	loa	bm	kts	pass	car	HGV	Type	Former Names

FG-Shipping Oy Ab
Finland

Funnel:	White or black with black 'F' on white disc interupting narrow blue band on broad white band.
Hull:	White or blue with 'FINNCARRIERS', red boot topping.
Routes:	Various.

Name	Flag	Year	GRT	loa	bm	kts	pass	car	HGV	Type	Former Names
Astrea	Fin	1991	9,528	129	21	13	-	-	-	F	
Aurora **	Nis	1982	21,381	155	25	18	12	-	179	F	ex Arcturus-91
Finnmaster	Fin	1973	11,839	138	22	17	12	-	112	F	ex Fennia-92, Sirius-87
Finnmerchant	Fin	1983	21,195	155	25	18	12	-	179	F	
Finnseal *	Fin	1991	7,395	123	19	16	6	-	37	F	ex Bore Nordia-97
Transnordica *	Fin	1977	8,188	129	19	17	-	-	-	F	ex Bore Song-97, Seaboard Horizon-93, Key Biscayne-91, Bore Song-91, Abha-79

*owned by Oy Bore Lines AB or ** by Actinor Shipping, Norway*

FinnLink

Routes:	Naantali - Kapellskar.

Name	Flag	Year	GRT	loa	bm	kts	pass	car	HGV	Type	Former Names
Finnarrow	Swe	1996	25,996	168	28	21	200	800	0	F	ex Gotland-98
Finnfellow	Fin	1973	14,297	137	25	19	48	170	55	Fr	
Finnmaid	Fin	1972	13,730	137	25	17	48	170	105	F	ex Capella av Stockholm-88, Capella-86, Hand Gutzeit-82
Finnsailor	Fin	1987	20,783	158	25	20	119	230	-	P	

Finnanglia Ferries

Funnel:	As above (Finncarriers) or cream with black anchor inside black ring, black top (United Baltic).
Hull:	As above (Finncarriers) or light grey.
Routes:	Felixstowe - Helsinki - Hamina; Hull - Helsinki - Hamina.

Name	Flag	Year	GRT	loa	bm	kts	pass	car	HGV	Type	Former Names
Baltic Eagle	Iom	1979	14,738	137	26	18	12	580	112	F	
Baltic Eider	Iom	1989	20,865	158	25	19	-	-	180	F	
Finnbirch **	Swe	1978	15,396	156	23	17	12	-	143	F	ex Bore Gothica-97, Stena Gothica-88, Stena Ionia-85, Merzario Ionia-82, Stena Ionia-81, Atlantic Prosper-81 (wid-79)
Finnforest **	Swe	1978	15,525	151	23	17	12	-	143	F	ex Bore Britannica-96, Stena Britannica-88, Stena Hispania-86, Kotka Violet-85, Stena Hispania-84, Merxario Hispania-83, Atlantic Project-81 (wid-79)
Finnriver ***	Swe	1979	20,172	165	26	16	-	-	136	F	ex Celia-96, Hesperus-86, Vasaland-83
Finnrose ***	Swe	1978	20,169	165	26	16	-	-	136	F	ex Cortia-96, Hektos-86, Timmerland-84
Transbaltica *	Cyp	1990	21,224	158	25	19	12	-	182	F	ex Ahlers Baltic-95

*operated by Poseidon Schiffahrt AG and owned by subsidiary of Ahlers Line or ** on charter from Oy Bore Lines AB or *** B&N Rederi*
Joint service of Finncarriers Oy Ab, Finland and United Baltic Corporation (Andrew Weir Shipping) UK.

Finncarriers

Funnel:	White with blue over white, red and blue wavy bands, above black 'POSEIDON', black top.
Hull:	Red with white 'FINNCARRIERS-POSEIDON.'
Routes:	Lubeck - Helsinki; Lubeck/Travemunde - Turku.

Name	Flag	Year	GRT	loa	bm	kts	pass	car	HGV	Type	Former Names
Finnhansa	Fin	1994	32,531	183	30	18	112	-	250	F	
Finnpartner	Fin	1994	32,534	183	29	18	112	-	250	F	
Finntrader	Fin	1995	32,534	183	29	18	112	-	250	F	
Transeuropa	Deu	1995	32,534	183	29	18	90	-	250	F	
Translubeca	Deu	1990	24,727	158	25	20	84	220	175	F	
Transfinlandia	Deu	1981	19,524	158	25	19	24	190	183	F	

on charter from previous joint owners of service Poseidon Schiffahrt AG

Finncarriers Finnpartner. *M. D. J. Lennon*

FG-Shipping Oy Ab Aurora. *J. Krayenbosch*

Name	Flag	Year	GRT	loa	bm	kts	pass	car	HGV	Type	Former Names

Fjord Line AS Norway

Funnel:	White with red 'F' and black 'L' interupting red and black wavy bands, black top.										
Hull:	Double blue with white 'Fjord Line', red boot-topping.										
Routes:	Hanstholm - Egersund - Bergen; Newcastle - Stavanger - Haugesund - Bergen;										

Name	Flag	Year	GRT	loa	bm	kts	pass	car	HGV	Type	Former Names
Bergen	Nor	1993	16,551	135	24	18	882	350	-	P	
Jupiter	Nor	1975	20,581	175	22	22	1300	285	0	P	ex Color Viking-99, King of Scandinavia-94, Dana Gloria-89, Svea Corona-85, Dana Gloria-84, Wellamo-81 (len-88)

Forde Reederei Seetouristik Germany

Funnel:	Yellow with black 'FRS', black top.										
Hull:	White with black boot-topping.										
Routes:	Cuxhaven - Helgoland; Travemunde - Warnemunde; Burgstaaken - Rodby; Travemunde - Rodby;										

Name	Flag	Year	GRT	loa	bm	kts	pass	car	HGV	Type	Former Names
Baltic Star	Deu	1963	2,890	92	15	18	1300	0	0	P	ex Stena Finlandia-75, Helgoland-72, Larvikspilen-66, Helgoland-64
Poseidon	Deu	1964	1,240	66	12	-	827	0	0	P	
Wappen von Hamburg	Deu	1965	4,192	110	15	15	1800	0	0	P	ex Lucaya-66, Wappen von Hamburg-65

Faaborg Gelting Linien/Denmark

Funnel:	Red with yellow compass points outside horizontally split black globe on white disc, black top.										
Hull:	Red with white ships name.										
Routes:	Faaborg - Gelting.										

Name	Flag	Year	GRT	loa	bm	kts	pass	car	HGV	Type	Former Names
Gelting Syd	Dmk	1974	6,672	115	18	17	800	140	-	P	ex Stella Scarlett-81

Gotlandstrafik AB Sweden
Destination Gotland

Funnel:	Red with large white 'G'.										
Hull:	White with black 'Destination Gotland' separated by two red or red/grey arrows, red boot-topping.										
Routes:	Nynashamn - Visby; Oskarshamn - Visby;										

Name	Flag	Year	GRT	loa	bm	kts	pass	car	HGV	Type	Former Names
Gotland	Swe	1999	5,230	113	16	35	700	150	-	M	
Gute *	Swe	1979	6,643	119	17	16	52	-	60	F	ex Sea Wind II-98, Sally Sun-95, Gute-92
Thjelvar	Swe	1981	16,829	137	23	18	1859	625	137	P	ex Sally Star-97, Travemunde Link-88, Travemunde-87
Visby	Swe	1980	23,775	146	25	21	1872	515	45	P	ex Stena Felicity-98, Felicity-90, Visby-90

Formed jointly by Silja Line and Rederi AB Gotland.
* managed by Sea Wind Line OY AB q.v.

E. H. Harms GmbH Germany
Elbe Ferry GmbH & Co. KG

Funnel:	B										
Hull:	W										
Routes:	Cuxhaven - Brunsbuttel (service due to commence summer 1999).										

Name	Flag	Year	GRT	loa	bm	kts	pass	car	HGV	Type	Former Names
Hinrich Kopf	Dmk	1964	5,148	103	17	18	1125	105	-	P	ex Prinsesse Elizabeth-98
Jochen Steffen	Dmk	1960	5,293	103	17	18	1500	105	-	P	ex Prinsesse Anne-Marie-98
Wilhelm Kaisen	Dmk	1967	2,402	85	13	12	450	60	-	P	ex Najaden-98

Hurtigruten Norway

Funnel:	* Black with white band on broad red band; ** Yellow with blue 'O' on white diamond on red band.										
Hull:	Black or black with red band.										
Routes:	Coastal service Bergen - Aalesund - Trondheim - Bodo - Svolvaer - Hammerfest - Kirkenes.										

Name	Flag	Year	GRT	loa	bm	kts	pass	car	HGV	Type	Former Names
Harald Jarl *	Nor	1960	2,632	87	13	16	595	0	0	P	

Gotlandstrafik AB Gute . *M. D. J. Lennon*

Gotlandstrafik AB Visby. *M. D. J. Lennon*

Name	Flag	Year	GRT	loa	bm	kts	pass	car	HGV	Type	Former Names
Kong Harald *	Nor	1993	11,204	122	23	18	691	50	0	P	
Lofoten **	Nor	1964	2,621	87	13	16	500	0	0	P	
Midnatsol *	Nor	1982	6,167	109	17	17	410	40	0	P	
Narvik **	Nor	1982	6,257	109	17	19	410	40	-	P	
Nordkapp **	Nor	1996	11,386	123	24	15	883	50	-	P	
Nordlys *	Nor	1994	11,204	122	24	15	691	50	-	P	
Nordnorge **	Nor	1997	11,386	123	20	18	690	40	-	P	
Polarlys *	Nor	1996	11,341	123	20	15	737	50	-	P	
Richard With **	Nor	1993	11,205	122	23	15	691		-	P	
Vesteralen	Nor	1983	6,262	109	17	17	314	40	-	P	

*owned by Troms Fylkes D/S A/S or ** by Ofotens Og Vesteraalens Dampskibsselskap ASA*

Irish Ferries   Eire

Funnel:	Green with white shamrock symbol on pale blue, green and dark blue angled square edged white.
Hull:	White with dark blue 'IRISH FERRIES' and pale blue, green and dark blue wavy symbol, green boot-topping.
Routes:	Dublin - Holyhead; Rosslare - Pembroke; Cork - Le Havre; Rosslare - Cherbourg; Rosslare - Le Havre; Rosslare - Roscoff.

Name	Flag	Year	GRT	loa	bm	kts	pass	car	HGV	Type	Former Names
Isle of Inishfree	Irl	1995	22,365	182	24	19	1650	600	0	P	
Isle of Inishmore	Irl	1997	34,031	183	28	21	2200	800	122	P	
Jonathan Swift	Irl	1999	5,992	87	24	40	800	200	10	Te	
Normandy *	Gbr	1982	17,043	149	26	20	2060	480	107	P	ex Stena Normandy-97, St. Nicholas-91, Prinsessan Birgitta-83

on charter from Rederi AB Gotland

Isles of Scilly Steamship Co.   UK

Funnel:	Yellow, blue waving flag with white cross and red 'ISSC' in corners.
Hull:	White.
Routes:	Scilly Isles - Penzance.

Name	Flag	Year	GRT	loa	bm	kts	pass	car	HGV	Type	Former Names
Scillonian III	Gbr	1977	1,256	68	12	15	600	0	0	P	

Jacobs Holdings   UK
Dart Line

Funnel:	Blue with red/white/blue 'J' symbol or white with blue 'J' interupting two narrow blue bands.
Hull:	Blue with blue 'DART' (red dart symbol within 'D') on white superstructure, red boot-topping.
Routes:	Dartford - Vlissingen; Dartford - Zeebrugge.

Name	Flag	Year	GRT	loa	bm	kts	pass	car	HGV	Type	Former Names
Dart 1	Rom	1984	9,071	120	21	15	0	49	94	F	ex Jolly Arancione-98, Bazias 1-96, Balder Fjord-86
Dart 2	Rom	1986	9,080	120	21	15	0	49	94	F	ex Bazias 2-95, Balder Hav-85
Dart 4 *	Bhs	1985	9,082	120	21	15	12	0	90	F	ex Sally Eurolink-97, Bazias 4-93, l/a Balder Bre
Dart 5	Rom	1986	9,080	120	21	15	0	49	94	F	ex Perseus-96, Bazias 5-95, l/a Balder Ra
Dart 6 **	Est	1998	7,606	122	20	17	0	0	96	F	ex Lembitu-99
Dart 7 **	Est	1998	7,606	122	20	17	0	0	96	F	ex Varbola-99

on charter to Belfast Freight Ferries q.v.
**on charter from Estonian Shipping q.v.*

Lithuanian Shipping Co.   Lithuania

Funnel:	White with yellow 'L' on red edged dark green band, black top.
Hull:	Black with white 'LISCO BALTIC SERVICE'.
Routes:	Klaipeda - Kiel.

Name	Flag	Year	GRT	loa	bm	kts	pass	car	HGV	Type	Former Names
Kaunas	Ltu	1989	25,606	190	28	16	202	460	-	F	
Palanga	Ltu	1979	11,630	127	21	18	36	440	-	F	ex Monte Stello-96
Panevezys	Ltu	1985	6,894	126	16	15	-	370	-	F	
Vilnius	Ltu	1987	21,800	191	28	16	122	460	-	F	ex Vilnyus

Hurtigruten Nordnorge. *J. Krayenbosch*

Jacobs Holdings (Dart Line) Dart 1. *M. D. J. Lennon*

Maersk Lines (A.P.Moller Group)   Denmark
Norfolk Line/Netherlands

Funnel:	Black with white 7-pointed star on broad pale blue band.
Hull:	Pale blue with black 'NORFOLK LINE'.
Routes:	Schevengen - Felixstowe;
	also Esbjerg - Immingham and Esbjerg - Harwich routes operated with DFDS as Brit Line.

Name	Flag	Year	GRT	loa	bm	kts	pass	car	HGV	Type	Former Names
Bolero *	Rom	1985	10,243	140	24	14	12	0	65	F	ex Tuzla-96, l/a Spiegelberg
Atlantic Freighter	Bhs	1978	13,117	151	22	16	12	0	0	F	ex Stena Grecia-86, Merzario Grecia-83, Tor Felicia-78
Maersk Anglia	Iom	1977	6,862	123	21	15	-	60	75	F	ex Duke of Anglia-90, Saint Remy-86, Admiral Caribe-82, Admiral Nigeria-79, Admiral Caribe-77
Maersk Exporter	Nld	1996	13,017	143	23	17	12	0	120	F	
Maersk Flanders	Nld	1978	7,199	123	21	16	0	0	90	F	ex Duke of Flanders-90, Romira-86, Admiral Atlantic-84
Maersk Importer	Nld	1996	13,017	143	23	17	12	0	120	F	

Newbuildings - two 18 knot freight ferries from Chinese builder.
* chartered

Mercandia Linierne I/S   Denmark

Funnel:	Silver stovepipes only.
Hull:	Blue with red 'HH Ferries' on white superstructure, red boot-topping.
Routes:	Helsingor - Helsingborg.

Name	Flag	Year	GRT	loa	bm	kts	pass	car	HGV	Type	Former Names
Mercandia IV	Dmk	1989	4,296	96	15	12	300	85	16	P	l/a Superflex November
Mercandia VIII	Dmk	1987	4,296	96	18	12	303	85	16	P	ex Svea Scarlett-96, Superflex Bravo-93

Rederi AB Nordo-Link   Sweden

Funnel:	Black with black 'link' symbol on broad white band.
Hull:	Black with white 'MALMO-TRAVEMUNDE', red boot-topping; black 'NORD LINK' on white superstructure.
Routes:	Malmo - Travemunde.

Name	Flag	Year	GRT	loa	bm	kts	pass	car	HGV	Type	Former Names
Lubeck Link	Swe	1980	33,163	193	27	19	240	800	250	P	ex Finnrose-90
Malmo Link	Swe	1980	33,163	193	27	19	240	800	250	P	ex Finnhawk-90

Norse Irish Ferries Ltd.   UK

Funnel:	White with bowed vertical narrow yellow, blue and wide red panels.
Hull:	Red with white ' NORSE IRISH FERRIES', blue boot-topping.
Routes:	Liverpool - Belfast.

Name	Flag	Year	GRT	loa	bm	kts	pass	car	HGV	Type	Former Names
Lagan Viking	Ita	1997	21,500	186	26	24	340	100	164	P	
Mersey Viking	Ita	1997	21,500	186	26	24	340	100	164	P	

OHG-TT Line   Germany
TT-Line

Funnel:	White with large yellow over blue rectangles, narrow black top.
Hull:	White with blue 'TT-Line' or ' TT-Line Clipper' and yellow over blue rectangles interrupting blue band, blue boot-topping.
Routes:	Rostock - Trelleborg; Travemunde - Trelleborg.

Name	Flag	Year	GRT	loa	bm	kts	pass	car	HGV	Type	Former Names
Delphin	Bhs	1996	5,333	82	23	37	600	175	-	Te	
Nils Dacke	Bhs	1995	26,790	179	28	18	308	0	150	F	
Nils Holgersson	Deu	1989	24,728	177	27	20	1045	280	98	P	ex Robin Hood-93
Peter Pan	Bhs	1988	30,825	177	27	20	1044	280	86	P	ex Nils Dacke-93
Robin Hood	Deu	1995	26,800	179	28	18	308	0	150	F	
Saga Star	Bhs	1981	17,672	146	24	18	250	96	117	F	ex Girolata-93, Saga Star-89
TT-Traveller *	Swe	1992	18,332	154	24	18	120	0	120	F	ex Stena Traveller-96, TT-Traveller-95, Stena Traveller-92

* on charter from Stena Line q.v.

Maersk Lines (Norfolk Line) Maersk Exporter. *J. Krayenbosch*

Rederi AB Nordo-Link Lubeck Link. *M. D. J. Lennon*

Orkney Island Shipping Co. UK
Orkney Ferries Ltd.

Funnel: Red with white 'I' inside white 'O' beneath two narrow white bands.
Hull: Black with red boot-topping.
Routes: Kirkwall - Eday - Sanday.

Small vessels Earl Sigurd *(90/771 g. 140 px)*, Earl Thorfinn *(90/771 g. 140 px)*.

P&O European Ferries Ltd. UK

Funnel: Dark blue with diagonally quartered (white over yellow with blue and red sides) houseflag;
(P&O Stena Line joint service vessels with overlapping flags on dark blue).
Hull: Dark blue with white 'P&O' or 'P&O Stena'.
Routes: Dover - Calais; Portsmouth - Le Havre; Portsmouth - Cherbourg; Portsmouth - Bilbao; Felixstowe - Rotterdam;
Felixstowe - Zeebrugge; Cairnryan - Larne; Ardrossan - Larne; Fleetwood - Larne; Liverpool - Dublin;
Liverpool - Dublin.

Name	Flag	Year	GRT	loa	bm	kts	pass	car	HGV	Type	Former Names
Bison	Gbr	1975	14,387	140	23	18	60	0	180	F	(wid-95, len-81)
European Endeavour	Gbr	1978	8,097	118	20	18	107	30	76	F	ex European Enterprise-88
European Envoy	Bmd	1979	18,653	150	22	19	12	0	125	F	ex Ibex-98, Norsky-95, Norsea-86, Ibex-80
European Freeway	Grb	1977	21,162	185	25	16	180	280	163	F	ex Cerdic Ferry-91, Stena Transporter-86, Syria-83, Alpha Enterprise-79 (len-81, wid-79)
European Highlander	Bhs	1978	5,897	116	18	15	12	37	71	F	ex Lion-98, Merchant Valiant-95, Salahala-90
European Leader	Bmd	1975	10,987	142	20	18	80	0	100	F	ex Buffalo-98 (len-98)
European Navigator	Bmd	1977	9,085	137	18	18	76	0	70	F	ex Leopard-98, Viking Trader-96, Oyster Bay-83, Manuare VII-83, Caribbean Sky-81, Federal Nova-81, Goya-79, l/a Stena Trader
European Pathfinder	Bmu	1975	8,023	118	20	18	107	30	76	F	ex Panther-98, European Clearway-96
European Seafarer	Bmu	1975	10,957	142	19	18	40	0	93	F	ex Puma-98, Union Trader-80, Union Melbourne-80
European Tideway	Gbr	1977	21,162	185	25	16	180	280	163	F	ex Doric Ferry-92, Hellas-86, Alpha Progress-79, l/a Stena Runner
European Trader	Gbr	1975	8,007	118	20	18	132	30	76	F	
Gabrielle Wehr **	Deu	1978	7,635	141	17	17	12	80	91	F	ex Sari-93, Gabrielle Wehr-92, Tor Anglia-85, Gabrielle Wehr-82 (len-82)
Jetliner	Bhs	1996	4,563	95	18	35	600	160	0	Mk	l/d Djursland
Pride of Bilbao	Gbr	1986	37,583	177	28	26	2461	600	62	P	ex Olympia-93
Pride of Cherbourg	Gbr	1975	14,760	144	23	21	1200	192	40	P	ex Pride of Le Havre-94, Viking Valiant-89 (rblt-86)
Pride of Flanders	Gbr	1978	16,776	151	24	17	124	207	81	F	ex Nordic Ferry-92, Merzario Hispania-79, Merzario Espania-78
Pride of Hampshire	Gbr	1975	14,760	144	23	21	1200	192	40	P	ex Viking Venturer-89 (rblt-86)
Pride of Le Havre	Gbr	1989	33,336	161	30	21	1720	590	118	P	ex Olau Hollandia-94
Pride of Portsmouth	Gbr	1989	33,336	161	30	21	1720	575	118	P	ex Olau Britannia-94
Pride of Rathlin	Gbr	1973	12,503	139	22	17	1200	370	50	P	ex Pride of Walmer-92, Free Enterprise VII-88 (len/wid-86)
Pride of Suffolk	Gbr	1978	16,776	151	22	17	124	207	81	F	ex Baltic Ferry-92, Stena Transporter-80, Finnrose-80, Stena Transporter-79
Superstar Express *	Mys	1997	5,517	87	26	39	776	200	0	Ti	ex SuperStar Express Langkawi-98, Superstar Express-97

OHG-TT Line (TT-Line) Peter Pan. *Bettina Rohbrecht*

P&O European Ferries Ltd Pride of Bilbao. *M. D. J. Lennon*

P&O European Ferries Ltd Pride of Suffolk. *J. Krayenbosch*

Name	Flag	Year	GRT	loa	bm	kts	pass	car	HGV	Type	Former Names
Thomas Wehr **	Deu	1977	7,628	141	17	17	12	80	91	F	ex Hornlink-94, Fuldatal-94, Santa Maria-93, Maria-93, Thomas Wehr-93, Dana Germania-86, Tor Neerlandia-85, Thomas Wehr-82, Wacro Express-78, l/a Thomas Wehr

* on short seasonal charter from Star Cruises,
** on charter from Oskar Wehr KG GmbH & Co., Germany.

P&O Stena

Funnel:	Dark blue with overlapping P&O and Stena flags.
Hull:	Dark blue with white 'P&O Stena'.
Routes:	Dover - Calais.

Name	Flag	Year	GRT	loa	bm	kts	pass	car	HGV	Type	Former Names
European Highway	Gbr	1992	22,986	180	28	21	200	0	124	F	
European Pathway	Gbr	1992	22,986	180	28	21	200	0	124	F	
European Seaway	Gbr	1991	22,986	180	28	21	200	0	124	F	
P&OSL Burgundy	Gbr	1993	28,138	179	28	21	1420	600	-	P	ex Pride of Burgundy-99, l/d European Causeway
P&OSL Calais	Gbr	1987	26,433	170	28	22	2290	650	104	P	ex Pride of Calais-99
P&OSL Canterbury	Bhs	1980	25,122	164	28	18	1800	650	0	P	ex Stena Fantasia-99, Fantasia-90, Fiesta-90, Tzarevetz-88, Scandinavia-82
P&OSL Dover	Gbr	1987	26,433	170	28	22	2290	650	104	P	ex Pride of Dover-99
P&OSL Kent	Gbr	1980	20,446	163	26	20	1825	461	64	P	ex Pride of Kent-98, Spirit of Free Enterprise-87 (len-92)
P&OSL Picardy	Gbr	1980	13,601	132	23	21	1326	200	50	P	ex Pride of Bruges-99, Pride of Free Enterprise-88
P&OSL Provence	Gbr	1983	28,559	155	28	21	2300	550	82	P	ex Stena Empereur-98, Stena Jutlandica-96
P&O Stena Elite	Bhs	1996	4,113	81	26	45	782	173	0	Ti	ex Elite-98, Stena Lynx III-98

Formed jointly by P&O and Stena Line.

P&O Ferrymasters

Routes:	Middlesborough - Gothenburg/Helsingborg.

Name	Flag	Year	GRT	loa	bm	kts	pass	car	HGV	Type	Former Names
Elk	Gbr	1978	14,374	164	22	18	12	0	142	F	(len-86)
Norse Mersey *	Ita	1995	16,009	175	24	19	61	0	149	F	

* on 3-year charter

P&O North Sea Ferries

Routes:	Hull - Rotterdam; Hull - Zeebrugge; Middlesborough - Zeebrugge.

Name	Flag	Year	GRT	loa	bm	kts	pass	car	HGV	Type	Former Names
Norbank	Nld	1993	17,464	167	24	23	114	0	156	F	
Norbay	Gbr	1994	17,464	167	24	23	114	0	156	F	
Norcape	Nld	1979	14,087	150	21	19	12	125	133	F	ex Tipperary-89, l/a Puma
Norcove	Swe	1977	10,279	142	19	18	12	1041	105	F	ex Cupria-95, Canopus-92, Finnforest-82, Rolita-79
Norking *	Fin	1980	17,884	171	23	19	12	0	145	F	ex Bore King-91 (len-95)
Norland	Gbr	1974	26,290	173	25	18	1042	519	134	P	(len-87)
Norqueen *	Fin	1980	17,884	171	23	19	12	0	145	F	ex Bore Queen-91 (len-95)
Norsea	Gbr	1987	31,785	179	25	18	1250	850	180	P	
Norsky *	Fin	1999	60,500	-	-	20	0	0	210	F	
Norstar	Nld	1974	26,919	173	25	18	1042	519	134	P	(len-87)
Norstream *	Fin	1999	60,500	-	-	20	0	0	210	F	
Norsun	Nld	1987	31,598	179	25	18	1250	850	180	P	
Tidero Star **	Nis	1978	9,698	152	20	17	6	0	206	F	

Newbuildings - two 22-knot 60,600 grt 1360 px passenger ferries for 2001 delivery.
* on charter from Oy Rettig Ab (Bore Line)
** on charter

P&O European Ferries Ltd Superstar Express. *M. D. J. Lennon*

P&O Stena European Highway. *M. D. J. Lennon*

Name	Flag	Year	GRT	loa	bm	kts	pass	car	HGV	Type	Former Names

P&O Scottish Ferries

Routes: Aberdeen - Lerwick; Aberdeen - Stromness - Lerwick; Scrabster - Stromness; Aberdeen - Lerwick - Bergen (summer).

Name	Flag	Year	GRT	loa	bm	kts	pass	car	HGV	Type	Former Names
St. Clair	Gbr	1971	8,696	118	20	18	600	160	38	P	exTreg-92, Tregastel-91, Njegos-85, Travemunde-80
St. Ola	Gbr	1971	4,833	86	17	16	950	180	39	P	ex Eck-92, Eckero-91, Svea Scarlett-82
St. Rognvald	Gbr	1970	5,297	104	19	16	12	0	47	F	ex Marino Torre-90, Rhone-87, Rhonetal-75, Norcape-74, I/a Rhonetal
St. Sunniva	Gbr	1972	6,350	104	19	16	400	200	28	P	ex N.F. Panther-87, Lasse II-79, Djursland-74

Polska Zegluga Baltycka SA   Poland
Polish Baltic Shipping Co.

Funnel: Blue with white' PZB' on shield interrupting red band.
Hull: White with blue 'Polferries', red boot-topping.
Routes: Swinoujscie - Copenhagen; Swinoujscie - Ronne; Gdansk - Nynashamn; Gdansk - Oxelosund; Swinoujscie - Malmo.

Name	Flag	Year	GRT	loa	bm	kts	pass	car	HGV	Type	Former Names
Nieborow	Pol	1973	8,697	119	19	20	984	225	-	P	ex Stena Baltica-88, Prins Hamlet-88, Prinz Hamlet-87
Pomerania	Pol	1978	10,550	127	19	20	984	277	0	P	
Rogalin	Pol	1972	10,241	127	20	21	988	146	-	P	ex Celtic Pride-92, Rogalin-91, Celtic Pride-89, Rogalin-87, Edda-83, Rogalin-83, Aallotar-78
Silesia	Pol	1979	10,553	128	19	20	984	277	0	P	

Provinciale Stoombootdiensten in Zeeland   Netherlands

Funnel: Buff.
Hull: White with black lower part.
Routes: Vlissingen - Breskens; Kruiningen - Perkpolder.

Name	Flag	Year	GRT	loa	bm	kts	pass	car	HGV	Type	Former Names
Koningen Beatrix	Nld	1993	7,910	114	19	17	1000	210	-	P	
Prins Johan Friso	Nld	1997	7,865	114	19	14	1000	210	0	P	
Prins Willem-Alexander	Nld	1970	7,038	114	19	16	1000	234	22	P	
Prinses Christina	Nld	1968	6,831	114	19	16	1000	234	22	P	
Prinses Juliana	Nld	1986	8,166	114	19	14	570	106	79	P	

Samso Linien Aps   Denmark

Funnel: Black with white band on broad red band.
Hull: Black with ships name in white.
Routes: Samso - Kalundborg.

Name	Flag	Year	GRT	loa	bm	kts	pass	car	HGV	Type	Former Names
Holger Dansk	Dmk	1976	2,779	86	13	11	600	60	-	R	

On charter from Scandlines AG until end 1998.

Scandlines AG   Germany
Scandlines A/S

Funnel: Black with inverted triangle having red top, yellow and blue sides; some vessels with earlier colours of black with red over white over red equal band (DSB) or white with blue, yellow and red bands on forepart (Sweferry)
Hull: White with black 'Scandlines' and 'Vogelflug' on white superstructure, black lower section above red boot-topping or white with blue/black 'HANSA'; Black or dark blue with vessels name in white, red boot-topping.
Routes: Aarhus - Kalundborg; Helsingor - Helsingborg; Puttgarden - Rodby; Rostock - Gedser; Arhus-Liepaja;*** Kalundborg - Kolby Kas; *** Korsor - Lohals.

Polish Baltic Shipping Co. Silesia. *M. D. J. Lennon*

Provinciale Stoombootdiensten in Zeeland Prins Johan Friso. *M. D. J. Lennon*

Name	Flag	Year	GRT	loa	bm	kts	pass	car	HGV	Type	Former Names
Arveprins Knud *	Dmk	1963	8,548	130	17	19	1500	400	0	P	
Ask **	Dmk	1982	11,160	151	20	18	610	-	69	P	ex Arka Marine-91, Nordic Hunter-91, Serdica-90, Seafreight Freeway-88, Stena Driver-85, Lucky Rider-84
Aurora af Helsingborg	Swe	1992	10,918	111	28	13	1250	238	-	P	
Berlin Express	Dmk	1995	4,675	95	17	30	600	160	0	Mk	ex Kattegat-96
Danmark *	Dmk	1968	10,350	145	17	17	1500	260	-	P	
Dronning Margrethe II *	Dmk	1973	10,850	140	18	18	1500	260	0	R	(len-82)
Felix											
Hamlet	Swe	1968	3,638	74	17	14	800	85	0	P	
Heimdal ****	Dmk	1983	9,975	132	20	16	540	764	111	P	ex Mercandian Admiral II-89, Ferrymar I-88, Mercandian Admiral II-88
Kraka	Dmk	1982	9,986	132	19	16	500	111	414	P	ex Mercandian Governor-88, Governor-85, Mercandian Governor-84
Kronprins Frederik	Dmk	1981	16,071	148	23	19	2280	420	18	R	
Lodbrog *	Dmk	1982	10,404	132	19	16	500	111	414	P	ex Mercandian President-88, President-86, Mercandian President-84
Ofelia	Swe	1968	3,638	74	17	14	800	-	-	P	
Prins Henrik *	Dmk	1974	10,850	145	18	18	1500	260	0	P	(len-81)
Prins Joachim *	Dmk	1980	16,071	152	23	18	2280	420	18	R	
Prins Richard	Dmk	1997	14,621	142	25	18	900	286	0	R	
Prinsesse Benedikte	Dmk	1997	14,621	142	25	18	900	286	0	R	
Romso *	Dmk	1973	9,401	130	17	18	1500	335	0	P	
Rostock Link	Bhs	1975	11,335	133	20	18	12	1000	350	P	ex Travemunde Link-92, Travemunde Link I-89, Flavia-88, European Gateway-83, I/a European Express
Scania	Swe	1972	3,474	74	17	14	800	-	-	P	
Skane	Swe	1998	42,705	200	30	21	600	500	165	R	
Sprogo *	Dmk	1962	6,590	109	17	18	1200	210	0	R	
Tranekaer	Dmk	1973	1,273	62	11	15	235	-	-	P	ex Lundeborg-96, Porsangerfjord-92, Stavanger-82
Trelleborg	Swe	1982	20,028	170	24	18	800	108	75	R	
Tycho Brahe	Dmk	1991	10,845	111	28	13	1250	238	-	P	
Urd **	Dmk	1981	11,030	151	20	17	610	-	69	P	ex Aktiv Marine-91, Boyana-90, Seafreight Highway-89, Easy Rider-85

* currently laid up following opening of Great Belt road bridge/rail tunnel and introduction of new vessels on Rodby-Puttgarten service.
** managed by Blaesbjerg Marine A/S.
*** operated with other minor routes by Sydfyenske Dampskibsselskab subsidiary.
**** on charter from Mercandia.

Deutsche Fahrgesellschaft Ostsee mbH (DFO), Germany

Funnel: White with black/blue 'DFO', black top.
Hull: White with black/blue 'VOGELFLUGLINIE'.
Routes: Sassnitz - Trellborg; Rostock - Trelleborg; Sassnitz - Ronne; Puttgarden - Rodby; Rostock - Gedser.

Name	Flag	Year	GRT	loa	bm	kts	pass	car	HGV	Type	Former Names
Deutschland	Deu	1997	15,187	143	25	18	900	305	-	R	
Karl Carstens **	Deu	1986	12,829	165	17	15	1500	177	25	R	
Mecklenburg-Vorpommern	Deu	1996	36,185	200	29	18	887	90	120	R	
Rugen	Deu	1972	12,289	156	19	20	1468	145	43	R	
Sassnitz	Deu	1989	21,154	172	24	17	800	140	0	R	
Schleswig-Holstein	Deu	1997	15,187	143	25	18	900	305	-	R	

** laid up in reserve.

Scandlines A/S Aurora af Helsingborg. *Bettina Rohbrecht*

Scandlines A/S (DFO) Schleswig-Holstein. *Bettina Rohbrecht*

Name	Flag	Year	GRT	loa	bm	kts	pass	car	HGV	Type	Former Names

Cat-Link A/S, Denmark

Hull: White with red 'whiskers', red 'CatLink' and black 'Scandlines'.

Name	Flag	Year	GRT	loa	bm	kts	pass	car	HGV	Type	Former Names
Max Mols	Dmk	1998	5,617	92	26	43	900	220	0	Ti	ex Cat-Link IV-99
Mads Mols	Dmk	1998	5,619	91	26	43	900	220	0	Ti	ex Cat-Link V-99

Service now merged with Mols-Linien A/S (K/S Difko) q.v.

Sea Containers Group   UK
Hoverspeed Ltd.

Funnel: Red
Hull: White with red/blue/red 'superseacat' or blue/red 'seacat', blue lower hull or boot-topping
Routes: Dover - Calais; * Dover - Ostend; ** Stranraer - Belfast; *** Frederikshavn - Gothenburg; Heysham - Belfast; Newhaven - Dieppe (seasonal).

Name	Flag	Year	GRT	loa	bm	kts	pass	car	HGV	Type	Former Names
Diamant *	Lux	1996	4,305	81	26	47	700	180	0	Ti	ex Holyman Diamant-98, Holyman Express-97
Hoverspeed Great Britain	Bhs	1990	3,003	74	26	35	600	84	0	Ti	I/a Christopher Columbus
Rapide *	Lux	1996	4,112	81	26	43	782	180	0	Ti	ex Holyman Rapide-98, Condor 12-97
Seacat Danmark ***	Gbr	1992	3,003	74	26	35	450	80	0	Ti	ex Seacatamaran Danmark-95, Hoverspeed Boulogne-93, I/a Hoverspeed Belgium
Seacat Isle of Man	Gbr	1991	3,003	74	26	35	450	80	0	Ti	ex Seacat Norge-97, Seacat Isle of Man-96, Seacat Boulogne-94, Hoverspeed France-94, Sardegna Express-92, Hoverspeed France-92
Seacat Scotland **	Urg	1992	3,003	74	26	35	431	84	0	Ti	ex Q Ship Express-95, Seacat Scotland-94
Superseacat One ***	Ita	1997	4,700	100	17	38	800	175	0	Mf	
Superseacat Two	Ita	1997	4,700	100	17	38	800	175	0	Mf	
Superseacat Three	ita	1999	4,700	100	17	38	800	175	0	Mf	
The Princess Anne	Gbr	1969	-	56	23	50	390	55	0	H	(len-78)
The Princess Margaret	Gbr	1968	-	56	23	50	390	55	0	H	(len-79)

* operated by Hoverspeed Holyman Ltd., formed jointly by Hoverspeed with Holyman, Silja and Belgian Government.
** operated by Sea Containers Ferries Scotland Ltd. or *** by SeaCat AB.

Isle of Man Steam Packet Co. Ltd.

Funnel: Red, some with white three legged symbol within white ring.
Hull: Blue with red boot-topping;
Routes: Fleetwood - Douglas; Heysham - Douglas;

Name	Flag	Year	GRT	loa	bm	kts	pass	car	HGV	Type	Former Names
Belard	Iom	1979	5,801	106	19	16	0	0	54	F	ex Mercandian Carrier II-85, Carrier II-85, Mercandian Carrier II-84, Alianza-83, Mercandian Carrier II-83
Ben-My-Chree	Iom	1998	12,504	125	23	19	500	200	-	P	
King Orry	Iom	1975	7,555	115	19	19	1000	170	34	P	ex Channel Entente-90, Saint Eloi-89
Lady Of Mann	Iom	1976	4,482	104	17	21	1064	130	-	P	
Peveril	Iom	1971	5,254	106	16	14	0	38	45	F	ex N.F. Jaguar-82, Penda-80, ASD Meteor-75, Holmia-73

Argyll and Antrim Steam Packet Co.

Name	Flag	Year	GRT	loa	bm	kts	pass	car	HGV	Type	Former Names
Claymore *	Gbr	1978	1,871	77	16	12	500	47	0	P	

Scandlines A/S (Cat-Link A/S) Cat-Link IV (since renamed Max Mols). *M. D. J. Lennon*

Sea Containers Group (Hoverspeed) Superseacat Two. *M. D. J. Lennon*

Name	Flag	Year	GRT	loa	bm	kts	pass	car	HGV	Type	Former Names

SeaFrance SA
France

Funnel:	White with blue above red 'SF' symbol, narrow red band below broad blue top.
Hull:	White with blue above red 'SF' symbol and blue 'SEAFRANCE', narrow red band above blue boot-topping.
Routes:	Calais - Dover.

Name	Flag	Year	GRT	loa	bm	kts	pass	car	HGV	Type	Former Names
Seafrance Cezanne	Fra	1986	25,122	164	28	18	1800	650	0	P	ex Fiesta-96, Channel Seaway-90, Fantasia-89, Trapezitza-89, Soca-82, Ariadne-80
Seafrance Manet	Fra	1984	15,093	130	23	20	1800	330	54	P	ex Stena Parisien-96, Champs Elysees-92
Seafrance Monet *	Fra	1974	12,962	127	24	18	1800	340	95	P	ex Stena Londoner-96, Versailles-92, Stena Nautica-87, Stena Nordica-83, Stena Danica-81, l/a Stena Nordica (wid/deep-77)
Seafrance Nord Pas-De-Calais	Fra	1987	13,727	160	23	21	80	0	90	F	ex Nord Pas-De-Calais-96
Seafrance Renoir	Fra	1981	15,612	130	23	18	1400	330	-	P	ex Cote d'Azur-96

* laid up in reserve.

Seatruck Ferries
UK

Funnel:	Blue with yellow 'sun' symbol.
Hull:	Dark blue with red.blue 'SeaTruckFerries' on white superstructure, red boot-topping.
Routes:	Heysham - Warrenpoint.

Name	Flag	Year	GRT	loa	bm	kts	pass	car	HGV	Type	Former Names
Moondance	Bhs	1978	5,881	116	18	15	0	37	71	F	ex Merchant Victor-97, Emadala-90
Riverdance	Bhs	1977	6,041	116	18	15	0	40	71	F	ex Sally Eurobridge-96, Eurobridge-94, Sally Eurobridge-94, Schiffino-93, Tikal-89, Halla-88, Mashala-86

Silja Oy AB
Finland

Funnel:	White with dark blue 'seal' outline beneath blue bands.
Hull:	White with dark blue 'SILJA LINE', blue boot-topping.
Routes:	Helsinki - Stockholm;Turku - Mariehamn - Stockholm; Helsinki - Rostock - Tallinn; Helsinki - Travemunde; Pietarsaari - Skelleftea; Pietarsaari - Umea; Wasa - Umea.

Name	Flag	Year	GRT	loa	bm	kts	pass	car	HGV	Type	Former Names
Fennia	Fin	1966	10,542	128	20	18	1200	215	82	P	
Finnjet	Fin	1977	32,940	213	24	30	1812	380	50	P	
Silja Europa	Fin	1993	59,912	202	33	21	3736	350	60	P	l/a Europa
Silja Festival	Fin	1985	34,414	163	32	22	2000	360	60	P	ex Wellamo-91
Silja Serenade	Fin	1990	58,376	203	32	21	2656	450	52	P	
Silja Symphony	Fin	1991	58,377	203	32	21	2656	470	52	P	
Wasa Jubilee *	Gbr	1985	19,763	134	25	19	2000	152	30	P	ex Stena Invicta-98, Peder Paars-91
Wasa Queen	Fin	1975	16,546	153	20	23	1400	240	0	P	ex Orient Sun-92, Eurosun-91, Club Sea-89, Orient Express-86, Silja Star-86, Bore Star-81

* on charter from Stena.
Parent company now 51% owned by Sea Containers group q.v.

SeaWind Line Oy Ab

Funnel:	White with blue band.
Hull:	Blue with blue 'SeaWind' on white superstructure, black boot-topping.
Routes:	Turku - Stockholm.

Name	Flag	Year	GRT	loa	bm	kts	pass	car	HGV	Type	Former Names
Sea Wind	Swe	1972	15,879	154	21	18	300	60	40	R	ex Saga Wind-89, Svealand-84
Star Wind *	Swe	1976	13,788	159	23	18	70	0	67	R	ex Rostock-99

* to be lengthened 25 metres in late 1999.

SeaFrance SA Seafrance Nord Pas-De-Calais. *M. D. J. Lennon*

Silja Oy AB Silja Europa. *M. D. J. Lennon*

Silja Oy AB Silja Festival. *M. D. J. Lennon*

Name	Flag	Year	GRT	loa	bm	kts	pass	car	HGV	Type	Former Names

Smyril Line Faeroes

Funnel:	Black with 'seal head' inside wide red ring inscribed with 'SMYRIL LINE'.										
Hull:	White with black 'SMYRIL LINE', black boot-topping.										
Routes:	Esbjerg - Torshavn - Bergen - Seydisfjordur.										

Name	Flag	Year	GRT	loa	bm	kts	pass	car	HGV	Type	Former Names
Norrona	Far	1973	11,999	129	21	22	1050	250	44	P	ex Gustav Vasa-83
Smyril	Far	1969	3,937	93	17	19	500	120	16	P	ex Morten Mols-75

Southampton, Isle of Wight
and South of England Royal Mail Steam Packet PLC UK
Red Funnel Ferries

Funnel:	Red with black top.										
Hull:	Red with black 'RED FUNNEL' interupting broad grey band between narrow red bands on white superstructure.										
Routes:	Southampton - Cowes;										

Name	Flag	Year	GRT	loa	bm	kts	pass	car	HGV	Type	Former Names
Red Eagle	Gbr	1996	3,028	82	18	13	910	140	-	P	
Red Falcon	Gbr	1994	2,881	84	18	13	895	140	-	P	
Red Osprey	Gbr	1994	2,881	84	18	13	895	140	-	P	

also high-speed catamarans Red Jet 1 and Red Jet 2 (both 1991/169 g. 120 px) and Red Jet 3 (1998/213 g. 190 px)
Owned by Associated British Ports PLC.

Stena Line AB Sweden

Funnel:	Red with large white 'S' symbol, narrow white and dark blue top and bottom bands or dark blue with joint houseflags (P&O Stena);										
Hull:	White with blue 'Stena Line' and red band above blue boot-topping (passenger) or blue with white 'STENA LINE' (freight).										
Routes:	Frederikshavn - Oslo; Frederikshavn - Gothenburg; Gothenburg - Kiel; Halmstad - Grenaa; Varberg - Grenaa; Karldkrona - Gdynia; Dover - Calais; Newhaven - Dieppe; Harwich - Hook of Holland; Fishguard - Rosslare; Holyhead - Dun Laoghaire; Holyhead - Dublin; Stranraer - Belfast.										

Name	Flag	Year	GRT	loa	bm	kts	pass	car	HGV	Type	Former Names
Medferry Express	Bmu	1978	15,406	148	24	18	-	-	-	F	ex Stena Trailer-93, Trailer-91, Stena Trailer-91, Chester-87, Balder Carrier-85, Ventuari-81
Koningen Beatrix	Nld	1986	31,189	162	28	21	2100	220	80	P	
P&OSL Aquitane	Bmu	1991	28,833	163	28	21	1350	710	-	P	ex Stena Royal-99, Prins Filip-98
Sea Centurion ***	Gbr	1998	21,104	183	26	22	12	-	100	F	l/a Stena Ausonia
Sea Chieftain ***	Gbr	1999	21,104	183	26	22	12	-	100	F	
Stena Caledonia	Gbr	1981	12,619	130	22	19	1200	306	62	P	ex St. David-91
Stena Carisma	Swe	1997	8,631	88	30	40	900	210	0	Ts	
Stena Carrier	Cym	1978	13,117	151	20	16	12	0	-	F	ex Jolly Smerald-83, Jolly Bruno-82, Stena Carrier-82, Imparca Miami-81, Stena Carrier-80, Imparca Express I-80
Stena Challenger	Gbr	1990	18,523	157	24	17	592		120	P	
Stena Danica	Swe	1983	28,727	155	28	21	2300	550	82	P	
Stena Discovery	Nld	1997	19,638	126	40	42	1500	375	50	Ts	
Stena Europe	Pol	1981	24,828	149	27	20	2076	500	47	P	ex Lion Europe-98, Stena Europe-97, Stena Saga-94, Kronsprinsessan Victoria-88
Stena Explorer	Gbr	1996	19,638	126	40	40	1520	375	50	Ts	
Stena Galloway	Gbr	1980	12,175	129	22	19	1000	144	26	P	ex Galloway Princess-90
Stena Germanica	Swe	1987	38,772	175	29	20	2400	540	26	P	
Stena Gothica	Swe	1975	14,406	189	21	16	12	0	150	F	ex Monawar L-90, Stena Project-88, Railro 2-88, Melbourne Trader-88
Stena Invicta	Gbr	1985	19,763	134	25	16	2000	152	30	P	ex Peder Paars-91
Stena Jutlandica	Swe	1996	29,691	182	28	22	1700	-	122	P	ex Stena Jutlandica III-96
Stena Lynx	Bhs	1993	3,231	74	26	35	450	90	0	Ti	ex Stena Sea Lynx-93, l/d Condor 11
Stena Nautica	Swe	1986	19,763	134	25	18	2000	152	30	P	ex Lion King-96, Isle of Innisfree-95, Stena Nautica-92, Niels Klim-91

Red Funnel Ferries Red Falcon. *Philip Kempsey*

Stena Line AB Stena Discovery. *J. Krayenbosch*

Name	Flag	Year	GRT	loa	bm	kts	pass	car	HGV	Type	Former Names
Stena Prince	Swe	1969	8,909	123	20	20	1400	250	40	P	ex Lion Prince-98, Europafarjan I-87, Stena Nordica-85, Prinsessan Christina-83, Safe Christina-82, Prinsessan Christina-81
Stena Saga	Swe	1981	33,750	166	29	22	2000	450	55	P	ex Stena Britannica-94, Silvia Regina-91
Stena Scandinavica	Swe	1988	38,756	175	29	18	2400	540	26	P	l/a Stena Germanica
Stena Scanrail	Swe	1973	7,504	141	16	19	36	0	-	R	ex Stena Searider-87, Trucker-85, Stena Searider-84, Searider-84, Stena Searider-83, Bahjah-81, Seatrader-76, l/a Stena Seatrader
Stena Searider	Swe	1969	20,914	172	25	18	120	0	200	F	ex Norse Mersey-95, Stena Searider-92, Searider-92, Stena Searider-91, Scandinavia Link-90, Scandinavia-87, Polaris-84, Finncarrier-75 (len-87)
Stena Seatrader	Nld	1973	17,991	183	22	17	36	0	130	F	ex Svea Link-90, Svealand av Malmo-87, Svealand-82 (len-82)
Stena Shipper	Bhs	1979	12,337	169	20	17	-	-	154	F	ex Nestor-94, Caribbean Stream-91, Nestor-90, African Gateway-89, Nestor-87, Nestor I-85, Nestor-84
Stena Voyager	Gbr	1996	19,638	127	40	40	1500	360	50	Ts	

* laid up
** on charter from Denval Shipping
*** on charter to Bitish Government (Ministry of Defence)
See also OHG-TT Line.

Swansea Cork Ferries

Eire

Funnel:	White with three red diagonal stripes, centre being interupted by blue 'E' symbol in blue rectangle.
Hull:	White with blue 'SWANSEA CORK FERRIES', red boot-topping.
Routes:	Swansea - Cork; Pembroke - Cork.

Name	Flag	Year	GRT	loa	bm	kts	pass	car	HGV	Type	Former Names
Super Ferry	Grc	1972	14,797	138	23	21	2700	250	46	P	ex Ionian Express-91, Izu No.3-91, Cassiopeia-76

Owned by Briar Star Ltd., Eire and vessel on charter from Strintzis Lines, Greece.

Tallink

Estonia

Funnel:	White with red dot over blue 'i' or white with white 'ESCO' on blue band or white with red 'V' shape at base and blue 'V' above.
Hull:	White with black 'TALLINK' or blue with white 'TALLINK'.
Routes:	Helsinki - Tallinn.

Name	Flag	Year	GRT	loa	bm	kts	pass	car	HGV	Type	Former Names
Fantaasia	Swe	1979	16,630	136	24	21	1700	549	58	P	ex Lion King-98, Stena Nordica-96, Turella-89
Georg Ots	Est	1980	12,549	134	21	16	600	150	0	P	
Meloodia	Est	1979	17,955	137	28	21	1300	480	42	P	ex Meloodia 1-96, Mare Balticum-96, Vironia-94, Diana II-94
Vana Tallinn	Est	1974	12,192	154	24	18	1065	300	48	P	ex Thor Heyerdahl-94, Nord Estonia-93, Dana Regina-90

Owned by Hansatee Ltd. (formed principally by Estonian Shipping Co and Inreko Laevad Ltd).

BV Terschellinger Stoomboot Maatschappij NV

Netherlands

Funnel:	Blue, some with white vertical bands.
Hull:	White with blue 'seal' and three blue angled bands.
Routes:	Harlingen - Terschelling-West; Harlingen - Vlieland.

Name	Flag	Year	GRT	loa	bm	kts	pass	car	HGV	Type	Former Names
Friesland	Nth	1989	3,583	69	17	13	1750	122	16	P	
Midsland	Nth	1974	1,812	78	13	15	1600	65	-	P	ex Rheinland-93 (len-80)
Oost Vlieland	Nth	1970	765	63	13	15	1100	-	-	P	ex Schellingerland-94, Ostfriesland-82

Owned by BV Rederij Doeksen.

Stena Line AB Stena Saga. *J. Krayenbosch*

BV Terschellinger Stoomboot Maatschappij NV Friesland. *M. D. J. Lennon*

Name	Flag	Year	GRT	loa	bm	kts	pass	car	HGV	Type	Former Names

Texels Eigen Stoomboot Onderneming — Netherlands

Funnel: Buff with green over black bands, black top.
Hull: broad buff band above black lower section.
Routes: Den Helder - Den Hoorn.

Name	Flag	Year	GRT	loa	bm	kts	pass	car	HGV	Type	Former Names
Molengat	Nld	1980	6,170	88	18	13	1200	126	19	P	
Schulpengat	Nld	1990	8,311	110	19	11	1320	156	25	P	

TransEurope Shipping Lines — UK/Belgium

Funnel: Yellow with red/black 'D' symbol.
Hull: White or ** blue with red boot-topping.
Routes: Ramsgate - Dunkirk.

Name	Flag	Year	GRT	loa	bm	kts	pass	car	HGV	Type	Former Names
Eurocruiser **	Cyp	1976	13,700	135	22	17	63	-	135	F	ex Rosebay-99, Eurocruiser-98, Eurostar-97, Rosebay-97, Transgermania-93
Eurovoyager *	Cyp	1978	12,110	118	21	22	1300	250	55	P	ex Prins Albert-98
Juniper **	Cyp	1977	5,610	110	18	16	12	280	47	F	ex Cap Benat-86
Larkspur *	Bhs	1976	14,558	144	21	17	1155	300	56	P	ex Eurotraveller-99, Sally Star-97, Viking-2-88, Gedser-86
Primrose *	Cyp	1975	12,110	118	23	22	1400	420	68	P	ex Princesse Marie-Christine-98 (rblt-85)

*on charter from Denval Shipping or ** from Dexterson Shipping Co. Ltd.*
Joint venture service set up to continue route following withdrawl of Sally Line.

Transfennica — Finland

Funnel: Blue with black 'U' on broad white band, (United) or cream with black 'B' and 'H' above and below narrow red band.
Hull: White with 'TRANSFENNIA', blue or red boot-topping.
Routes: Kotka - London; Rauma - London; Oulu/Kemi - Antwerp - London/Felixstowe; Lotka - Blythe.

Name	Flag	Year	GRT	loa	bm	kts	pass	car	HGV	Type	Former Names
Degero **	Fin	1985	10,215	135	21	14	-	-	-	F	
Grano **	Fin	1991	6,620	122	19	16	-	-	-	F	
Hamno **	Fin	1992	6,620	122	19	16	-	-	-	F	
Styrso **	Fin	1992	6,620	122	19	16	-	-	-	F	
Transgard *	Fin	1996	10,570	139	23	20	12	-	96	F	
United Carrier **	Fin	1998	12,251	155	23	20	12	-	-	F	
United Express **	Fin	1997	12,251	155	23	20	12	-	-	F	
United Trader **	Fin	1998	12,251	155	23	20	12	-	-	F	

*owned by Bror Husell Chartering AB or ** by United Shipping Ab (Birka Line Ab).*
Numerous other vessels on charter from various owners, including Godby Shipping A/B and Ernst Russ GmbH q.v.

Unity Line Co. Ltd. — Poland

Funnel: White with two diagonal blue stripes; * white with black 'SWINOUJSCIE-YSTAD', red boot-topping.
Hull: White with 'UNITY LINE' (blue 'I', otherwise black) above black band; * cream with black 'ESL' outline on shield interrupting red band.
Routes: Swinoujscie - Ystad.

Name	Flag	Year	GRT	loa	bm	kts	pass	car	HGV	Type	Former Names
Jan Sniadecki *	Cyp	1988	14,417	155	21	16	50	-	88	Fr	
Mikolaj Kopernik *	Vct	1974	8,734	126	17	15	41	-	20	Fr	
Polonia	Bhs	1995	29,875	170	28	17	900		110	P	

*Jointly formed by Polish Steamship Co. and by privatised * Euroafrica Shipping Lines Co. Ltd., both Poland.*

Viking Line — Finland

Funnel: Red with black 'V' at base of white edged yellow diamond, black top.
Hull: Red with white 'VIKING LINE', white band above blue boot-topping.
Routes: Helsinki - Tallinn; Helsinki - Stockholm; Turku - Mariehamn - Stockholm; Mariehamn - Kapellskar.

Name	Flag	Year	GRT	loa	bm	kts	pass	car	HGV	Type	Former Names
Alandsfarjan	Swe	1972	6,172	104	19	17	1004	200	46	P	ex Tiger-86, N.F. Tiger-85, Kattegat-78
Amorella	Fin	1988	34,384	158	28	21	2300	630	53	P	
Cinderella	Fin	1989	46,398	191	29	22	2810	480	60	P	
Gabriella	Swe	1992	35,492	169	28	21	2400	400	68	P	ex Silja Scandinavia-97, Frans Suell-94
Isabella	Fin	1989	34,937	169	28	21	2200	630	53	P	

Unity Line Co. Ltd. Polonia. *M. D. J. Lennon*

Viking Line Cinderella. *J. Krayenbosch*

Name	Flag	Year	GRT	loa	bm	kts	pass	car	HGV	Type	Former Names
Mariella	Fin	1985	37,799	176	28	22	2500	580	0	P	
Rosella	Fin	1980	16,850	136	24	21	1700	145	43	P	

Wagenborg Passagierdiensten BV Netherlands

Funnel:	Black with two white bands.
Hull:	White with red band and black 'WAGENBORG', red boot topping.
Routes:	Ameland - Holerd; Lauwersoog - Schiermonnikoog.

Name	Flag	Year	GRT	loa	bm	kts	pass	car	HGV	Type	Former Names
Oerd	Nld	1985	1,121	58	14	12	1000	46	12	P	
Rottum	Nld	1985	1,121	58	14	12	1140	46	12	P	
Sier	Nld	1995	2,286	73	16	10	1463	72	-	P	ex Sier-95

Reederei Warrings GmbH Germany
Bremerhaven - Helgoland Linie GmbH & Co. KG

Routes:	Bremerhaven - Helgoland; Wilhelmshaven - Helgoland.

Name	Flag	Year	GRT	loa	bm	kts	pass	car	HGV	Type	Former Names
Helgoland	Deu	1962	3,464	104	15	22	1980	0	0	P	ex Alte Liebe-84, Wappen-66, Wappen von Hamburg-64
Wilhelmshaven *	Deu	1963	1,496	76	12	14	1100	0	0	P	

* managed by Harle Express Seetouristik GmbH & Co. KG

Wightlink Ltd. UK

Funnel:	Blue with white edged blue flag having red diamond on white rectangle.
Hull:	White with blue/red 'WIGHTlink' and flag symbol, red band above blue boot-topping.
Routes:	Portsmouth - Ryde; Portsmouth - Fishbourne; Lymington - Yarmouth.

Name	Flag	Year	GRT	loa	bm	kts	pass	car	HGV	Type	Former Names
St. Catherine	Gbr	1983	2,036	77	17	12	680	142	-	P	
St. Cecilia	Gbr	1987	2,968	77	17	13	1000	142	-	P	
St. Faith	Gbr	1990	3,009	76	17	12	1000	142	-	P	
St. Helen	Gbr	1983	2,983	77	17	12	680	142	-	P	

smaller ferries Caedmon, Cenred and Cenwulf (all 73/761 g. 756 px. 76 cars) also high-speed catamarans Our Lady Pamela (86/313 g. 470 px) and Our Lady Patricia (86/312 g. 470 px.)

Wagenborg Passagierdiensten BV Sier. *J. Krayenbosch*

PART TWO

Coastal Cargo Vessels

Name	Flag	Year	GRT	DWT	Loa	Bm	Draft	Kts	Type	Former names

Ahlers NV

Belgium

Funnel: Blue with blue triangular symbol on broad white band.
Hull: Blue.

Name	Flag	Year	GRT	DWT	Loa	Bm	Draft	Kts	Type	Former names
Ahlers Belgica	Atg	1984	4,489	6,158	106.0	17.6	7.0	13	Cc	ex Cam Bubinga-97, Ahlers Belgica-96, Kent Trader-93, Ahlers Belgica-92, ScanDutch Levant-91, Insulano-89, Shetland-86, Scol Broker-86, Shetland-84
Breeze *	Lux	1983	5,450	6,687	113.7	19.3	6.5	14	CC	ex X Press Makalu-98, Breeze-96, Ahlers Breeze-95, Pegasus Pioner-89, Bandama-88, Cape York-87, Taabo-86, Ruth Borchard-85, Ahlers Breeze-84
Mopa Daniel	Bhs	1982	5,209	9,093	110.1	18.3	8.1	13	Tch	ex Chemical Harmony-92, Gogo Chemstar-91
Oram Bridge *	Atg	1984	5,450	6,687	113.7	19.3	6.5	14	Cc	ex Lhotse-98, Tiger Ocean-94, Ahlers Bridge-93, Judith Borchard-91, Cam Azobe-88, Norasia Adria-87, Buyo-86, Ahlers Bridge-84

* owned by subsidiary European Maritime Services AG, Luxembourg.

Ahlmark Lines AB

Sweden

Funnel: Black with black 'A' on broad white band.
Hull: White or blue with black or red boot-topping.

Name	Flag	Year	GRT	DWT	Loa	Bm	Draft	Kts	Type	Former names
Alstern	Swe	1984	4,451	6,021	105.9	17.6	7.0	13	Cc	ex Scol Trader-86, Friesland-85
Fryken *	Ant	1989	4,059	6,260	99.5	17.0	6.5	12	Cc/T	ex Coldstream Shipper-96, Norrsundet-93
Mangen *	Nld	1984	2,580	3,171	87.0	13.2	6.0	14	Cc	
Noren	Swe	1985	4,483	6,154	106.0	17.5	6.9	13	Cc	ex Scol Carrier-86, Nordland-85
Saxen *	Ant	1989	4,059	6,275	99.6	17.0	6.5	12	Cc/T	ex Coldstream Merchant-96, Skutskar-93
Skagern	Swe	1983	4,426	6,021	106.0	17.6	7.0	13	Cc	ex Icecrystal-95, Skagern-85
Sommen	Swe	1983	4,426	6,150	106.0	17.6	7.0	13	Cc	
Unden *	Nld	1984	2,577	3,171	87.0	13.2	6.0	14	Cc	
Visten *	Ant	1990	4,059	6,275	99.6	17.0	6.5	12	Cc/T	ex Coldstream Trader-96, Aldabi-93

Managed by Ferm Marine AB, except * owned by Ahlmarco BV, Netherlands (Barber Ship Management AS, Norway).

Christian F. Ahrenkiel GmbH & Co.

Germany

Funnel: Buff or buff with houseflag on blue band, or charterers.
Hull: Black, red or grey with red boot-topping.

Name	Flag	Year	GRT	DWT	Loa	Bm	Draft	Kts	Type	Former names
Alstergas	Lbr	1991	4,200	5,694	100.0	15.9	7.2	14	Lpg	
Elbegas	Lbr	1983	5,958	7,656	116.5	17.4	8.4	15	Lpg	ex Wesergas-88, l/a Norge
Luna Azul	Phl	1997	8,359	8,244	(108.0)	19.6	7.5	13	Ro	
Moselgas	Deu	1998	5,870	6,050	(108.3)	17.2	-	-	Lpg	l/a Odergas
Multitank Adria	Tuv	1981	2,780	3,561	102.8	14.0	5.4	13	Tch	(len-85)
Multitank Arcadia	Tuv	1981	2,780	4,036	102.8	14.0	5.5	13	Tch	(len-86)
Multitank Armenia	Tuv	1981	2,780	4,051	102.9	14.0	5.5	13	Tch	(len-85)
Multitank Ascania	Tuv	1981	2,780	4,034	102.8	14.0	5.5	13	Tch	(len-85)
Multitank Badenia	Lbr	1997	3,726	5,846	99.9	16.5	6.8	15	Tch	
Multitank Bahia	Lbr	1996	3,726	5,846	100.0	16.5	6.7	15	Tch	
Multitank Balearia	Lbr	1998	3,726	5,846	99.9	16.5	6.8	15	Tch	
Multitank Batavia *	Lbr	1998	3,726	5,846	99.9	16.5	6.8	15	Tch	
Multitank Bolognia	Lbr	1997	3,726	5,846	100.0	16.5	6.8	15	Tch	
Multitank Bracaria	Lbr	1997	3,726	5,846	99.9	16.5	6.8	15	Tch	
Multitank Brasilia	Lbr	1997	3,726	5,846	99.9	16.5	6.8	15	Tch	
Multitank Britannia	Deu	1996	3,726	5,846	100.0	16.5	6.8	15	Tch	
Multitank Calabria	Lbr	1984	2,690	4,028	91.7	13.6	6.4	12	Tch	ex Southern Island-87
Multitank Catania	Lbr	1983	2,690	3,885	91.7	13.6	6.2	12	Tch	ex Crest Island-87
Rheingas	Lbr	1992	4,200	5,650	100.0	15.9	7.2	14	Lpg	
Wesergas	Deu	1999	4,950	5,200	-	-	-	-	Lpg	

* owned by Martime-Gesellschaft fur Maritime Dien. GmbH.

Ahlmark Lines AB Saxen. *J. Krayenbosch*

Christian F. Ahrenkiel GmbH & Co. Multitank Batavia. *J. Krayenbosch*

Name	Flag	Year	GRT	DWT	Loa	Bm	Draft	Kts	Type	Former names

Alba Shipping Ltd. A/S
Funnel: Colours not confirmed.
Hull: Colours not confirmed.

Denmark

Name	Flag	Year	GRT	DWT	Loa	Bm	Draft	Kts	Type	Former names
Astra	Pan	1972	1,843	3,460	82.7	13.0	6.4	12	Tch	ex Perko-91, Selma-90, Pointe de Lervily-74, Bras-74
Baltic Breeze	Hnd	1952	397	585	49.5	7.6	3.2	9	C	ex New Sea-97, Sea Glory I-92, Vanerfjord-91, Hamnfjord-76, Westfjord-69
Bravur	Pan	1975	2,139	3,575	83.0	13.0	6.6	13	Tch	ex Al Sabah I-88, Bravur-82
Breeze	Bhs	1977	2,021	3,153	83.0	14.3	5.9	13	Tch	ex Mare Bonum-93
Buna	Iom	1979	1,561	1,760	73.4	12.3	4.9	13	Tch	
Dan Carrier	Bhs	1970	465	635	41.1	9.2	3.4	10	C	ex Neo-94
Dan Trader	Dis	1958	296	478	44.9	7.6	3.2	11	C	ex Janto-85, Rosenvold-65 (len-64)
Dan Trimmer	Dis	1976	499	772	50.2	9.0	3.4	9	C	ex Angela Helen-98, Westanvind-95, Bulk Sea-89, Esperanza-87, Bulk Sea-85, Angela Helen-81, Frendo Norden-77
Dan Viking	Dis	1957	412	540	50.8	8.3	3.2	10	C	ex Vivi-97, Stina B-92, Vivi-90, Lone Baand-90, Kongsaa-81, Jorna-75, Herfrid-70, Mogens S.-66
Fajal II	Pan	1967	500	1,392	68.6	11.5	3.7	11	T	ex Brix-90, Gorce-87, Alecto-73
Kasla	Iom	1974	4,724	6,863	130.3	17.6	6.3	14	Tch	ex Kiisla-96 (len-79)
Lisa	Nis	1965	2,633	4,813	103.5	12.9	5.8	11	T	ex Kaprifol-99, Tarnfors-91, Winjona-75, Rubistream-68, (len/deep-78)
Maxim	Mlt	1976	1,975	3,100	83.5	14.1	5.2	12	C	ex G. Roussos II-95, Mishnish-87
Mermaid Eagle	Dis	1977	2,196	4,034	82.2	13.3	6.5	9	C	ex Monzabon-95, Agate Progress-82, Panstar-82, Danstar-78 (len-82)
Mermaid Hawk	Dis	1977	2,201	4,083	82.2	13.3	6.5	9	C	ex Maroi-95, Agate Pioneer-82, Atlantic Pioneer-82, Danboat-78 (len-82)
Reda	Mlt	1976	1,949	3,109	83.5	14.1	5.2	12	Cc	ex Marathon-96, Chivas-88, Whitehall-85, Bloempoort-83, Flowergate-82
Sunbeam	Pan	1975	318	420	43.3	8.1	3.0	9	T	ex Nosal-91
Tinka	Pan	1972	2,097	3,205	91.3	13.7	5.3	12	T	ex Inka-90

Torkel Alendal Rederi AS
Funnel: White with blue 'A' on red flag, black top.
Hull: Red with dark red boot-topping.

Norway

Name	Flag	Year	GRT	DWT	Loa	Bm	Draft	Kts	Type	Former names
Bulk Trader	Mlt	1973	6,049	8,001	121.8	17.7	7.7	13	Cc	ex Marsa-93, Brunhorn-86
Early Bird	Bhs	1973	3,809	7,044	106.0	15.2	7.4	12	C	ex Sete-73 (len-81)
Moon Trader	Bhs	1969	2,555	4,196	99.0	12.6	6.4	12	Tch	ex Otaru-91
North Trader	Mlt	1974	3,133	4,651	106.0	14.7	6.7	14	Tch	ex Arcturus-95, Okiti-82
Queen Trader	Nis	1980	2,783	3,726	89.5	14.0	6.2	13	Tch	ex Proof Gallant-98
Sky Trader	Bhs	1969	1,589	2,991	87.2	12.0	5.0	12	Tch	ex Thuntank 10-90, Credo-74 (len/deep-77)
Spirit Trader	Bhs	1975	2,246	3,124	96.8	12.0	6.2	11	Tch	ex Proof Trader-95 (len-81)
Star Trader	Mlt	1980	1,815	2,710	79.2	14.1	5.0	12	Tch	ex Listraum-90, Alk-87
Sun Trader	Mlt	1981	2,092	3,020	79.6	14.0	5.6	12	Tch	ex Solstraum-90, Aun-85
West Trader	Mlt	1975	3,787	5,984	105.4	15.9	7.0	15	Tch	ex Inox-99, Snow Queen-95, Chemical Discoverer-91, Bow Queen-82

Amasus Shipping BV
Funnel: Various owners markings.
Hull: Various colours, mainly blue with black boot topping.

Netherlands

Name	Flag	Year	GRT	DWT	Loa	Bm	Draft	Kts	Type	Former names
Aldeboorn	Nld	1984	997	1,506	78.9	10.1	3.1	12	C	ex Aldebaran-97, Bornrif-94
Antares	Nld	1984	1,172	1,576	78.9	10.1	3.4	9	C	ex Oldehove-94

Alba Shipping Ltd. A/S Reda. *M. D. J. Lennon*

Amasus Shipping BV Vesting. *J. Krayenbosch*

Name	Flag	Year	GRT	DWT	Loa	Bm	Draft	Kts	Type	Former names
Auriga	Ant	1978	1,589	1,670	84.2	10.8	3.7	10	Cc	ex Algerak-90, German-86
Compaen	Nld	1975	935	1,458	80.1	9.0	3.2	10	Cc	ex Argo-93, Inez V-83, Cargo-Liner V-82
Daan	Nld	1979	726	1,163	62.5	9.4	3.4	10	C	ex Ideaal-96, Meran-90, Sambre-89, Carpe Diem II-81, Carpe Diem-79
Diamant	Nld	1985	998	1,497	78.0	10.0	3.2	10	C	ex Watum-95
Dina Jacoba ‡	Nld	1977	945	1,473	64.4	10.7	4.0	11	C	ex Anne-87, Dependent-82
Eemshorn †	Nld	1995	2,735	4,250	89.6	13.8	5.7	12	Cc	
Fast Wil	Nld	1985	1,391	2,285	80.0	11.1	4.1	10	Cc	ex Christina-97
Geertje	Nld	1986	1,139	1,601	79.1	11.4	3.3	12	Cc	ex Anne S-98
Gitana	Nld	1970	605	830	67.0	8.1	2.6	11	C	ex Aldebaran-93, Gesina-90, Banjaard-??
Hansa Bremen	Nld	1999	1,999	2,815	89.5	12.4	4.3	10	Cc	
Hansa Kampen	Nld	1998	2,056	2,953	89.5	12.4	4.3	10	Cc	
Hansa Lubeck	Nld	1998	1,999	2,815	89.5	12.4	4.3	10	Cc	
Henk Van Otterloo	Nld	1978	736	1,163	62.5	9.9	3.4	10	C	ex Elisabeth G-97, Vera-95, Frisian-90, Frisiana-89, Thalassa-79
Heyst	Bel	1985	752	998	63.4	10.0	3.1	11	C	ex Zuiderzee-97
Koerier	Nld	1996	1,546	2,346	85.8	10.8	4.8	10	C	
Laurina-Neeltje	Nld	1995	1,546	2,310	85.1	10.8	4.1	11	C	
Miska	Nld	1963	404	507	55.6	7.3	2.5	10	C	ex Rola-90, Corry II-86
Morgenstond	Nld	1967	439	530	62.1	7.2	2.2	10	C	ex Texel-81
Njord	Nld	1985	998	1,490	78.8	10.6	3.1	10	C	ex Deo Juvante-95, Huibertje Jacoba-87
Omega 4	Nld	1972	1,472	2,159	71.3	11.6	5.0	11	C	ex Isabel-97
Omega III	Nld	1973	967	1,371	80.0	9.0	3.0	10	C	ex Noorderling-97, Tasman-92, Bielefeld-84, Cargoliner I-82
Orion	Nld	1985	978	1,411	70.0	10.4	3.5	10	C	ex Ariel-98, Vita Nova-92
Polar Sky	Nld	1999	2,800	3,700	-	-	-	-	Cc	
Polar Star	Nld	1999	2,625	3,740	-	-	-	-	Cc	
Polar Sun	Nld	1999	2,625	3,740	-	-	-	-	Cc	
Quo-Vadis	Ant	1983	1,130	1,564	79.0	10.0	3.5	11	C	
Sea Charente	Nld	1996	1,638	2,270	82.3	11.4	4.0	11	C	
Soli Deo Gloria	Nld	1997	2,377	3,462	89.0	12.5	5.0	10	Cc	
Thalassa	Nld	1999	2,625	3,740	-	-	-	-	Cc	
Vega	Nld	1992	1,576	2,500	82.0	11.0	4.1	12	Cc	
Veritas	Nld	1999	2,625	3,600	-	-	-	-	C	
Vesting	Nld	1992	1,587	2,166	88.0	11.9	3.6	11	C	
Warber	Nld	1965	455	571	60.5	7.5	2.2	10	C	ex Zeus-90
Vahalis *	Nld	1984	998	1,485	78.0	10.1	3.2	10	C	ex Vios-97
Vikingbank **	Nld	1978	1,596	3,040	81.7	14.3	5.4	13	C	

*managed by Wijnne & Barends B.V., ** by Wagenborg Shipping B.V., † by Poseiden Chartering B.V. or ‡ by Unity Chartering B.V.*

Amons & Co. Netherlands

Funnel: Blue with red top or individual owners markings.
Hull: Blue.

Name	Flag	Year	GRT	DWT	Loa	Bm	Draft	Kts	Type	Former names
Marathon	Ant	1976	1,655	2,575	78.7	12.4	5.0	11	C	ex Vrouwe Alida-90
Mariner *	Ant	1966	1,148	1,821	73.0	12.1	5.0	11	C	ex Armada Mariner-83, Dicky-79, Kraftca-75, I/a Jan F. Spliethoff
Voyager	Nld	1975	1,746	2,790	78.4	12.4	5.4	10	C	ex Baron-96, Barok-95, Audrey Johanna-81

owned by subsidiary Ocean-Dolphin Ship Management NV, Netherlands Antilles.

Amur Shipping Co. Russia

Funnel: White with blue over red bands, black top.
Hull: Various.

Name	Flag	Year	GRT	DWT	Loa	Bm	Draft	Kts	Type	Former names
Baltiyskiy-106 (2)	Rus	1979	1,926	2,554	95.0	13.2	4.0	12	Cc	
Omskiy-114 (2)	Rus	1983	2,360	2,923	108.4	14.8	3.0	10	C	
Omskiy-116 (2)	Rus	1984	2,360	2,933	108.4	14.8	3.0	10	C	
Sormovskiy-117 (2)	Rus	1979	2,478	3,134	114.0	13.2	3.7	10	C	
Sormovskiy-40 (2)	Rus	1978	2,478	3,147	114.0	13.2	3.7	10	C	

Name	Flag	Year	GRT	DWT	Loa	Bm	Draft	Kts	Type	Former names
Sormovskiy-58 (2)	Rus	1978	2,478	3,734	114.0	13.2	3.7	10	C	ex XVIII Syezd VLKSM-92
Volga-4007 (2)	Rus	1989	4,911	5,845	139.8	16.6	4.5	10	Cc	
Volga-4009 (2)	Rus	1990	4,966	5,985	139.8	16.6	4.5	10	C	
Volga-4011 (2)	Rus	1991	4,966	5,985	139.8	16.6	4.5	10	Cc	

About 9 other dry cargo and 3 coastal tankers.

Anchor Line plc
George Gibson & Co. Ltd.

UK

Funnel: Black with red 'GG' on broad white band beneath deep red top.
Hull: Red with red boot-topping.

Name	Flag	Year	GRT	DWT	Loa	Bm	Draft	Kts	Type	Former names
Eildon	Lbr	1982	6,808	8,738	114.4	18.3	7.6	14	Lpg	ex Norgas Transporter-98, Etienne Schlumberger-89
Ettrick	Lbr	1991	3,023	3,621	88.0	14.8	6.0	13	Lpg	
Lanrick	Lbr	1992	3,023	3,620	88.0	14.9	6.0	14	Lpg	
Quentin	Lbr	1977	1,709	2,088	76.1	12.4	5.4	12	Lpg	ex Pentland Moor-79
Traquair	Lbr	1982	5,992	7,230	113.8	18.4	8.1	16	Lpg	
Yarrow	Cym	1982	6,356	7,850	115.1	18.5	8.5	14	Lpg	ex Norgas Mariner-98, Sigurd Jorsalfar-88, Nopal Norte-87

Controlled jointly by Erik Thun AB and Transmark AB.
Associated with Unigas International (United Gas Carriers BV).

Armada Shipping APS

Denmark

Funnel and Hull: Colours not confirmed.

Name	Flag	Year	GRT	DWT	Loa	Bm	Draft	Kts	Type	Former names
Eastern Glory	Pan	1984	4,073	6,711	107.7	17.0	7.0	-	Tch	ex Panam Dorado-97, Sea Princess-90, Sarah Kathryn-89
Ice Bird	Dis	1990	3,625	3,043	92.9	15.4	5.2	13	Rc	ex San Carlos Pride-93, Ice Clipper-92
Ice Crystal	Dis	1991	3,625	3,043	92.9	15.4	5.2	13	Rc	
Ice Field	Cyp	1988	5,966	6,959	118.4	18.8	7.3	18	Rc	ex Prins Casimir-96
Ice Star	Dis	1990	3,625	3,039	92.9	15.4	5.2	13	R	
Scan Eagle	Dis	1991	1,964	2,750	83.2	13.0	4.7	13	Cc	
Scan Falcon	Dis	1992	1,964	2,784	83.2	13.0	5.4	13	Cc	
Scan Hawk	Dis	1992	1,964	2,784	83.2	13.0	4.7	13	Cc	
Scan Swan	Dis	1991	1,964	2,600	83.2	13.0	5.4	13	Cc	

Armawa Shipping & Trading

Netherlands

Funnel: Blue with red 'A' and blue water symbol on white square, red top.
Hull: Blue with red boot-topping.

Name	Flag	Year	GRT	DWT	Loa	Bm	Draft	Kts	Type	Former names
Bermuda Islander	Nld	1995	2,035	2,800	90.6	13.8	4.3	13	CC	
Emmaplein	Nld	1998	2,039	3,210	89.4	12.5	4.8	11	Cc	
Emmasingel	Nld	1998	2,039	3,100	89.4	12.5	4.8	11	Cc	
Heerebrug	Nld	1999	2,035	2,850	90.5	13.8	4.3	13	Cc	
Heereplein	Nld	1996	2,035	2,800	90.6	13.8	4.3	13	CC	
Heerestraat	Nld	1997	2,035	2,850	90.6	13.9	4.3	13	Cc	
Lys Ranger	Nld	1997	2,035	2,780	90.0	14.0	4.6	13	Cc	I/a Heerepoort
Lys Rover	Nld	1996	2,035	2,850	90.6	13.8	4.2	13	CC	ex Heeresingel-96
Lys Viking	Nld	1996	2,036	2,800	90.0	13.8	4.6	13	C	ex Heereweg-96
Radeplein	Nld	1999	2,560	3,500	92.8	15.9	4.9	15	Cc	
Radepoort	Nld	1998	2,560	3,500	92.8	15.9	4.9	15	Cc	
Radesingel	Nld	1999	2,560	3,500	92.8	15.9	4.9	15	Cc	

Newbuildings: two further 2,560 grt 3,500 dwt and three 7,589 grt 8,430 dwt due 1999/2000.

Arpa Shipping BV

Netherlands

Funnel: Blue.
Hull: Blue, some with white 'ARPA', red boot-topping.

Name	Flag	Year	GRT	DWT	Loa	Bm	Draft	Kts	Type	Former names
Berys Trader	Atg	1985	1,291	1,548	74.9	10.6	3.4	10	C	ex Katharina Charlotte-96, Sea Thames-93, Katharina Charlotte-92, Sea Thames-91, I/a Katharina Charlotte
Claudia Trader	Atg	1983	1,300	1,506	74.8	10.6	3.3	10	C	ex Claudia L-96
Dominique Trader	Atg	1985	1,521	1,740	82.5	11.3	3.5	10	Cc	ex Provence-98, Pero-96

Name	Flag	Year	GRT	DWT	Loa	Bm	Draft	Kts	Type	Former names
Dorothy Trader	Atg	1986	1,680	2,142	82.5	10.8	4.2	10	Cc	ex Claudia-97, Lys Clipper-91, Neidenburg-90
Eliane Trader	Mlt	1978	1,384	1,623	81.6	10.0	3.4	10	C	ex Konigssee-95
Johanna Trader	Atg	1983	1,980	3,008	81.7	14.1	5.4	13	Cc	ex Vrouwe Johanna-95
Louise Trader (2)	Mlt	1981	1,716	2,319	80.3	11.4	4.3	11	C	ex Katharina-94, Selene-89
Marc Trader	Atg	1983	1,301	1,501	74.9	10.6	3.3	10	C	ex Marc L-96
Marcel	Atg	1993	2,449	3,710	87.9	12.8	5.5	10	Cc	
Michelle Trader	Mlt	1983	994	1,591	63.7	11.8	3.9	10	C	ex Paola-95, Paul Brinkman-88
Oxana Trader	Atg	1985	1,680	2,144	82.5	10.8	4.3	10	Cc	ex Stephanie-97, Lys Cape-91, Herta H-90
Samin Trader	Mlt	1979	1,456	1,703	81.9	10.0	3.6	10	C	ex Sea Mosel-94, Huberna-89
Steel Trader	Atg	1984	1,521	1,720	82.5	11.3	3.5	10	Cc	ex Pirat-98, Haithabu-94

Aspen Shipping & Trading BV   Netherlands
Funnel: Black with white 'M'.
Hull: Black or grey with white 'MUNDIAL LINE', red boot-topping.

Name	Flag	Year	GRT	DWT	Loa	Bm	Draft	Kts	Type	Former names
Bassma	Hnd	1965	499	1,145	66.2	10.6	4.0	11	C	ex Arosandra-91, Hannes Lunstedt-??
Cedar Car	Lbn	1972	6,623	5,599	126.6	16.0	6.0	15	Ro	ex Algol-92 (len-81)
Kessma	Hnd	1965	399	1,065	61.7	10.0	4.0	11	C	ex Ocean Sun-88, Santana-87, Ruthensand-80, Martha Ahrens-75
Liban Car	Lbn	1976	9,998	4,728	137.3	18.3	6.3	15	V	ex Wild Rose-88
Mundial Car	Lbn	1965	2,588	2,133	81.8	14.0	5.3	13	V	ex Passat-82
O'Shea Express	Lbn	1970	9,592	1,054	91.5	16.8	3.9	14	V	ex Clearway-78, Speedway-70
Tony Car	Lbn	1973	3,495	1,194	92.6	14.8	4.3	14	V	ex Feedermate-97, Tony Car-95, Tony Safi-87, Ramsgate-84

Atlantic-Rhederei F. & W. Joch KG   Germany
Funnel: Black with white over blue bands.
Hull: Red with green boot-topping.

Name	Flag	Year	GRT	DWT	Loa	Bm	Draft	Kts	Type	Former names
Apache	Lbr	1980	2,804	3,659	97.9	13.7	5.8	13	Tch	
Aztek	Lbr	1978	2,801	3,659	97.9	13.8	5.8	12	Tch	
Cheyenne	Lbr	1983	1,734	2,593	85.0	13.0	4.7	12	T	
Sioux	Lbr	1981	4,270	6,400	115.0	15.9	7.2	14	Tch	
Unkas	Lbr	1981	4,270	6,390	115.8	15.8	7.2	14	Tch	

B&N Nordsjofrakt AB   Sweden
Funnel: Blue with yellow 'B&N' between narrow yellow bands.
Hull: Various.

Name	Flag	Year	GRT	DWT	Loa	Bm	Draft	Kts	Type	Former names
Bergon	Nis	1978	3,700	5,514	100.8	16.4	6.2	13	Cc	ex Mini Star-83
Bremon	Nis	1976	5,312	8,650	120.1	16.6	7.7	14	C	(deep-82, len-79)
Britta Oden (2)	Swe	1979	16,947	8,412	170.3	21.0	5.4	16	Ro	ex Tor Scandia-98, Britta Oden-88 (len-88)
Corner Brook	Swe	1976	7,587	7,173	135.8	18.6	7.0	16	Cp	
Eva Oden (2)	Swe	1979	16,948	8,400	170.3	21.0	5.4	16	Ro	ex Tor Belgia-99, Eva Oden-88 (len-88)
Falcon	Nis	1993	4,081	5,697	104.4	16.2	6.4	14	Cc	ex Stella Pacific-98
Humber Arm	Swe	1976	7,587	7,173	130.0	18.6	6.7	16	Rop	
Ivan Gorthon	Bmu	1974	5,173	3,500	118.2	15.6	5.0	12	Rop	ex Bravik-82 (len/conv Ro-82)
Macado	Nis	1985	6,996	9,650	123.4	20.0	7.9	16	Ccp	ex Abitibi Macado-96
Nordon	Nis	1977	5,420	7,884	113.0	19.2	7.1	14	C	ex Pasila-93
Southern Carrier (2)	Swe	1979	16,947	8,400	170.3	21.0	5.4	15	Ro	ex Tor Flandria -98, Anna Oden-88 (len-88)
Stig Gorthon	Swe	1979	10,165	7,607	119.9	21.1	6.0	13	Ro	

Owned or managed by subsidiaries B&N Sea Partner A/S or B&N Sea Partner Sweden AB.

B&N Kustvaartbedrijf Moerman BV,   Netherlands
Funnel: Yellow with green 'M' on white disc interrupting green/white/green bands
Hull: Red with black or green boot-topping.

Name	Flag	Year	GRT	DWT	Loa	Bm	Draft	Kts	Type	Former names
Dyggve **	Nld	1987	2,673	3,004	88.0	13.0	4.7	11	Cc	ex Domaide-95, Petuja-94
Eemnorge	Nld	1980	2,052	2,730	82.5	12.8	5.1	12	Cc	ex Delta B-98, Westgard-97, Laura-92, Lavola-84

Aspen Shipping & Trading BV Mundial Car. *J. Krayenbosch*

Atlantic-Rhederei F. & W. Joch KG Aztek. *J. M. Kakebeeke*

Name	Flag	Year	GRT	DWT	Loa	Bm	Draft	Kts	Type	Former names
Ferro *	Cyp	1991	1,986	3,504	88.2	14.2	5.0	12	Cc	
Forte	Nld	1989	3,998	4,001	90.8	16.2	6.4	15	Rop	
Jumbo *	Nld	1987	1,998	3,697	88.2	14.2	5.0	12	C	
Largo †	Nld	1989	3,998	4,001	90.8	16.2	6.4	15	Rop	
Libra **	Nld	1980	2,201	2,208	79.8	12.8	4.5	12	Cc	ex Allgard-89, Melton Challenger-88
Pluto *	Nld	1986	1,998	3,697	88.1	14.0	5.0	10	C	
Roelof	Nld	1983	1,600	3,152	81.6	14.1	5.4	12	C	ex Viking-92
Salvinia	Nld	1986	1,986	2,798	79.8	12.1	4.7	-	Cc	ex Alblas-94
Swallow	Nld	1996	2,848	4,251	90.5	13.2	5.8	12	Cc	
Swan	Nld	1995	2,839	4,304	90.5	13.2	5.7	12	Cc	
Swift	Nld	1993	2,825	4,148	90.5	13.4	5.6	11	C	
Tinno	Bhs	1991	1,986	3,504	88.2	14.2	5.0	12	Cc	
Torpo	Bhs	1990	1,986	3,504	88.2	14.2	4.9	12	Cc	
Sweder	Nld	1996	2,848	4,264	90.5	13.2	5.8	12	Cc	

* managed by Paal Wilson Management A/S, Norway q.v.or ** by Marin Ship Management BV, Netherlands.
† on charter to Transfennica (see ferry section).

Reederei Karl-Heinz Baase　　　　　　　Germany

Funnel: Buff or charters colours.
Hull: Blue with red boot-topping.

Name	Flag	Year	GRT	DWT	Loa	Bm	Draft	Kts	Type	Former names
Birkenwald	Atg	1969	1,387	1,355	76.3	11.2	3.8	12	C	ex Henriette Isa-83, Christopher Meeder-75
Eastwind	Cyp	1976	3,006	3,844	93.5	14.5	6.0	14	Cc	ex Caribbean Sun-94, Santa Rosa-92, Patricia I-89, Zim Napoli I-88, Trans Luso I-87, Patricia I-86, Nordic I-83, Zim Northland-83, Nordic-79
Godewind	Pmd	1977	3,622	4,415	97.5	16.1	5.7	14	Cc	ex UB Panther-97, Geranta-94, Gracechurch Star-91, Geranta-89, Karen Oltmann-89, Neerlandia-85, Karen Oltmann-78
Kiefernwald	Atg	1971	2,498	2,453	88.5	13.9	5.3	14	Cc	ex Ingeborg II-92, Norrsundet-83, Ursa-77
Ostwind	Atg	1979	1,624	1,660	79.2	13.5	3.5	12	Cc	ex Agila-91, St. Antonius-89, Aros Mistley-86, St. Antonius-85
Passatwind	Atg	1977	1,920	2,240	80.4	12.8	4.9	13	Cc	ex Irina-96, Rugard-95, Veerhaven-92, Rugard-91
Polarwind	Atg	1983	3,504	3,126	97.5	16.0	5.0	13	Cc	ex Freesia-95
Seebrise	Atg	1974	1,990	1,530	82.2	13.0	4.2	13	Cc	ex Lindaunis-85, Hispania-84, Lindaunis-83, Isle of Man-81, Lindaunis-80
Sudwind	Atg	1978	1,624	1,659	79.2	13.5	3.5	12	Cc	ex Alrek-91, Sudwind-89
Traveberg	Cyp	1975	2,287	2,560	81.4	13.4	5.0	13	Cc	ex Patria-94, American Comanche-78
Westwind	Atg	1985	3,539	3,177	101.0	16.8	5.0	13	Cc	ex Tertia-95

Baltic Group International Ltd.　　　　Estonia

Funnel: Blue with white top.
Hull: Blue with red boot-topping.

Name	Flag	Year	GRT	DWT	Loa	Bm	Draft	Kts	Type	Former names
Alvina M.	Est	1969	1,427	1,723	77.9	11.5	4.9	12	C	ex Russobalt 1-96, Alvi-92, Sten Ranger-69
Anne Timber	Est	1966	786	1,200	62.3	9.8	3.1	11	C	ex Amanda-98, Amigo-91, Padberg-87, Heljo-78
Eevi	Est	1955	556	772	51.1	8.8	3.8	9	C	ex Thorsten-94, Jan Suhr-71
Fiina Timber	Est	1970	996	2,464	77.3	12.8	5.5	12	Cc	ex Rolf D-97, Euro Sailer-87, Jenny Graebe-83, Heidberg-78, Skeppsbron-72, I/a Heidberg
Goga	Khm	1965	657	760	53.6	9.3	3.3	9	C	ex Karin-98, Karin Knorr-90, Sea Odin-80, Widor-75
Iida	Est	1968	828	785	59.5	10.1	4.2	12	C	ex Ida-94, Siv Hege-94, Havblik-92, Citra-85, Arnholt-78, Jolita-71

B&N Kustvaartbedrijf Moerman BV Salvinia. *M. D. J. Lennon*

Reederei Karl-Heinz Baase Eastwind. *J. Krayenbosch*

Name	Flag	Year	GRT	DWT	Loa	Bm	Draft	Kts	Type	Former names
Inna	Est	1972	1,427	1,847	77.9	11.5	4.9	12	C	ex Jenny-98, Kabala-97, Kabona-92
Irina Trader	Est	1976	2,002	1,530	82.2	13.0	4.2	13	Cc	ex Westwind-95, Ilni-88, Boknis-86
Kati K	Est	1958	486	720	52.3	9.0	3.5	9	C	ex Crystal V-95, Vasant-91, Star Libra-90, Hohensee-85, August von Allworden-82, Ernst de Buhr-65
Maria M	Est	1969	698	930	55.0	9.3	3.8	9	C	ex Havhelt-94, Nuni-89, Louise A-87, Annette Dania-83
Mila Timber	Est	1966	1,340	1,280	71.5	12.5	3.7	13	C	ex Fallwind-96, Heidi P-91, Westwind-85, Ruth Dieter-77

Baltic Tramp Ltd. Estonia

Funnel: Colours not confirmed.
Hull: Colours not confirmed.

Name	Flag	Year	GRT	DWT	Loa	Bm	Draft	Kts	Type	Former names
Komet	Vct	1979	1,181	1,690	68.0	11.8	4.3	9	C	ex South Med-96, Albatross 1-95, Janet C-93, Fastnet Rock-90
Ladoga-3 (2)	Blz	1973	1,511	1,968	81.0	11.9	4.0	12	C	
Ladoga-5 (2)	Blz	1973	1,511	1,968	81.0	11.9	4.0	12	C	
Ladoga-8 (2)	Blz	1974	1,511	1,885	81.0	12.0	4.0	12	C	ex Norppa-81, Ladoga-8-74
Multi Carrier	Vct	1977	721	1,010	60.0	9.6	3.2	10	C	ex Snipe-96, Petrel-92, Union Pearl-89
Multi Coaster	Vct	1977	721	1,018	60.0	9.5	3.2	10	C	ex Tern-96, Prion-92, Union Jupiter-89
Multi Trader	Vct	1977	721	1,010	60.0	9.5	3.2	10	C	ex Seagull II-96, Osprey-92, Union Saturn-89
Niral (2)	Blz	1964	1,948	2,121	96.0	13.2	3.3	10	C	ex Yelena-94, Baltiyskiy-8-94
Tramp	Blz	1978	1,181	1,690	68.0	11.6	4.3	11	C	ex North Med-96, Sea Eagle 1-96, Eileen C-93, Tuskar Rock-90

Baltimar ApS Denmark

Funnel and Hull: Colours not confirmed.

Name	Flag	Year	GRT	DWT	Loa	Bm	Draft	Kts	Type	Former names
Baltimar Boreas	Bhs	1989	2,854	2,657	91.3	15.0	4.6	12	Cc	ex Superseven-98, Perla-95, Superseven-92
Baltimar Neptune	Bhs	1988	2,854	2,742	91.3	15.1	4.6	13	Cc	ex Saigon Neptune-92, Mary Durack-91, Baltimar Neptune-88
Baltimar Nereus	Bhs	1986	3,790	4,250	106.6	16.1	5.5	14	CC	ex Lirena-97, Azapa-96, Lirena-95, Pacheco-92, ScanDutch Corsica-90, Pacheco-89, Gracechurch Gem-89, Pacheco-88, Gerrans Bay-87, Pacheco-86
Baltimar Notos	Bhs	1988	2,854	3,168	91.3	15.5	5.0	12	Cc	ex Industrial Navigator-97, Baltimar Notos-96, Permint Suria-94, Baltimar Venus-91, Jon Sanders-91, Baltimar Venus-88
Baltimar Okeanos	Bhs	1985	3,790	4,250	106.6	16.1	5.5	14	CC	ex Alina I-97, Eagle magnolia-95, Alina-93, Palacio-92, Ville de Kuwait-92, Palacio-92, Vira Bhum-90, Palacio-90, Oyster Bay-90, Global Express-86, Palacio-86
Baltimar Orion	Bhs	1990	2,854	3,168	91.2	15.1	5.0	12	Cc	
Baltimar Saturn	Bhs	1992	2,850	2,700	91.2	15.1	5.0	12	Cc	ex Orient Vision-96, Baltimar Comdiflate-??, Aotea Link II-92, Baltimar Comdiflate-92
Baltimar Sirus	Bhs	1991	2,854	3,181	91.2	15.1	5.0	13	Cc	ex Moresby Chief-99, Baltimar Sirius-98, Mekong Sirius-98, IAL President-97, Baltimar Sirius-94, Kirk Pride-92, Baltimar Sirius-91
Baltimar Venus	Bhs	1990	2,854	2,700	91.3	15.0	5.0	12	Cc	ex Lae Chief-98, Mekong Venus-98, Baltimar Venus-98, Superten-94
Industrial Carrier	Bhs	1991	2,854	3,181	91.3	15.1	5.0	13	Cc	ex Baltimar Euros-94

Name	Flag	Year	GRT	DWT	Loa	Bm	Draft	Kts	Type	Former names

Baltway Shipping Ltd. Russia

Funnel: Colours not confirmed.
Hull: Colours not confirmed.

Name	Flag	Year	GRT	DWT	Loa	Bm	Draft	Kts	Type	Former names
Antonina II	Blz	1976	2,344	2,706	84.3	13.5	5.0	14	Cc	ex Lagard-96, Lady Ulrike-88, Hejo-83
Celtic Venture	Bhs	1971	1,285	1,533	79.0	11.1	4.1	12	Cc	ex Norman Commodore-91 (len-77)
Celtic Voyager	Bhs	1975	1,015	1,519	65.7	10.8	4.1	10	C	ex Alannah Weston-84
Donna	Blz	1972	557	905	55.8	9.9	3.3	10	C	ex Fordonna-96
Star Anna	Blz	1976	1,044	1,558	65.8	10.9	4.3	11	C	ex Lough Mask-96, Rockford-95, Canford-94, Viscount-88
Star Maria	Blz	1974	1,586	2,399	75.5	11.8	5.0	11	Cc	ex Majgard-96, Tajami-84, Rie Bres-80

J. H. Barr Befrachtungs-und Reedereikontor GmbH Germany

Funnel: Blue with red 'JB' on white disc, black top.
Hull: Black or blue with red boot-topping.

Name	Flag	Year	GRT	DWT	Loa	Bm	Draft	Kts	Type	Former names
Anita B	Tuv	1985	2,564	3,050	87.9	12.8	5.0	11	Cc	ex Spica-94
Brake	Atg	1957	603	817	57.5	8.5	3.4	9	C	ex Marlies-90 (len-78)
Claus	Tuv	1987	2,006	2,723	82.0	12.7	4.5	10	Cc	
Norderfeld	Tuv	1996	2,345	3,992	82.5	12.7	5.3	11	Cc	ex Oyat-98
Ruth-W	Tuv	1984	2,119	3,500	92.1	11.5	5.2	10	Cc	
Sandfeld	Tuv	1984	1,547	1,735	82.5	11.3	3.5	10	Cc	ex Paloma I-97, Paloma-96, Landkirchen-93
Smaland	Cyp	1983	3,075	3,219	92.4	15.2	4.4	12	Cc	ex Anita Maria-97, Gerd Schepers-94
Suderfeld	Rus	1995	2,345	3,400	82.5	12.7	5.3	11	Cc	ex Pasha-98

Gerd Bartels Germany

Funnel: Cream with black top.
Hull: Black with green boot-topping.

Name	Flag	Year	GRT	DWT	Loa	Bm	Draft	Kts	Type	Former names
Francop	Atg	1991	3,818	4,654	103.5	16.2	6.1	14	Cc	ex Aquitaine Spirit-97, CMBT Cutter-96, Emma-96, Rhein Lagan-94, Francop-94, Manchester Trader-92, Francop-91
Merkur	Deu	1991	3,815	4,155	103.5	16.3	6.1	14	Cc	
Nincop	Atg	1991	3,818	4,650	103.5	16.2	6.1	15	Cc	ex OPDR Tejo-99, Nincop-95, Norasia Alexandria-95, Nincop-93, City of Valletta-92, Nincop-91

Kustenschiffahrt Bauer & Hauschildt KG Germany
Reederei Heinz-Gerog Voge KG

Funnel: Various colours.
Hull: Various colours.

Name	Flag	Year	GRT	DWT	Loa	Bm	Draft	Kts	Type	Former names
Condock IV ** (2)	Deu	1984	6,786	4,490	106.0	19.6	3.7	13	Cc/bg	ex Submerger II-93, Este Submerger II-92
Frieda	Deu	1993	3,992	5,336	100.0	18.4	6.5	15	Cc	ex Scandinavian Bridge-99, Frieda-92
Jan Fabian	Deu	1998	3,999	5,215	101.8	18.5	6.5	16	Cc	
Penhir * (2)	Fra	1983	6,705	4,390	106.1	19.6	4.8	12	Cc/bg	ex Condock III-99
Rita	Deu	1995	3,999	5,314	101.1	18.5	6.6	15	Cc	
Robert	Deu	1983	3,435	4,188	98.7	15.5	5.5	14	Cc	ex Rhein Partner-93, Robert-92, ECL Commander-92, Robert-91, Gracechurch Crown-86, Akak Success-84, Robert-84 (len-91)
Yvette	Deu	1996	6,362	7,225	121.4	18.5	6.7	16	CC	ex Partnership-96

* owned by Condock Befrachtungs GmbH and ** managed by Aug. Bolten Wm. Miller's Nachfolger GmbH & Co.

Name	Flag	Year	GRT	DWT	Loa	Bm	Draft	Kts	Type	Former names

Baum & Co. GmbH KG

Germany

Funnel: Blue with dark and light blue horizontal bands on flag on white diamond on broad light blue bands.
Hull: Blue with red boot-topping.

Name	Flag	Year	GRT	DWT	Loa	Bm	Draft	Kts	Type	Former names
Britta	Atg	1968	1,229	2,032	74.0	10.8	5.1	12	Cc	ex Latona-92, Corvus-85, Impala-75, l/a Obotrita
HMS Portugal	Atg	1996	3,821	4,766	-93.0	16.5	5.9	15	Cc	ex Karin-96, l/a Vera
Jan-Rasmus	Atg	1969	1,223	2,017	74.0	10.8	5.1	13	Cc	ex Arosita-91, John Wulff-76

Nordenhamer Bereederungs GmbH

Name	Flag	Year	GRT	DWT	Loa	Bm	Draft	Kts	Type	Former names
Anja II	Atg	1991	2,705	4,056	89.5	13.5	5.3	12	Cc	
Athens	Atg	1983	3,780	4,110	97.0	17.8	5.6	15	CC	ex Turakina-98, HMS Portugal-95, WEC Portugal-94, Akak Star-85, Arnd Becker-84
Elke	Atg	1986	1,473	2,111	79.0	10.9	4.0	10	Cc	
Emma	Atg	1985	3,412	4,104	96.1	16.2	6.0	14	Cc	ex Einswarden-98, Rangitata-98, Christa Thielemann-92, Nedlloyd Shuttle-91, Christa Thielemann-89
Gudrun II	Atg	1987	1,599	2,262	80.3	11.3	4.4	11	Cc	ex Gudrun-90 (len-94)
Hajo	Atg	1983	3,780	4,646	97.0	17.6	6.0	14	Cc	ex Takitimu-98, Ocean-94, Velazquez-91, City of Salerno-87, Ocean-86, Akak
Helga	Atg	1984	1,472	2,131	79.0	10.9	4.0	10	Cc	ex Fast Karel-98, Helga-94, Hanne-90
Hella	Atg	1985	1,473	2,100	79.0	10.9	3.9	10	Cc	ex Hel-92
Kirsten	Atg	1985	1,473	2,127	79.0	10.9	4.0	10	Cc	ex Fast Wal-98, Kirsten-93, Sabine-93
Maersk Beira	Atg	1992	7,361	9,410	128.5	20.5	8.3	16	Cc	ex Alexandra-97, Rachel Borchard-97, City of Limassol-94, Alexandra-93, Sylvia-93
Monte Verde	Cpv	1980	5,589	7,954	126.3	20.1	6.6	15	CC	ex Luso-97, Medipas Sun-89, EA Princess-88, Independent Pursuit-87, Tauria-87, Holcan Maas-87, BCR King-86, Tauria-85, Merzario Saudi-85, Louisiane-84, Tauria-83, Arabian Eagle-83, Tauria-82
MSC Frisia	Atg	1997	4,128	5,184	100.6	16.2	6.4	14	Cc	ex Tettens-98
MSC Vigo	Atg	1998	4,115	4,656	100.6	16.3	6.4	15	Cc	ex Volkers-98
Nordland	Atg	1986	7,562	9,050	127.0	20.1	8.1	16	Cc	
Portlink Caravel	Atg	1996	3,821	4,695	100.6	16.5	5.9	15	Cc	ex CMBT Caravel-98, Blexen-96, Heike-96
Sarah	Atg	1991	2,705	3,982	89.5	13.6	5.3	12	Cc	ex Cortes-96, Sarah-96
Scotia	Atg	1987	1,473	2,097	79.0	10.9	3.9	10	Cc	l/a Meise
Waddens	Atg	1984	3,784	5,189	99.5	17.2	6.5	14	Cc	ex Rangiora-98, Nedlloyd Trindad-95, Weser Guide-94, Zim Kingston-88, Weser Guide-84 Ocean-86, Ocean-84

See also James Fisher Tankships Ltd.

Beck Scheepvaartkantoor BV

Netherlands

Funnel: Blue with white italic 'B' inside white ring.
Hull: Light grey with black boot-topping.

Name	Flag	Year	GRT	DWT	Loa	Bm	Draft	Kts	Type	Former names
Alert	Nld	1984	2,970	4,830	87.0	15.4	6.7	12	C	
Arrow	Nld	1988	2,986	5,150	92.1	15.2	6.7	11	C	
Comtesse	Nld	1994	3,968	6,630	100.7	16.0	7.0	11	C	
Electron	Nld	1983	1,923	3,145	80.6	13.6	5.7	12	C	
Electron	Nld	1983	1,923	3,145	80.6	13.6	5.7	12	C	
Triton	Nld	1986	997	1,544	63.8	11.9	3.9	11	Cc	
Triumph	Nld	1986	997	1,544	63.8	11.7	3.9	11	C	
Valiant	Nld	1977	1,839	3,048	80.4	13.6	5.5	12	C	
Vedette	Nld	1990	2,033	3,502	86.0	14.2	5.3	-	Cc	
Velox	Nld	1992	2,033	3,502	86.0	14.2	5.3	-	Cc	

J. H. Barr Befrachtungs-und Reedereikontor GmbH Brake. *M. D. J. Lennon*

Baum & Co. GmbH KG (Nordenhamer Bereederungs GmbH) Anja II. *J. Krayenbosch*

Beck Scheepvaartkantoor BV Velox. *M. D. J. Lennon*

Name	Flag	Year	GRT	DWT	Loa	Bm	Draft	Kts	Type	Former names
Verona	Nld	1982	1,923	3,095	80.0	13.4	5.6	12	C	
Victress	Nld	1982	1,095	1,622	66.2	11.6	4.5	11	C	
Viscount	Nld	1997	4,999	8,130	116.6	16.8	6.9	-	Cc	

Bergen Shipping A/S Norway

Funnel: White with blue wavy band.
Hull: Blue with red boot-topping.

Name	Flag	Year	GRT	DWT	Loa	Bm	Draft	Kts	Type	Former names
Borealnes	Bhs	1998	4,197	6,260	112.7	15.2	6.5	13	C	
Elianna	Bhs	1996	4,197	6,254	112.7	15.2	6.6	13	B	ex Langenes-98
Isnes	Nor	1999	4,200	6,000	112.7	15.2	6.5	13	B	
Linito	Nis	1969	840	925	61.5	10.6	3.9	22	Cu	ex Aastun-95, Tromsbulk-91, Aasland-85, Venlo-81 (conv C-85)
Marble Bay	Nor	1999	3,092	4,200	89.9	15.2	5.2	-	C	
Marble Fjord	Nor	1999	3,500	4,250	89.9	15.2	5.2	-	C	
Marmorbulk	Nor	1979	3,423	5,210	80.8	16.5	7.2	12	Ccp	ex Markborg-95, Meran-93, Unit Sky-91, Unit Link-90, Germa Pride-82
Sava Ocean	Pan	1993	2,026	3,080	74.7	12.7	6.0	11	Cc	
Senator *	Nor	1967	687	832	55.3	9.3	3.5	10	C	ex Myraas-96, Kviksholm-85, Lady-84, Pollen-83, Pulpa-81, Clover Bres-74, Sligo-74, Clover Bres-72

*Managed by subsidiary BSHIP Management AS, except * by Mera A/S*

W. Bockstiegel Reederei KG Germany

Funnel: White with 'B' on white disc on yellow/blue diagonally quartered houseflag, black top.
Hull: Blue with red boot-topping.

Name	Flag	Year	GRT	DWT	Loa	Bm	Draft	Kts	Type	Former names
A.B.Amsterdam	Deu	1997	2,844	4,250	89.9	13.2	5.7	12	Cc	ex Saar Amsterdam-97
A.B.Bilbao	Deu	1997	2,844	4,212	89.8	13.2	5.7	12	Cc	l/a Saar Bilbao
A.B.Dublin	Deu	1997	2,844	4,211	89.9	13.2	5.7	12	Cc	l/a Saar Dublin
A.B.Liverpool	Atg	1996	2,844	4,224	89.9	13.2	5.7	12	Cc	ex Saar Liverpool-96
A.B.Lubeck	Deu	1997	2,844	4,212	89.9	13.2	5.7	12	Cc	l/a Saar Lubeck
A.B.Valencia	Deu	1996	2,844	4,250	89.9	13.2	5.7	12	Cc	ex Saar Valencia-97
Canum	Atg	1994	2,072	3,010	88.3	12.5	4.6	12	Cc	ex Saar Rouen-96, Canum-95
Dornum	Atg	1993	1,662	2,450	81.8	11.5	3.8	10	Cc	ex Saar Madrid-96
Eilsum	Atg	1992	1,662	1,920	81.8	11.4	3.8	10	Cc	ex Saar Lisboa-96, l/a Eilsum
Enno B	Atg	1983	2,649	3,525	90.4	14.0	5.9	14	Cc	ex Torm Assinie-98, Enno B-98, Karin B-98, Marina Heeren-85
Freepsum	Atg	1994	1,990	3,041	88.3	12.5	4.6	12	Cc	ex Saar Genoa-96, l/a Freepsum
Groothusen	Atg	1991	1,961	2,767	88.3	12.5	4.4	11	Cc	ex Saar London-96, Rex-91
Heiko B	Atg	1993	1,662	2,358	81.8	11.4	4.3	10	Cc	ex Pilsum-98, Saar Rotterdam-96, l/a Pilsum
Lydia B	Atg	1991	2,497	4,173	88.3	13.2	5.4	12	Cc	ex Venlo-97
Malte-B	Atg	1998	2,300	3,440	86.4	12.8	5.5	12	Cc	l/a Oldeoog
Nils B	Svk	1998	2,528	3,440	86.4	12.8	5.5	12	Cc	ex Boreas-98
Osterhusen	Atg	1985	1,297	1,527	74.9	10.6	3.4	10	C	ex-Jessica S-94
Petra	Atg	1985	5,608	7,130	117.0	19.6	6.1	13	Cc/Ro	ex CGM Saint Elie-97, Helene-97, Carib Faith-96, Helene-92, Ville du Mistral-89, Helene-88, BCR Dusseldorf-87, Bacol Rio-86, BCR Helene-85, Helene-85
Rysum	Atg	1992	1,662	2,450	81.8	11.4	4.4	10	Cc	ex Saar Emden-96, Rysum-92
Sina B	Atg	1984	1,298	1,537	74.9	10.6	3.4	10	C	ex Heike-97, Neil B-96, Sea Tiber-91, Line-88, Webo-Liner-86, Neil B-86
Sonja B	Atg	1989	1,984	2,818	89.3	12.5	4.3	11	Cc	
Suurhusen	Atg	1996	2,805	4,256	89.9	13.2	5.7	11	Cc	ex Saar Roma-96
Uphusen	Atg	1996	2,846	4,334	89.0	13.7	5.9	11	Cc	ex Saar Bremen-96
Utturn	Atg	1993	1,662	1,935	81.8	11.5	4.3	10	Cc	ex Saar Antwerp-97
Waldtraut B	Atg	1989	1,984	2,829	89.3	12.5	4.3	11	Cc	
Wirdum	Atg	1993	2,446	3,709	87.9	12.9	5.2	10	Cc	ex Saar Breda-96, Wirdum-93, Comet-93, l/a Preussen
Wolthusen	Atg	1995	2,846	4,342	90.3	13.7	5.9	11	Cc	ex Saar Hamburg-96

Bockstiegel Reederei KG Petra. *M. D. J. Lennon*

Bockstiegel Reederei KG Sonja B. *M. D. J. Lennon*

Name	Flag	Year	GRT	DWT	Loa	Bm	Draft	Kts	Type	Former names

Kapitan Siegfried Bojen-Schiffahrtsbetrieb   Germany
Funnel and Hull: Colours not confirmed.

Name	Flag	Year	GRT	DWT	Loa	Bm	Draft	Kts	Type	Former names
Baccara	Deu	1998	2,997	4,450	99.9	12.8	5.7	13	Cc	
Bosporus	Deu	1996	2,997	4,431	99.9	12.8	5.6	13	Cc	ex Saar Bosporus-96, I/a German Trader
Casablanca	Atg	1994	2,061	3,002	88.5	11.4	4.9	10	Cc	ex Saar Casablanca-97
Helsinki	Atg	1997	2,810	4,221	89.9	13.2	5.7	13	Cc	
Ibiza	Deu	1999	2,997	4,450	99.9	12.8	5.7	13	Cc	
Jacaranda	Deu	1999	2,997	4,450	99.9	12.8	5.7	13	Cc	
Johann	Atg	1993	1,589	2,682	82.4	11.4	4.8	9	Cc	
Kopenhagen	Deu	1998	2,810	4,218	89.8	13.2	5.7	12	Cc	
Korsika	Deu	1999	2,997	4,450	99.9	12.8	5.7	13	Cc	
Mallorca	Deu	1999	2,997	4,450	99.9	12.8	5.7	13	Cc	
Memel	Deu	1999	2,997	4,450	99.9	12.8	5.7	13	Cc	
Neermoor	Atg	1993	1,589	2,694	82.6	11.4	4.8	9	C	
Oslo	Atg	1996	2,805	4,245	89.9	13.2	5.7	11	C	
Riga	Deu	1997	2,810	4,220	99.9	12.8	5.7	13	Cc	
Sardinia	Deu	1998	2,997	4,450	99.9	12.8	5.7	13	Cc	
Tallin	Atg	1997	2,810	4,221	89.9	13.2	5.7	13	Cc	
Taranto	Atg	1995	2,061	3,009	88.5	11.4	5.0	-	Cc	

Hermann C. Boye & Co.   Denmark
Funnel: Various.
Hull: Black with red boot-topping.

Name	Flag	Year	GRT	DWT	Loa	Bm	Draft	Kts	Type	Former names
Andreas Boye	Dis	1979	1,167	1,304	69.8	10.4	3.6	11	Cc	
Anne Boye	Dis	1985	1,501	1,680	76.6	11.2	5.3	10	Cc	
Birthe Boye	Dis	1983	1,510	1,630	72.5	11.3	3.8	11	Cc	
Cetus	Dis	1958	201	298	41.7	6.5	3.0	9	C	ex Rio-78 (len-67)
Cimber	Dis	1956	622	645	56.5	9.1	3.2	10	C	ex Karna-82, Catrin-77
Elisabeth Boye	Dis	1990	1,652	2,650	76.7	11.2	5.3	13	Cc	
Hanne Hansen	Dis	1958	199	298	40.5	6.5	-	9	C	(len-66)
Lindholm	Dis	1952	375	580	52.4	8.1	2.9	10	C	ex Ingrid-59 (len-84)
Hermann C. Boye	Dis	1980	1,167	1,525	69.8	10.4	3.6	11	Cc	
Industrial Leader	Dis	1996	3,030	4,100	88.4	15.1	6.0	13	Cc	ex Hans Boye-96
Lette Lill	Dis	1966	1,068	1,296	66.2	10.7	4.0	11	Cc	ex Britta-91, Ortrud-89, Carina-84, Regine-75, City of Antwerp-71, Regine-66
Lis Weber	Dis	1978	991	1,050	60.0	10.4	3.6	11	Cc	ex Erria-97, Long Island-90, Thor-85
Lone Boye	Dis	1967	544	715	49.7	8.3	3.5	10	C	ex Camilla Weber-97, Johanne Ege-94, Hanne Fyn-89, Hanne Frank-87, Cito-79, Else Lindinger-76 (len-90)

Claus Braack GmbH. & Co. KG   Germany
Funnel: Various.
Hull: Blue with red boot-topping.

Name	Flag	Year	GRT	DWT	Loa	Bm	Draft	Kts	Type	Former names
Anke Bettina	Atg	1980	1,499	1,561	82.5	11.4	3.6	10	Cc	ex Pelikan-92, Hammaburg-89
Claudia-Isabell	Atg	1997	2,905	4,490	88.2	13.7	6.1	12	Cc	
Delta	Deu	1999	3,999	5,050	100.7	16.4	6.3	16	Cc	
Echo Trader	Deu	1998	3,999	5,050	100.7	16.4	6.3	16	Cc	
Emja	Atg	1990	2,497	4,161	88.3	13.2	5.5	12	Cc	
Piano	Atg	1987	1,392	1,570	72.0	11.5	3.6	11	Cc	ex Sullberg-88
Ruthensand	Atg	1981	1,834	2,623	78.6	12.8	4.6	10	Cc	ex Echo Trader-90, Ruthensand-87

Reederei Rord Braren   Germany
Funnel: Various.
Hull: Blue with red boot-topping.

Name	Flag	Year	GRT	DWT	Loa	Bm	Draft	Kts	Type	Former names
Aros News	Atg	1985	2,816	2,923	91.2	13.9	4.4	12	Cc	ex Nioba-97, Bremer Import-91, Nioba-89, Rudolf Karstens-87

Kapitan Siegfried Bojen-Schiffahrtsbetrieb Oslo. *J. Krayenbosch*

Hermann C. Boye & Co. Andreas Boye. *J. Krayenbosch*

Name	Flag	Year	GRT	DWT	Loa	Bm	Draft	Kts	Type	Former names
Brar Braren	Deu	1999	4,230	6,350	-	-	-	-	Cc	
Cellus	Deu	1978	3,081	3,798	93.3	14.5	6.1	14	Cc	ex Hildegard Wulff-83
Figaros	Atg	1980	2,050	3,254	80.3	13.9	6.6	13	Cc	ex Unamar-92, Figaros-89
Forester	Deu	1995	4,110	6,471	100.0	17.2	7.3	14	Cc	I/a Ute Braren
Heike Braren	Deu	1999	4,230	6,350	-	-	-	-	Cc	
Timbus	Deu	1983	4,043	6,231	95.0	17.6	7.4	14	Cc	I/a Hans-Gunther Bulow

Rederi AB Brevik Sweden

Funnel: Cream with white 'B' on blue diamond, blue top.
Hull: Black, some with yellow 'BREVIK TANKERS', red or green boot-topping.

Name	Flag	Year	GRT	DWT	Loa	Bm	Draft	Kts	Type	Former names
Brevik	Swe	1981	2,160	3,889	86.0	12.7	5.8	12	Tch	ex United Tiger—97, Nordic Tiger-97, United Tina-91, Luro-91
Domar **	Swe	1976	2,216	2,471	81.5	13.4	5.0	13	C	ex Hove-91
Forsvik	Swe	1981	2,409	3,889	86.0	12.7	6.0	12	T	
Marie *	Swe	1974	2,632	3,750	93.2	13.8	5.7	13	C	ex Junior Lone-83
Marina **	Swe	1980	4,155	6,385	106.2	14.9	6.9	13	Cc	ex Albona-96
Ramona	Swe	1974	4,270	6,825	111.3	16.0	7.8	14	T	ex Ramona af Donso-98, Tarnhav-96
Tankvik	Swe	1975	2,117	3,511	82.7	13.2	6.6	12	Tch	ex Chess-87, Fredensborg-85

* owned by Aste Brevik or ** by subsidiary AB Rederi Marie

Briese-Schiffahrts GmbH & Co. Germany

Funnel: White with 'b' outline, centre black/red/blue.
Hull: Grey or blue or red boot-topping.

Name	Flag	Year	GRT	DWT	Loa	Bm	Draft	Kts	Type	Former names
Alta Mar	Pmd	1995	2,840	4,137	89.7	13.6	5.7	13	Cc	ex Senator-96
Annlen-G	Atg	1995	2,061	3,004	88.5	11.4	5.0	11	Cc	ex Duisburg-96, Annlen G-95
Bavaria	Deu	1996	2,550	3,800	88.0	12.8	5.5	11	Cc	
Boreas	Deu	1999	2,300	3,440	-	-	-	-	C	
Bremer Flagge	Atg	1985	3,062	3,840	99.4	14.2	5.1	12	Cc	ex Santa Helena-97
Bremer Forest	Deu	1998	2,528	3,442	85.6	12.8	5.5	12	C	ex Leda-98, I/a Oster Till
Bremer Timber	Deu	1997	4,078	4,900	101.3	16.8	6.4	15	Cc	ex Ranzel-97
Bremer Uranus	Cyp	1993	2,478	3,834	85.4	13.3	4.8	13	Cc	
Dollart	Pmd	1995	2,532	3,560	88.0	12.8	5.5	11	Cc	
Franz Keller	Atg	1992	1,960	3,041	88.3	12.5	4.3	11	Cc	ex Tima Jupiter-92
Frigga	Pmd	1987	3,230	3,938	100.6	14.2	5.3	12	Cc	ex Sun Bird-96, Ines-93, Sun Bird-93, Ines-92, Deepsea Merchant-88, Sina-88, I/a Thule
Hanse	Atg	1990	1,508	1,688	79.7	10.9	3.5	10	Cc	ex Hanse Contor-92, Elena-90
Heimatland	Vct	1984	1,372	1,550	75.0	10.8	3.7	11	C	ex Athos-97, Heimatland-96
Helgoland	Atg	1998	4,453	6,300	105.0	16.2	7.0	14	Cc	
Industrial Alliance	Deu	1997	4,078	4,900	100.6	16.6	6.4	15	Cc	ex Bremer Forest-97, Wilgum-97
Industrial Explorer	Atg	1991	3,236	4,595	(100.0)	14.2	5.4	13	C	ex Mekong Swift-97, Coringle Bay-96, I/a Ditzum
Industrial Harmony	Deu	1997	4,078	4,900	100.6	16.8	6.4	15	Cc	I/a Torum
Kopersand	Atg	1993	1,960	3,036	88.1	12.5	4.7	11	Cc	
Leysand	Atg	1993	1,960	3,042	88.3	12.5	4.6	11	Cc	
Memmert	Deu	1999	4,100	4,900	-	-	-	-	Cc	
Miramar	Deu	1996	2,840	4,135	89.7	13.7	5.7	13	Cc	ex Geestborg-96
Musketier *	Pmd	1997	2,820	4,135	89.7	13.6	5.7	13	Cc	
Odin	Deu	1997	4,050	4,900	100.6	16.8	6.4	15	Cc	ex Industrial Unity-98. Odin-98
Paapsand	Deu	1999	2,532	3,380	-	-	-	-	C	
Porthos	Vct	1977	2,351	2,378	86.5	13.0	4.9	12	Cc	ex Thor-96, Flensburger Flagge-95, Bremer Flagge-95, Schwinge-77
Remmer	Atg	1990	1,552	2,412	79.6	11.3	4.4	10	Cc	
Santiago	Deu	1997	2,528	3,525	85.6	12.8	5.5	12	Cc	I/a Janssand
Sea Clyde	Atg	1984	1,843	2,348	80.1	12.7	4.2	11	Cc	ex Petena-98
Sina	Atg	1990	3,236	3,944	100.0	14.2	5.8	13	Cc	ex Emma Helene-90
Sjard	Atg	1989	5,753	8,224	107.4	19.3	8.3	15	ChL	ex Sea Breeze-98, Antje-97
Star	Pmd	1991	2,237	2,707	82.5	12.6	4.7		Cc	ex Huberna-91
Sudstrand	Atg	1986	3,113	4,279	88.6	15.7	6.6	13	Cc	ex Ranginui-99, Zim Bangkok-94, Anke-93, Global Express 4-89, Anke-88, Falcon-88, Anke-87
Tanja	Pmd	1989	2,190	2,735	82.5	12.6	4.7	11	CC	

Briese-Schiffahrts GmbH & Co. Bremer Uranus. *J. Krayenbosch*

Briese-Schiffahrts GmbH & Co. Franz Keller. *M. D. J. Lennon*

Name	Flag	Year	GRT	DWT	Loa	Bm	Draft	Kts	Type	Former names
Tornator	Pmd	1995	2,840	4,178	87.7	13.7	5.7	12	Cc	
Venture	Atg	1994	2,446	3,717	87.9	12.8	5.5	12	Cc	ex MSC Venture 99, Lys Trader-96
Wangeroege	Deu	1999	4,100	4,900	-	-	-	-	Cc	
Weser	Pmd	1986	3,219	4,257	100.6	14.3	5.3	12	Cc	ex Industrial Grace-98, Amke-97, Norbrit Weser-87
Wilke	Cyp	1994	2,901	4,223	91.2	13.8	5.7	13	Cc	ex Leknes-99

owned by subsidiary Briese Nederland BV, Netherlands.
Newbuildings: nine others between 2,000-3,000 grt due for 1999/2000 delivery.

Brink & Wolffel GmbH & Co. Germany
Christian Jurgensen, Brink & Wolffel Schiffahrt. Gmbh & Co

Funnel:	Various.
Hull:	Red with red boot-toping.

Name	Flag	Year	GRT	DWT	Loa	Bm	Draft	Kts	Type	Former names
Barbara	Deu	1996	2,984	4,850	98.7	16.9	5.9	15	CC	
Bonnie Rois	Deu	1998	2,990	4,791	99.6	16.9	5.9	15	CC	
Coastal Isle	Deu	1991	3,125	2,973	89.1	16.2	6.1	14	Cc	ex Johanna-97
Eider	Deu	1978	1,934	2,495	91.8	13.5	4.0	12	C	(len-94)
Eugen Rothenhoefer	Deu	1965	492	1,315	65.0	9.9	4.0	10	C	ex Katharina S-84, Gerd Sibum-76 (len/deep-68)
Eva-Maria Mueller	Deu	1998	2,446	3,680	88.0	13.0	-	10	Cc	
Inga	Deu	1985	1,584	1,783	82.0	11.5	3.5	10	C	
Jenna Catherine	Deu	1995	2,986	4,830	98.4	16.9	5.9	15	Cc	
Leona	Deu	1987	1,593	1,900	82.0	11.5	3.7	10	C	ex Scot Carrier-94, I/a Leona
Monika Mueller	Deu	1998	2,446	3,750	88.0	13.0	-	10	Cc	
Rhein Merchant	Deu	1991	3,125	4,485	89.1	16.2	6.1	14	Cc	ex Sybille-95, Baltic Bridge-93, Sybille-93
Ute Johanna	Deu	1995	2,984	4,850	96.6	17.1	5.9	15	Cc	
Wotan	Deu	1996	2,997	4,450	99.8	12.8	5.6	13	Cc	

Brise Schiffahrts GmbH Germany

Funnel and Hull:	Colours not confirmed.

Name	Flag	Year	GRT	DWT	Loa	Bm	Draft	Kts	Type	Former names
Boxter	Cyp	1981	2,023	2,840	79.7	13.0	5.7	12	Cc	ex Baltic Bridge-97, Eliza Heeren-95, Akak Success-86, Eliza Heeren-86
Cemsea	Atg	1979	2,657	4,400	86.5	14.4	6.1	13	Ce	ex Coral Sea-95, Coral-91, Puerto de Aguilas-83, Duro Seis-82
Gatje	Atg	1984	1,857	2,200	80.7	12.7	4.2	10	Cc	ex Gama-99, Lys Captain-96, Gama-95
Lark	Atg	1976	1,972	2,463	79.0	12.4	4.8	11	Cc	ex Hoogen-94, Aland II-87, Aland-83
Margareta	Ant	1984	1,781	2,515	83.2	11.5	4.4	10	Cc	
Solar	Atg	1977	2,361	2,680	86.5	13.0	5.2	12	Cc	ex Marburg-92, Solar-85
Sunnanhav	Atg	1977	2,351	2,350	86.5	13.0	4.9	12	Cc	
Svendborg	Atg	1984	2,730	2,931	98.3	13.5	4.3	10	Cc	ex Navaro-93
Swallow	Atg	1977	1,968	2,051	87.0	15.9	6.9	14	Cc	I/a Swallow II
Vanerland	Atg	1977	2,351	2,669	86.5	13.0	5.2	12	Cc	ex Vanerhav-96, Rebena-96

The British Petroleum Co. plc UK
BP Oil UK Ltd.

Funnel:	Red with narrow white and green bands.
Hull:	Black with red boot-topping.

Name	Flag	Year	GRT	DWT	Loa	Bm	Draft	Kts	Type	Former names
Border Battler	Gbr	1968	1,410	2,257	76.0	12.5	4.7	11	T	ex BP Battler-97, Inverness-76
Border Jouster	Gbr	1972	1,568	2,734	79.0	12.6	5.2	12	T	ex BP Jouster-97, Swansea-76
Border Springer	Gbr	1969	1,071	1,538	65.5	11.3	4.5	11	T	ex BP Springer-97, Dublin-76
Border Warrior	Gbr	1968	1,410	2,257	76.0	12.5	4.7	11	T	ex BP Warrior-97, Grangemouth-76

BP Gas Tankers A/S, Denmark

Name	Flag	Year	GRT	DWT	Loa	Bm	Draft	Kts	Type	Former names
Danish Arrow	Dis	1976	926	759	66.5	10.7	3.3	12	Lpg	
Danish Dart	Dis	1976	926	759	66.5	10.7	3.3	12	Lpg	

Brink & Wolffel GmbH & Co. Rhein Merchant. *J. Krayenbosch*

Broere Shipping BV Dutch Mariner. *M. D. J. Lennon*

Name	Flag	Year	GRT	DWT	Loa	Bm	Draft	Kts	Type	Former names

Broere Shipping BV Netherlands

Funnel: Black with white 'GB' on broad blue band.
Hull: Orange with black boot-topping.

Name	Flag	Year	GRT	DWT	Loa	Bm	Draft	Kts	Type	Former names
Bastiaan Broere	Nld	1988	3,693	5,098	104.3	17.0	6.2	15	Tch	
Dutch Engineer	Nld	1986	2,183	2,570	80.9	14.5	5.1	14	Tch	
Dutch Faith	Nld	1996	3,419	4,442	99.9	17.1	5.5	14	Tch	
Dutch Glory	Nld	1975	1,640	2,321	80.2	12.1	5.4	13	Tch	
Dutch Mariner	Nld	1986	2,183	2,570	81.0	14.5	5.2	14	Tch	
Dutch Master	Nld	1975	1,640	2,321	80.2	12.1	5.4	13	Tch	
Dutch Mate	Nld	1989	4,297	6,250	118.0	17.1	6.2	15	Tch	
Dutch Navigator	Nld	1991	3,693	5,098	104.3	17.1	6.2	15	Tch	
Dutch Pilot	Nld	1984	2,137	3,052	91.2	13.7	5.1	12	Tch	ex Jacqueline Broere-93 (new forepart-93)
Dutch Progress	Nld	1984	2,137	3,052	91.1	13.7	5.1	12	Tch	ex Neeltje Broere-93 (new forepart-93)
Dutch Sailor	Nld	1981	3,427	4,387	91.0	16.0	6.3	14	Tch	ex Broere Aquamarine-87
Dutch Spirit	Nld	1996	3,419	4,442	99.9	17.1	5.5	14	Tch	
Engelina Broere	Nld	1975	1,807	2,610	82.4	12.7	5.7	13	Tch	ex Chemtrans Arcturus-80
Jacobus Broere	Nld	1989	3,693	5,098	104.3	17.0	6.2	15	Tch	

Newbuildings: three 4,500 grt 6,500 dwt tankers due for 2000 delivery.
Part of Koninklijke Pakhoed Holdings NV.

Brostroms Rederi AB Sweden

Funnel: Blue with yellow entwined rope symbol.
Hull: Blue.

Name	Flag	Year	GRT	DWT	Loa	Bm	Draft	Kts	Type	Former names
CT Sky	Swe	1981	3,568	5,280	101.4	15.7	6.7	13	Tch	ex Brage Nordic-96, Alpine Rose-89, Brage Nordic-87
CT Star	Swe	1981	6,060	8,706	129.6	19.4	7.0	14	Tch	ex Sulphur-87, Stena Sulphur-87, OT Sulphur-83
CT Sun	Swe	1980	3,554	4,641	96.8	15.5	6.6	13	Tch	ex Coppelia-92

Managed by Ferm International Ship Management AB.

United Tankers AB

Funnel: Yellow with blue 'U' above yellow 'T' on blue square;
Hull: Blue with red boot-topping.

Name	Flag	Year	GRT	DWT	Loa	Bm	Draft	Kts	Type	Former names
United Nadja	Swe	1996	4,128	5,752	99.8	16.4	6.7	12	Tch	
United Nelly	Swe	1997	4,137	5,767	99.8	16.4	6.7	12	Tch	
United Nora	Swe	1997	4,137	5,811	99.8	16.4	6.7	13	Tch	
United Tony *	Swe	1982	2,593	4,165	88.0	13.1	6.4	13	Tch	ex Lecko Av Lidkoping-91

* owned by AB Shipinvest and managed by Ferm International Ship Management AB, both Sweden.

Brugse Scheepssoperij NV Belgium

Funnel: Blue with overlapping white 'B' and 'S'.
Hull: Black with red boot-topping.

Name	Flag	Year	GRT	DWT	Loa	Bm	Draft	Kts	Type	Former names
Sunny Jane	Bhs	1974	1,327	1,666	74.1	11.1	4.8	13	R	ex Fisko-95
Sunny Lady	Bhs	1970	1,547	2,538	80.8	11.3	5.3	11	C	ex Lady Patricia-95, Orchid Wave-85, Diabas-83 (len-75)
Sunny Lisa	Bhs	1975	1,327	1,666	74.2	11.1	4.7	13	R	ex Igloo Lion-95, Lindo-86
Sunny Sarah	Bhs	1971	1,178	1,542	73.5	10.7	4.7	12	R	ex Igloo Star-95, Herro-84
Sunny Tina	Bhs	1979	1,328	1,660	74.6	11.1	4.7	13	R	ex Igloo King-95, Asko-86

Hermann Buss GmbH & Cie. Germany

Funnel: White with broad blue band, narrow black top.
Hull: Light grey with green over red boot-topping.

Name	Flag	Year	GRT	DWT	Loa	Bm	Draft	Kts	Type	Former names
Amrum Trader	Pan	1997	5,941	8,081	132.3	19.5	6.9		CC	ex Seaboard Unity-98, Amrum Trader-97
Barten	Atg	1998	3,239	4,803	95.9	13.7	6.1	12	Cc	
Christa *	Cyp	1983	2,795	2,852	95.6	13.6	4.3	13	C	
Edda *	Cyp	1985	2,729	2,812	98.3	13.5	4.5	11	Cc	

Brostroms Rederi AB CT Sun. *J. Krayenbosch*

Brugse Scheepssoperij NV Sunny Lady. *J. Krayenbosch*

73

Name	Flag	Year	GRT	DWT	Loa	Bm	Draft	Kts	Type	Former names
Frieda	Atg	1996	2,901	4,515	88.0	13.7	6.1	10	Cc	
Gracechurch Comet	Atg	1995	4,984	6,928	116.4	19.5	7.1	16	CC	ex Northsea Trader-97, Texel Bay-96, Northsea Trader-95
Huemmling *	Cyp	1985	2,730	2,947	98.3	13.6	4.3	10	Cc	ex Belida-96, Helena I-96, Almaris-94
Jonas *	Cyp	1985	2,729	2,814	98.3	13.5	4.5	11	Cc	ex Pegwell Bay-98, Altair-95
Noort	Atg	1989	910	1,086	69.1	9.5	2.8	9	Cc	
Norasia Adria	Atg	1994	4,984	7,014	116.4	19.5	7.1	16	CC	ex Frisian Trader-98, Ems Bay-96, Frisian Trader-95
Norasia Attica	Atg	1995	4,984	6,974	116.4	19.5	7.1	15	CC	ex Baltic Trader-98, Zim Napoli I-97, Baltic Trader-97, Armada Trader-96, Baltic Trader-95
Olivia *	Cyp	1978	1,990	3,050	80.7	14.3	5.1	12	C	ex Fjord Star-95, Caroline-93, Cindy-89, Altappen-86
Ruth	Atg	1991	2,873	4,566	88.2	13.7	6.1	12	Cc	
Transportor	Atg	1990	2,873	4,566	88.2	13.7	6.1	11	Cc	
Vento di Ponente	Atg	1993	7,361	9,517	128.5	20.5	8.3	17	CC	ex Charlotte Borchard-97, Eastern Trader-93
Western Trader	Atg	1991	4,164	4,744	111.1	16.1	6.0	14	Cc	ex Gracechurch Meteor-97, Western Trader-91

* owned by subsidiary Medstar Shipmanagement Ltd., Cyprus.
Newbuildings: two 4,300 grt 6,300 dwt part containerships due for 1999 delivery.

Campbell Maritime Ltd.   UK

Funnel:	Colours not confirmed.
Hull:	Colours not confirmed.

Name	Flag	Year	GRT	DWT	Loa	Bm	Draft	Kts	Type	Former names
Alice PG *	Bhs	1994	3,627	6,248	102.1	16.1	6.5	-	T	
Eliza PG *	Iom	1992	3,338	5,440	96.2	16.1	6.3	12	T	
Emily PG *	Iom	1997	3,627	6,249	102.1	16.1	6.5	12	T	
Forth Bridge **	Gbr	1992	3,338	5,800	96.2	16.1	6.6	12	T	
Lesley PG *	Iom	1998	3,630	6,249	102.1	16.1	6.5	12	T	

* managed for Giles W. Pritchard-Gordon & Co. Ltd. or ** for Forth Tankers plc (Benmarine Ltd.)
See also Union Navale SA.

Carisbrooke Shipping plc   UK

Funnel:	Buff with buff 'CS' on blue rectangle.
Hull:	Light grey.

Name	Flag	Year	GRT	DWT	Loa	Bm	Draft	Kts	Type	Former names
Anja C	Brb	1991	2,230	3,222	99.7	12.5	4.3	10	Cc	ex Tima Saturn-92, I/a Union Saturn
Cheryl C	Brb	1983	1,636	2,367	70.1	13.1	5.0	10	Cc	ex Catarina Caldas-91, Catarina-89, Norbrit Rijn-87, Norbrit Hope-85
Elizabeth C	Brb	1971	1,768	2,823	85.0	12.8	5.1	-	C	ex Mark C-96, Mark-86, Security-86
Emily C *	Brb	1996	2,741	4,650	89.8	13.2	6.0	-	C	
Janet C	Gbr	1998	2,748	4,290	89.9	13.2	6.0	11	Cc	
Johanna C	Gbr	1998	2,748	4,290	89.9	13.2	5.6	11	Cc	
Klazina C	Brb	1983	1,633	2,554	81.3	12.0	4.3	10	C	ex Lasina-88, Klazina H-88, Klazina-85 (len-88)
Mark C *	Brb	1996	2,744	4,620	89.9	13.2	6.0	-	Cc	
Mary C	Brb	1977	1,522	2,440	66.1	13.1	5.1	12	C	ex Fiducia-89, Ligato-88
Minka C	Brb	1975	1,655	2,657	78.7	12.5	5.0	12	C	ex Victory-95
Nordstrand	Brb	1991	1,960	2,800	88.3	12.5	4.4	11	Cc	ex Nicole-93
Tina C	Brb	1974	1,655	2,591	78.8	12.5	5.0	12	C	ex Vanda-95
Vanessa C	Brb	1974	1,853	3,165	80.1	13.6	5.5	12	C	ex Vanessa-93
Vectis Falcon	Brb	1978	2,431	3,564	87.0	13.8	5.7	12	B	ex Fribourg-93, Clarknes-83
Vectis Isle *	Nld	1990	2,230	3,222	99.7	12.5	4.3	11	Cc	ex Lesley-Jane C-93, Union Mercury-90

* owned by subsidiary Carisbrooke Shipping (Holland) BV, Netherlands.
Newbuildings: two 2,850 grt 4,650 dwt dry cargo vessels due for 1999 delivery.

Name	Flag	Year	GRT	DWT	Loa	Bm	Draft	Kts	Type	Former names

Gastankvaartmaatschappij Chemgas BV   Netherlands

Funnel: White with red houseflag on blue panel.
Hull: Blue with red boot-topping.

Name	Flag	Year	GRT	DWT	Loa	Bm	Draft	Kts	Type	Former names
Salmon	Nld	1987	1,605	1,294	92.8	11.4	2.9	10	Lpg	
Sturgeon	Nld	1988	1,605	1,294	92.5	11.4	2.9	11	Lpg	
Trout	Nld	1990	1,997	1,520	105.6	11.9	2.9	-	Lpg	
Twaite (2)	Nld	1991	1,997	1,640	105.6	12.0	3.0	11	Lpg	
Zephyr	Nld	1985	1,621	1,800	92.6	11.4	3.2	11	Lpg	

Chr. Jensen, Soeborg og Benthin's Eftf. A/S   Denmark

CJ Shipping

Funnel: White or charterers.
Hull: Black with red boot-topping.

Name	Flag	Year	GRT	DWT	Loa	Bm	Draft	Kts	Type	Former names
Askholm	Dis	1961	836	1,430	67.5	9.6	3.6	12	Ce	ex Eastcoast-97, Kirsten Tholstrup-88 (conv Lpg-96)
Bette-Lyn	Dis	1967	640	830	54.9	9.3	3.3	10	C	ex Limfjord-90, Jens Rand-86, Balder Buur-74
Birkholm	Dis	1976	1,882	3,100	80.1	13.8	5.3	12	C	ex Vibro Star-98, Alantes-88, Ragni-80
Draco	Dis	1973	2,787	2,661	93.2	14.5	4.9	14	Cc	ex Rhein Agent-92, Gitta-91, Sagitta I-89, Sagitta-82
Egholm	Dis	1958	803	1,019	65.0	9.8	4.2	11	Ce	ex Eastwind-97, Eva Tholstrup-89 (conv Lpg-90)
Hirsholm	Dis	1983	3,504	3,126	97.5	16.0	5.0	13	Cc	ex Nordia-96, Anna-89
Katholm	Dis	1974	2,709	2,660	93.2	14.6	4.9	14	Cc	ex Elbe-96
Klintholm	Dis	1977	1,793	2,930	80.2	11.5	5.6	11	C	ex Fortuna-97, Ijsselmeer-95, Norrbotten-82, I/a Mallarsee
Kongsholm	Dis	1969	958	1,400	70.9	9.3	4.1	11	C	ex Kongsaa-97, Anne C-94, Garmo-91 (len-76)
Korsholm	Dis	1979	1,958	2,544	95.1	11.4	4.2	12	Cc	ex Guimaraes-97, Almuth-90, Petra-82, Almuth-81
Kronholm	Dis	1974	2,709	3,981	93.2	14.6	6.2	14	Cc	ex Weser-99
Lone Baand	Dis	1968	924	1,190	59.3	10.6	3.7	11	C	ex Miquelon-90, Prince of Gotland-87, Birgit T-83, Miquelon-82, Pep Miquelon-79, Miquelon-76, Karelli Coast-74, Jytte Bewa-73, Merc Jytte-70
Marina-S	Dis	1970	494	555	41.1	9.2	3.4	9	C	ex Asoy-90, Saaoy-87, Warvik-85, Ringen-80, Basel-75
Polaris	Dis	1965	686	833	55.0	9.3	3.5	12	C	ex Skirner-92, Kongsaa-85, Skirner-85, Susanne Jors-78, Eske-73, Dori Bres-72
Uranus	Dis	1977	1,440	1,510	72.0	13.1	3.9	13	C	ex Finlith-97
Vest	Dis	1951	283	488	46.0	7.5	2.8	8	C	ex Oleto-72, Holger Andreasen-68, Christa Griese-60 (len-65 & 55)

Clipper Denmark ApS   Denmark

Funnel: Colours not confirmed.
Hull: Colours not confirmed.

Name	Flag	Year	GRT	DWT	Loa	Bm	Draft	Kts	Type	Former names
Maersk Savannah	Bhs	1997	6,714	8,874	100.5	20.4	8.2	16	Cc	ex Seaboard Pacific-98, Clipper Confidence-97
Mint Accord	Bhs	1998	3,838	5,119	100.7	16.0	6.2	-	CC	
Mint Ace	Bhs	1997	3,838	5,200	100.7	16.0	6.2	-	CC	

Crescent Shipping Ltd/UK

Funnel: Black with white cresent on broad red or blue band between narrow white bands.
Hull: Brown or black with red boot-topping.

Name	Flag	Year	GRT	DWT	Loa	Bm	Draft	Kts	Type	Former names
Bardsey	Gbr	1981	1,144	1,767	69.5	11.8	4.3	10	T	ex Sten-86
Ambience	Bhs	1982	664	1,020	58.3	9.3	3.2	9	C	(len-94)

Name	Flag	Year	GRT	DWT	Loa	Bm	Draft	Kts	Type	Former names
Banwell	Gbr	1980	1,023	1,710	71.9	11.1	3.7	10	T	
Barmouth	Gbr	1980	1,144	1,771	69.5	11.8	4.3	10	T	ex Per-86
Blackfriars	Gbr	1985	992	1,677	69.9	11.2	3.8	10	T	
Blackheath	Gbr	1980	775	1,098	60.0	11.3	3.4	11	T	
Blackrock	Gbr	1989	1,646	2,675	78.5	12.7	4.9	10	T	
Boisterence	Bhs	1983	664	1,020	58.3	9.3	3.2	10	C	(len-94)
Brabourne	Gbr	1988	1,646	2,675	78.5	12.7	4.9	10	T	
Breaksea	Gbr	1985	992	1,570	69.9	11.3	3.8	10	T	
Brentwood	Gbr	1980	1,004	1,640	69.8	11.3	3.8	11	T	
Crescence	Bhs	1982	664	1,020	59.6	9.3	3.2	10	C	(len-94)
Kindrence	Bhs	1976	2,206	3,210	91.2	13.5	5.1	10	C	
Laguna *	Bhs	1980	2,465	3,845	87.2	14.0	6.2	13	C	ex Kristianne Elisa-99, Maran-96, Uralar Cuarto-90
Luminence	Bhs	1977	1,928	3,210	91.2	13.5	5.1	10	C	
Stridence	Bhs	1983	1,426	1,821	84.7	11.5	3.4	10	C	
Tarquence	Bhs	1980	664	1,020	59.6	9.3	3.2	10	C	(len-94)
Turbulence	Bhs	1983	1,426	1,821	84.8	11.5	3.5	10	C	
Urgence	Bhs	1981	1,425	1,842	84.8	11.5	3.4	10	C	
Vibrence	Bhs	1981	1,425	1,842	84.8	11.5	3.4	10	C	

* managed by Crescent Ship Management Ltd.
Jointly owned by Clipper ApS and London & Wessex Ltd., UK.

NV CMB SA   Belgium
Exmar NV

Funnel: Colours not confirmed.
Hull: Colours not confirmed.

Name	Flag	Year	GRT	DWT	Loa	Bm	Draft	Kts	Type	Former names
Lady Hilde	Lbr	1999	2,998	3,183	96.0	15.5	5.6	13	Lpg	
Lady Elena *	Lbr	1998	3,465	4,288	99.6	15.5	5.8	13	Lpg	ex Elena-98
Lady Kathleen	Lbr	1998	3,465	4,288	99.6	15.5	5.8	13	Lpg	
Lady Martine *	Lbr	1998	2,998	3,183	96.0	15.5	5.6	13	Lpg	
Lady Stephanie	Lbr	1991	3,415	4,240	(92.0)	15.8	5.8	13	Lpg	

* managed by Anglo-Eastern Ship Management Pte. Ltd., Singapore

Transportes Maritimos Insulares SARL, Portugal

Name	Flag	Year	GRT	DWT	Loa	Bm	Draft	Kts	Type	Former names
Atlantis *	Prt	1984	4,319	6,173	105.9	17.6	6.9	13	Cc	ex Hooghly Pioneer-87, Emsland-85
Pemba *	Prt	1986	2,726	2,958	92.5	13.9	4.4	-	Cc	ex Jetty-96, Karola-S-92
Ponta Sao Lourenco	Prt	1980	4,222	6,392	106.2	14.9	6.9	13	Ce	ex Valluga-96 (conv C-96)
Vitorino Nemesio	Prt	1980	2,485	3,777	86.1	14.0	5.7	14	Cc	ex Nicolette-90, Nicole-87

* managed by S & C Shipmanagement & Crewing Ltd., Portugal.

Columbia Shipmanagement (Netherlands) BV   Netherlands

Funnel: Colours not confirmed.
Hull: Colours not confirmed.

Name	Flag	Year	GRT	DWT	Loa	Bm	Draft	Kts	Type	Former names
Flottbek	Atg	1981	2,690	3,914	91.7	13.6	6.2	12	Tch	
Lauenburg	Atg	1982	2,690	3,926	91.7	13.9	6.2	12	Tch	
Reinbek	Atg	1982	2,690	3,914	91.7	13.9	6.3	12	Tch	
Rodenbek	Atg	1981	1,599	3,914	91.7	13.6	6.2	12	Tch	

C. Crawley Ltd.   UK

Funnel: Green/black.
Hull: Green.

Name	Flag	Year	GRT	DWT	Loa	Bm	Draft	Kts	Type	Former names
Aquatic	Gbr	1963	199	315	35.1	7.5	2.3	-	T	ex Busby-85
Aqueduct	Gbr	1964	594	908	62.3	10.2	3.0	10	T	ex Charcrest-91
Bruce Stone (2)	Gbr	1964	357	375	43.7	9.2	2.3	-	T	ex Viaduct-78, Bruce Stone-76
K-Toulson	Gbr	1966	614	833	52.9	10.3	3.1	9	T	ex Beechcroft-90 (len-77)
Marpol	Gbr	1957	200	360	36.6	6.5	2.6	8	T	ex Snydale H-??
Tommy	Gbr	1963	217	315	35.1	7.5	2.3	8	T	ex Batsman-87
Torduct	Gbr	1959	65	100	28.1	5.3	2.1	8	T	ex Wakefield-70

Other small ships include Charlton, Stefan Scott and Varsseveld.

Columbia Shipmanagement (Netherlands) BV Flottbek. *M. D. J. Lennon*

Dala Rederi Och Forvaltnings AB Matisse. *J. Krayenbosch*

Name	Flag	Year	GRT	DWT	Loa	Bm	Draft	Kts	Type	Former names

Dala Rederi Och Forvaltnings AB

Sweden

Funnel: Black.
Hull: Black or blue with red boot-topping.

Name	Flag	Year	GRT	DWT	Loa	Bm	Draft	Kts	Type	Former names
Chagall	Swe	1982	4,311	6,400	115.9	15.9	7.2	14	Tch	ex Indio-94
Dala Corona	Swe	1976	4,520	8,205	116.3	15.2	7.8	13	T	ex Vinga Corona-89, Corona-86 (len-78)
Dalanas	Swe	1972	2,907	5,150	110.4	12.7	6.3	12	T	ex Hai-81 (len/deep-87)
Dalcor	Swe	1991	4,095	6,209	99.6	17.0	6.5	12	Cc/T	ex Talcor-96, Alcor-91
Dalhena	Swe	1991	4,095	6,209	99.6	17.0	6.5	12	Cc/T	ex Talhena-96, Alhena-91
Dali	Swe	1988	6,506	9,939	119.8	19.0	8.0	12	Tch	ex Rava-95
Dalnati	Swe	1991	4,095	6,209	99.6	17.0	6.5	12	Cc/T	ex Talnati-96, Alnati-91
Matisse	Nis	1978	3,370	4,866	105.5	14.3	6.2	13	Tch	ex Rantum-98, Eider-88 (conv C-88)
Monet	Nis	1978	3,370	4,935	105.5	14.3	6.2	13	Tch	ex Keitum-98, Hever-88 (len/conv C-88)

Rederiet Otto Danielsen

Denmark

Funnel: Green with white 'OD'.
Hull: Grey with red boot-topping.

Name	Flag	Year	GRT	DWT	Loa	Bm	Draft	Kts	Type	Former names
Blue Bird	Bhs	1986	3,113	4,285	88.6	15.7	6.6	13	Cc	ex Saigon Progress-95, Blue Bird-92, Mexico Express-91, Tequila Sunburst-90, Blue Bird-89, Gretl-87
Bongo Danielsen	Bhs	1980	2,391	2,910	83.1	14.0	5.2	13	C	ex Grete Danielsen-90
Gudrun Danielsen	Bhs	1977	2,675	3,705	82.8	15.0	6.1	13	C	ex Kaloum-84, Gudrun Danielsen-82
Hermod	Dis	1980	2,854	3,124	95.7	13.6	4.1	10	Cc	ex Herm J-89
Maj Danielsen	Bhs	1985	3,120	4,107	88.6	15.7	6.5	13	Cc	ex Tinto-96, Band Aid Star-86, I/a Tinto
Otto Danielsen	Bhs	1985	3,120	4,100	88.6	14.5	6.5	13	Cc	ex Libra-96, Dorado-93, Band Aid Express-86, Dorado-85

Danz und Tietjens Schiffahrts KG

Germany

Funnel and Hull: Colours not confirmed.

Name	Flag	Year	GRT	DWT	Loa	Bm	Draft	Kts	Type	Former names
Anglia	Cyp	1977	3,160	3,765	95.3	14.6	5.9	14	Cc	ex Lucy Borchard-91, Baldur-84, Contship Four-79, Baldur-78
Ottar	Deu	1974	1,948	1,929	77.5	13.0	3.9	13	Cc	ex Siegeria-90, Siegerland-88, Varberg-84, Siegerland-83
P&O Nedlloyd Dover	Atg	1984	2,472	3,065	90.0	13.7	4.5	11	Cc	ex Dithmarsia-98, Zim Colombia-96, Nevis-95, Dithmarsia-90, Azrou-89, Dithmarsia-90
P&O Nedlloyd Calais	Atg	1985	2,472	3,050	90.0	13.7	4.4	11	Cc	ex Point Lisas-98, Lys Carrier-91, Holsatia-89
Sea Rover	Atg	1996	5,963	6,885	121.0	18.6	7.0	16	Cc	ex Fortunia-96

Managed by BBC-Burger Bereederungs Contor GmbH.

Scheepvaartsbedrijf K. De Groot
Q-Shipping BV

Netherlands

Funnel: Owners markings.
Hull: Blue with black boot-toppings.

Name	Flag	Year	GRT	DWT	Loa	Bm	Draft	Kts	Type	Former names
Breezand	Nld	1983	1,560	2,401	87.8	11.1	4.1	11	Cc	
Cast Bass (2)	Cyp	1992	2,882	2,250	108.9	15.1	2.8	11	Cc	ex Mirka-92, I/a Nevskiy 37
Cast Salmon (2)	Cyp	1992	2,691	2,845	108.9	15.1	3.2	10	Cc	I/a Nevskiy 36
Ems-Liner	Nld	1977	1,300	1,450	84.8	9.5	3.3	11	C	
Llano	Nld	1981	1,010	1,448	70.0	11.3	3.4	11	C	ex Union Pluto-94
Rhine Trader	Nld	1982	1,859	2,607	88.5	12.2	4.1	-	Cc	ex River Trader-95, I/a Sea River
Waterway	Nld	1981	1,010	1,448	69.9	11.3	3.4	11	C	ex Union Venus-94

Rederiet Otto Danielsen Gudrun Danielsen. *J. Krayenbosch*

Scheepvaartsbedrijf K. De Groot (Q-Shipping BV) Cast Bass. *J. Krayenbosch*

Name	Flag	Year	GRT	DWT	Loa	Bm	Draft	Kts	Type	Former names

Peter Dohle Schiffahrts-KG
Germany

Funnel: Black with black 'PD' on white diamond on white edged red band.
Hull: Various.

Name	Flag	Year	GRT	DWT	Loa	Bm	Draft	Kts	Type	Former names
Agatha	Atg	1998	5,381	6,750	107.6	18.3	6.2	12	B	
Aida	Atg	1997	4,927	6,918	107.0	18.6	6.2	12	Cc	
Alexandria	Atg	1994	4,927	6,918	107.1	18.3	6.2	12	Cc	
Alina	Atg	1998	5,381	6,750	107.6	18.2	6.2	12	B	
Anglia	Atg	1995	4,927	6,918	102.9	18.4	6.2	12	Cc	ex Arabia-96
Aurelia	Atg	1998	5,381	6,790	107.6	18.3	6.2	12	B	
Christa Kerstin	Atg	1982	1,939	2,890	88.0	11.3	4.7	11	Cc	ex Esteburg-90, Bilbao-89, Sea Este-88, Esteburg-83
Cosmea †	Deu	1990	1,985	2,620	82.5	12.5	4.5	11	Cc	
Doris T	Atg	1977	1,973	2,150	79.0	12.4	4.8	12	Cc	ex Libra II-97, Libra-85
Felix	Atg	1980	2,610	4,510	86.5	14.4	6.8	13	Cc	ex Leveche-94, Pacifico-94, Eve Pacific-93, Svea Pacific-93, Burro-88, Burro Bulk-86, Astillero-86, Cabados-85, Duro Ocho-82
Margret Knuppel	Atg	1984	8,639	9,282	133.4	21.8	7.6	16	Cc	ex Sea Expedition-98, Sea Pilot-98, Cielo di Venezuela-97, Christine Delmas-96, Maersk Caracas-95, Sea-Land Salvador-94, Maya Tikal-94, Sleipner-93, Wiking-93, Karyatein-92, City of Salerno-92, Kahira-89, Wiking-87, Woermann Ulanga-86, Wiking 1-86
Sagitta ‡	Deu	1990	1,985	2,620	82.5	12.5	4.5	11	Cc	l/a Rosemarie
Sea Cloud	Atg	1996	8,633	9,200	132.9	23.1	7.7	17	CC	ex FAS Odessa-97, Alida-96
Xandrina *	Atg	1986	1,567	1,750	81.2	11.4	3.4	9	Cc	
Zim Caribe 1	Atg	1993	7,361	9,410	128.5	20.5	8.3	17	CC	ex Cerrina-97, Lucy Borchard-97, City of Liverpool-94, Cerrina-93

* managed for Kapt. Peter Theilsiefje or † for Christian Trost Schiffahrtsges.mbH KG, both Germany.
‡ managed by Uwe von Allworden KG.
Newbuildings: five 4,000 grt 5,500 dwt roll-on roll-off vessels due for 1999 delivery.

Kapitan Manfred Draxl Schiffahrts GmbH
Germany

Funnel: White with light blue top or with black 'D' between two pairs of narrow blue bands.
Hull: Blue with red boot-topping.

Name	Flag	Year	GRT	DWT	Loa	Bm	Draft	Kts	Type	Former names
Anne	Atg	1980	1,588	1,604	79.7	11.4	3.3	10	C	ex Anda-91
Antina	Atg	1989	2,292	2,750	(84.7)	12.8	4.4	11	Cc	
Assiduus	Atg	1990	2,292	2,706	84.9	12.8	4.4	11	Cc	ex Lehship-90, Assiduus-90
Diana-Maria	Atg	1989	2,249	2,728	81.9	12.7	4.5	11	Cc	ex Betula-94
Elisabeth	Deu	1993	3,958	5,350	108.0	16.4	6.0	16	CC	
Emma	Atg	1995	4,628	5,660	113.0	16.4	6.1	16	CC	ex Gertrud-96
Kirsten	Deu	1996	5,522	6,850	118.0	19.4	7.3	17	CC	
Maersk Mombasa	Deu	1997	5,549	7,060	118.0	19.4	7.5	17	CC	ex Ingrid-99, Maersk Mombasa-99, Ingrid-97
Marman	Atg	1985	1,782	2,350	83.2	11.5	4.4	10	Cc	
Mathilda	Atg	1994	3,957	5,388	102.0	16.4	6.0	16	CC	ex Dorte-94
Panda II	Deu	1992	2,326	2,752	84.9	12.9	4.3	11	Cc	ex Edith-92
Pelayo	Atg	1995	4,628	5,660	113.1	16.4	6.1	16	CC	ex City of Oporto-98, Jane-98, Gudrun-95

Elite-Shipping A/S
Denmark

Funnel: Cream with green 'ES' and 'club' on white playing card on broad green band.
Hull: Green with red boot-topping.

Name	Flag	Year	GRT	DWT	Loa	Bm	Draft	Kts	Type	Former names
Arktis Atlantic	Dis	1992	2,815	4,110	88.4	15.2	5.3	13	Cc	ex Mekong Sentosa-96, Arktis Atlantic-94, Vigour Atlantic-94, Arktis Atlantic-93
Arktis Blue	Dis	1992	2,815	4,110	88.4	15.2	5.3	13	Cc	
Arktis Breeze	Dis	1987	1,808	2,671	79.5	13.4	5.2	11	Cc	
Arktis Carrier	Dis	1988	1,829	2,671	77.6	13.5	5.2	11	Cc	ex Delmas Carrier-95, Arktis Carrier-95

Name	Flag	Year	GRT	DWT	Loa	Bm	Draft	Kts	Type	Former names
Arktis Crystal	Dis	1994	3,810	5,400	97.4	16.4	6.7	14	Cc	
Arktis Dream	Bhs	1993	2,815	4,110	88.4	15.2	6.0	13	Cc	ex Mekong Dream-95, Arktis Dream-94, Vigour Penang-93, ex Arktis Dream-93
Arktis Faith	Dis	1994	4,980	7,120	101.1	19.2	7.3	14	Cc	ex Melfi Faith-99, Melbridge Faith-97, Arktis Faith-97
Arktis Fantasy	Dis	1994	4,980	7,120	101.1	19.2	7.3	14	CC	
Arktis Fighter	Dis	1994	4,980	7,120	101.1	19.2	7.3	14	CC	ex Ville de Rodae-96, Arktis Fighter-96
Arktis Force	Dis	1995	4,980	7,225	101.1	19.2	7.3	16	Cc	ex Melfi Force-99, Melbridge Force-97, Arktis Force-96, Melbridge Force-96, Arktis Force-95
Arktis Future	Dis	1994	4,980	7,120	101.1	19.2	7.3	16	Cc	ex Melbridge Flash-96, Arktis Future 94
Arktis Grace	Dis	1988	1,829	2,671	79.6	13.5	5.2	11	Cc	ex Aotea Link-92, Arktis Grace-91
Arktis Hope	Dis	1994	3,810	5,400	97.4	16.4	6.7	14	Cc	
Arktis Hunter	Dnk	1995	3,810	5,401	97.4	16.4	6.7	14	Cc	
Arktis Light	Dis	1993	3,810	5,401	97.4	16.4	6.7	14	Cc	
Arktis Mariner	Dis	1996	6,285	8,972	100.8	20.2	8.2	15	C	ex Melfi Halifax-98, Melbridge Major-97, Arktis Mariner-96
Arktis Mayflower	Dis	1996	6,310	8,973	100.8	20.4	8.2	15	Cc	ex Melfi Venezuela-98, Arktis Mayflower-96
Arktis Meadow	Dis	1995	6,285	8,970	100.8	20.2	8.2	15	Cc	ex Melfi Azteca-97, Melbridge Main-97, Arktis Meadow-95
Arktis Mermaid	Dis	1995	6,216	8,943	100.8	20.2	8.2	15	Cc	ex Maersk Salvador-99, Arktis Mermaid-98, Nedlloyd Corfu-97, Arktis Mermaid-96
Arktis Meridian	Dis	1996	6,310	8,900	100.8	20.5	8.2	15	Cc	
Arktis Mirage	Dis	1998	6,310	8,970	100.8	20.5	8.2	15	Cc	
Arktis Morning	Dis	1996	6,310	8,947	100.8	20.4	8.2	15	Cc	ex Maersk Luanda-99, Arktis Morning-98
Arktis Ocean	Dis	1987	1,598	2,428	76.3	11.7	5.2	11	Cc	
Arktis Pearl	Dis	1984	1,557	2,300	74.3	11.4	4.6	9	Cc	
Arktis Pride	Dis	1991	2,815	4,110	88.4	15.2	5.3	13	Cc	
Arktis Princess	Dis	1989	1,829	2,677	79.6	13.5	5.2	11	Cc	ex Queen Amelia-98, Arktis Princess-96
Arktis Queen	Dis	1989	1,829	2,676	79.6	13.5	5.2	11	Cc	ex Clearwater Bay-97, Arktis Queen-95, Queen Amelia-95, Rarotongan Rover-94, Ocean Link-92, Arktis Queen-91
Arktis River	Dis	1986	1,599	2,430	79.1	11.7	5.1	11	Cc	
Arktis Sea	Dis	1984	1,557	2,298	74.3	11.4	4.6	9	Cc	
Arktis Sky	Dis	1987	1,829	2,680	79.6	13.4	5.2	11	Cc	ex P&O Nedlloyd Coral-98, P&O Nedlloyd Eritrea-97, Arktis Sky-97
Arktis Sirius	Dis	1989	1,829	2,671	79.6	13.5	5.2	11	Cc	
Arktis Spring	Dis	1993	2,815	4,125	88.4	15.2	6.0	13	Cc	ex Mekong Spring-95, Arktis Spring-94
Arktis Trader	Dis	1987	1,591	2,470	76.3	12.3	5.2	11	Cc	
Arktis Venture	Dis	1992	2,815	4,140	88.4	15.2	6.0	12	Cc	ex Industrial Venture-96, Arktis Venture-92
Arktis Vision	Dis	1995	3,810	5,401	97.4	16.4	6.7	15	Cc	
Industrial Ace	Dis	1993	2,815	4,111	88.4	15.2	6.0	13	Cc	ex Arktis Ace-94, Elsborg-93, Arktis Ace-93
Industrial Caribe	Dis	1992	2,815	4,117	88.4	15.2	5.3	13	Cc	ex-Arktis Pacific-??, I/a Arktis Swan
Industrial Frontier	Atg	1993	2,815	4,110	88.4	15.2	6.0	13	Cc	ex Arktis Pioneer-97, Industrial Pioneer-95, Arktis Pioneer-95
Industrial Pioneer	Dis	1991	2,815	4,110	88.4	15.2	5.3	13	Cc	ex Arktis Dawn-96

Rederi AB Engship
Finland

Funnel: Cream with white 'E' on broad blue band, narrow black top.
Hull: White, black or green with green or red boot-topping.

Name	Flag	Year	GRT	DWT	Loa	Bm	Draft	Kts	Type	Former names
Aila †	Fin	1989	3,826	4,402	104.8	16.3	5.8	15	Ccp	

Name	Flag	Year	GRT	DWT	Loa	Bm	Draft	Kts	Type	Former names
Borden (2)	Fin	1977	10,100	6,615	142.2	19.3	7.2	17	Ro	ex Blue Sky-92, Bore Sky-91
Christina †	Fin	1991	3,828	4,452	103.5	16.2	6.7	15	Cc	
Fjardvagen * (2)	Fin	1972	6,040	2,607	109.5	20.4	4.9	19	Ro	ex Norman Commodore-95, Pride of Portsmouth-91, Mads Mols-89, Mols Trader-87, Merchant Trader-87, Sir Lamorak-86, Lakespan Ontario-83, Lady Catherine-81, Lune Bridge-80, Anu-80, Norcliff-74, Anu-73
Heralden	Fin	1997	10,572	7,619	138.8	22.7	7.1	20	Rop	
Hjordis †	Fin	1996	5,239	6,526	119.9	18.1	6.8	17	C	
Klenoden	Fin	1991	3,828	4,455	103.5	16.2	6.7	15	Cc	
Laura †	Fin	1996	5,239	6,410	119.9	18.1	6.8	17	Cc	
Lillgard *	Fin	1973	2,062	1,596	78.1	12.8	4.2	12	Cc	ex Gabriella-88
Linda †	Fin	1989	3,826	4,402	104.8	16.2	5.6	14	Cc	
Marjatta †	Fin	1996	5,239	6,527	119.9	18.2	6.8	17	Cc	
Najaden	Fin	1989	3,826	4,402	104.8	16.3	5.6	14	Ccp	
Outokumpu	Fin	1985	3,702	4,694	99.0	16.0	6.0	-	Cc	
Passaden	Fin	1991	3,828	4,452	103.5	16.0	6.1	15	Cc	ex ECL Captain-92, Passaden-91
Serenaden	Fin	1998	10,585	7,490	138.8	22.7	7.1	20	Rop	
Smaragden	Fin	1991	3,828	4,452	103.5	16.2	6.1	15	Cc	
Sofia †	Fin	1989	3,826	4,402	104.8	16.3	5.6	15	Ccp	
Trenden	Fin	1989	3,826	4,402	104.8	16.3	5.8	15	Ccp	
Winden	Fin	1989	3,826	4,401	104.8	16.3	5.6	15	Ccp	

* owned by Rederi AB Lillgaard or † by Oy Langh Ship AB.

Rederiaktiebolaget Gustaf Erikson   Finland

Funnel: Black with black 'GE' on broad white band, or charterers colours.
Hull: White with red boot-topping.

Name	Flag	Year	GRT	DWT	Loa	Bm	Draft	Kts	Type	Former names
Green Cooler	Bhs	1990	5,084	6,123	109.0	18.0	7.4	16	Rc	ex Erikson Cooler-96
Green Freezer	Bhs	1991	5,084	6,120	109.0	18.0	7.4	16	Rc	ex Erikson Freezer-96
Wisida Arctic	Bhs	1989	5,084	6,120	109.0	18.0	7.4	16	Rc	ex Belinda-96, Erikson Arctic-94

Ermefer S.A.   Switzerland
Vinalmar S.A.

Funnel: Red with red 'E' on broad white band.
Hull: Light grey with red boot-topping.

Name	Flag	Year	GRT	DWT	Loa	Bm	Draft	Kts	Type	Former names
Cervin	Che	1982	4,076	6,930	106.5	16.0	7.8	13	Tch	
Geneve	Che	1992	4,433	6,280	106.8	17.7	6.7	13	Tch	
Leman IV	Che	1994	5,401	9,108	113.6	17.7	8.0	13	Tch	
Rhin	Vct	1975	1,843	3,141	90.6	13.6	5.5	14	Tw	
Rhone	Che	1974	2,222	3,641	90.1	13.6	5.7	13	Tw	

John T. Essberger GmbH & Co.   Germany
Transocean Shipmanagement GmbH

Funnel: Black with large blue 'E' on broad white band.
Hull: Orange with red boot-topping.

Name	Flag	Year	GRT	DWT	Loa	Bm	Draft	Kts	Type	Former names
Alcoa Chemist	Pmd	1992	2,634	3,743	90.0	14.5	6.2	14	Tch	ex Annette Essberger-97
Aspia	Pan	1974	5,987	9,560	128.3	18.3	7.6	-	Ce	
Bernd	Deu	1967	607	993	65.7	8.3	3.5	11	T	(len-69)
Cementia	Pan	1967	3,739	5,335	106.6	15.6	6.7	14	Ce	
Coral Essberger **	Prt	1981	1,941	2,893	81.3	13.4	5.3	12	Tch	
Dalia	Pan	1970	3,739	5,300	106.6	15.6	6.8	14	Ceu	
Douro Chemist	Pmd	1992	2,634	3,741	90.0	14.5	6.1	14	Tch	ex Roland Essberger-97
Ebro	Prt	1986	2,238	2,898	81.0	14.0	5.5	12	Tch	ex Eberhard Essberger-95
Essberger Pioneer *	Sgp	1975	1,616	2,456	77.1	12.6	4.8	12	Tch	ex Alpha Lady-92, Ellen Essberger-86, Solvent Venturer-81, Essberger Pioneer-77

Rederi AB Engship Winden. *J. Krayenbosch*

Ermefer S.A. (Vinalmar SA) Leman IV. *J. Krayenbosch*

John T. Essberger GmbH & Co. (Transocean Shipmanagement GmbH) Tejo Chemist. *J. Krayenbosch*

Name	Flag	Year	GRT	DWT	Loa	Bm	Draft	Kts	Type	Former names
Essberger Progress	Sgp	1981	3,798	6,162	108.3	16.0	6.9	13	Tch	ex Golden Kyosei-96, Golden Kyosei Maru-91
Floria	Pan	1976	6,023	9,560	128.3	16.3	7.6	15	Ce	
Koralia	Pan	1995	5,929	8,811	119.5	19.0	7.0	14	Ce	
Lima Chemist	Pmd	1992	2,634	3,687	90.0	14.5	6.2	14	Tch	ex Liselotte Essberger-97
Reno	Prt	1986	2,238	2,898	81.0	13.8	5.5	13	Tch	ex Heinrich Essberger-94
Tejo Chemist	Pmd	1992	2,634	3,750	90.0	14.5	6.2	13	Tch	ex John Augustus Essberger-97
Tom Elba †	Prt	1980	1,958	2,544	80.9	13.4	5.1	12	Tch	ex Helga Essberger-92
Tom Lis †	Prt	1981	1,958	2,541	80.9	13.4	5.1	12	Tch	ex Liesel Essberger-92

* owned or ** managed by associated Transocean Shipmanagement Pte. Ltd.

† managed by Transocean Shipmanagement G.m.b.H., Germany for Trasfegas E Operacoes Maritimas Ltds., Portugal.

Estonian Shipping Co.
Estonia

Funnel: White with white 'ESCo' on light blue band.

Hull: Black or green with red boot-topping.

Name	Flag	Year	GRT	DWT	Loa	Bm	Draft	Kts	Type	Former names
Abruka	Est	1977	3,464	6,072	80.3	16.1	8.5	11	Cc	ex Khudozhnik Pimenov-92, Lijnbaansgracht-86
Amber I	Mlt	1973	6,876	7,400	135.4	18.0	7.5	15	Cc	ex Paldiski-96, Unitrader-92, Pyotr Krasikov-91
Amber II	Mlt	1973	6,876	7,400	135.4	18.0	7.5	15	Cc	Kunda-95, Andrey Andreyev-92
Arula (2)	Est	1965	1,948	2,193	95.9	13.2	3.4	11	C	ex Baltiyskiy-37-97
Calibur	Mlt	1976	9,737	5,675	126.4	19.4	6.6	18	Ro	ex Excalibur-97, Stena Mariner-95, Senator-94, Salah L-93, Stena Mariner-90, Dana-83, Seaspeed Dana-81
Dirhami	Est	1996	2,658	3,200	91.0	15.8	4.6	16	Cc	
Donata (2)	Est	1972	6,609	3,625	128.1	16.0	5.6	19	Ro	ex Saga Skane-91, Feederteam-90, Misana-87, Coastal Trader-87, Silvia-73 (len-83)
Haapsalu	Est	1985	9,489	5,500	152.7	19.2	6.6	16	Ro	ex Eemhaven-93, Nikolai Janson-91
Kalana	Est	1996	2,658	3,274	90.7	15.9	4.6	16	Cc	
Kapten (2)	Est	1967	1,595	2,157	87.9	12.4	3.3	11	C	ex Kapitan Senkevich-97, Morskoy-5-97
Kapten Konga	Est	1981	2,120	2,684	82.5	12.8	5.1	12	Cc	ex Yuriy Klementyev-91
Kapten Voolens	Est	1981	2,120	2,673	82.5	12.8	5.1	12	Cc	ex Kapitan Voolens-92
Kassari	Est	1976	3,466	6,072	80.2	16.1	8.5	11	Cc	ex Friscohaven-96, Kassari-93, Ivan Rabchinskiy-92, Leidsegracht-86
Kurkse	Est	1997	2,658	3,250	90.7	15.9	4.6	14	Cc	
Lani (2)	Est	1974	1,511	1,885	81.0	11.9	4.0	12	C	ex Ladoga-9-98
Lehola (2)	Est	1997	7,606	5,758	122.3	19.8	6.2	17	Ro	
Maira	Est	1972	1,160	1,120	71.1	10.3	3.7	12	C	ex Voosi-94, Fritsis Rozin-92
Mehaanik Krull	Est	1981	2,120	2,680	82.5	12.8	5.1	12	Cc	ex Mekhanik Krull-92
Muhu	Est	1976	3,466	6,072	80.2	16.1	8.5	11	Cc	ex Arnold Sommerling-92, Leliegracht-86
Muuga	Est	1995	2,658	3,200	90.7	15.9	4.6	16	Cc	
Naissaar	Est	1976	3,466	6,072	80.2	16.1	8.5	11	Cc	ex Unicarrier-93, Osvald Tuul-91, Lindengracht-86
Narva	Est	1979	8,545	4,600	140.1	19.2	6.6	17	Ro	ex Narahhaven-93, Timur Frunze-91
Pihtla	Est	1975	6,876	7,400	135.4	18.0	7.5	15	Cc	ex Vera Lebedyeva-92
Rakke	Est	1975	6,876	7,400	135.4	18.0	7.5	15	Cc	ex Mikhail Kedrov-92
Rakvere	Est	1977	8,545	4,600	139.6	19.2	6.6	17	Ro	ex Tallinnhaven-93, Nikolay Vilkov-91
Sindi (2)	Est	1966	1,948	2,140	95.9	13.2	3.9	10	C	ex Seagull-98, Whitenight-97, Baltiyskiy-59-96
Sompa	Est	1974	6,876	7,400	135.4	18.0	7.5	15	Cc	ex Nikolay Shvernik-92
Tiskre (2)	Est	1977	2,478	2,925	114.0	13.2	3.4	10	C	ex Voznesenye-98, Leningradskiy Komsomolets-92
Vaida (2)	Vct	1966	1,865	2,121	96.0	13.2	3.3	10	C	ex Baltiyskiy-32-98
Vaindlo	Est	1976	3,464	6,072	80.2	16.1	8.5	11	Cc	ex Khudozhnik Nesterov-92, Lauriergracht-86
Valga	Mlt	1979	8,545	4,600	139.6	19.2	6.6	17	Ro	ex Waalhaven-94, Aleksandr Osipov-92

Name	Flag	Year	GRT	DWT	Loa	Bm	Draft	Kts	Type	Former names
Valkla	Mlt	1975	6,876	7,400	135.4	18.0	7.5	15	Cc	ex Ivan Byelostotskiy-92
Viljandi	Est	1978	8,545	4,600	139.6	19.2	6.6	17	Ro	ex Merwehaven-93, Viljandi-92, Boris Buvin-92, Uniroller-91, Boris Buvin-91
Vilsandi	Est	1976	3,464	6,072	80.2	16.1	8.0	11	Cc	ex Khudozhnik Koryn-92, Looiersgracht-86
Virtsu	Est	1995	2,658	3,285	90.7	15.9	4.6	14	Cc	

F.T. Everard & Sons Ltd. UK

Funnel: Cream or black with red/white diagonally quartered rectangle.
Hull: Cream or light grey with red boot-topping.

Name	Flag	Year	GRT	DWT	Loa	Bm	Draft	Kts	Type	Former names
Ability	Gbr	1979	1,696	2,550	79.3	13.2	5.0	13	T	
Agility	Gbr	1990	1,930	3,144	80.0	14.6	5.6	11	T	
Alacrity	Gbr	1990	1,930	3,144	80.0	14.6	5.6	12	T	
Amenity	Gbr	1980	1,696	2,528	79.2	13.2	5.0	13	T	
Amity	Bhs	1980	1,147	1,767	69.5	11.8	4.3	11	T	ex Christian-88
Annuity	Gbr	1988	1,711	3,294	83.5	13.5	5.5	10	Tch	ex Janne Terkol-95
Asperity	Gbr	1997	2,965	3,778	88.6	16.5	5.6	13	T	
Audacity	Gbr	1997	2,965	3,778	88.6	16.5	5.6	13	T	
Authenticity	Gbr	1979	1,696	2,550	79.3	13.2	4.9	12	T	
Averity	Bhs	1981	1,144	1,770	69.5	11.8	4.3	11	T	ex Natalie-88
North Sea Trader *	Gbr	1991	2,230	3,222	99.7	12.5	4.3	11	Cc	
Pamela Everard	Gbr	1984	1,892	2,887	79.0	12.7	5.1	10	Cc	
Sagacity	Bhs	1973	1,926	3,238	91.3	13.3	5.1	12	C	
Sanguity	Gbr	1984	1,892	2,887	79.0	12.7	5.1	10	Cc	ex Willonia-88
Selectivity	Gbr	1984	1,892	2,887	79.0	12.7	5.1	10	Cc	
Seniority	Gbr	1991	3,493	5,163	99.5	16.6	5.4	11	C	
Short Sea Trader *	Gbr	1991	2,230	3,263	99.7	12.5	4.3	11	Cc	
Sociality	Gbr	1986	1,892	2,887	79.0	12.8	5.1	10	Cc	ex Stevonia-87
Speciality	Bhs	1977	2,822	4,245	89.7	14.3	6.0	12	Cc	
Stability	Bhs	1978	2,822	4,245	91.1	14.3	6.4	12	Cc	
Superiority	Gbr	1991	2,230	3,212	100.0	12.5	4.3	11	Cc	

* owned by Short Sea Europe plc.

Exxon Corp. USA
Standard Marine Services Ltd./UK

Funnel: Black with narrow white bands bordering broad red band.
Hull: Dark grey with red boot-topping.

Name	Flag	Year	GRT	DWT	Loa	Bm	Draft	Kts	Type	Former names
Petro Avon	Gbr	1981	2,386	3,215	91.3	13.1	5.6		Tb	ex-Esso Avon-94

Fabricius & Co. A/S Denmark

Funnel: Various.
Hull: Red with black boot-topping.

Name	Flag	Year	GRT	DWT	Loa	Bm	Draft	Kts	Type	Former names
Caroline K	Dis	1983	1,516	2,166	72.5	11.4	3.8	11	Cc	ex Jeanie Brown-98, Sagaland-93, Karolina-88, Carimed Wave-86, Karolina-85
Emilie K	Dis	1982	1,510	2,150	72.5	11.4	3.8	11	Cc	ex Arktis Star-95
Gimo One	Bhs	1986	4,896	7,310	106.8	16.6	7.6	13	C	ex Kartal 7-94
Greenland Saga	Dis	1989	2,469	3,200	87.1	14.6	6.2	18	R	
Laola	Dis	1980	2,275	2,920	99.8	11.4	4.2	10	Cc	ex Emsdeich-95
Malene	Dis	1984	845	922	53.9	9.6	3.7	11	Cc	ex Markland Saga-90
P&O Nedlloyd Jeddah	Dis	1987	3,277	4,330	94.4	15.5	5.6	12	Cc	ex Martin-97, FAS Naples-95, Tequila Sunrise-94, I/a Martin
Sea Flower	Dis	1982	1,512	1,630	72.5	11.3	3.8	10	Cc	ex Kirsten Frank-88
Sea Lion	Dis	1993	2,815	4,110	88.4	15.0	6.0	14	Cc	ex Industrial Faith-97, Sea Lion-95, IAL Premier-95, Sea Lion-93
Sea Maid	Dis	1984	1,510	1,632	72.5	11.2	3.6	10	Cc	ex Lottelith-96
Susan K.	Dis	1982	1,510	2,158	72.5	11.4	3.7	11	Cc	ex Nautilus-94, Svea Atlantic-93, Herborg-88, Carimed Sea-87, Naz-85, Hubert-85
Vinland Saga	Dis	1982	972	1,600	63.2	9.6	3.7	11	C	(len-87)

Name	Flag	Year	GRT	DWT	Loa	Bm	Draft	Kts	Type	Former names

Fll Fyffes plc

Eire

Funnel: Buff with black top.
Hull: White with red boot-topping.

Name	Flag	Year	GRT	DWT	Loa	Bm	Draft	Kts	Type	Former names
Coppename	Iom	1990	4,666	4,433	108.8	16.4	6.5	16	Rc	
Cottica *	Iom	1991	4,660	4,446	108.8	16.4	6.5	16	Rc	
Jarikaba	Iom	1986	4,238	4,277	108.0	16.0	5.9	16	R	

* managed by Marine Management Services Ltd.

James Fisher and Sons plc

UK

Funnel: Dark blue with yellow 'Fisher' (some with sea-bird).
Hull: Dark blue or black with red boot-topping.

Name	Flag	Year	GRT	DWT	Loa	Bm	Draft	Kts	Type	Former names
New Generation (me2)	Gbr	1966	2,330	2,233	86.7	16.5	4.6	11	Ro	ex Kingsnorth Fisher-90

Onesimus Dorey (Shipowners) Ltd.

Name	Flag	Year	GRT	DWT	Loa	Bm	Draft	Kts	Type	Former names
Briarthorn	Gbr	1980	1,576	2,435	74.6	12.9	4.9	12	C	ex Craigallian-89
Pentland	BRB	1980	909	1,315	60.0	11.3	3.9	12	C	ex Capacity-94, Lizzonia-89
Redthorn	Gbr	1978	2,025	3,070	85.3	13.8	5.0	12	C	ex Pinewood-90
Rockfleet **	Irl	1979	1,095	1,622	66.2	11.5	4.5	11	C	ex Globe-93
Rockisland	Irl	1978	1,279	1,467	80.4	10.1	3.3	11	Cc	ex Verena-92
Rosethorn	Gbr	1982	1,213	1,694	69.3	11.1	4.3	11	Cc	ex Shamrock Endeavour-90
Silverthorn	Gbr	1982	1,213	1,694	69.3	11.1	4.3	11	Cc	ex Shamrock Enterprise-90
Solway Fisher *	Irl	1977	1,597	2,753	73.3	13.2	5.1	11	Cc	ex Rockpoint-96, Arklow Valley-91, Procyon-84 (len-80)

* managed by James Fisher & Sons (Liverpool) Ltd, ** by Dundalk Shipowners Ltd, Eire or *** by Torbulk Ltd.

James Fisher Tankships Ltd.

Name	Flag	Year	GRT	DWT	Loa	Bm	Draft	Kts	Type	Former names
Anchorman †	Lbr	1993	4,842	6,417	101.6	17.5	6.9	12	T	
Chartsman	Lbr	1993	4,842	6,397	101.6	17.5	6.9	12	T	
Eastgate	Gib	1979	2,072	3,415	93.2	13.4	5.3	12	T	
Forth Fisher	Gbr	1997	3,368	3,628	91.0	15.6	5.1	12	T	l/a Quarterman
Galway Fisher	Gbr	1997	3,368	3,622	91.0	15.6	5.1	12	T	
Humber Fisher *	Gbr	1997	2,760	4,763	91.4	15.6	6.0	12	T	
Irishgate	Gib	1981	2,071	3,284	93.2	13.4	5.2	12	T	
Lough Fisher	Gib	1980	4,777	8,496	117.2	17.5	7.2	12	T	ex Cableman-98
Mersey Fisher	Gbr	1998	2,760	4,765	91.4	15.6	6.0	12	T	
Michael M *	Gbr	1980	2,077	3,120	82.0	15.0	5.8	14	Tch	ex BP Hunter-91
Milford Fisher	Gbr	1998	3,368	3,700	91.0	15.6	5.1	12	T	
Northgate	Gib	1981	2,071	3,290	93.2	13.4	5.2	12	T	
Oarsman	Gib	1980	1,449	2,547	76.1	12.5	4.9	10	T	
Rudderman †	Lbr	1994	4,842	6,419	101.6	17.5	6.9	12	T	
Severn Fisher	Gib	1983	5,646	10,716	119.7	19.2	7.8	11	T	ex Tankerman-98
Solent Fisher	Gbr	1997	3,368	3,700	91.0	15.6	5.0	12	T	
Steersman †	Lbr	1994	4,842	6,404	101.6	17.5	6.9	12	T	
Stellaman	Gib	1980	2,804	3,680	97.8	13.8	5.8	12	Tch	ex Navajo-94, Richard-88
Thames Fisher *	Gbr	1997	2,760	4,781	91.4	15.6	6.0	12	T	
Tyne Fisher *	Gbr	1980	1,803	2,924	75.2	13.3	5.8	12	Tch	ex Frederick M-98
Wear Fisher *	Gbr	1980	2,077	3,120	82.0	15.0	5.8	14	Tch	ex David M-98, BP Harrier-91
Westgate	Gib	1979	2,071	3,368	93.2	13.6	5.3	12	T	

* managed for James Fisher & Sons (Liverpool) Ltd,
† owned by Nordenhamer Bereederungs GmbH (Baum & Co. GmbH), Germany.

British Nuclear Fuels Ltd., UK

Funnel: Blue with white 'BNFL' beneath white ring containing yellow pattern.
Hull: Black with yellow band, grey boot-topping.

Name	Flag	Year	GRT	DWT	Loa	Bm	Draft	Kts	Type	Former names
European Shearwater (2)	Gbr	1981	2,493	1,583	80.0	12.6	5.1	11	Cn	ex Mediterranean Shearwater-94
Pacific Crane (2)	Gbr	1980	4,800	3,804	103.0	16.1	6.0	13	Cn	ex Akatsuki Maru-93, Pacific Crane-92
Pacific Pintail (2)	Gbr	1987	5,087	3,865	103.9	16.6	6.0	13	Cn	
Pacific Sandpiper (2)	Gbr	1985	5,050	3,775	103.9	16.7	6.0	13	Cn	
Pacific Swan (2)	Gbr	1979	4,473	3,792	103.0	16.1	6.0	13	Cn	
Pacific Teal (2)	Gbr	1982	4,710	3,702	103.9	16.7	6.0	13	Cn	

Fabricius & Co. A/S Greenland Saga. *J. Krayenbosch*

James Fisher Tankships Ltd. Rudderman. *M. D. J. Lennon*

Name	Flag	Year	GRT	DWT	Loa	Bm	Draft	Kts	Type	Former names

KG Fisser & Van Doornum Gmbh & Co.   Germany

Funnel: Black with three vertical markings on white disc on broad dark green band edged with narrow white bands.
Hull: Black with red boot-topping.

Name	Flag	Year	GRT	DWT	Loa	Bm	Draft	Kts	Type	Former names
Antigua *	Cyp	1981	3,253	4,613	98.9	15.5	6.0	14	Tch	
Bonaire *	Cyp	1982	3,253	4,563	98.9	15.5	6.0	14	Tch	
Camira	Irl	1997	4,107	3,960	100.0	16.2	6.4	15	Cc	
Connemara	Irl	1997	4,095	4,800	100.0	16.2	6.4	15	Cc	
Corona	Cyp	1998	4,095	4,800	100.0	16.2	6.4	15	Cc	
Cosa	Cyp	1972	4,255	6,329	101.5	16.0	7.2	13	Cc	ex Ventus-85, Erika Fisser-79 (len/rblt-90)
Innes	Cyp	1976	4,372	6,300	106.6	16.6	6.8	12	Cc	ex Conticarib-96, Innes-94, Inn-92, Ventus-79, Josun-78
Kenmare	Atg	1975	5,306	8,110	117.6	18.1	7.2	14	C	ex Raute-86, Singapura-83, Raute-78
Kinsale	Cyp	1976	5,306	8,150	117.6	18.1	7.3	15	Cc	ex Rhombus-86, Wachau-84, Bayu-83, Rhombus-78
Kronoborg	Cyp	1998	4,128	4,800	100.0	16.2	6.4	15	Cc	
Miriam	Deu	1998	4,163	4,800	100.0	16.2	6.4	15	Cc	
Okapi	Cyp	1972	4,255	6,348	101.5	16.0	7.2	13	Bc	ex Tabla-86, Boca Tabla-82, Imela Fisser-73 (len/rblt-90)
Wasaborg	Cyp	1997	4,128	5,400	100.6	16.2	6.4	15	Cc	ex P&O Nedlloyd Belem-98, Wasaborg-98
Pyrgos	Cyp	1972	4,255	6,364	101.5	16.0	7.2	13	Bc	ex Villiers-86, Elisabeth Fisser-79 (len/rblt-91)

owned by subsidiary Kompass Reederei GmbH.

Edmund Halm & Co. GmbH

Name	Flag	Year	GRT	DWT	Loa	Bm	Draft	Kts	Type	Former names
Angus	Cyp	1977	1,989	2,767	79.1	12.4	4.8	12	C	ex Andros-93, Alsterberg-86
Drax	Cyp	1977	2,205	3,927	82.5	13.4	6.6	9	C	ex Drau-91, Santana-81, Santa Teresa-81
Kells	Cyp	1977	1,986	2,657	79.2	12.4	4.8	10	Cc	ex Gotaland-88
Killarney	Irl	1978	2,563	2,908	96.3	12.4	4.8	12	Cc	ex Anholt-86, Neuwerk-81 (len-78)
Kylemore	Irl	1977	2,563	2,908	96.3	12.4	4.7	10	Cc	ex Borssum-95, Bregenz-92, Bornholm-86, Neukloster-81
Melissa	Cyp	1977	1,989	2,772	79.1	12.4	5.4	12	Cc	ex Messberg-86
Murray	Cyp	1977	2,201	3,963	82.2	13.4	6.5	9	C	ex Mur-91, Agate Prosperity-82, Atlantic Prosperity-81, Danship-77, l/a Frendo Danship (len-82)
Salamander	Cyp	1974	2,197	4,005	82.2	13.4	6.5	9	Cc	ex Salzach-91, Hilary Weston-83, Frendo Hope-76 (len-83)
Sterakovou	Cyp	1974	2,197	4,006	82.2	13.4	6.5	9	Cc	ex Steyr-91, Monitor-82, Caroline Weston-82, Frendo Grace-76 (len-82)

H. Folmer & Co.   Denmark

Funnel: Red with white 'D'.
Hull: Black with red boot-topping.

Name	Flag	Year	GRT	DWT	Loa	Bm	Draft	Kts	Type	Former names
Danalith	Dis	1976	1,440	1,300	72.0	13.1	3.9	12	C	
Danica Brown	Dis	1986	997	1,563	61.6	10.3	3.4	9	Cc	
Danica Four	Dis	1984	997	1,563	61.6	10.3	3.3	9	Cc	
Danica Green	Dis	1981	902	1,130	60.0	9.6	3.4	11	Cc	
Danica Rainbow	Dis	1987	1,087	1,718	66.8	10.2	3.7	11	Cc	
Danica Red	Dis	1983	902	1,130	60.0	9.7	3.4	11	Cc	
Danica Sunbeam	Dis	1988	1,087	1,787	66.8	10.2	3.5	10	Cc	
Danica Sunrise	Dis	1989	1,087	1,778	66.8	10.2	3.5	11	Cc	
Danica Violet	Dis	1986	1,087	1,718	66.8	10.2	5.6	9	Cc	
Danica White	Dis	1985	997	1,563	61.6	10.3	3.4	10	Cc	
Hanne Danica	Dis	1992	1,409	2,191	71.8	11.7	4.9	12	Cc	
Karina Danica	Dis	1991	1,352	2,130	69.4	11.6	4.9	13	Cc	
Marianne Danica	Dis	1993	1,409	2,200	71.8	11.7	4.9	11	C	

KG Fisser & Van Doornum Gmbh & Co. Sterakovou. *M. D. J. Lennon*

H. Folmer & Co. Danica Sunbeam. *M. D. J. Lennon*

Name	Flag	Year	GRT	DWT	Loa	Bm	Draft	Kts	Type	Former names

Furness NV   Netherlands
Rederij Theodora BV
Funnel: White with two green swallow-tail flags.
Hull: Grey with red boot-topping.

Name	Flag	Year	GRT	DWT	Loa	Bm	Draft	Kts	Type	Former names
Orion	Vct	1973	1,986	3,212	82.9	13.5	5.7	12	Tb	ex Stella Orion-99
Stella Lyra	Nld	1989	2,874	3,480	95.8	14.5	5.7	12	Tb	
Stella Pollux	Nld	1981	2,523	4,200	93.1	13.9	5.8	14	Tb	
Stella Procyon	Nld	1978	2,697	4,520	83.6	15.6	6.6	12	Tb	
Stella Rigel	Nld	1988	2,456	3,682	93.0	14.0	5.5	-	Tb	ex Francesca S-98
Stella Wega	Nld	1996	3,983	4,350	105.6	15.9	6.0	15	Tb	
Theodora	Nld	1991	4,098	6,616	110.6	17.0	7.1	14	T	

Gard Shipping A/S   Norway
Funnel: Red with black 'W' on white disc, black top.
Hull: Red.

Name	Flag	Year	GRT	DWT	Loa	Bm	Draft	Kts	Type	Former names
Gardpoint	Nis	1979	2,062	2,525	88.0	12.7	4.6	13	Cc	ex Lys-Point-97, Gardpoint-96, Lys-Point-95 (len-87)
Gardsky	Nis	1976	2,978	4,001	91.1	14.6	6.8	13	Cc	ex Isnes-94, Dollart-87
Gardsun	Nis	1977	3,026	4,281	91.0	14.6	6.8	14	R	ex Selfoss-93, Osterems-87 (len/conv C-87)
Gardway	Nis	1978	2,978	4,145	91.1	14.6	6.8	14	Cc	ex Hvassafell-95, Luhe-88
Gardwill	Nis	1978	2,020	2,250	88.0	12.7	5.3	13	Cc	ex Lys-Wind-96, Gardwill-96, Ullero-92, Lys-Tind-88 (len-93)

J. & A. Gardner & Co. Ltd.   UK
Funnel: Black with white band.
Hull: Light Grey.

Name	Flag	Year	GRT	DWT	Loa	Bm	Draft	Kts	Type	Former names
Saint Brandan	Gbr	1976	1,017	1,394	63.8	10.8	4.1	10	C/Ro	
Saint Kearan	Gbr	1978	439	775	50.4	9.1	3.3	9	Tch	
Saint Oran	Gbr	1981	621	719	53.3	9.2	3.4	10	C/Ro	

Gefo Gesellschaft fur Oeltransporte mbH & Co.   Germany
Funnel: Black with black 'GEFO' on yellow band between narrow blue bands, or blue with white 'C' on red band.
Hull: Grey, blue or red with red boot-topping.

Name	Flag	Year	GRT	DWT	Loa	Bm	Draft	Kts	Type	Former names
Bellini	Deu	1999	2,195	2,750	93.6	12.3	4.4	12	Tch	
Coralwater	Nld	1998	1,895	3,357	93.4	10.9	5.0	10	Tch	I/a Jeanine Theresa (1992)
Clearwater	Nld	1995	1,620	2,304	79.9	10.9	4.4	11	Tch	
Crystalwater	Nld	1997	1,655	2,683	80.0	11.1	5.1	12	Tch	
Donizetti	Deu	1999	2,195	2,750	93.6	12.3	4.4	12	Tch	
Gefo Baltic	Atg	1972	1,198	1,757	74.0	10.8	4.6	11	Tch	ex Tarpenbek-80
Mozart	Deu	1999	2,195	2,750	93.6	12.3	4.4	12	Tch	
Puccini	Deu	1999	2,195	2,750	93.6	12.3	4.4	12	Tch	
Rossini	Deu	1999	2,195	2,750	93.6	12.5	4.7	12	Tch	
Verdi	Deu	1999	2,195	2,750	93.6	12.3	4.4	12	Tch	

H. Glahr & Co. GmbH & Co. KG   Germany
Funnel: Colours not confirmed.
Hull: Colours not confirmed.

Name	Flag	Year	GRT	DWT	Loa	Bm	Draft	Kts	Type	Former names
Baltic Champ	Pan	1977	1,660	2,060	72.0	12.8	4.5	12	Cc	ex Pico Ruivo-95, Nordlicht II-83
Baltic Courier	Cyp	1977	1,667	2,060	72.0	12.8	4.5	12	Cc	ex Jorn Dede-95, Akak Progress-86, Jorn Dede-83, Bell Variant-78, I/a Joern Dede
Baltic Meteor	Pan	1971	1,817	1,223	75.0	13.2	4.2	15	Ro	ex Rivagijon-94
Baltic Sprinter (2)	Cyp	1980	4,291	3,580	92.1	18.4	4.6	12	Ro	ex Oparis-96, Golden Oparis-92, Oparis-91, Obotrita-87, Ville de Syrte-83, Obotrita-81

Furness NV (Rederij Theodora BV) Stella Rigel. *J. Krayenbosch*

Gard Shipping A/S Gardway. *J. Krayenbosch*

Name	Flag	Year	GRT	DWT	Loa	Bm	Draft	Kts	Type	Former names
Olga I	Pan	1973	2,595	3,689	90.4	14.8	4.7	14	Cc	ex Resolute-94, Gimo Tellus-92, Sira Ocean-90, Mare Pride-88, Nedlloyd Pride-83, Mare Pride-82, Atlantic Duke-81, Stuart Prince-79, Atlantic Duke-77, Joachim-75

Godby Shipping A/B   Finland

Funnel: White with white 'S' on green 'G', narrow black top, or charterers colours.
Hull: Green.

Name	Flag	Year	GRT	DWT	Loa	Bm	Draft	Kts	Type	Former names
Link Star	Fin	1989	5,627	4,453	106.5	17.2	6.1	15	Rop	
Mimer	Fin	1990	5,873	4,232	108.4	17.5	5.8	15	Rop	ex Bore Star-93
Mini Star	Fin	1989	5,627	4,452	107.5	17.2	6.1	15	Cc/Rop	
Miniforest	Fin	1972	2,016	2,545	88.5	12.8	5.6	11	C	ex Ilse Wulff-79
Miranda *	Fin	1999	10,471	7,250	153.5	20.9	§7.0	20	Ro	
Mistral *	Fin	1998	10,471	7,250	153.5	20.9	§7.0	20	Ro	

* on charter to Transfennica q.v.

Reederei Gerd A. Gorke   Germany

Funnel: Various.
Hull: Various.

Name	Flag	Year	GRT	DWT	Loa	Bm	Draft	Kts	Type	Former names
Corinna	Atg	1974	2,130	2,450	81.4	13.4	4.9	13	Cc	ex Vantage-93, Bell Vantage-78
Lucas	Atg	1984	2,472	3,065	90.0	13.7	4.5	11	Cc	ex Oriental Dragon-98, Sonja-95, Martini-94, Paul-92, Tiger Wave-90, Paul-89, Band Aid I-86, Paul-85
Marianne	Atg	1974	2,765	3,318	93.2	14.5	5.5	14	Cc	ex OPDR Cartagena-98, Casablanca-97, Francop-90, Manchester Faith-83, Francop-78, Manchester Faith-77, Francop-76
Nautila	Atg	1974	2,075	2,488	81.4	13.4	4.9	13	Cc	ex Leana-95, Cranz-90, Aros Olympic-81, Ute Wulff-80, Galway-79, Ute Wulff-80, American Apache-77, I/a Ute Wulff
Philipp	Atg	1978	2,567	2,937	88.4	15.5	4.9	14	Cc	ex Karat-94, Rhein Lagan-94, Ile de France-93, Karat-82, Magnolia-78, I/a Karat
Swift	Atg	1976	1,599	3,850	93.5	14.5	6.0	14	Cc	ex Bell Swift-97, Jan-91, Arfell-90, Jan-87
Tinka	Atg	1976	2,219	2,560	81.4	13.5	5.0	13	Cc	ex Taras-96, Ikaria-86

H. C. Grubbe I/S   Denmark

Funnel: Various.
Hull: Various.

Name	Flag	Year	GRT	DWT	Loa	Bm	Draft	Kts	Type	Former names
Artemis	Dis	1926	287	457	45.4	7.1	3.8	10	C	ex Lister-77, Pol II-48 (len-51)
Hanne Catharina	Dis	1970	1,729	2,035	76.6	11.3	4.8	12	C	ex Anne Catharina-91, Katharina-87, Mignon-84, Anne Catharina-82
Jenbo	Dis	1966	688	838	55.5	9.4	3.5	9	Cc	ex Alma Koppelmann-85
Jenclipper	Dis	1976	548	710	49.7	8.3	3.7	10	Cc	ex Aries Trigon-82
Jenka	Dis	1970	520	710	49.7	8.3	3.5	11	C	ex Great Circle-84, Bokul-79
Jenlil	Dis	1971	1,188	1,954	74.0	10.9	5.1	11	Cc	ex Renate-93, Renate Omega-92, Renate-87, Annette-86, Osteriff-82
Kim	Dis	1977	1,213	1,535	72.2	10.4	3.6	10	C	ex Sine Bres-89 (len-80)

Hagland Shipping A/S   Norway

Funnel and Hull: Colours unconfirmed.

Name	Flag	Year	GRT	DWT	Loa	Bm	Draft	Kts	Type	Former names
Michelle	Mlt	1975	3,123	4,240	94.2	15.4	6.0	12	Cc	ex Amulet-94
Millenium	Pan	1978	6,355	8,139	121.0	18.0	7.6	14	Ccp	ex Aquarius 2-98, Aquarius-97, Boxy-89

Godby Shipping A/B Mimer. *M. D. J. Lennon*

Hammann & Prahm Reederei Sheila Hammann. *M. D. J. Lennon*

Name	Flag	Year	GRT	DWT	Loa	Bm	Draft	Kts	Type	Former names
Mina	Nis	1972	1,923	3,272	91.1	13.3	5.1	12	C	ex Mira Bulk-96, Tara Bulk-87, Fred Everard-85
Minerva	Nor	1973	1,480	2,378	70.0	13.2	5.3	12	C	ex Ronita-86, Brunita-84
Mira Nor	Nor	1981	2,343	3,241	80.9	13.5	6.1	11	Cc	ex Corriente-93, Anglo-89, Corconte-86

Hammann & Prahm Reederei Germany

Funnel: Black 'H P' seperated by green diamond on white band between upper green and lower red bands.
Hull: Blue.

Name	Flag	Year	GRT	DWT	Loa	Bm	Draft	Kts	Type	Former names
Eric Hammann	Deu	1991	1,156	1,323	58.8	11.7	3.6	9	Cc	
Evert Prahm	Deu	1996	1,598	2,390	78.3	11.7	4.5	11	C	
Gerhard Prahm	Deu	1982	1,022	1,089	74.5	9.5	2.9	10	C	ex RMS Bavaria-96, Gerhard Prahm-92
Lore Prahm	Deu	1989	1,156	1,323	58.0	11.8	3.6	9	Cc	
Martha Hammann	Deu	1985	1,832	2,287	80.7	12.7	4.2	11	Cc	
Rebecca Hammann	Deu	1995	1,595	2,420	76.4	11.7	4.5	10	C	
Selene Prahm	Deu	1994	1,584	2,422	75.1	11.7	4.5	10	C	
Sheila Hammann	Deu	1983	1,022	1,113	74.5	9.5	2.9	10	C	ex RMS Anglia-96, Sheila Hammann-92
Walter Hammann	Deu	1988	1,156	1,323	58.8	11.7	3.5	9	Cc	
Wilhelmine Steffens	Deu	1981	1,022	1,092	74.3	9.5	2.9	10	C	ex RMS Scotia-96, Wilhelmine Steffens-92, Lucky Star-91

Heinrich Hanno & Co. BV Germany

Funnel: Blue with white 'HOS' beneath cargo symbol.
Hull: Various colours with red boot-topping.

Name	Flag	Year	GRT	DWT	Loa	Bm	Draft	Kts	Type	Former names
Bengalen	Ant	1978	1,951	3,265	81.7	14.1	5.5	12	C	ex Zomerhof-93, Sylvia Omega-85
Caspic	Nld	1978	1,599	3,265	81.7	14.1	5.5	12	C	ex Vijverhof-93, Sylvia Gamma-85
Cemile	Nld	1991	2,370	4,270	88.3	13.2	5.7	12	C	
Combi Trader	Nld	1975	1,399	2,807	71.5	13.0	5.7	12	Cc	ex Ocean Coast-75
Ikiena	Nld	1993	2,735	4,266	89.6	13.2	5.7		Cc	
Katja	Nld	1993	2,735	4,200	89.6	13.2	5.7	-	C	
Magdalena	Nld	1990	2,371	4,247	88.3	13.2	5.5	12	C	
Marja	Nld	1993	2,715	4,293	89.8	13.2	5.5	-	C	
Marjolein	Ant	1994	2,715	4,293	89.8	13.2	5.6	12	C	
North Sea	Nld	1978	1,931	3,214	81.7	14.1	5.5	12	C	ex Elise-92, Sylvia Beta-85
Scotia	Nld	1977	1,951	3,214	81.7	14.1	5.5	12	C	ex Vredehof-93, Katja-91, Carib Bird-88, Reestland-87, Sylvia Alpha-85

Hanson Aggregates Marine Ltd. UK

Funnel: Blue with 'mermaid' on blue 'A' symbol on white band.
Hull: Black with red boot-topping, or brown (Cambrook).

Name	Flag	Year	GRT	DWT	Loa	Bm	Draft	Kts	Type	Former names
Arco Adur	Gbr	1988	3,498	5,360	98.3	17.7	6.3	12	Dss	
Arco Arun	Gbr	1987	3,476	5,360	98.3	17.5	6.3	12	Dss	
Arco Avon	Gbr	1986	3,474	5,360	98.3	17.5	6.3	12	Dss	
Arco Axe	Gbr	1989	3,498	5,348	98.3	17.7	6.3	12	Dss	
Arco Beck (2)	Gbr	1989	3,325	4,745	99.6	17.0	6.3	12	Dss	ex Cambeck-97
Arco Bourne (2)	Gbr	1981	3,249	4,557	97.5	17.1	6.3	12	Dss	ex Cambourne-97
Arco Dart (2)	Gbr	1990	1,309	1,700	67.7	13.0	4.1	10	Dss	
Arco Dee (2)	Gbr	1990	1,309	1,812	67.7	13.0	4.1	10	Dss	
Arco Dijk (2)	Gbr	1992	4,960	9,823	113.2	19.6	7.7	12	Dss	ex Camdijk-97
Arco Humber *	Gbr	1972	5,487	8,962	107.0	20.0	7.4	14	Dss	ex Deepstone-86
Arco Severn	Gbr	1974	1,915	2,806	81.5	14.1	5.0	12	Dss	
Arco Thames	Gbr	1974	2,645	4,357	98.5	15.5	5.4	12	Dss	
Arco Trent	Gbr	1971	594	835	63.6	9.9	3.3	10	Dss	ex Amey I-74 (len-72)
Arco Tyne	Gbr	1975	2,684	4,357	98.5	15.5	5.4	13	Dss	
Cambrae * (2)	Gbr	1973	4,107	5,202	99.8	17.1	7.3	12	Dss	
Cambrook	Bhs	1982	2,318	3,020	99.8	11.4	4.3	10	Cc	ex Lena Wessels-87

* laid up

Heinrich Hanno & Co. BV Combi Trader. *M. D. J. Lennon*

Hanson Aggregates Marine Ltd. Arco Dart. *Philip Kempsey*

Name	Flag	Year	GRT	DWT	Loa	Bm	Draft	Kts	Type	Former names

E.H.Harms GmbH & Co. Car Feeder Service   Germany

Funnel: Blue with white disc, narrow black top.
Hull: Grey with red boot-topping.

Name	Flag	Year	GRT	DWT	Loa	Bm	Draft	Kts	Type	Former names
Feedercadet	Prt	1972	6,722	4,665	113.5	19.2	6.2	16	Ro	ex Aschberg-96, Bore IX-77
Feedercaptain *	Mlt	1993	8,659	3,222	99.9	20.5	5.6	14	V	
Feederchief *	Mlt	1993	8,659	3,222	99.9	20.5	5.6	14	V	
Feedercrew	Prt	1972	3,641	2,100	88.2	14.6	4.8	13	V	ex Hallstavik-91 (conv Rop-91)
Feederman	Prt	1972	6,712	4,700	113.5	19.2	6.2	16	Ro	ex Beerberg-96, Bore X-78,
Feedermaster (2)	Prt	1972	4,603	839	100.5	16.0	4.0		Ro	ex Orakali-87, Kalidora-84, Monza-83
Feedermate (2)	Pmd	1998	9,233	3,346	99.9	19.5	5.5	15	V	
Feederpilot	Pmd	1999	9,000	2,500	99.9	19.5	5.5	15	V	
Feedersailor	Prt	1972	3,641	2,100	88.2	14.6	4.8	14	V	ex Carola Schulte-91 (conv Rop-91)

* owned by Kawasaki Kisen KK, Japan.

Harren & Partner Schiffahrts GmbH   Germany

Funnel: Various.
Hull: Blue or green with red boot-topping.

Name	Flag	Year	GRT	DWT	Loa	Bm	Draft	Kts	Type	Former names
Helen	Cyp	1992	2,446	3,735	87.9	12.8	5.5	10	Cc	ex Pandora-99
Nenufar Atlantico	Esp	1996	5,544	7,200	118.0	19.7	7.3	17	CC	ex Pan Tau-98, Medfeeder Malta-98, Pan Tau-97
Niklas	Cyp	1992	2,446	3,735	87.9	12.8	4.5	10	Cc	ex Padua-99
OPDR Douro	Deu	1995	3,791	4,766	100.6	16.5	5.9	15	Cc	ex Emstal-95
Palatin	Atg	1990	5,753	7,640	107.4	19.3	8.3	15	Cchl	ex Calypso-98, Lena-98, I/a Annegret
Pampero *	Atg	1995	4,628	5,660	113.4	16.4	6.1	16	Cc	ex Cari Sun-97, Pampero-96, Cari Sun-96, Pampero-95
Paramar	Deu	1998	2,820	4,023	89.7	13.6	5.7	13	Cc	
Rhein Master	Atg	1994	3,790	4,766	100.6	16.5	5.9	12	Cc	ex Rhein Lagan-96, Paranga-95
Rheintal †	Deu	1996	3,830	4,766	100.5	16.5	5.9	12	Cc	ex Calderon-97, Rheintal-96
Scan Pacific **	Deu	1997	5,752	5,100	100.3	19.0	6.6	16	CC/Ro	
Scan Partner **	Deu	1997	5,752	5,147	100.9	19.0	6.6	16	CC/Ro	
Solymar	Pmd	1998	2,820	4,023	89.7	13.6	5.7	13	Cc	
Spirit of Resolution	Ant	1997	3,379	4,766	100.6	16.5	5.9	12	Cc	ex Pasadena-98
Stadt Augsburg	Deu	1997	4,004	5,270	104.8	16.6	6.6	16	Cc	
Transmar	Pmd	1998	2,840	4,023	89.7	13.6	5.7	13	Cc	
Ultramar	Pmd	1997	2,820	4,128	89.7	13.6	5.7	13	Cc	I/a Papagena

* managed by RMS Schiffahrtskontor Bremen GmbH, or ** on charter to Scanscot Shipping Services q.v.
† owned by subsidiary Ems-Fracht Schiffahrts GmbH & Co. KG.

Hartmann Schiffahrts. GmbH & Co. KG   Germany

Funnel: Various.
Hull: Blue with red boot-topping.

Name	Flag	Year	GRT	DWT	Loa	Bm	Draft	Kts	Type	Former names
Castor	Nld	1996	4,178	5,905	110.4	15.9	6.1	15	CC	ex Iberian Bridge-98, Castor-97
Danubegas	Deu	1998	4,201	4,300	98.5	15.2	6.5	14	Lpg	
Dollart Gas	Cyp	1990	4,200	5,688	99.9	15.9	7.2	14	Lpg	
Emsgas	Lbr	1984	5,284	5,670	114.8	17.4	6.7	14	Lpg	
Garmo	Cyp	1994	2,901	4,206	91.2	13.8	5.8	12	Cc	I/a Ilka
Germania	Deu	1993	8,721	9,355	125.2	19.0	8.0	16	Cc/Ro	
Haugo	Cyp	1994	2,811	4,206	91.2	13.9	5.8	12	Cc	I/a Niels
Isargas	Lbr	1991	4,200	5,688	100.0	15.9	7.2	14	Lpg	
Jadegas	Lbr	1992	4,822	6,240	113.0	15.9	7.0	14	Lpg	
Jummegas	Lbr	1993	4,822	6,292	113.7	15.9	7.0	14	Lpg	
Ledagas	Lbr	1984	5,284	5,686	114.8	17.4	6.7	14	Lpg	
Maido	Deu	1999	4,000	4,500	-	-	-	-	Lpg	ex Travegas-99
Max Planck	Lbr	1992	4,429	5,560	(99.9)	16.2	7.2	14	Lpg	I/a Oriongas
Norgas Traveller	Nor	1980	6,684	7,770	130.0	17.8	7.6	14	Lpg	ex Chem Olefine-91, Olefine Gas-90, Crusader Point-87, Beate-80 (len/conv C-87)
Odergas	Deu	1999	4,000	4,500	-	-	-	-	Lpg	
P&O Nedlloyd Capri	Deu	1996	6,114	7,697	125.5	19.8	6.4	16	Cc	ex Antares-97

96

Harren & Partner Schiffahrts GmbH OPDR Douro. *J. Krayenbosch*

Harren & Partner Schiffahrts GmbH Scan Pacific. *J. Krayenbosch*

Name	Flag	Year	GRT	DWT	Loa	Bm	Draft	Kts	Type	Former names
P&O Nedlloyd Corinth	Deu	1996	6,114	7,761	126.6	20.2	6.4	16	CC	ex TMM Jalisco-97, Neptun-96
P&O Nedlloyd Corsica	Deu	1996	6,114	7,761	126.6	20.0	6.4	16	CC	ex Nedlloyd Corsica-98, Aries-96
Phoenix Gas	Lbr	1993	4,484	5,500	(99.9)	16.2	6.8	15	Lpg	
Rio Gas	Lbr	1986	7,581	7,840	136.3	19.0	6.8	15	Lpg	
Santa Clara	Lbr	1985	7,581	7,850	136.3	19.1	6.8	15	Lpg	

Newbuildings: six 3,000 grt 4,050 dwt Lpg tankers due for 1999/2000 delivery.

Feederlines BV, Netherlands

Name	Flag	Year	GRT	DWT	Loa	Bm	Draft	Kts	Type	Former names
Amsteldiep	Nld	1996	4,099	5,916	110.4	15.9	6.1	15	CC	ex Tyne Bridge-98, Amsteldiep-97, Emily Borchard-97, I/a Amsteldiep
Borndiep	Nld	1998	3,454	5,020	106.6	13.8	5.6	-	Cc	
Commandant l'Alexandre	Nld	1999	2,050	2,250	-	-	-	-	Cc	
Eemsdiep	Nld	1996	3,170	4,680	98.8	13.8	5.7	-	Cc	
Hoendiep	Nld	1995	1,998	3,662	88.2	14.0	5.0	11	Cc	
Ijsseldiep	Nld	1998	3,600	5,000	106.6	13.8	5.6	12	Cc	
Lengai	Cyp	1997	3,266	4,150	91.0	15.7	5.7	14	Cc	
Marnediep	Nld	1999	3,300	4,575	106.6	13.8	5.6	12	Cc	
Reitdiep	Nld	1995	2,901	4,198	91.2	13.8	5.8	12	Cc	ex Mercator-98, Reitdiep-95
Santa Luzia	Nld	1998	3,620	4,513	98.3	15.4	5.7	15	CC	ex Merwediep-98
Tyr	Cyp	1997	3,601	4,649	98.3	15.7	5.7	15	Cc	
UAL Africa	Nld	1997	5,296	6,853	118.2	18.8	6.5	16	Cc	ex Cielo del Brasile-98, I/a Maasdiep
UAL Angola	Nld	1997	6,114	8,160	126.5	19.8	6.4	16	Cc	ex Johannes Boele-98, Seaboard Atlantic-98, Johannes Boele-97

KG Paul Heinrich GmbH & Co.　　　　Germany

Funnel: Buff with red 'PH' on white diamond on red panel.
Hull: Light grey with white 'SAL', green boot-topping.

Name	Flag	Year	GRT	DWT	Loa	Bm	Draft	Kts	Type	Former names
Annegret	Atg	1992	5,780	8,224	107.4	19.3	8.3	14	Chl	
Calypso	Atg	1990	5,753	7,640	107.4	19.3	8.3	14	Cc	ex Lena-98, I/a Annegret
Frauke	Atg	1994	5,782	7,713	107.4	19.7	8.3	15	Cchl	
Gloria	Atg	1997	8,388	9,400	151.5	20.7	7.8	20	Cchl	
Lena	Atg	1998	8,388	9,630	151.6	20.6	7.8	20	Cchl	
Margaretha	Atg	1992	5,782	7,802	107.4	19.9	8.3	15	Cc	
Paula	Atg	1992	5,783	7,520	107.4	19.9	8.3	14	Cchl	
Regine	Atg	1996	5,799	7,713	107.4	19.7	8.3	15	Cchl	
Steinkirchen	Atg	1991	5,780	7,910	107.4	19.6	8.3	15	Cchl	ex Grietje-98
Svenja	Atg	1996	5,799	7,713	107.5	19.7	7.9	15	Cchl	
Trina	Atg	1995	5,799	7,380	107.4	19.7	8.3	15	Cchl	
Wiebke	Atg	1993	5,782	8,200	107.4	19.9	8.3	14	Cchl	
Wilma	Atg	1997	8,388	9,549	151.6	20.6	7.9	20	Cchl	

Newbuildings: four 8,400 grt 9,270 dwt semi-container/heavy lift vessels due for 1999 delivery.

Helmsing & Grimm GmbH & Co.　　　　Germany

Funnel: White with black toothed top.
Hull: Black with red boot-topping.

Name	Flag	Year	GRT	DWT	Loa	Bm	Draft	Kts	Type	Former names
Adelaide	Cyp	1972	5,202	7,470	124.5	16.4	7.1	15	C	ex Leo Schroder-83
Elisabeth	Cyp	1969	2,851	4,179	96.1	14.7	5.9	14	C	ex Eskdalegate-77, Fredericksgate-74, Bruni-74
Fione	Pan	1967	2,348	3,770	96.2	13.5	5.9	13	C	ex Abdul Razaak Sanusi-79, Gratia-77
John C. Helmsing	Cyp	1967	2,451	3,780	96.1	13.5	5.9	13	C	ex Fiducia-75
Mariann	Pan	1972	1,953	3,015	91.4	13.3	5.1	14	C	
Senya	Cyp	1973	5,202	7,470	124.5	16.4	7.1	15	C	ex Lutz Schroder-86
Therese	Cyp	1972	1,953	3,015	91.4	13.3	5.1	14	C	

Hartmann Schiffahrts. GmbH & Co. KG Danubegas. *J. Krayenbosch*

Helmsing & Grimm GmbH & Co. John C. Helmsing. *J. Krayenbosch*

Name	Flag	Year	GRT	DWT	Loa	Bm	Draft	Kts	Type	Former names

C. J. Helt & Co. {Denmark}

Funnel: Colours not confirmed.
Hull: Blue with red boot-topping.

Name	Flag	Year	GRT	DWT	Loa	Bm	Draft	Kts	Type	Former names
Alka II	Vct	1969	525	726	49.7	8.3	3.5	10	C	ex Carbas-94, Minna-88, Jonny af Karlshamn-86, Toveland-85, Tovelil-79
Cemida	Vct	1966	684	1,156	55.0	9.3	3.5	11	C	ex Laguna-93, Ulla-89, Ulla Lonnie-86, Gitte Steen-77, Bidjovagge-72, Liss-70
Embla	Dis	1968	699	848	55.0	9.3	3.5	10	C	ex Grollen-89, Susanne Dania-78
Lucie	Blz	1968	919	1,021	59.3	10.6	3.7	12	C	ex Dragso-91, Ingrid af Stockholm-89, Merc Mariner-79
Othonia	Dis	1965	465	670	52.1	8.7	3.3	11	C	ex Fionia-77
Uno	Dis	1971	1,937	2,443	77.3	12.8	5.5	12	Cc	ex Saaoy-91, Euro Broker-87, Jan Graebe-83, Munkbron-73, I/a Jan Graebe
Skantic	Swe	1974	1,081	1,094	64.6	11.1	3.6	11	C	ex Skanlill-99, Skanlith-83

Tankskibsrederiet Herning A/S {Denmark}

Funnel: Red with black top, some with shield.
Hull: Red.

Name	Flag	Year	GRT	DWT	Loa	Bm	Draft	Kts	Type	Former names
Anette Theresa	Dis	1976	1,440	2,093	73.6	11.5	4.6	12	T	ex Birgitta-86
Bitten Theresa	Iom	1999	2,900	5,250	-	-	-	-	Tch	
Ditte Theresa	Dis	1977	2,813	4,501	92.8	14.7	6.8	13	Tch	ex Bravado-96
Grete Atlantic *	Bhs	1968	915	1,591	78.1	11.0	3.6	11	Tch	ex Rims Mariner-97, Sally Schmidt-92, Kathe H-90 (len-77)
Grete Theresa	Iom	1968	772	1,061	64.0	9.9	3.8	11	Tch	ex Unicorn Michael-91, Onabi-77
Maria Theresa	Dis	1972	805	1,132	65.8	9.8	3.9	11	Tch	ex Unicorn Odabo-91, Odabo-81
Marianne Theresa	Dis	1991	1,716	3,232	83.5	13.7	5.5	11	Tch	ex Else Terkol-95
Pia Theresa	Dis	1976	563	795	49.7	8.3	3.5	11	Tch	ex Limfjord-84, Arroi-82 (conv C-85)
Sara Theresa	Dis	1974	2,114	3,646	82.7	13.0	6.6	13	Tch	ex Hvalrossen-87, Bragd-87
Sofie Theresa	Dis	1981	2,551	3,512	87.0	14.0	6.3	14	Tch	ex Amanda-88
Vitta Theresa	Dis	1991	1,892	2,294	97.5	10.9	4.4	10	Tch	(len-97)

* managed by BR Shipmanagement A/S

A/B Broderna Hoglund {Sweden}

Funnel: Various.
Hull: Various.

Name	Flag	Year	GRT	DWT	Loa	Bm	Draft	Kts	Type	Former names
Argonaut	Atg	1960	1,068	1,930	74.8	10.8	4.9	11	C	ex Johann I-87, Argonaut II-83, Argonaut-78, Anita Adele-70
Bleking	Swe	1966	1,210	1,115	68.1	10.8	3.8	12	C	ex Bremer Mercur-84
Key	Swe	1967	1,219	1,115	68.2	10.9	3.8	11	C	ex Bremer Saturn-84
Lea	Swe	1970	1,345	1,430	76.4	11.9	3.6	12	C	ex Clipper I-85, Martha I-83, Dynacontainer II-72, I/a Liselotte Bos
Lissa	Swe	1956	491	671	53.1	8.4	3.2	9	C	ex Nea-79, Solklint-77
Ostfart	Swe	1950	366	559	45.5	7.4	3.2	11	C	ex Tranvik-85, Gemini-81, Westvag-79, Nysater-57 (len-63)
Pavona	Swe	1951	286	370	42.4	7.4	2.7	9	C	ex Carlso-73, Pavona-61, Pavonis-60
Turi	Blz	1955	498	1,212	65.2	9.5	4.0	11	C	ex Utklippan-92, Grimskar-90, Egaria-87, Hoburgen-85, Isgard-85, Britmari-79, Beluna-61 (len-69)

C. J. Helt & Co. Alka II. *M. D. J. Lennon*

Tankskibsrederiet Herning A/S Pia Theresa. *M. D. J. Lennon*

Name	Flag	Year	GRT	DWT	Loa	Bm	Draft	Kts	Type	Former names

H.S.S. Holland Ship Service BV Netherlands

General Shipping & Chartering Services V.o.F. 'GENCHART'

Funnel: White with blue 'G'.
Hull: Blue with red boot-topping.

Name	Flag	Year	GRT	DWT	Loa	Bm	Draft	Kts	Type	Former names
Carola I	Cyp	1983	5,934	9,620	113.5	17.1	8.6	13	C	ex Carola Smits-93
Steel Shuttle	Nld	1985	993	1,715	64.8	11.1	4.3	12	C	
Steel Sprinter	Nld	1985	993	1,715	64.8	11.1	4.3	12	C	

Holwerda Shipmanagement BV Netherlands

Funnel: Blue with white 'H' symbol crossed by two blue wavy arrows.
Hull: Blue with red boot-topping.

Name	Flag	Year	GRT	DWT	Loa	Bm	Draft	Kts	Type	Former names
Agnes *	Nld	1978	1,008	1,559	65.8	11.1	4.3	11	C	ex Expansa II-85
Elsa	Nld	1985	3,986	6,025	106.6	18.1	6.6	14	Cc	ex UB Lynx-96, Elsa-96, Umag Cayenne-93, Clement-92, Frisian Glory-86, Samsun Glory-85
Fenja	Nld	1985	3,727	4,152	103.5	16.5	5.6	13	Cc	ex Meteor-95, Maersk Tinto-91, Uwe Kahrs-90, Maersk Tinto-90, Uwe Kahrs-89, Gracechurch Gem-88, Uwe Kahrs-86
Gera	Nld	1988	2,749	3,146	94.5	16.1	5.0	14	Cc	ex Inishowen-98, Angela Jurgens-96
Tanja	Nld	1986	3,801	4,636	103.5	16.2	5.6	14	Cc	ex Kate-96, Containerships II-90, I/a Kate
Tina	Nld	1985	3,727	4,185	103.5	16.5	5.6	14	Cc	ex Wega-96

* managed by Vertom Scheepvaart en Handelsmaatschappij BV.

Bror Husell Chartering AB Ltd. Finland

Funnel: Cream.
Hull: Red with black boot-topping.

Name	Flag	Year	GRT	DWT	Loa	Bm	Draft	Kts	Type	Former names
Anette	Fin	1973	569	890	56.2	10.0	3.3	11	C	ex Marygard-84, Mary Weston-81
Midgard	Fin	1985	2,932	3,050	95.7	14.4	4.3	12	Cc	ex Artemis-98, Marlen-L-92
Ostgard	Fin	1980	2,718	2,866	95.0	13.5	4.3	12	Cc	ex Navisara-94, Norma-90
Sydgard	Fin	1981	2,225	2,574	80.8	13.4	5.1	13	Cc	ex Verena-93, Ina Lehmann-89,
Transgard	Fin	1996	10,570	7,629	138.5	22.7	7.1	20	Rop	

Newbuildings: four 2,800 grt 3,700 dwt dry cargo vessels due for 2000 delivery.

Hydroship Services A/S Norway

Funnel: Orange with white viking ship and 'HYDRO' on blue square.
Hull: Orange or grey with blue/orange 'HYDRO-GAS' and logo, red boot-topping.

Name	Flag	Year	GRT	DWT	Loa	Bm	Draft	Kts	Type	Former names
Balina	Nis	1975	4,226	6,153	106.6	15.8	7.5	16	Lpg	ex Tarquin Ranger-82, Deltagas-86
Haugvik	Nis	1973	2,076	2,489	79.7	13.0	6.8	13	Lpg	ex Sigurd Jorsalfar-85
Hydrobulk	Mlt	1986	3,088	4,319	94.4	15.5	6.1	12	Ccu	
Hydrogas *	Nis	1977	1,744	2,060	72.0	12.8	4.5	11	Lpg	ex Este-89 (conv C-89)
Hydrogas II *	Nis	1977	1,744	1,964	72.0	12.8	4.4	12	Lpg	ex Britta II-92, Britta I-87, American Cheyenne-79, Britta-77 (conv Cc-92)
Hydrogas III *	Nis	1975	2,198	2,645	81.5	13.4	5.0	13	Lpg	ex Coburg-96, Nautilus-88, American Cherokee-79, I/a Nautilus (conv Cc-96)

* managed by Larvik Shipping A/S.

The Iceland Steamship Co. Ltd Iceland

Funnel: Light blue and broad white band beneath black top.
Hull: Black with white 'EIMSKIP', red boot-topping.

Name	Flag	Year	GRT	DWT	Loa	Bm	Draft	Kts	Type	Former names
Bakkafoss	Atg	1982	5,424	7,782	106.5	19.0	7.7	15	Cc	ex Helios-88, Cape Henry-87, Helios-86, Katherine Borchard-85, Helios-83, Asian Eagle-82, I/a Helios
Dettifoss	Cyp	1982	5,424	7,752	106.5	19.1	7.7	14	Cc	ex Rachel Borchard-91, Ilse Wulff-87, Convoy Ranger-87, Ilse Wulff-86

Holwerda Shipmanagement BV Fenja. *J. Krayenbosch*

Hydroship Services A/S Hydrogas II. *J. Krayenbosch*

Name	Flag	Year	GRT	DWT	Loa	Bm	Draft	Kts	Type	Former names
Godafoss	Atg	1982	5,503	7,787	106.5	19.3	7.7	15	CC	ex Nedlloyd Dragon-94, Oriolus-93, CCNI Antartico-89, Oriolus-83
Lagarfoss	Atg	1983	6,670	8,340	117.5	20.2	7.5	15	CC	ex Sea Navigator-97, Levant Weser-97, Birte Ritscher-94, Rachel Borchard-94, Birte Ritscher-91, Independent Concept-89, Kartagena-87, Concorde Tide-84, I/a Birte Ritscher
Maersk Georgetown	Atg	1979	4,226	5,840	110.0	16.1	5.4	13	Cc	ex Skogafoss-98, Ostebay-84, Kalymnos-81, I/a Ostebay
Reykjafoss	Atg	1979	4,226	4,070	109.9	16.1	5.4	13	CC	ex Regulus-84

Interscan Schiffahrtsgellschaft m.b.H. Germany

Funnel: Colours not confirmed.
Hull: Green with red boot-topping.

Name	Flag	Year	GRT	DWT	Loa	Bm	Draft	Kts	Type	Former names
Caribbean Trader	Deu	1999	4,320	6,366	100.0	17.2	7.3	15	Cc	
Christina Star	Deu	1997	4,320	6,366	100.0	17.2	7.3	15	Cc	ex Christina-97, I/a Papagena
Industrial Millenium	Deu	1998	4,246	6,288	100.0	17.0	7.3	15	Cc	I/a Karin
Pamela	Deu	1985	1,586	1,738	83.4	11.3	3.5	10	Cc	ex Boberg-88
Patria	Cyp	1996	2,210	3,519	82.5	12.5	5.7	-	C	
Patriot	Cyp	1994	2,163	3,086	82.4	12.6	5.2	12	Cc	
Peikko	Cyp	1983	1,521	1,756	82.5	11.4	3.6	10	Cc	ex Sabine L-98, RMS Germania-95, Sabine L-92
Pinta	Deu	1993	2,190	2,795	82.3	12.6	4.9	11	Ccp	
Pionier †	Cyp	1989	2,270	2,801	82.3	12.5	4.9	11	Cc	
Premiere	Deu	1985	1,649	1,631	82.5	11.3	3.5	10	Cc	
Sooneck *	Atg	1986	1,616	2,019	82.5	11.3	3.9	10	Cc	

* managed for Horst Striesow Schiffahrtsges. KG or † for Pioner Wolter Schiffahrtsgesellschaft m.b.H. & Co.

Th. Jacobsen & Co. A/S Norway

Funnel: Colours not confirmed.
Hull: Colours not confirmed.

Name	Flag	Year	GRT	DWT	Loa	Bm	Draft	Kts	Type	Former names
Adra	Nis	1968	1,656	2,264	83.9	12.0	4.6	12	C	ex Bammen-93, Sommen-79 (len-73)
Bremer Norden	Nis	1977	1,896	1,400	80.9	12.9	3.4	11	Cp	ex Capella-90
Bremer Saturn	Nis	1994	2,854	3,895	89.7	13.8	5.7	12	Cc	
Concord	Nis	1985	6,994	9,260	123.4	20.0	8.0	16	Ccp	ex Abitibi Concord-96, Concord-94, Abitibi Concord-92
Coralli	Nis	1971	2,397	2,554	88.5	13.9	6.5	14	Cc	ex Bremer Banken-98, Coralli-96, Carina-93, Hacklin Blue-92, Skanden-91, Margret-84, Margret Knuppel-76, Pinto-73, Hannes Knuppel-73
Emma	Nis	1969	2,621	4,235	98.4	14.0	6.0	14	T	ex Malik II-98, Pom Baltica-92, Vinga Baltica-89, Tebonia-87
Etzel	Nis	1971	2,397	3,704	88.5	13.9	6.5	14	Cc	ex Bremer Stauer-97, Etzel-96, Eve-93, Hanklin White-92, Eden-91, Eve-86, Heino-82, Scol Venture-76, Baltic Unit-73, Heino-71
Harmon	Nis	1991	2,641	3,628	88.0	13.8	5.4	13	Cc	ex Bremer Export-97, Nedlloyd Caribbean -94, Bremer Export-93
Julie	Nis	1970	2,029	3,556	82.0	12.5	5.1	13	C	ex Seaction-93, Sannida-90, Scheldeborg-89
Riga Merchant	Pan	1980	5,590	6,070	130.3	17.4	6.9	14	C	ex Pioner Uzbekistana-98
Sarah	Nis	1971	2,390	2,568	88.5	13.8	5.3	14	Cc	ex Bremer Handel-97, Sarah-95, Sabine D-88, Twiehausen-83, Ibesca Algeria-80, Ibesca Espana-78, Twiehausen-77
Vivaldi	Nis	1982	3,922	6,125	104.3	16.7	6.8	12	Tch	ex Echoman-97

The Iceland Steamship Co. Ltd. Dettifoss. *J. Krayenbosch*

Jungerhans & Co. Reedereiverwaltung Angela J. *J. Krayenbosch*

Name	Flag	Year	GRT	DWT	Loa	Bm	Draft	Kts	Type	Former names

Jaczon Rederij En Haringhandel B.V.   Netherlands

Funnel: Colours not confirmed.
Hull: Colours not confirmed.

Name	Flag	Year	GRT	DWT	Loa	Bm	Draft	Kts	Type	Former names
Holland Klipper	Nld	1989	3,999	5,363	107.7	16.2	7.6	18	R	
Orange Klipper	Nld	1991	4,091	5,416	108.2	16.2	7.9	17	R	
Oceaan Klipper	Nld	1992	4,091	5,416	108.2	16.2	7.9	17	R	

Jungerhans & Co. Reedereiverwaltung   Germany

Funnel: Colours not confirmed.
Hull: Blue with red boot-topping

Name	Flag	Year	GRT	DWT	Loa	Bm	Draft	Kts	Type	Former names
Amisia J	Deu	1999	4,370	5,400	100.8	18.8	6.7	15	Cc	
Angela J	Atg	1995	3,806	4,766	99.8	16.5	5.8	14	Cc	ex CMBT Cruiser-96, I/a Angela J
Bremer Handel	Atg	1994	3,806	4,766	100.6	16.5	5.9	15	Cc	ex Regina J-97
Cagema St. Lucia	Deu	1997	3,833	4,766	100.6	16.5	5.9	15	Cc	I/a Gerd J
Cagema St. Vincent	Deu	1997	3,850	4,766	100.6	16.5	5.9	15	Cc	I/a Tim
Canis J.	Deu	1998	6,400	8,800	132.3	19.4	7.3	-	CC	
Coastal Bay	Atg	1991	2,463	3,269	87.4	13.0	5.1	12	Cc	ex Rhein Feeder-96, Rhein Lee-94, Rhein Feeder-93, Liesel I-91
Coastal Breeze	Atg	1990	2,463	3,200	87.4	13.0	5.1	12	Cc	ex Hanni J-98, Herm J-97, Cari-Star-94, Primo-92, Medeur Primo-92, Rhein carrier-91, Herm J-90,
Doris J	Deu	1997	3,840	4,766	100.6	15.5	5.9	15	Cc	
Harun	Deu	1985	5,608	7,130	117.0	19.6	6.1	13	Cc/Ro	ex Cam Iroko Express-96, Carib Navigator-95, Navigare-94, Ville de Byblos-93, Navigare-92, Seacrest Achiever-91, Navigare-89, Bacol Santos-87, BCR Jane-85, Naviagre-85
Heimar J	Atg	1985	5,608	7,120	116.5	19.6	6.2	13	Cc/Ro	ex Flensburg-98, FAS Austria-97, FAS Var-96, Nedlloyd Rose-95, Heinrich J-92, Ville du Levant-92, Heinrich J-90, Lido Adriatico-90, Seacrest Pioneer-89, Heinrich J-88, Bacol King-87, BCR King-87, RMS Laguna-86, Heinrich H-85
Hydra J.	Deu	1999	4,370	5,400	100.8	18.8	6.7	15	Cc	
Maria J	Atg	1983	4,827	6,028	102.6	18.2	6.1	11	Cc/Ro	ex EWL Guyana-91, Marie J-89, RMS Laguna-88, Maria J-86, Ville de Surte II-84, Maria J-84
MF Carrier	Atg	1992	2,481	3,221	87.4	13.0	5.1	12	Cc	ex Intermodal Carrier-96, Rhein Carrier-95, Heide J-93
MF Egypt	Atg	1993	2,480	3,269	87.5	13.0	5.1	12	Cc	ex Intermodal Egypt-96, Anna J-93
MF Levant	Atg	1991	2,480	3,237	87.4	13.0	4.7	12	Cc	ex Intermodal Levant-96, Diana J-93, Queensee-93
MF Mare	Atg	1991	2,463	3,200	87.5	13.0	5.0	12	Cc	ex Intermodal Mare-96, Trident Star-95, Adele J-93, Medeur Secondo-93, Adele J-92
Seaboard Spirit	Atg	1985	2,295	2,596	95.9	14.1	4.1	10	Ro	ex Anke S-97, Dyggve-94, RMS Alemannia-94, Anke S-92
Simone J	Deu	1997	3,840	4,635	100.6	16.5	5.9	15	Cc	
Stephan J	Atg	1995	3,833	4,635	100.6	16.5	5.9	15	Cc	
VAL Rooach	Deu	1997	6,393	8,750	133.5	19.7	7.3	17	CC	ex Lauritzen Ecuador-99, I/a Mira J
Vanguard	Atg	1994	3,806	4,766	100.6	16.5	5.9	15	Cc	ex Cari Sea-95, Angela J-94

Kahn Scheepvaart BV   Netherlands
Jumbo Shipping Co. SA

Funnel: Colours not confirmed.
Hull: Colours not confirmed.

Name	Flag	Year	GRT	DWT	Loa	Bm	Draft	Kts	Type	Former names
Daniella	Nld	1989	5,818	7,600	98.4	20.9	7.1	-	Chl	ex Stellaprima-90
Fairlift	Nld	1990	6,953	7,780	100.3	21.0	7.4	13	Cchl	
Fairload	Nld	1995	4,962	7,500	95.7	17.8	6.8	14	Chl	
Fairmast	Ant	1983	6,792	6,833	110.0	20.4	7.3	13	Chl	(conv Ro/hl-86)
Jumbo Challenger	Ant	1983	6,555	6,375	109.9	19.2	7.3	13	Chl	(conv Ro/hl-86)
Jumbo Spirit	Nld	1995	4,962	5,200	95.7	18.4	6.8	14	Chl	
Stellamare	Ant	1982	2,368	2,850	88.2	15.6	5.6	14	Chl	ex Valkenswaard-87
Stellanova	Nld	1996	4,962	5,198	99.8	18.0	6.4	14	Cchl	
Stellaprima	Ant	1991	6,902	7,600	100.3	21.0	7.4	13	Cchl	

Newbuildings: two 4,900 grt 7,300 dwt heavy-lift vessels due for 1999 delivery.

KiL Management A/S   Denmark

Funnel: Dark blue with red outlined /white 'KiL' inside red ring.
Hull: Light blue with red boot-topping.

Name	Flag	Year	GRT	DWT	Loa	Bm	Draft	Kts	Type	Former names
Anne Sif	Sgp	1993	6,544	9,214	116.4	19.0	7.8	14	Tch	
Baltic Sif	Bhs	1984	4,509	6,733	113.3	18.0	6.3	13	Tch	ex Shoun Marigold-89
Celtic Sif	Sgp	1985	4,509	6,743	113.3	18.0	6.3	13	Tch	ex Shoun Salute-89
Charlotte Sif	Sgp	1981	4,317	4,486	102.5	17.0	5.4	13	Cc	ex Salif Bay-94, Lotte Sif-93, C.R.Kourou-92, Lotte Sif-90, Lotte Scheel-89
Coleen Sif	Sgp	1991	8,908	9,766	133.7	23.0	7.6	18	CC	ex Sea-Land Costa Rica-99, Colleen Sif-94
Hanne Sif	Sgp	1991	7,676	8,609	126.6	20.7	6.3	15	CC	ex Vento di Ponente-96, Elisabeth Delmas-96, Hanne Sif-95, Maersk Euro Tertio-94, I/a Hanne Sif
Holger Sif	Sgp	1984	4,085	6,692	107.6	17.0	7.0	12	Tch	ex Stephanie-91, Pacific Prince-90, Stephanie-90
Hong Bang	Vct	1983	4,953	5,500	115.0	17.5	5.4	14	Cc	ex Bravo Sif-96, Tiger Pearl-94, Bravo Sif-93, Hornsee-86, Bravo Sif-85
Kilchem Acid	Cyp	1979	5,011	8,418	111.5	17.5	8.0	13	Tch	ex Tivoli-94, Kilchem Pacific-92, Uranus-88, Panam Trader-86
Kilchem Adriatic	Bhs	1984	4,509	6,721	113.3	18.0	6.3	13	Tch	ex Andreas Z-90, Shoun Jupiter-89
Kilchem Baltic	Sgp	1985	4,269	7,177	106.5	18.2	6.7	12	Tch	ex Dansborg-89, Golden Arrow-87
Kilchem Biscay	Bhs	1984	4,479	6,791	113.4	18.0	6.3	13	Tch	ex Southern Navigator-90, Shoun Maru No.8-89
Kilchem Bothnia	Bhs	1985	4,072	6,730	107.6	17.0	7.0	12	Tch	ex Ace Chemi-91, I/a Ace
Kilchem Caribbean	Sgp	1984	4,215	6,815	108.5	16.5	7.1		Tch	ex Eastern Pride-90
Kilchem Labrador	Sgp	1985	4,509	6,764	113.3	18.0	6.3	13	Tch	ex Dixie Queen-91, Shoun Universe-90
Kilchem Mediterranean	Sgp	1984	4,462	7,340	114.1	16.5	7.0	12	Tch	ex Pacific Rica-90, Tomoe 6-87
Kilchem Navigator	Sgp	1984	4,509	6,715	113.3	18.0	6.3	13	Tch	ex Golden Navigator-90, Shoun Fujiyama-89
Kilchem Oceania	Bhs	1984	4,497	6,748	113.4	18.0	6.3	13	Tch	ex Oceania Glory-90, Shoun Maru No.11-89
Kilgas Champion	Sgp	1995	2,458	2,347	74.0	14.1	4.8	11	Lpg	
Kilgas Commander	Sgp	1996	2,458	2,347	74.0	14.1	4.8	11	Lpg	
Kilgas Crusader	Sgp	1996	2,458	2,284	74.0	14.0	4.8	12	Lpg	
Kilgas Discovery	Sgp	1965	1,403	2,266	71.2	11.5	5.5	12	Lpg	ex Happy Falcon-92, Sunny Baby-81, Kings Star-70 (conv C-71)
Maersk Euro Quarto	Sgp	1992	7,676	8,609	126.6	20.8	6.3	15	CC	I/a Maersk Forto
Maersk Lamentin	Dis	1990	8,908	9,766	133.7	23.0	7.6	17	CC	ex Sea-Land Guatemala-99, Kathrine Sif-94
Malene Sif	Sgp	1996	6,544	9,214	116.6	19.0	7.8	14	Tw	(conv. Tch-95)

Name	Flag	Year	GRT	DWT	Loa	Bm	Draft	Kts	Type	Former names
Martin Sif	Sgp	1984	4,409	7,088	107.8	17.6	6.9	12	Tch	ex Chemical Trader I-91, White Atlas-89
Nathalie Sif	Dis	1993	6,544	9,176	116.6	19.0	7.8	14	Tch	
Sea-Land Honduras	Dis	1990	8,908	9,766	133.7	23.0	7.6	17	CC	ex Flemming Sif-94
Van Lang	Vct	1983	4,953	5,223	115.5	17.0	5.4	13	Cc	ex Ocean Sif-96, Mekong Vitesse-96, Ocean Sif-93, Nowshera-93, Oyster Bay-92, Ocean Sif-90, ScanDutch Corsica-89, Ocean Sif-87, Hornberg-86, Ocean Sif-85 (len-89)
Vento di Tramontana	Sgp	1991	7,676	8,609	126.6	20.5	6.3	15	CC	ex Lotte Sif-98, P&O Nedlloyd Cyclops-98, Maersk Euro Primo-98, Maersk Primo-91, I/a Lotte Sif
Ville de Damiette	Bhs	1982	4,317	4,508	102.5	17.1	5.4	13	Cc	ex Peter Sif-94, Melaka Bay-91, Peter Sif-91, Global Express

Kopervik Shipping As
Friborg Management AS

Norway

Funnel: Colours not confirmed.
Hull: Colours not confirmed.

Name	Flag	Year	GRT	DWT	Loa	Bm	Draft	Kts	Type	Former names
Friborg	Nis	1972	807	825	55.3	10.5	3.3	10	C	ex Dana Guro-94, Dana-81, Hellelil-81, Helle Steen-77, I/a Hanna Steen
Frihav	Cyp	1978	1,089	1,528	65.8	10.8	4.4	12	C	ex Atlantic Wave-95, Udo-84, Pechudo-83
Frisnes	Nis	1972	906	1,150	62.9	10.1	3.6	11	C	ex Line-94, Ringen-84, Okla-80, Rokur-80, I/a Joff (len-85)
Frifjord	Bhs	1986	1,212	1,131	63.0	11.6	3.4	10	Cc	ex Eros-97

Krey Schiffahrts GmbH & Co. KG
Phoenix Reederei GmbH

Germany

Funnel: Colours not confirmed.
Hull: Blue with red boot-topping.

Name	Flag	Year	GRT	DWT	Loa	Bm	Draft	Kts	Type	Former names
Addi L	Cyp	1995	2,876	4,557	88.2	13.6	-	11	Cc	ex Blinke-97, Apis-96
Boltentor	Deu	1998	4,620	5,650	116.1	16.6	6.1	16	Cc	
Carina	Cyp	1983	1,988	2,858	88.0	11.4	4.5	11	Cc	ex Intermare-97, Voga-94, Vanernsee-92
Delmas Kourou	Atg	1995	3,572	5,030	96.7	15.8	6.2	14	C	ex Delphina-97, Ledator-95
Delmas Mahury	Atg	1996	3,572	5,030	96.7	15.8	6.2	14	C	ex Ivaran Primero-97, Falderntor-96
Eversmeer	Atg	1990	2,374	4,161	88.3	13.2	5.7	12	C	ex Cady-97, Skagern-93
Hannah	Atg	1987	3,236	4,244	99.4	14.1	5.4	12	Cc	ex Paapsund-97, Paapsand-95, Sun Bay-95, Enno B-94, Myanmar Pioneer-92, Tiger Cliff-91, Enno B-90, Nouakchott-90, Karin B-89, A.I.M. Voyager-87, I/a Karin B
Herrentor	Deu	1998	4,620	5,650	116.1	16.6	6.1	16	Cc	
Hilde K	Atg	1998	4,453	6,375	105.0	16.2	7.4	14	Cc	
Maersk Bridgetown	Deu	1997	4,180	4,950	107.7	16.4	6.3	-	CC	ex Maersk Cartagena-98, Jummetor-97
Maersk Castries	Deu	1997	4,180	4,953	107.7	16.4	6.3	-	CC	ex Maersk Maracaibo-98, Emstor-97
Maersk Coral	Deu	1997	4,180	4,985	110.0	16.4	6.3	15	Cc	I/a Evenburg
Maersk Kingston	Deu	1998	5,025	5,650	116.1	16.6	6.1	16	Cc	ex Hafentor-98
Nesse	Cyp	1991	3,186	4,139	93.0	15.0	6.3	12	Cc	ex Wila Buck-98, FAS Colombo-97, Wila Buck-94
Neutor	Deu	1997	5,025	5,450	116.1	16.6	6.2	16	Cc	ex P&O Nedlloyd Manaus-99, Neutor-98
Nordertor	Deu	1998	4,620	5,650	116.1	16.6	6.1	16	Cc	

Krey Schiffahrts GmbH & Co. KG (Phoenix Reederei GmbH) Wiebke K. *M. D. J. Lennon*

R Lapthorn & Co Ltd. Hoo Willow. *M. D. J. Lennon*

Name	Flag	Year	GRT	DWT	Loa	Bm	Draft	Kts	Type	Former names
Ratstor	Deu	1999	4,620	5,650	116.1	16.6	6.1	16	Cc	
Sandwater	Atg	1993	1,950	3,038	88.3	12.5	4.6	11	Cc	ex Oxelosund-96, Sandwater-95
Sieltor	Deu	1999	4,620	5,650	116.1	16.6	6.1	16	Cc	
Sirius P	Atg	1990	2,440	3,181	87.5	13.0	4.8	12	Cc	ex Highland-99, Sirrah-95
Southern Cross	Cyp	1990	3,186	4,150	93.0	15.0	6.3	12	Cc	ex Bartok-95
Sudertor	Deu	1999	4,620	5,650	116.1	16.6	6.1	16	Cc	
Svenja	Deu	1996	2,060	3,000	88.5	11.4	5.0		Cc	
Wiebke K	Atg	1994	1,589	2,735	82.5	11.6	4.8	10	Cc	

R Lapthorn & Co Ltd.   UK

Funnel: Black with yellow 5-pointed star on black band.
Hull: Black with red boot-topping.

Name	Flag	Year	GRT	DWT	Loa	Bm	Draft	Kts	Type	Former names
Anna Meryl	Gbr	1991	999	1,704	69.1	10.0	3.9	9	C	ex Anna Maria-94
Carole T * (2)	Gbr	1980	613	1,120	49.6	9.5	3.9	9	C	ex Emily PG -93 (len-80)
Hoo Beech (2)	Gbr	1989	794	1,399	58.3	9.5	3.6	9	C	
Hoo Dolphin (2)	Gbr	1986	794	1,412	58.3	9.6	3.9	9	C	
Hoo Falcon (2)	Gbr	1991	1,382	2,225	78.0	11.0	4.0	9	C	
Hoo Finch (2)	Gbr	1988	794	1,377	58.3	9.5	3.9	9	C	
Hoo Kestrel (2)	Gbr	1993	1,382	2,225	77.8	11.1	4.0	10	C	
Hoo Larch (2)	Gbr	1992	1,382	2,225	78.0	11.1	4.0	10	C	
Hoo Laurel (2)	Gbr	1984	794	1,394	58.3	9.5	3.9	8	C	
Hoo Maple (2)	Gbr	1989	794	1,399	58.3	9.5	3.9	9	C	
Hoo Marlin (2)	Gbr	1986	794	1,412	58.3	9.5	3.9	9	C	
Hoo Plover (2)	Gbr	1983	671	1,234	50.0	9.5	4.0	8	C	
Hoo Robin (2)	Gbr	1989	794	1,400	58.3	9.5	3.9	9	C	
Hoo Swan (2)	Gbr	1986	794	1,412	58.3	9.5	3.9	8	C	
Hoo Swift (2)	Gbr	1989	794	1,399	58.3	9.5	3.9	9	C	
Hoo Tern (2)	Gbr	1985	794	1,394	58.3	9.5	3.9	8	C	l/a Hoo Gannet
Hoo Venture (2)	Gbr	1982	671	1,230	50.0	9.5	4.1	8	C	
Hoo Willow (2)	Gbr	1984	671	1,234	50.0	9.5	4.0	8	C	
Hoocreek (2)	Gbr	1982	671	1,236	50.0	9.4	4.1	8	C	
Hoocrest (2)	Gbr	1986	794	1,400	58.3	9.6	3.9	9	C	
Hoopride (2)	Gbr	1984	794	1,394	58.3	9.5	3.9	9	C	
Nicky L *	Gbr	1976	1,220	1,897	78.4	10.8	4.1	11	C	ex Magrix-98, The Dutch-87, Tanja Holwerda-87, Roelof Holwerda-81 (len-87)

* managed for Waveney Shipping Ltd.

Latvian Shipping Co.   Latvia

Funnel: Brown with white 'LAT'.
Hull: Blue with red boot-topping.

Name	Flag	Year	GRT	DWT	Loa	Bm	Draft	Kts	Type	Former names
Baltic Horizon	Mlt	1977	1,939	2,992	83.4	14.3	5.1	12	C	ex Atlantic Horizon-94, Marion Bosma-78
Juris Avots	Cyp	1983	9,479	5,500	152.7	19.2	6.6	16	Ro	ex Yuriy Avot-91
Kasira	Cyp	1984	5,191	6,269	113.0	18.3	7.2	15	T	ex Kashira-91
Komponists Caikovskis (2)	Cyp	1986	6,960	4,673	125.9	16.2	5.7	16	Ro	ex Kompozitor Chapkovskiy-91
Leo	Mlt	1973	1,597	2,987	87.5	12.0	5.4	12	C	ex Adriatic-88, Moidart-86
Omodos (2)	Cyp	1992	2,870	3,089	122.8	15.3	3.0	10	T	ex Kala I-96, Skala-95, Klints-2-94
Petrochem Valour	Mlt	1975	1,686	2,507	80.7	12.3	5.9	13	Tch	ex Bima-96, rainbow Chaser-95, Tom Mira-92, Solvent Discoverer-87, Ochre Point-77
Razna	Lbr	1984	5,154	6,269	112.0	18.3	7.2	15	T	ex Razdolnoye-91
Renda	Cyp	1984	5,191	6,269	112.0	18.3	7.2	15	T	ex Aleiska-96, Aleysk-91
Taganroga	Lbr	1983	5,154	6,297	112.0	18.3	7.2	15	T	ex Taganrog-92
Ventspils	Cyp	1983	5,154	6,297	113.0	18.3	7.2	15	T	

Latvian Shipping Co. Baltic Horizon. *J. Krayenbosch*

Lauritzen Kosan Tankers Greta Kosan. *J. Krayenbosch*

Name	Flag	Year	GRT	DWT	Loa	Bm	Draft	Kts	Type	Former names

J. Lauritzen Holding A/S

Denmark

Lauritzen Kosan Tankers

Funnel: Yellow with blue 'K' on yellow diamond on blue band.
Hull: Yellow with blue 'KOSAN', black or red boot-topping.

Name	Flag	Year	GRT	DWT	Loa	Bm	Draft	Kts	Type	Former names
Cavo Greco	Vct	1982	5,804	7,113	122.6	15.5	7.5	14	Lpg	ex Christoph Schulte-99, Kurt Illies-90
Cervantes	Pmd	1992	3,669	4,630	97.6	15.3	6.8	15	Lpg	
Fenja Kosan	Dis	1974	2,077	2,035	79.5	13.4	5.8	13	Lpg	ex Sorine Kosan-96, Sorine Tholstrup-90, Devon-81 (rblt-96)
Gitta Kosan	Dis	1990	4,086	4,828	98.3	16.2	6.7	14	Lpg	
Greta Kosan	Dis	1990	4,086	4,811	98.3	16.2	6.7	14	Lpg	
Henriette Kosan	Dis	1982	2,323	2,528	82.0	13.8	5.6	13	Lpg	ex Henriette Tholstrup-90
Henrik Kosan	Dis	1984	1,687	1,941	70.9	12.9	5.4	13	Lpg	ex Henrik Tholstrup-90, Vinland-87
Jakob Kosan	Dis	1985	1,692	1,929	70.9	12.9	5.4	13	Lpg	ex Jakob Tholstrup-90, Markland-87
Knud Kosan	Dis	1982	2,252	2,978	76.7	14.0	6.8		Lpg	ex Knud Thostrup-91, Traenafjord-82
Laura Kosan	Dis	1992	2,223	2,004	73.6	14.0	5.0	12	Lpg	
Laurits Kosan	Dis	1983	2,252	2,950	76.7	14.1	6.8	12	Lpg	ex Laurits Tholstrup-90, Traenafjell-83
Linda Kosan	Dis	1992	2,223	2,003	74.6	14.0	5.0	12	Lpg	
Lotta Kosan	Dis	1992	2,223	2,004	73.6	14.0	5.0	12	Lpg	
Lydia Kosan	Dis	1993	2,224	2,004	74.0	14.0	5.0	12	Lpg	
Mette Kosan	Dis	1981	2,323	2,530	82.0	13.8	5.6	13	Lpg	ex Mette Tholstrup-90
Poul Kosan	Dis	1978	3,063	3,886	92.7	14.0	6.5	13	Lpg	ex Poul Tholstrup-91, Chemtrans Capella-85
Selma Kosan	Pmd	1976	5,807	6,680	101.8	19.0	7.7	-	Lpg	ex Sunny Lady-95, Lady-81, Leikvin-79 (conv C-81)
Tenna Kosan	Dis	1998	4,700	6,130	112.5	16.0	8.3	16	Lpg	
Tessa Kosan	Dis	1999	4,700	6,130	112.5	16.0	8.3	16	Lpg	
Virgo Gas 1 *	Dis	1978	2,198	2,989	75.7	14.0	6.8	13	Lpg	ex Erik Kosan-98, Erik Tholstrup-90, Francis Drake-85

* on charter to Transgas, Peru.

Gasnaval S.A.

Name	Flag	Year	GRT	DWT	Loa	Bm	Draft	Kts	Type	Former names
Becquer	Esp	1987	2,796	3,659	84.6	14.5	6.6	14	Lpg	
Berceo	Pmd	1991	4,691	4,380	105.0	15.1	6.1	13	Lpg	
Fernando Clariana	Pmd	1991	4,691	4,380	104.5	15.1	6.1	13	Lpg	
Gongora	Esp	1987	2,796	3,659	84.6	14.5	6.6	14	Lpg	

Reederei M. Lauterjung KG

Germany

Funnel: Colours not confirmed.
Hull: Colours not confirmed.

Name	Flag	Year	GRT	DWT	Loa	Bm	Draft	Kts	Type	Former names
Arion	Atg	1999	1,846	2,500	89.7	12.7	4.5	13	Cc	
Beluga Spirit *	Atg	1997	6,358	8,359	130.9	17.7	8.1	15	Cc	ex Annika L-98, Adnan Kalkavan-97, I/a Macin (1990)
Berit L *	Atg	1989	1,307	1,529	74.9	10.6	3.4	10	C	
Gorch Fock *	Atg	1986	1,525	1,506	74.3	12.4	3.3	10	Cc	
Hestia	Atg	1999	1,846	2,500	89.7	12.7	4.5	13	Cc	
Jerome H *	Atg	1985	1,297	1,525	74.9	10.6	3.4	10	C	
Jupiter	Atg	1991	2,450	3,710	87.8	12.9	5.5	10	Cc	
Kay L	Atg	1984	1,298	1,537	74.9	10.6	3.3	10	C	
MSC Bahamas	Atg	1992	2,450	3,720	87.9	12.8	5.5	12	Cc	ex Saturn-98
RMS Anglia *	Atg	1984	1,298	1,537	74.9	10.6	3.3	10	C	ex Richard C-98
Sunrise	Atg	1992	2,449	3,710	88.0	12.8	5.5	10	Cc	ex Stadt Wilhelmshaven-92, I/a Castor
Thebe	Atg	1999	1,846	2,500	89.7	12.7	4.5	13	Cc	
Uranus	Atg	1992	2,449	3,710	87.9	12.8	5.5	12	Cc	
Zeus	Atg	1999	1,846	2,500	89.7	12.7	4.5	13	Cc	

* owned by subsidiary Sunship Schiffahrtskontor KG.

Name	Flag	Year	GRT	DWT	Loa	Bm	Draft	Kts	Type	Former names

Reederei Lehmann GmbH   Germany

Funnel: Yellow with red castle on blue edged white disc.
Hull: Black or grey with red boot-topping.

Name	Flag	Year	GRT	DWT	Loa	Bm	Draft	Kts	Type	Former names
Agila	Atg	1995	2,997	4,550	97.3	16.2	5.9	14	Cc	l/a Alessandra Lehmann
Alrek	Atg	1995	2,997	3,182	97.3	16.2	5.9	15	Cc	l/a Julia Lehmann
Hans Lehmann *	Mmr	1978	2,359	3,182	94.8	12.8	4.7	12	Cc	(len-88)
Heike Lehmann	Atg	1985	2,564	3,070	87.9	12.8	4.5	11	C	
Ina Lehmann *	Atg	1985	2,472	3,055	90.0	13.7	4.4	11	Cc	ex Werner-91, Sea Louise-87, Werner-86
Lisa Lehmann	Deu	1989	2,643	3,200	88.0	13.0	4.9	11	Cc	
Marie Lehmann	Deu	1987	2,642	3,017	88.0	13.0	4.4	11	Cc	
Siegfried Lehmann *	Mmr	1980	2,225	2,570	80.8	13.4	5.0	13	Cc	

* managed by Harmstorf Shipping Co. Ltd., Cyprus.

Liquid Gas Shipping Ltd.   UK

Funnel: Blue with blue 'U' on broad red band (Unigas International).
Hull: Red with grey boot-topping.

Name	Flag	Year	GRT	DWT	Loa	Bm	Draft	Kts	Type	Former names
Tarquin Brae	Lbr	1997	5,420	7,246	113.5	16.5	7.6	15	Lpg	
Tarquin Dell	Lbr	1999	4,720	5,900	107.9	15.7	-	16	Lpg	
Tarquin Forth	Pan	1998	6,051	7,950	118.5	17.2	-	16	Lpg	
Tarquin Glen	Lbr	1991	2,985	3,590	88.4	14.2	5.1	15	Lpg	
Tarquin Grove	Lbr	1992	2,985	3,590	88.4	14.2	6.2	15	Lpg	
Tarquin Loch	Pan	1999	4,900	5,900	-	-	-	-	Lpg	
Tarquin Mariner	Lbr	1992	3,693	4,444	99.4	15.0	6.4	15	Lpg	
Tarquin Moor	Lbr	1997	5,420	7,241	113.5	16.5	7.6	15	Lpg	
Tarquin Navigator	Lbr	1995	5,821	5,632	115.3	16.8	8.1	-	Lpg	
Tarquin Pride	Pan	1998	6,051	7,950	118.5	17.2	-	16	Lpg	
Tarquin Ranger	Lbr	1994	4,317	5,771	105.4	15.7	7.0	15	Lpg	
Tarquin Rover	Lbr	1994	5,821	5,704	115.3	16.8	8.1	-	Lpg	l/a Val Metavro
Tarquin Trader	Lbr	1988	3,595	4,320	98.3	15.0	6.6	15	Lpg	
Tarquin Vale	Pan	1999	4,693	5,900	-	-	-	-	Lpg	

Managed by Acomarit (UK) Ltd.

Lithuanian Shipping Co.   Lithuania

Funnel: White with yellow 'L' on red-edged dark green band below black top.
Hull: Black or blue with red or green boot-topping.

Name	Flag	Year	GRT	DWT	Loa	Bm	Draft	Kts	Type	Former names
Akvile	Ltu	1997	3,893	5,600	102.8	15.9	6.1	13	Cc	
Algirdas	Ltu	1991	3,936	4,168	97.8	17.3	5.6	12	Cc	ex Boshnyakovo-92
Apuole	Ltu	1973	3,450	4,471	97.3	16.3	6.7	14	C	ex Abram Arkhipov-91
Asta	Ltu	1996	3,891	5,805	102.8	15.9	6.6	13	Cc	
Audre	Ltu	1997	3,893	6,085	102.8	15.9	6.6	13	Cc	
Aukse	Ltu	1996	3,893	5,820	102.8	15.9	6.5	13	Cc	
Daina	Lyu	1998	3,893	5,820	102.4	15.9	6.6	13	Cc	
Gediminas	Ltu	1996	3,097	4,502	99.0	16.5	6.2	13	Cc	
Kernave	Ltu	1973	3,450	4,466	97.3	16.2	6.7	14	C	ex Nikolay Kasatkin-92
Kreva	Ltu	1974	3,450	4,471	97.3	16.2	6.7	14	C	ex Mitrofan Grekov-92
Medininkai	Ltu	1974	3,450	4,471	97.3	16.2	6.7	14	C	ex Vasiliy Polenov-92
Merkine	Ltu	1973	3,450	4,464	97.3	16.2	6.7	14	C	ex Nikolay Yaroshenko-92
Mindaugas	Ltu	1992	3,936	4,168	97.8	17.3	5.6	13	Cc	l/a Chaplanovo
Musa (2)	Ltu	1993	4,110	4,485	117.5	16.6	4.5	10	C	
Nida	Ltu	1976	2,111	2,180	88.8	12.8	5.2	12	Cc	ex Marat Kozlov-91
Palanga (2)	Ltu	1979	11,630	3,000	126.5	21.0	5.9	18	Ro	ex Monte Stello-96
Panevezys (2)	Ltu	1985	6,894	4,673	125.9	16.2	5.6	15	Ro	ex Kompozitor Musorgskiy-97
Rasa	Cyp	1998	3,893	6,085	102.8	16.1	6.7	13	C	
Rusne	Ltu	1976	2,111	2,180	88.8	12.8	5.2	12	Cc	ex Vanya Kovelyev-92
Siauliai (2)	Ltu	1985	6,894	4,673	125.9	16.2	5.6	15	Ro	ex Kompozitor Borodin-92
Sventoji	Ltu	1975	2,111	2,180	88.8	12.8	5.2	12	C	ex Khendrik Kuyvas-92
Veliuona	Ltu	1973	3,450	4,471	97.3	16.2	6.7	14	C	ex Vladimir Favorskiy-92
Voke (2)	Ltu	1990	4,966	5,985	139.8	16.6	4.5	10	Cc	ex Sormovo-93
Vytautas	Ltu	1995	3,097	4,500	99.0	15.5	6.2	13	C	

Name	Flag	Year	GRT	DWT	Loa	Bm	Draft	Kts	Type	Former names

Loewer Schiffahrtsges. mbH & Co. KG   Germany

Funnel: Colours not confirmed.
Hull: Blue with red boot-topping.

Name	Flag	Year	GRT	DWT	Loa	Bm	Draft	Kts	Type	Former names
Anja *	Deu	1985	1,476	1,770	77.4	11.4	3.8	11	C	ex Anna-90, Butjadingen-88 (len-92)
Birgit *	Deu	1985	1,474	1,770	77.4	11.4	3.8	11	C	ex Margit-90, Wesermarsch-88 (len-93)
Brigitta	Deu	1979	1,578	2,045	84.2	10.8	4.1	10	Cc	ex Emstal-89, Ostergotland-81, Emstal-80
Eberstein **	Atg	1979	1,713	1,640	79.5	12.8	3.5	11	Cc	
Emsbroker	Deu	1991	2,450	3,710	87.9	12.8	5.5	12	Cc	ex Katharina D-96
Maersk Salerno	Deu	1998	3,999	5,272	100.0	17.9	6.6	16	CC	ex Gerd Sibum-98
Noumea Express	Atg	1984	3,120	3,654	88.6	15.7	6.4	12	Cc	ex Rangitoto-97, Blue Wave-92, Sleipner-91, Brynmore-88, Sleipner-87

* managed by BD Shipsnavo GmbH or ** by Baum & Co. GmbH & Co. KG or † by Zirkel Verwaltungsges. mbH.

LMG Marin (Lund, Mohr & Giaever-Enger AS)   Norway

Funnel: Colours not confirmed.
Hull: Pale blue with red boot-topping.

Name	Flag	Year	GRT	DWT	Loa	Bm	Draft	Kts	Type	Former names
Bewa	Nis	1975	1,920	3,220	79.9	13.0	5.6	10	C	ex Havso-93, Karin Bewa-76 (len-79)
Blue Sky	Nis	1974	5,086	2,926	115.7	15.6	5.0	13	Rop	ex Flipper-94, Monaco-86, Tuulia-85, Iggesund-81 (len-84)
Blue Sun	Nis	1975	5,186	3,525	118.2	15.6	5.0	15	Ro	ex Kalmarsund-93, Merzario Olimpia-81, Kalmarsund-77 (len-83)
Hanna	Nis	1971	1,616	1,475	76.9	12.8	4.1	12	C	ex Johanna Catharina-89,
Indian	Nis	1975	1,920	3,220	79.9	13.0	5.7	12	C	ex Tina-93, Indian Coast-79 (len-80)
Karin	Nis	1970	2,135	2,530	81.6	14.3	5.0	14	CC	ex Samo-90, Scot Venture-90, Samo-90, Novia-86, Samo-86, Anja-86, Novia-85, Mercia-81, Brage-79
White Sea (2)	Nis	1972	7,037	5,913	127.2	17.7	6.4	13	Ro	ex Svano-95, Ocean Link-85, Fragaria-80 (len-75)
Windfjord	Nis	1977	1,678	2,060	72.0	12.8	4.5	13	Cc	ex Baltic Bonita-97, Norrland-96, Falkenstein-90

Lys-Line AS   Norway

Funnel: White with linked white 'SS' symbol between small blue diagonals.
Hull: Dark blue with white 'LYS-LINE'.

Name	Flag	Year	GRT	DWT	Loa	Bm	Draft	Kts	Type	Former names
Lys-Skog	Nor	1991	3,852	3,728	90.1	17.0	5.9	14	Ccp	
Lysekil	Nor	1979	1,927	2,080	85.0	12.9	4.4	13	Ccp	(len/conv C-82)
Lysfoss	Nor	1989	3,852	3,600	90.0	17.0	5.9	14	Ccp	
Lyshav	Nor	1985	3,179	3,040	85.0	16.0	5.9	14	Ccp	
Lysholmen	Nor	1981	2,876	3,319	94.7	13.8	5.1	12	Ccp	(len-94)
Lyskraft *	Deu	1981	3,060	3,154	95.7	13.5	4.4	11	Ccp	ex Golf-96
Lystind	Nor	1990	3,852	3,728	90.1	17.0	5.9	14	Ccp	
Lysvik	Nor	1998	5,570	7,000	-	18.0	-		Cc	

* owned by Rolf Witt, Germany.
Newbuildings: two further 7,000 dwt vessels due during 1999

Meerpahl & Meyer Bereederungs GBR   Germany

Funnel: White with black 'M' on white diamond on flag, black top.
Hull: Colours not confirmed.

Name	Flag	Year	GRT	DWT	Loa	Bm	Draft	Kts	Type	Former names
Buxtehude	Cyp	1985	2,565	3,020	89.1	13.0	4.6	11	C	ex Rita-95
Cranz II	Cyp	1980	1,527	1,782	82.5	11.4	3.6	10	Cc	ex Cranz-98, Matthias-93, Vouksi-91, Matthias-91, Echo Matthias-90, Elbe-89

LMG Marin (Lund, Mohr & Giaever-Enger AS) Blue Sun. *M. D. J. Lennon*

Lys-Line AS Lysekil. *J. Krayenbosch*

Name	Flag	Year	GRT	DWT	Loa	Bm	Draft	Kts	Type	Former names
Leeswig	Cyp	1985	2,561	3,065	87.9	12.9	4.6	11	Cc	ex Claus Jurgens-93
Radesforde	Atg	1990	2,606	3,647	88.0	13.0	5.2	11	Cc	ex Johanna-98
Sierksdorf	Atg	1983	1,963	2,827	88.0	11.5	4.7	11	Cc	ex Montania-96, Meike-92, Faun-89, Frauke-88
Wahlstedt	Cyp	1985	2,568	3,070	88.0	12.8	4.3	10	Cc	ex Monika Ehler-95

Walther Moller & Co. GmbH Germany

Funnel and Hull: Colours not confirmed.

Name	Flag	Year	GRT	DWT	Loa	Bm	Draft	Kts	Type	Former names
Castor I *	Pan	1977	2,139	2,109	86.9	12.8	4.7	13	Cc	ex Thor-98, Brigitte Graebe-86
Charlotte Borchard	Deu	1997	6,362	7,225	121.4	18.5	6.7	16	CC	ex Inga Lena-98, I/a Hoheriff
Komet *	Atg	1976	3,006	3,882	93.5	14.5	6.1	14	Cc	ex Steinkirchen-92, DFL Hamburg-90, Steinkirchen-88, Mosta-88, Regine-86
Marlin *	Atg	1979	2,354	2,604	84.3	13.5	4.9	14	Cc	ex Reliant-93, Johanna-91
Pinguin *	Atg	1977	1,773	2,380	81.6	12.8	4.9	13	Cc	ex Pinguin Ocean District-97, Mekong Venture-94, Pinguin-93, Barbara Chris-90 (len-82)

* owned by subsidiary Reederei Martin Spaleck KG.

Moscow River Shipping Co. Russia

Funnel: White with red above blue bands, blacktop
Hull: Various.

Name	Flag	Year	GRT	DWT	Loa	Bm	Draft	Kts	Type	Former names
Leonid Bykov	Rus	1991	4,096	4,540	138.5	16.8	3.1	10	C	
Ruza-1 (2)	Rus	1987	1,627	1,223	86.7	12.3	2.4	-	Cc	ex ST-1310-??
Ruza-2 (2)	Rus	1987	1,627	1,223	86.7	12.3	2.5	-	Cc	ex ST-1312-??
Ruza-3 (2)	Rus	1987	1,627	1,223	86.7	12.3	2.5	-	Cc	ex ST-1314-??
Ruza-4 * (2)	Rus	1987	1,719	1,750	86.7	12.3	2.9	-	Cc	ex Lidiya-??, ST-1318-93
Ruza-5 (2)	Rus	1987	1,627	1,223	86.7	12.3	2.4	-	Cc	ex ST-1320-94
Ruza-6 (2)	Rus	1987	1,719	1,223	86.7	12.3	3.0	-	Cc	ex ST-1324-??
Ruza-7 (2)	Rus	1987	1,627	1,223	86.7	12.3	2.5	-	Cc	ex ST-1326-??
Ruza-8 (2)	Rus	1987	1,627	1,223	86.7	12.3	2.5	-	Cc	ex ST-1328-??
Strelets *	Rus	1990	3,390	4,540	138.5	16.8	3.1	10	C	ex Kapitan Solyanik-97
Vladimir Filkov (2)	Rus	1991	4,096	4,540	138.5	16.8	3.1	10	C	ex Volzhskiy-46-94
Volzhskiy-32 (2)	Rus	1990	3,070	3,977	107.4	16.7	3.5	11	C	(short-93)
Volzhskiy-35 (2)	Rus	1990	3,070	3,977	107.4	16.7	3.5	11	C	(short-93)
Volzhskiy-37 (2)	Rus	1990	3,070	3,977	107.4	16.7	3.5	11	C	(short-93)
Volzhskiy-38 (2)	Rus	1990	3,070	3,977	107.4	16.7	3.5	11	C	(short-93)

* managed by Baltcom Shipping Co.

Ewald Muller & Co. GmbH Germany

Funnel: Owners markings
Hull: Various colours.

Name	Flag	Year	GRT	DWT	Loa	Bm	Draft	Kts	Type	Former names
Alissa	Nld	1996	1,143	1,490	81.4	9.5	3.1	8	Cc	
Birgit	Nld	1995	3,430	4,831	93.5	15.1	6.1	12	Cc	
Confidence *	Nld	1984	1,399	2,280	79.8	11.1	4.1	9	Cc	ex Christiaan-98, Mouna-93
Duiveland	Nld	1983	998	1,463	78.9	10.1	3.4	12	C	
Frisiana	Nld	1991	1,256	1,820	76.1	10.8	3.6	-	C	
Geminus	Nld	1965	402	564	55.0	7.2	2.2	-	C	ex Zuiderzee-85, Bornrif-83, Veritas-79, Dolfijn-75
Johanna	Nld	1984	1,280	1,558	74.9	10.6	3.4	10	C	ex Sea Trent-95, Echo Venture-90, Sea Trent-90
Meander	Nld	1973	804	1,130	76.4	8.1	3.0	-	C	ex Latona-95
Rio-y-Mar	Nld	1973	555	721	60.4	7.9	2.4	-	C	
Scout Marin	Nld	1983	1,035	1,063	74.6	9.5	2.9	10	Cc	ex Wilke-93, Sea Dart-89, Wilke-88
Simwer	Nld	1986	1,272	1,500	81.2	10.4	3.5	10	Cc	ex Bolder-98, Eben Haezer-96
Veritas *	Nld	1993	1,666	1,590	82.0	12.4	3.9	11	C	
Willy	Nld	1986	851	1,281	64.2	10.5	3.3	10	C	
Willy II	Nld	1991	1,189	1,891	64.7	11.5	4.4	10	C	

* managed for Poseidon Chartering BV, Netherlands.

Name	Flag	Year	GRT	DWT	Loa	Bm	Draft	Kts	Type	Former names

Mikkal Myklebusthaug Rederi

Norway

Funnel and Hull: Colours not confirmed.

Name	Flag	Year	GRT	DWT	Loa	Bm	Draft	Kts	Type	Former names
Edmy *	Nor	1956	573	582	53.5	8.5	3.2	-	C	ex Tarajoq-85, Edmy-80, Olter-67
Fonnland	Nis	1962	597	765	53.2	9.0	3.7	10	C	ex Gardegg-71, Bonn-68
Grinna **	Nis	1972	1,562	1,306	76.6	12.3	3.5	12	Cc	ex Freida-95, Dilshan-91, Jenna-90, Dilshan-90, Meriem-89, Eco Sado-81, Merc Asia-73
Langefoss *	Nis	1968	811	1,060	56.2	10.1	4.3	-	Cp	ex Sea West-94, Hilmo-89, East Coast-87, Gulf Countess-84, Gabriela-81, Ariadne-80, Gabriela-79
Langeland	Nis	1971	1,881	2,439	70.0	13.2	5.4	13	C	ex Langefoss-90, Langeland-90, Janneland-78, Langeland-74
Langesund	Nis	1979	5,060	7,906	106.8	16.5	7.2	13	Cc	ex United Way-96, Mary W-93, Retala-89, Kephill-87, Katawa-84
Sava Hill *	Pan	1991	2,026	3,080	74.7	12.7	6.0	12	Cu	
Sava River *	Nis	1990	2,030	3,050	74.7	12.7	6.0	12	Cu	

* owned or ** managed by subsidiary Haugship A/S.

Navale Francaise SA

France

Funnel: White with blue horizontal wavy line inside grey ring, black top.
Hull: Dark blue with green over red boot-topping.

Name	Flag	Year	GRT	DWT	Loa	Bm	Draft	Kts	Type	Former names
Odet	Atf	1975	2,146	3,641	90.1	13.6	5.7	13	Tw	
Pic Saint Loup	Atf	1974	1,599	1,934	89.2	13.6	5.3	-	Tw	
Pointe de Lesven	Pan	1975	2,123	3,130	91.0	13.5	5.4	13	Tw	
Pointe de Morgat	Pan	1975	2,128	3,200	91.0	13.5	5.5	13	Tw	ex Commandant Henry-90
Pointe du Castel	Atf	1992	3,224	4,216	87.5	15.2	6.2	14	Tch	
Pointe du Cormoran	Atf	1987	3,446	5,453	100.5	15.9	6.4	14	Tch	ex Domenico Ievoli-96
Pointe du Sablon	Atf	1991	2,910	4,470	86.5	15.2	6.5	12	Tch	ex Matagrifone-97
Pointe du Van	Atf	1974	1,735	3,002	85.9	12.1	5.5	11	Tch	ex Pointe de Penharn-76
Saint Brice *	Pan	1975	3,883	6,258	103.5	16.1	7.6	12	B	ex Rossnes-82

* managed by Wilson Ship Management (Bergen) AS, Norway.

Neste OY

Finland

Funnel: Black with diamond divided green over blue.
Hull: Black with red boot-topping.

Name	Flag	Year	GRT	DWT	Loa	Bm	Draft	Kts	Type	Former names
Sirri (2)	Fin	1981	4,468	6,954	107.0	18.0	7.3	13	Tch	ex Pinja-95, Esso Finlandia-92
Suula	Fin	1980	4,462	6,679	112.4	16.6	7.0	15	Tch	ex Carupano-90, Emden-86, Bomin Emden-83
Vikla	Fin	1982	6,763	8,388	133.3	19.3	7.2	15	Tch	

Rederiet Nielsen Og Bresling

Denmark

Funnel and Hull: Colours not confirmed.

Name	Flag	Year	GRT	DWT	Loa	Bm	Draft	Kts	Type	Former names
Astrid Bres	Dis	1977	1,275	2,210	72.2	10.4	4.8	11	C	(len-81)
Dori Bres	Dis	1974	1,872	1,372	75.5	11.8	5.0	11	C	
Nina Bres	Dis	1975	1,872	1,372	75.5	11.8	5.0	12	C	
Silke Polax	Dis	1975	1,889	2,035	75.4	11.8	5.0	11	Cc	

Nomadic Shipping ASA

Norway

Green Chartering AS and Green Management AS

Funnel: Green with white 'GR'
Hull: Green.

Name	Flag	Year	GRT	DWT	Loa	Bm	Draft	Kts	Type	Former names
Green Atlantic	Mlt	1985	3,402	3,073	93.8	16.3	6.0	12	R	ex Anais-97, Jokulfell-93
Green Bergen	Nis	1983	6,182	4,200	128.1	18.0	5.6	20	Rc	ex Bentago-98
Green Eskimo	Mlt	1984	4,427	5,438	109.0	16.4	7.7	16	Rc	ex Garnet Reefer-96, Winter Reefer-95, Atlas Rex-95
Green Flake	Mlt	1976	2,688	1,284	84.5	16.6	4.9	15	R	ex Mare Freezer-96, Atle Jarl-95

Name	Flag	Year	GRT	DWT	Loa	Bm	Draft	Kts	Type	Former names
Green Freesia	Bhs	1978	3,624	4,348	107.7	14.7	5.5	14	R	ex Pacific Freesia-94, Gomba Victoria-80, Santo Alakhram-79, Alakhram-78, l/a Gomba Challenger (len/conv C-84)
Green Frost	Nis	1985	3,398	2,979	85.9	16.0	6.0	15	R	ex Nidaros-93, Olavur Gregersen-88
Green Ice	Nis	1985	3,398	2,900	84.6	16.2	5.9	15	Rc	ex Tinganes-93, Svanur-88
Green Igloo	Mlt	1983	1,313	1,525	67.3	12.0	4.4	13	R	ex Frio Skagen-96, Vestlandia-93
Green Rose	Bhs	1979	3,624	4,348	107.7	14.7	5.5	14	R	ex Pacific Rose-94, Gomba Endeavour-80 (len/conv C-84)
Green Snow	Mlt	1987	2,913	2,686	95.3	14.9	5.1	14	R	ex Karen-96
Green Spring	Mlt	1989	4,970	6,522	124.7	17.8	7.3	17	R	ex Frio Naruto-96
Green Summer	Mlt	1988	4,970	6,489	124.7	17.8	7.3	17	R	ex Frio Hellenic-96
Green Tulip	Bhs	1977	3,624	4,352	107.7	14.7	5.5	14	R	ex Pacific Tulip-94, Gomba Endurance-80, Santo Vastiram-79, l/a Gomba Venture (len/conv C-84)
Green Violet	Bhs	1978	3,618	4,348	107.7	14.7	5.5	14	R	ex Pacific Violet-94, Mechi Venture-81, Gomba Venture-80 (len/conv C-83)
Green Winter	Mlt	1989	4,970	6,526	124.7	17.8	7.3	17	R	ex Frio Canarias-96

Nor-Cargo International A/S Norway

Funnel: Various colours.
Hull: Various colours.

Name	Flag	Year	GRT	DWT	Loa	Bm	Draft	Kts	Type	Former names
Cometa *	Nis	1981	4,610	4,450	102.5	16.5	6.2	13	Rop	
Nordfjell † (2)	Nor	1978	4,578	3,043	108.8	16.6	5.5	14	Rop	ex Fast One-87 (len-80)
Nordhav ‡	Nis	1980	2,865	4,469	103.0	19.7	6.6	16	Ro	ex Cres-98
Nordjarl	Nor	1985	3,968	2,607	95.5	17.6	5.2	15	Rc	ex Ice Pearl-95
Nordskott †(2)	Nor	1979	4,578	2,600	108.8	16.6	5.5	14	Ro	ex Fast Two-87 (len-81)
Nordvaer	Nor	1986	2,731	2,050	79.9	15.0	5.0	13	Cp	ex Victoriahamn-93

* managed by Stavangerske Linjefart AS, † by Ofotens og Vesteraalens Dampskibs or ‡ Troms Fylkes Dampskibs.

Nordane Shipping A/S Denmark

Funnel: White with white 'castle' outline on red shield, black top.
Hull: Green.

Name	Flag	Year	GRT	DWT	Loa	Bm	Draft	Kts	Type	Former names
Gerda Vesta	Dis	1983	1,407	2,610	74.2	11.2	5.3	11	Cc	
Hanne Mette	Dis	1978	768	850	53.8	9.6	3.3	11	Cc	ex Horneland-87
Helle Stevns	Dis	1980	5,224	7,909	106.6	16.5	7.3	11	Ccp	ex Christina W-92, Sintala-90, Mare Garant-88, Germa Garant-81, Germa Lina-80, l/a Lina (len-89)
Nadia J *	Dis	1984	1,042	1,040	65.8	10.0	3.4	10	Cc	
Stevns Bulk	Hnd	1975	2,005	3,320	75.0	13.3	6.5	10	C	ex Mikos I-96, Carib-96, Frendo Carib-77, Frendo United-76
Stevns Pearl	Dis	1984	4,366	5,907	99.9	17.8	7.0	13	Cc	ex CPC Holandia-95, Conti Holandia-87
Stevns Sea	Atg	1972	2,433	3,610	88.5	13.8	5.3	14	Cc	ex Urridafoss-91, Vesterland-85, Estebogen-84, Scol Unit-78, Estebogen-75
Stevns Trader	Dis	1970	2,433	2,245	88.5	13.9	5.3	14	Cc	ex Baltic Trader-93, Patric-88, Patricia I-85, Patricia-85, Scol Action-77, Patricia-76
Stevnsland	Atg	1972	2,433	2,510	88.5	13.9	5.3	14	Cc	ex Oslobank-90, Ostebank-83, Scol Action-75, Ostebank-74

* managed by J. Poulsen Shipping A/S.

Nordtank Shipping ApS Denmark

Funnel: Black.
Hull: Black with red boot-topping.

Name	Flag	Year	GRT	DWT	Loa	Bm	Draft	Kts	Type	Former names
Arctic Swan †	Pan	1970	2,428	4,237	98.9	12.5	6.4	-	Tch	ex Nordstar-96, Lindtank-91, Ottawa-89, Jessica-88, Ottawa-84

Nor-Cargo International A/S Nordjarl. *J. M. Kakebeeke*

North-Western Shipping Joint Stock Co. Ladoga-104. *M. D. J. Lennon*

North-Western Shipping Joint Stock Co. ST-1321. *J. Krayenbosch*

Name	Flag	Year	GRT	DWT	Loa	Bm	Draft	Kts	Type	Former names
Baltic Swan †	Iom	1969	2,615	4,924	105.2	12.6	6.4	12	T	ex Furetank-97, Tarntank-84 (len/deep-86)
Croma *	Swe	1975	4,417	7,293	107.9	17.3	8.1	14	Ta	ex Tanit-88, Essi Atlantic-79, Joatlantic-78
Furevik **	Swe	1990	5,774	8,575	120.3	17.8	7.8	14	Tch	
Haahr Bridge †	Iom	1967	1,131	2,104	74.6	10.2	4.9	11	T	ex Brevik-95, l/a Venern (len/deep-72)
Haahr Trumf †	Iom	1964	1,133	1,946	74.4	10.2	4.9	12	T	ex Candy I-95, Candy-90, Arholma-85, Smaragd-80, Sibell-79, Cortina-77, Tarnsjo-70 (len-71)
Matvik ‡	Swe	1991	5,245	8,952	103.5	17.5	8.4	12	Tch	

*managed for Rederi Donsotank A/B, Sweden, ** for Furetank Rederi AB, Sweden, † for Uni-Tankers, Denmark, or ‡ for Hernrik Hermansen, Sweden*

North-Western Shipping Joint Stock Co.   Russia

Funnel: White with black anchor and 'N' or white with blue over red bands, black top.
Hull: Light grey or black with red boot-topping.

Name	Flag	Year	GRT	DWT	Loa	Bm	Draft	Kts	Type	Former names
Aleksandr Grin	Rus	1997	2,319	3,030	89.5	13.4	4.5	11	Cc	
Alexander Kuprin	Rus	1996	2,319	3,030	89.5	13.4	4.5	11	Cc	
Alexander Tvardovskiy	Rus	1995	2,319	3,030	89.5	13.4	4.5	11	Cc	
Amur-2507 (2)	Rus	1985	3,086	3,152	115.7	13.4	4.0	10	Cc	ex Volgo-Balt 255-85
Amur-2510 (2)	Rus	1986	3,086	3,159	115.7	13.4	4.0	10	Cc	
Amur-2514 (2)	Rus	1986	3,086	3,159	115.7	13.4	4.0	10	Cc	
Amur-2520 (2)	Rus	1987	3,086	3,148	115.7	13.4	4.0	10	Cc	
Amur-2521 (2)	Rus	1987	3,086	3,148	115.7	13.4	4.0	10	Cc	
Amur-2525 (2)	Rus	1988	3,086	3,148	116.0	13.4	4.0	10	Cc	
Amur-2527 (2)	Rus	1988	3,086	3,148	116.0	13.4	4.0	10	Cc	
Baltiyskiy-102 (2)	Rus	1978	1,926	2,554	95.0	13.2	4.0	12	Cc	
Baltiyskiy-107 (2)	Rus	1979	1,926	2,554	95.0	13.2	4.0	12	Cc	
Baltiyskiy-110 (2)	Rus	1980	1,926	2,554	95.0	13.2	4.0	12	Cc	
Baltiyskiy-201	Rus	1994	2,264	2,803	89.5	13.4	4.3	11	Cc	
Baltiyskiy-202	Rus	1994	2,264	2,803	89.5	13.4	4.3	12	Cc	
Geroi Oleynikov (2)	Rus	1971	2,457	2,907	114.0	13.2	3.9	10	C	ex Geroi V.S.Oleynikov-96
Konstantin Paustovskiy	Rus	1996	2,319	3,030	89.5	13.4	4.5	11	Cc	
Ladoga-1 (2)	Rus	1972	1,511	1,968	81.0	11.9	4.0	12	C	
Ladoga-2 (2)	Rus	1973	1,511	1,968	81.0	11.9	4.0	12	C	
Ladoga-6 (2)	Rus	1973	1,511	1,885	81.0	11.9	4.0	12	C	
Ladoga-11 (2)	Rus	1978	1,606	1,855	81.0	11.9	4.0	12	C	
Ladoga-12 (2)	Rus	1978	1,578	1,855	81.0	11.9	4.0	12	C	
Ladoga-13 (2)	Rus	1978	1,639	1,855	81.0	11.9	4.0	12	C	
Ladoga-14 (2)	Rus	1979	1,578	1,855	81.0	11.9	4.0	12	C	
Ladoga-15 (2)	Rus	1979	1,639	1,855	81.0	11.9	4.0	12	C	
Ladoga-16 (2)	Rus	1979	1,578	1,855	81.0	11.9	4.0	12	C	
Ladoga-17 (2)	Rus	1979	1,639	1,855	81.0	11.9	4.0	12	C	
Ladoga-18 (2)	Rus	1980	1,578	1,850	81.0	12.0	4.0	12	C	
Ladoga-19 (2)	Rus	1980	1,639	1,850	81.0	11.9	4.0	12	C	
Ladoga-101 (2)	Rus	1988	1,853	2,075	82.5	11.4	4.0	10	Cc	
Ladoga-102 (2)	Rus	1988	1,853	2,075	82.5	11.4	4.0	10	Cc	
Ladoga-103 (2)	Rus	1988	1,853	2,075	82.5	11.4	4.0	10	Cc	
Ladoga-104 (2)	Rus	1988	1,853	2,075	82.5	11.4	4.0	10	Cc	
Ladoga-105 (2)	Rus	1988	1,853	2,075	82.5	11.4	4.0	10	Cc	
Ladoga-106 * (2)	Rus	1989	1,853	2,075	82.5	11.4	4.0	10	Cc	
Ladoga-107 (2)	Cyp	1989	1,853	2,075	82.5	11.4	4.0	10	Cc	
Ladoga-108 * (2)	Rus	1989	1,853	2,075	82.5	11.4	4.0	10	Cc	
Leonid Leonov	Rus	1994	2,264	2,800	89.5	13.4	4.3	11	Cc	
Ligo (2)	Rus	1973	1,511	1,968	81.0	11.9	4.0	12	C	ex Ladoga-7-99
Lizori (2)	Rus	1972	2,478	2,925	114.0	13.2	3.7	10	C	ex Vytegra-99, Strana Sovetov-92
Mikhail Dudin	Rus	1996	2,319	3,030	89.5	13.4	4.3	11	Cc	
Omskiy-132 (2)	Rus	1988	2,551	2,853	108.4	15.0	3.1	10	C	
Omskiy-133 (2)	Rus	1988	2,551	2,853	102.0	15.0	3.1	10	C	
Omskiy-134 (2)	Rus	1988	2,550	2,853	108.4	14.8	3.1	10	C	

Name	Flag	Year	GRT	DWT	Loa	Bm	Draft	Kts	Type	Former names
Omskiy-135 (2)	Rus	1988	2,550	2,853	108.4	14.8	3.1	10	C	
Omskiy-137 (2)	Rus	1989	2,498	2,667	108.4	15.0	3.0	10	C	
Omskiy-140 (2)	Rus	1989	2,470	2,886	108.4	15.0	3.1	10	Cc	
Omskiy-141 (2)	Rus	1989	2,460	2,760	108.4	15.0	3.1	10	C	
Saymenskiy Kanal (2)	Rus	1978	1,639	1,855	81.0	11.9	4.0	12	C	ex Ladoga-10-78
Sheksna	Rus	1994	2,052	2,769	82.4	12.5	5.0	12	Cc	
Sibirskiy 2131 (2)	Rus	1982	3,978	3,507	129.5	15.8	3.7	10	C	
Sibirskiy 2132 (2)	Rus	1983	3,978	3,507	129.5	15.8	3.7	10	C	
Sibirskiy 2133 (2)	Rus	1983	3,978	3,507	129.5	15.8	3.7	10	C	
Smolnyy (2)	Rus	1992	4,510	4,056	113.1	16.6	4.8	10	T	
Sormovskiy-12 (2)	Mlt	1969	2,478	2,925	114.2	13.2	3.4	10	C	
Sormovskiy-3001 (2)	Rus	1981	2,491	3,100	114.1	13.2	3.7	10	C	
Sormovskiy-3003 (2)	Rus	1981	2,491	3,100	114.1	13.2	3.7	10	C	
Sormovskiy-3055 (2)	Rus	1986	3,041	3,134	119.2	13.4	3.7	10	Cc	
Sormovskiy-3056 (2)	Rus	1986	3,041	3,134	119.2	13.2	3.7	10	Cc	
Sormovskiy-3057 (2)	Rus	1987	3,041	3,134	119.2	13.4	3.7	10	Cc	
Sormovskiy-3058 (2)	Rus	1987	3,041	3,134	119.2	13.4	3.7	10	Cc	
Sormovskiy-3064 (2)	Rus	1989	3,048	3,391	118.7	13.4	4.8	10	Cc	
Sormovskiy-3067 ** (2)	Rus	1990	3,048	3,391	119.2	13.4	4.8	10	Cc	
ST-1311 (2)	Rus	1985	1,627	1,258	86.7	12.3	2.5	10	Cc	
ST-1313 (2)	Rus	1985	1,627	1,223	86.7	12.3	2.5	10	Cc	
ST-1315 (2)	Rus	1985	1,745	1,723	86.7	12.3	2.5	10	Cc	
ST-1317 (2)	Rus	1985	1,627	1,258	86.7	12.3	2.5	10	Cc	
ST-1321 (2)	Rus	1986	1,627	1,258	86.7	12.3	2.5	10	Cc	
STK-1001 (2)	Rus	1983	1,408	1,706	82.0	11.6	2.9	10	C	
STK-1003 (2)	Rus	1983	1,408	1,260	82.0	11.6	2.5	10	C	
STK-1004 (2)	Rus	1983	1,573	1,669	82.0	11.6	2.5	10	C	
STK-1009 (2)	Rus	1984	1,408	1,669	82.0	11.6	2.8	10	C	
STK-1012 (2)	Rus	1985	1,573	1,669	82.0	11.9	2.8	10	C	
STK-1016 (2)	Rus	1985	1,408	1,260	82.0	11.6	2.5	10	C	
STK-1017 (2)	Rus	1985	1,408	1,706	82.0	11.6	2.5	10	C	
STK-1019 (2)	Rus	1986	1,408	1,260	82.0	11.6	2.5	10	C	
STK-1023 (2)	Rus	1986	1,573	1,669	82.0	11.6	2.5	10	C	
STK-1028 (2)	Rus	1987	1,575	1,669	82.0	11.6	2.5	10	C	
STK-1031 (2)	Rus	1987	1,408	1,669	82.0	11.6	2.8	10	C	
STK-1036 (2)	Rus	1988	1,408	1,706	82.0	11.9	2.8	11	C	
Svir (2)	Rus	1980	2,794	3,345	105.9	16.7	3.4	10	C	ex Volgo-Don 5078-92
Universal 1 (2)	Cyp	1993	2,143	2,977	105.9	14.9	2.9	10	C	ex Nevskiy 40-96
Valentin Pikul	Rus	1994	2,264	2,917	89.5	13.4	4.3	11	Cc	
Vasiliy Malov (2)	Rus	1978	1,926	2,554	95.0	13.2	4.0	12	Cc	ex Baltiyskiy-104-81
Vasiliy Shukshin	Rus	1995	2,264	2,792	89.5	13.4	4.4	11	Cc	
Volga-4003 (2)	Rus	1987	4,911	5,845	139.8	16.6	4.5	10	C	
Volga-4008 (2)	Rus	1989	4,966	5,985	139.8	16.6	4.5	10	C	
Volgo-Balt 126 (2)	Rus	1970	2,457	2,907	114.0	13.2	3.5	10	C	
Volgo-Balt 131 (2)	Rus	1971	2,457	3,180	114.0	13.2	3.5	10	C	
Volgo-Balt 190 (2)	Rus	1975	2,554	3,173	113.9	13.2	3.6	10	C	
Volgo-Balt 204 (2)	Rus	1977	2,457	3,191	114.0	13.2	3.6	10	C	
Volgo-Balt 215 (2)	Rus	1978	2,457	2,893	114.0	13.2	3.6	10	C	
Volgo-Balt 238 (2)	Rus	1982	2,457	3,150	114.0	13.2	3.6	10	C	

* managed by Poseidon Schiffahrt GmbH or ** by Transchart Schiffahrts. Gmbh, both Germany.
About 57 other dry cargo coasters between 1,200-5,200 dwt.

Northern River Shipping Lines Joint-Stock Co.   Russia

Funnel: White with narrow blue over red band, light blue polar bear symbol, black top.
Hull: Blue with red boot-topping.

Name	Flag	Year	GRT	DWT	Loa	Bm	Draft	Kts	Type	Former names
Amur-2518 (2)	Rus	1987	3,086	3,159	117.7	13.4	4.0	10	Cc	
Amur-2526 (2)	Rus	1988	3,086	3,159	116.0	13.4	4.0	10	Cc	
Amur-2537 (2)	Rus	1991	3,086	3,159	116.0	13.4	4.0	10	Cc	
Kolguev (2)	Rus	1971	2,478	3,225	114.0	13.2	3.7	10	C	ex XXIV Syezd KPSS-92
Pur-Navolok	Cyp	1997	2,446	3,720	88.0	12.8	5.5	11	C	
Sormovskiy-3063 (2)	Rus	1989	3,048	3,391	119.2	13.4	3.9	10	Cc	
Sormovskiy-3068 (2)	Rus	1990	3,048	3,391	118.7	13.4	4.1	10	Cc	
STK-1005 (2)	Rus	1984	1,573	1,663	82.0	11.6	2.8	11	Cc	
STK-1020 (2)	Rus	1986	1,573	1,663	82.0	11.6	2.8	10	Cc	
STK-1026 (2)	Rus	1986	1,573	1,663	82.0	11.6	2.5	10	Cc	

Name	Flag	Year	GRT	DWT	Loa	Bm	Draft	Kts	Type	Former names
STK-1029 (2)	Rus	1987	1,573	1,660	82.0	11.6	2.5	10	Cc	
Viktor Koryakin (2)	Rus	1969	1,662	2,226	88.0	12.4	3.3	11	C	ex Morskoy-18-93
Volgo-Balt 153 (2)	Rus	1972	2,459	3,170	114.0	13.2	3.6	11	C	
Volgo-Balt 246 (2)	Rus	1984	2,516	3,150	113.0	13.2	3.7	10	C	

Newbuildings: five 2,446 grt 3,700 dwt dry cargo coasters due for 1999/2000 delivery.

Northern Shipping Co.   Russia

Funnel: White with blue over red bands, black top.
Hull: Various.

Name	Flag	Year	GRT	DWT	Loa	Bm	Draft	Kts	Type	Former names
Arnold Ikkonen § (2)	Cyp	1994	4,110	4,485	117.4	16.6	4.5	-	Cc	
Cherepovets	Rus	1970	1,531	1,857	80.3	11.9	4.9	12	C	
Igor Grabar	Rus	1973	3,527	4,054	97.3	16.2	6.4	14	C	
Ivan Ryabov	Rus	1979	5,370	6,070	130.3	17.4	6.9	16	Cc	ex Heidenau-93
Ivan Shadr	Rus	1973	3,527	4,054	97.3	16.2	6.4	14	C	
Horizon ‡	Mlt	1968	4,909	6,013	122.0	16.7	6.8	15	C	ex Pertominsk-95
Kapitan Drobinin †	Mlt	1995	2,446	3,680	88.0	12.8	5.5	11	Cc	
Kapitan Glotov	Mlt	1989	6,395	7,075	131.6	19.3	7.0	14	Cc	
Kapitan Kuroptev	Mlt	1998	4,998	4,345	98.2	17.6	6.7	12	C	
Kapitan Lus	Mlt	1994	4,998	4,678	93.6	17.6	7.0	12	C	
Kapitan Mironov	Mlt	1995	4,998	4,678	98.2	17.6	6.7	12	C	
Kapitan Ponomarev	Mlt	1990	6,395	7,075	131.6	19.3	7.0	14	Cc	
Kapitan Yakovlev	Mlt	1996	4,998	4,678	98.2	17.6	6.7	12	C	
Koida **(2)	Mlt	1995	4,955	5,885	140.0	16.6	4.5	10	Cc	ex Aleksandr Gutorov-97
Konstantin Yuon	Rus	1974	3,527	4,466	97.3	16.2	6.7	14	C	
Kotlas	Rus	1989	2,968	2,853	97.4	14.2	4.9	13	T	
Mekhanik Brilin	Rus	1991	2,489	2,636	85.2	14.5	5.1	12	C	
Mekhanik Fomin	Rus	1991	2,489	2,650	85.4	14.5	5.1	12	C	
Mekhanik Kottsov	Rus	1991	2,489	2,650	85.4	14.5	5.1	12	C	
Mekhanik Kraskovskiy	Rus	1992	2,489	2,650	85.4	14.5	5.1	12	C	
Mekhanik Makarin	Rus	1991	2,489	2,650	85.4	14.5	5.1	12	C	
Mekhanik Pustoshnyy	Rus	1992	2,489	2,650	85.4	14.5	5.1	12	C	
Mekhanik Pyatin	Rus	1992	2,489	2,650	85.4	14.5	5.1	12	C	
Mekhanik Semakov	Rus	1991	2,489	2,650	85.4	14.5	5.1	12	C	
Mekhanik Tyulenev	Rus	1992	2,489	2,650	85.4	14.5	5.1	12	C	
Mekhanik Yartsev	Rus	1990	2,489	2,650	85.2	14.5	5.1	12	C	
Mikhail Cheremnykh	Rus	1973	3,527	4,054	97.3	16.2	6.4	14	C	
Natalia	Vct	1970	4,909	6,090	122.0	16.7	6.8	14	C	ex Petrokrepost-98
Northern Coast *	Mlt	1998	2,446	3,680	87.9	12.9	5.5	10	Cc	
Northern Lady *	Mlt	1997	2,446	3,694	87.9	12.9	5.5	10	Cc	
Northern Lake *	Mlt	1998	2,446	3,750	87.9	12.9	5.5	10	Cc	
Northern Land *	Mlt	1997	2,446	3,695	87.9	12.9	5.5	10	Cc	
Northern Wind *	Mlt	1997	2,446	3,694	87.9	12.9	5.5	10	Cc	
Pavel Korchagin	Rus	1980	5,370	6,017	130.3	17.4	6.9	15	C	
Pioner Belorussii	Rus	1978	5,370	6,070	130.3	17.4	6.9	15	C	
Pioner Estonii	Rus	1976	5,370	6,070	130.3	17.3	7.3	15	C	
Pioner Karelil	Rus	1978	5,370	6,070	130.3	17.4	6.9	15	C	
Pioner Kazakhstana	Rus	1979	5,370	6,070	130.3	17.4	6.9	15	C	
Pioner Litvy	Rus	1977	4,814	6,070	130.3	17.4	6.9	15	C	
Pioner Moldavii	Rus	1979	4,814	6,070	130.3	17.4	6.9	15	C	
Pioner Severodvinska	Rus	1975	5,370	6,070	130.3	17.3	6.9	15	C	
Pioner Yakutii	Rus	1977	5,370	6,070	130.3	17.3	6.9	15	C	
Salavat Yulaev	Pan	1969	1,426	1,691	77.9	11.5	4.7	12	C	
Sosnovets	Rus	1970	1,582	1,857	80.2	11.9	4.9	12	C	
Sovietskaya Yakutiya (2)	Rus	1972	3,624	3,984	123.5	15.0	4.5	11	C	
Sovietskiy Moryak	Rus	1971	1,798	2,230	82.0	12.5	5.1	12	C	
ST-1338 §(2)	Rus	1990	1,804	1,761	86.7	12.3	3.0	10	Cc	
Streamer ‡	Mlt	1969	4,909	5,990	122.0	16.7	7.2	15	C	ex Pulkovo-96
Tama	Vct	1980	5,634	5,720	130.0	17.4	6.9	15	CC	ex Mekhanik Zheltovskiy-98
Tekhnolog Konyukhov	Rus	1979	5,370	6,095	130.0	17.4	6.9	16	Cc	ex Rabenau-93
Teodor Nette	Rus	1988	6,395	7,075	131.6	19.3	7.0	14	Cc	
Timber Express	Blz	1971	1,798	2,230	82.0	12.5	5.1	12	C	ex Aleksandr Miroshnikov-99
Timber Sun	Blz	1971	1,798	2,230	82.0	12.5	5.1	12	C	ex Yakov Reznichenko-98
Umba ** (2)	Mlt	1986	4,911	5,845	139.8	16.6	4.3	10	C	ex Volga 4001-97
Vera Mukhina	Rus	1973	3,527	4,054	97.3	16.2	6.4	14	C	
Yekaterina Belashova	Rus	1973	3,527	4,054	97.3	16.2	6.4	14	C	

Name	Flag	Year	GRT	DWT	Loa	Bm	Draft	Kts	Type	Former names
Vyborgskaya Storona	Rus	1970	1,798	2,230	82.0	12.5	5.1	12	C	
Whitesnow **(2)	Mlt	1969	2,478	2,925	114.2	13.2	3.4	10	C	ex 0050 Let Viksm-96
Zamoscvorechye	Mlt	1997	4,998	4,678	98.2	17.6	6.7	-	C	I/a Kapitan Ryntsyn

* managed by V. Ships (UK) Ltd., ** by Norchart BV, Netherlands, † by Wilson Ship Management (Bergen) AS, Norway or ‡ by Unimar Shipmanagement, Greece.
§ owned by subsidiary Norchart BV, Netherlands (formed jointly with Lumar Logistics BV).

Northwood (Fareham) Ltd.   UK

Funnel:	Black with two white bands
Hull:	Black with red boot-topping

Name	Flag	Year	GRT	DWT	Loa	Bm	Draft	Kts	Type	Former names
Donald Redford	Gbr	1981	681	964	53.5	10.7	3.4	-	Dss	(len-90)
Medina River	Gbr	1969	199	424	41.8	7.7	2.7	9	C	ex Colby River-91, Subro Vixen-87, Tower Marie-80
Norstone	Gbr	1971	1,143	1,803	67.2	12.5	4.5	10	Dss	ex Sand Skua-97
Wightstone	Gbr	1967	438	655	52.7	8.3	3.0	9	C	ex Michael Ane-98, Sanmark-95, Ilen-93, Patmarie-89, Sanmar-87, Union Sun-84, Andre-74

Owned jointly by Redland Ltd. and Westminster Gravels Ltd.

Ob-Irtysh River Shipping Co.   Russia

Funnel:	White with red over blue bands, black top.
Hull:	Light blue with red boot-topping.

Name	Flag	Year	GRT	DWT	Loa	Bm	Draft	Kts	Type	Former names
Breeze (2)	Khm	1978	1,522	1,650	82.0	11.6	3.4	11	C	ex Vakh-98
City of Chios † (2)	Pan	1984	2,068	3,060	108.4	15.0	3.0	8	C	ex Omskiy-29-92
City of Inousse † (2)	Pan	1984	2,068	3,060	108.4	15.0	2.8	8	C	ex Omskiy-30-92
City of Piraeus † (2)	Pan	1985	2,068	3,060	108.4	15.0	3.0	8	C	ex Omskiy-37-91
City of Sochi † (2)	Pan	1982	2,068	3,060	108.4	15.0	3.0	8	C	ex Omskiy-25-92
City of Taganrog † (2)	Pan	1986	2,068	3,060	108.4	15.0	3.0	10	C	ex Omskiy-38-91
City of Tumen † (2)	Pan	1985	2,068	3,060	108.4	15.0	3.0	8	C	ex Omskiy-34-91
City of Vergina † (2)	Pan	1983	2,068	3,060	108.4	15.0	3.0	8	C	ex Omskiy-28-92
Dvina * (2)	Rus	1983	2,426	2,797	108.4	15.0	2.8	-	C	ex Omskiy-111-94
Ishim * (2)	Rus	1978	1,522	1,755	81.9	11.9	3.4	8	C	
Izhora * (2)	Rus	1977	2,426	3,060	108.4	15.0	3.2	10	C	ex Omskiy-8-93
Lozva (2)	Rus	1979	1,430	1,640	82.0	11.6	3.4	-	Cc	
Nadym * (2)	Rus	1986	2,426	2,797	108.4	15.0	3.0	10	C	ex Omskiy-129-93
Ob * (2)	Rus	1983	2,426	2,797	108.4	15.0	3.0	10	C	ex Omskiy-112-94
Omskiy-14 * (2)	Rus	1980	2,426	2,500	108.4	15.0	2.8	10	C	
Omskiy-102 * (2)	Rus	1980	2,426	2,797	108.4	15.0	3.0	10	C	
Omskiy-109 * (2)	Rus	1981	2,426	2,500	108.4	15.0	2.8	10	C	
Pur * (2)	Rus	1979	1,522	1,755	82.0	11.8	3.4	10	Cc	
Refrizherator-602 (2)	Rus	1981	1,531	1,047	82.0	11.8	2.7	10	R	
Refrizherator-608 (2)	Rus	1983	1,492	1,190	82.0	11.6	2.6	10	R	
Sibirskiy 2104 (2)	Rus	1980	3,415	3,050	128.3	15.6	3.0	10	C	
Sibirskiy 2125 (2)	Rus	1982	3,415	3,050	127.5	15.4	3.0	10	C	
Slavyanka * (2)	Rus	1982	2,426	2,797	108.4	15.0	3.2	10	C	ex Omskiy-110-??
Svir * (2)	Rus	1977	2,426	2,797	108.4	15.0	2.8	10	C	ex Omskiy-9-93
Tobolsk * (2)	Rus	1986	2,426	2,500	108.4	15.0	2.8	10	C	ex Omskiy-128-94
Vuoksa * (2)	Rus	1978	2,426	2,400	108.4	15.0	2.8	10	C	ex Omskiy-11-93

* managed by Shipping Co. Sibnec or † by Eurostar Navigation Co. Ltd., Greece.

Jurgen Ohle   Germany

Funnel:	Various.
Hull:	Various.

Name	Flag	Year	GRT	DWT	Loa	Bm	Draft	Kts	Type	Former names
Baumwall	Deu	1998	3,999	5,215	101.1	18.5	6.6	15	CC	I/a Ragna
Janra	Deu	1995	3,999	5,214	100.6	18.5	6.6	15	Cc	
Norrland	Deu	1996	3,999	5,220	101.1	18.5	6.6	15	Cc	I/a Dornbusch
Rika	Deu	1978	1,925	2,271	79.8	12.8	4.4	12	C	ex Hanni-98, G.H.Ehler-90

Name	Flag	Year	GRT	DWT	Loa	Bm	Draft	Kts	Type	Former names

Oldenburg-Portugiesische Dampfschiffs-Rhederei GmbH

Germany

Funnel: Yellow with blue over red bands.
Hull: Grey with red boot-topping.

Name	Flag	Year	GRT	DWT	Loa	Bm	Draft	Kts	Type	Former names
Canarias Express	Esp	1984	3,041	7,200	131.7	19.4	6.2	14	Ro	ex Mercandian Duke-93, Duke-85, Mercandian Duke-85
OPDR Cadiz	Atg	1982	5,371	7,826	120.6	18.5	6.5	14	CC	ex Cadiz-97, Cape-84, Hellenic Cape-84
OPDR Cartagena	Cyp	1974	2,765	3,318	93.2	14.5	5.5	14	Cc	ex Casablanca-97, Francop-90, Manchester Faith-83, Francop-78, Manchester Faith-77, Francop-76
OPDR Casablanca	Cyp	1998	4,115	4,650	100.6	16.2	6.4	15	Cc	
OPDR Lisboa	Atg	1981	5,087	7,826	120.6	18.5	6.5	14	CC	ex Lisboa-97, Dawn-84, Hellenic Dawn-83
OPDR Tanger	Atg	1982	5,371	7,826	120.6	18.5	6.5	15	CC	ex Tanger-97, Canarias Express-93, Tanger-85, Island-84, Hellenic Island-83

Reederei 'NORD' Klaus E. Oldendorff Ltd.

Cyprus

Funnel: Blue with white 'N' inside white ring, black top or charterers colours.
Hull: grey with white boot-topping.

Name	Flag	Year	GRT	DWT	Loa	Bm	Draft	Kts	Type	Former names
Jakarta Star	Cyp	1980	5,148	7,652	120.4	17.8	6.5	13	CC	ex Nordsund-99, Eastmed King-82, Nordsund-81
Nordheim	Cyp	1976	5,306	8,183	117.6	18.1	7.3	14	C	
Nordholm	Cyp	1976	5,306	8,176	117.6	18.0	7.3	14	C	

Schiffahrtsgesellschaft Oltmann Verwaltung. mbH

Germany

Name	Flag	Year	GRT	DWT	Loa	Bm	Draft	Kts	Type	Former names
Aurora	Atg	1995	8,633	9,319	132.9	23.1	7.7	17	CC	ex Kent Merchant-98
Elisia	Atg	1984	1,547	1,735	82.5	11.4	3.5	10	Cc	
Hannes Oltmann	Atg	1993	7,361	9,198	128.5	20.5	8.3	17	Cc	ex Susan Borchard-97, Beaver Dimitra-93, Hannes Oltmann-93
Sven Oltmann	Atg	1992	5,006	6,620	116.8	18.2	6.9	16	Cc	

Oost-Atlantic Lijn B.V.

Netherlands

Funnel: Red with red 'OAL' on broad white over green bands.
Hull: Light grey, black or blue with red boot-topping.

Name	Flag	Year	GRT	DWT	Loa	Bm	Draft	Kts	Type	Former names
Atlantic Bay (2)	Bhs	1984	4,996	4,205	104.8	18.2	4.5	12	C/Ro	ex Flamares-96, Johanna-86
Atlantic Coast	Bhs	1977	1,943	3,124	81.7	14.2	5.4	13	C	ex Fivel-81
Atlantic Comet	Cyp	1971	1,465	1,971	82.1	12.2	4.5	13	C	ex Cornelia Bosma-78 (len-77)
Atlantic Island	Bhs	1983	5,417	6,930	119.1	19.3	6.2	14	Cc	ex Norasia Melita-93, Atlantic Island-92, EWL Paramaribo-92, Atlantic Island-90, Norasia Attica-89, Neustadt-87, Convoy Record-86, Americas Condor-86, Neustadt-85, Concorde Wave-84, I/a Neustadt
Atlantic Moon	Bhs	1976	3,339	2,999	96.5	16.0	5.7	12	Cc	ex Polydorus-88, Mercandian Admiral-79
Atlantic River	Cyp	1971	1,196	2,489	77.2	13.0	4.8	13	C	ex Munte-81, Norimo-74

'Orion' Schiffahrts-Gesellschaft Reith & Co.

Germany

Funnel: Black with blue 'O' on white disc at centre of white diagonal cross on broad red band.
Hull: Black with red boot-topping.

Name	Flag	Year	GRT	DWT	Loa	Bm	Draft	Kts	Type	Former names
Carola	Atg	1988	2,610	2,925	86.2	13.0	4.6	11	Cc	ex Tricolor Star II-96, Coringle Bay-91, Tiger Sea-90, Carola R-89
Concordia	Mlt	1985	4,254	8,881	115.2	18.6	7.6	13	C	ex Pronobis-93, Clipper Courage-87
Fortuna	Mlt	1984	5,586	8,875	115.2	18.6	7.6	12	Cc	ex Clipper Challenge-91

Oost-Atlantic Lijn B.V. Atlantic Bay. *J. Krayenbosch*

Osterreichischer Lloyd/Krohn Shipping Group Durnstein. *M. D. J. Lennon*

Name	Flag	Year	GRT	DWT	Loa	Bm	Draft	Kts	Type	Former names
Mekong Fortune	Atg	1987	2,610	2,871	87.0	13.0	4.6	11	Cc	ex Saigon Fortune-93, Fortune Bay-92, Markham Bay-91, Magdalena R-88
Patria	Mlt	1985	5,586	8,880	115.2	18.6	7.6	12	Cc	ex Sungreen-91, Clipper Maestro-87

Orion-Rederierne A/S   Denmark
P.E.P. Shipping (Scandinavia) ApS
Funnel: Various.
Hull: Various.

Name	Flag	Year	GRT	DWT	Loa	Bm	Draft	Kts	Type	Former names
Arnarfell *	Dis	1994	6,297	7,850	121.9	20.4	7.1	16	CC	ex Gertie-96, CGM St. Elie-96, Gertie-95
Helgafell *	Iom	1994	6,297	7,968	121.9	20.3	7.6	16	Cc	ex Heidi B-97, Maersk Euro Quinto-97, l/a Heidi B
Karin B (2)	Dis	1993	2,881	3,280	91.5	16.8	4.5	14	Cc/Ro	ex Pacific Ecuador-98, Karin B-94
Lisbeth C (2)	Dis	1993	2,881	3,288	91.6	16.8	4.5	14	Cc/Ro	ex Pacific Peru-98, Lisbeth C-94
Ocean Ady (2)	Dis	1990	2,762	3,036	91.5	16.8	4.3	14	Cc/Ro	
Ocean Hanne (2)	Dis	1991	2,762	3,095	91.5	16.8	4.3	14	Cc/Ro	ex Elisabeth-98, Ocean Hanne-97, Maersk Pacific-94, Ocean Hanne-93
Sophie (2)	Dis	1992	2,881	3,300	91.6	16.8	4.5	14	Cc/Ro	ex Pacific Chile-98, Sophie-93

* on charter to Samskip H/F, Iceland.

Osterreichischer Lloyd/Krohn Shipping Group   Austria
Funnel: Black with red 'A' on broad white band, or black with 7-leaf symbol on broad white band edged with narrow green bands.
Hull: Brown or blue with red boot-topping.

Name	Flag	Year	GRT	DWT	Loa	Bm	Draft	Kts	Type	Former names
Arabella C	Cyp	1994	2,818	4,216	91.5	13.6	5.8	12	B	
Bettina K	Aut	1994	2,449	3,713	88.0	12.8	5.5	10	Cc	
Blankenes	Cyp	1978	4,061	6,433	105.6	14.9	6.8	11	Bc	ex Black Sea-93
Claudia C	Cyp	1994	2,818	4,216	91.5	13.6	5.8	12	Cc	
Corona	Aut	1994	2,450	3,717	88.0	12.8	5.5	10	Cc	
Dellach	Cyp	1977	1,980	2,750	79.1	12.4	5.4	10	Cc	ex Dalsland-86
Durnstein	Aut	1986	2,367	3,812	87.9	12.8	4.5	9	Cc	ex Visurgis-95
Elisabeth K	Aut	1994	2,499	3,710	87.9	12.8	5.5	12	Cc	
Elke K	Aut	1993	2,440	3,712	87.9	12.8	5.5	11	Cc	
Hvitanes	Pan	1966	2,517	2,345	83.5	14.1	5.3	-	C	ex Saga I-87, Frengenfjord-85, Sunmore-85, Baltique-75
Innsbruck	Aut	1977	2,851	4,186	86.0	14.1	6.5	12	C	ex Conara-88
Klostertal	Aut	1996	5,622	7,000	108.8	17.8	7.2	12	Cc	
Lech	Aut	1977	4,372	6,300	106.2	16.6	6.8	12	Cc	ex Bora-79, Josky-78
Linz	Cyp	1970	3,133	4,481	102.9	14.6	5.8	10	C	ex Hvalnes-93, Hvalvik-88, Mambo-75, Samba-72
Natascha	Pan	1976	1,935	3,205	91.2	13.3	5.1	11	C	ex Stuben-99, Ettrick-82
Pitztal	Aut	1995	5,624	6,920	109.7	17.8	7.2	12	Cc	
Rautz	Aut	1976	1,935	3,205	91.2	13.3	5.1	12	C	ex Eildon-82
Scorpius	Atg	1993	2,449	3,329	87.9	12.8	5.5	11	Cc	ex Ursa-98
Selnes	Cyp	1975	3,658	5,790	102.3	15.6	6.8	14	B	ex Risnes-79
St. Anton	Aut	1976	2,300	4,028	91.7	13.6	6.0	13	C	ex Andrea-85, Cairnash-83 (len-83)
St. Christoph	Aut	1977	2,300	4,028	91.7	13.6	5.9	13	C	ex Christiane-85, Cairnelm-83 (len-83)
St. Jakob	Aut	1977	2,300	4,028	91.7	13.6	6.0	13	C	ex Leony-85, Cairnoak-83 (len/deep-83)
Stefan K	Aut	1995	2,449	3,710	88.0	12.8	5.5	12	Cc	
Ursula C	Cyp	1996	2,818	4,164	91.5	13.6	5.8	12	Cc	
Villach	Cyp	1970	4,769	7,611	123.3	17.1	6.8	13	B	ex Akranes-95, Fossnes-81, Midiboy-77, Brinknes-73
Vita	Vct	1990	3,749	5,444	110.0	16.5	5.0	12	Cc	ex Dolphin Z-99, Merkur-97, Commodore-95
Wachau	Aut	1985	2,367	3,810	87.9	12.9	4.5	9	Cc	ex Ruhrtal-94
Walsertal	Aut	1995	5,624	6,900	109.7	17.8	7.2	12	Bc	

Name	Flag	Year	GRT	DWT	Loa	Bm	Draft	Kts	Type	Former names
Werfen	Aut	1991	2,364	2,685	82.4	12.8	5.8	12	Cc	ex Amor-93, Ulla-93, Nordic Bridge-91
Zillertal	Aut	1996	5,602	7,142	109.7	17.8	7.2	12	Cc	
Zug	Aut	1977	2,583	4,252	96.7	13.6	5.3	14	Cc	ex Holmsland-88, Lina von Bargen-82 (len-83)
Zuppert	Aut	1978	2,578	4,252	96.6	13.6	5.3	13	Cc	ex Jylland-88, Anita von Bargen-82 (len-83)
Zurs	Aut	1977	2,577	4,254	96.6	13.6	5.9	13	Cc	ex Halland-88, Hein von Bargen-82 (len-83)

Pohl Shipping Schiffahrtsges.mbH　　　　　Germany

Funnel:　　　　　Blue.
Hull:　　　　　Blue with white 'P+C', black or red boot-topping.

Name	Flag	Year	GRT	DWT	Loa	Bm	Draft	Kts	Type	Former names
Alblas	Nld	1996	3,430	4,985	93.5	15.1	6.3		Cc	
Alteland	Deu	1991	5,999	4,300	114.0	17.2	5.9	15	Rop	ex Ortviken-96, Alteland-90
Baltic Carrier	Deu	1997	2,280	3,130	82.5	12.3	5.0	11	Cc	
Baltic Merchant	Deu	1997	2,280	3,110	82.5	12.3	5.0	11	Cc	
Baltic Sailor	Deu	1998	2,280	3,110	82.5	12.6	5.0	11	Cc	
Baltic Skipper	Deu	1997	2,280	3,110	82.5	12.5	5.0	11	Cc	
Baumwall	Deu	1995	3,999	4,500	100.2	15.5	6.5	14	Ccp	
Grimm	Deu	1992	3,564	4,050	104.8	15.4	4.1	12	Ccp	
Kajen	Deu	1989	3,555	3,027	103.7	15.2	4.1	12	Cc	I/a Edina
Lys Vista *	Deu	1979	2,096	2,240	83.8	12.8	4.4	12	Cc	ex Tista-98
Marschenland	Atg	1985	1,373	1,550	75.0	10.8	3.7	11	C	
Ness	Deu	1996	3,999	3,881	100.2	15.5	5.5	14	Ccp	
Rachel Borchard	Deu	1996	6,362	7,225	121.4	18.5	6.7	16	CC	ex Sound-97, Kalina-96
Tistedal *	Deu	1996	4,464	4,600	116.0	16.6	5.1	15	Ccp	ex Lyspol-99, Tistedal-98
Torne	Nld	1996	3,443	4,927	93.8	15.1	6.1	-	Cc	

* managed by Schiff. Wolfgang Hammann KG.

Reederei Heinz Corleis KG

Name	Flag	Year	GRT	DWT	Loa	Bm	Draft	Kts	Type	Former names
Gracechurch Sun	Deu	1992	5,006	6,541	116.7	18.2	6.9	16	Cc	ex Uranus-97
Jupiter *	Deu	1992	5,025	6,650	116.7	18.2	6.9	16	Cc	
Katrin *	Deu	1986	3,448	4,250	101.5	15.2	3.8	12	Cc	I/a Odin
Polaris	Deu	1988	7,944	6,494	123.9	20.4	6.2	14	Cc/Ro	I/a Odin

* managed for Heinrich Mahler.

Polish Baltic Shipping Co. (Polska Zegluga Baltycka SA)　　　Poland

Funnel:　　　　　Blue with white 'PZB' and trident on red shield interupting red band with narrow white bands.
Hull:　　　　　Black with red boot-topping.

Name	Flag	Year	GRT	DWT	Loa	Bm	Draft	Kts	Type	Former names
Fast Ann	Pol	1980	1,740	1,990	85.9	11.4	3.0	10	Cc	ex Saphir-92
Fast Catrien	Pol	1980	1,740	1,990	85.9	11.4	3.5	10	Cc	ex Rubin-92
Fast Filip	Pol	1980	1,740	1,990	85.9	11.4	3.5	10	Cc	ex Smaragd-92
Ner	Pol	1988	910	1,263	69.1	9.5	5.4	9	Cc	ex Monika-90
Nimfa II	Pol	1991	1,948	1,880	76.0	12.7	4.5	10	Cc	
Rusalka II	Pol	1991	1,948	2,063	76.0	12.8	4.5	10	Cc	
Sola	Pol	1988	910	1,258	69.1	9.5	3.3	9	Cc	ex Natascha-91

Polish Steamship Co. (Polska Zegluga Morska)　　　Poland
Polstream Shortramp Ltd.

Funnel:　　　　　Black with white 'PZM' and trident on red shield interupting red band with narrow red bands.
Hull:　　　　　Black with red boot-topping.

Name	Flag	Year	GRT	DWT	Loa	Bm	Draft	Kts	Type	Former names
Boleslawiec	Mhl	1979	3,127	4,390	95.1	14.6	6.1	12	C	
Bytom	Mhl	1980	3,127	4,459	95.0	14.6	6.1	12	C	
Chorzow	Mhl	1979	3,127	4,361	95.0	14.6	6.1	12	C	
Gniezno II	Mhl	1979	3,127	4,358	95.1	14.6	6.1	12	C	
Goleniow	Mhl	1979	3,127	4,449	95.1	14.6	6.1	12	C	
Koscierzyna	Mhl	1980	3,127	4,443	94.9	14.6	6.1	12	C	
Lomza	Mhl	1980	3,127	4,459	95.0	14.6	6.1	12	C	

Name	Flag	Year	GRT	DWT	Loa	Bm	Draft	Kts	Type	Former names
Malbork II	Mhl	1980	3,127	4,461	94.9	14.6	6.1	12	C	
Mielec	Mhl	1980	3,127	4,456	95.0	14.6	6.1	12	C	
Mlawa	Mhl	1979	3,122	4,415	94.9	14.0	6.0	12	C	
Sieradz	Mhl	1979	3,127	4,361	95.0	14.6	6.1	12	C	
Warka	Mhl	1980	3,127	4,451	95.0	14.6	6.1	12	C	
Wielun	Mhl	1980	3,127	4,442	95.0	14.6	6.1	12	B	
Wyszkow	Mhl	1979	3,127	4,378	95.1	14.6	6.1	12	C	
Zgorzelec	Mhl	1980	3,127	4,412	94.8	14.6	6.0	12	C	
Wejherowo *	Mlt	1975	4,120	3,408	106.4	16.0	6.2	14	Cc	

Formed jointly with Polish Shipping Co. and * managed for Polish Ocean Lines.

Poseidon Chartering BV
Netherlands

Funnel: Owners markings.
Hull: Various colours.

Name	Flag	Year	GRT	DWT	Loa	Bm	Draft	Kts	Type	Former names
Almenum	Nld	1992	1,425	1,830	74.0	11.6	4.0	11	C	
Aquarius	Nld	1996	1,996	3,246	84.8	12.6	4.8	10	Cc	
Banjaard	Nld	1993	5,299	7,485	126.8	16.6	6.9	15	CC	ex Texel Bay-95, Banjaard-94
Batavier VII	Nld	1998	2,560	3,480	92.8	15.9	4.9	-	CC	I/a Scheldedijk
Daniel	Nld	1996	1,999	3,420	91.2	11.9	5.1	11	Cc	
Emil-Nolde	Nld	1991	4,059	5,850	108.8	16.6	6.5	15	Cc	ex Mir-98, Admiraal-97, Sea Admiral-95, Admiraal-92
Empire	Nld	1991	1,981	3,260	90.0	11.9	4.9	11	C	
Fast Jef	Nld	1996	2,066	3,180	88.0	12.5	4.6	12	Cc	ex Breehorn-97
Gerarda	Nld	1994	2,650	4,200	89.6	13.2	5.7	12	C	
Harns	Nld	1994	1,909	2,350	89.2	11.4	4.1	12	Cc	
Holland	Nld	1963	634	780	67.1	8.3	2.2	9	C	ex Cum Deo-97, Via Maris-87 (len-73)
Kim	Cyp	1976	1,597	2,440	81.2	11.9	4.7	12	C	
Lisa	Deu	1985	1,587	2,380	82.0	11.5	4.2	10	C	ex Edith-90, Echo Lisa-90, Edith-89
Lumare	Nld	1998	2,780	3,700	89.3	13.4	5.7	12	Cc	
Marianne	Nld	1986	1,318	1,613	79.1	11.4	3.3	10	C	ex Harns-94
Marinier	Nld	1986	1,630	2,525	87.9	11.0	4.1	12	Cc	
Merak	Cyp	1976	1,472	2,340	76.4	11.9	4.8	13	C	ex Geziena-88, Meran-80, Merak-80
Oostzee	Nld	1978	815	1,150	63.0	9.4	3.4	10	C	ex Zwartewater-95, Almenum I-92, Almenum-92
Scorpio	Nld	1974	1,828	3,192	80.4	13.6	5.5	13	C	ex Proton-98, Swallow-80
Seabreeze	Nld	1995	1,996	3,246	84.8	12.4	4.8	10	C	
Sirenitas	Cyp	1977	906	1,373	63.0	10.0	3.6	10	C	ex Sandettie-93, Espero I-89, River Herald-88, Riosal-83
Tendo	Nld	1995	2,050	3,370	88.0	12.8	4.9	12	Cc	
Tharsis	Nld	1997	1,595	2,066	88.1	11.4	3.4	10	C	
Transmare	Nld	1999	2,800	3,700	-	-	-	-	C	
Troubadour	Nld	1992	1,789	2,450	90.0	11.4	3.9	11	Cc	
Vlieland	Nld	1994	1,937	3,150	82.4	12.4	4.8	12	C	
Waddenzee	Nld	1985	1,861	3,035	91.0	11.4	4.9	10	Cc	
Warfsum	Nld	1999	2,500	3,900	-	-	-	-	C	
Winsum	Nld	1999	2,500	3,900	-	-	-	-	C	
Zwartewater	Nld	1985	1,132	1,528	79.3	10.4	3.2	10	C	ex Marina-95, Veritas-92

Also see Wagenborg Shipping B.V.
Newbuildings: two 2,500 grt 3,900 dwt dry cargo coasters due for 2000 delivery.

J. Poulsen Shipping A/S
Denmark

Funnel and Hull: Colours not confirmed.

Name	Flag	Year	GRT	DWT	Loa	Bm	Draft	Kts	Type	Former names
Dansus	Dis	1985	1,042	1,050	65.5	10.1	3.6		Cc	
Hornestrand	Dis	1981	808	960	61.9	9.6	3.7	10	Cc	
Jens Munk	Dis	1988	1,501	1,742	76.6	11.2	3.9	11	Cc	
Karin Cat	Dis	1986	1,501	1,680	76.5	11.2	4.0	11	Cc	ex Puma-97, Faroe Island-88
Marsus	Dis	1986	1,091	1,122	67.9	10.1	3.4	10	Cc	
Moon Bird	Ant	1978	3,474	3,787	82.1	17.0	6.4	12	Cc	ex Protea Trader-90, Black Bird-90, Alamar-87, Alamak-85
Ocean Bird	Dis	1991	3,320	4,222	94.4	15.5	5.6	13	Cc	

Polish Baltic Shipping Co. (Polska Zegluga Baltycka SA) Nimfa II. *J. Krayenbosch*

Poseidon Chartering BV Oostzee. *M. D. J. Lennon*

Name	Flag	Year	GRT	DWT	Loa	Bm	Draft	Kts	Type	Former names
Peder Most	Dis	1984	1,475	1,654	74.8	11.2	3.9	10	Cc	
Pegasus	Dis	1981	1,161	1,275	62.9	11.2	3.9	11	Cc	
Sea Bird	Dis	1990	3,273	4,270	94.4	15.5	5.6	13	Cc	
Sky Bird	Ant	1977	2,978	4,305	91.1	14.5	6.8	14	Cc	ex Mirzam-89, Arai Ava-89, Mirzam-89, Jan Wilhelm-87
Star Bird	Dis	1993	3,351	5,215	96.7	15.8	6.3	15	Cc	ex Felston-94

Newbuildings: Two 3,500 grt 5,500 dwt dry cargo vessels on order for 1999 delivery.

Schiffahrtskontor Rendsburg GmbH   Germany

Funnel: Various ownership colours.
Hull: Red or black with red boot-topping.

Name	Flag	Year	GRT	DWT	Loa	Bm	Draft	Kts	Type	Former names
Annette-J	Nld	1978	1,034	1,408	72.3	11.3	3.3	11	C	ex Denfield-96, Almaty-95, Militence-93
Annika-M	Atg	1977	1,678	1,964	72.0	12.8	4.5	12	Cc	ex Loga-90, Anja-88
Betsy *	Deu	1998	2,986	4,830	98.4	16.9	5.9	14	CC	
Christine O	Deu	1978	1,925	2,262	79.8	12.8	4.4	12	Cc	ex John Bluhm-98
Heike *	Deu	1999	2,986	4,830	98.4	16.9	5.9	14	CC	
Henny *	Deu	1997	2,986	4,834	98.4	16.9	5.9	14	CC	
Maja-M	Deu	1979	1,624	1,638	79.2	13.5	3.5	12	Cc	
Mermaid	Deu	1985	1,856	2,302	80.7	12.7	4.2	10	Cc	
Somers Isles	Atg	1977	2,372	2,720	84.3	13.5	5.0	14	Cc	ex Theodor Storm-85, Baltic Heron-83, Theodor Storm-78
Zim Espana	Gbr	1977	3,807	4,150	97.5	16.0	5.7	14	Cc	ex West Moor-95, Westermoor-86, Essex Courage-83, Westermoor-83

* owned by subsidiary Reederei Karl Schluter GmbH & Co. KG.

Rhein-Maas-und See-Schiffahrtskontor GmbH   Germany

Funnel: White with blue 'RMS' inside blue diamond, or * orange with black 'H' inside black diamond outline.
Hull: Light grey, green or brown with red boot-topping.

Name	Flag	Year	GRT	DWT	Loa	Bm	Draft	Kts	Type	Former names
Carol Ann **	Atg	1994	3,992	5,331	100.0	18.4	6.6	15	CC	
Einstein	Atg	1968	1,229	2,030	74.1	10.8	5.1	13	Cc	ex Bismarckstein-86, Stephanie-80, Bismarckstein-78, Elbestroom-75, Eland-72, Bismarckstein-69
Eldor *	Deu	1981	1,441	1,795	81.0	11.3	3.3	10	Ccs	
Emily **	Atg	1990	2,190	3,283	82.5	12.6	5.3	10	Cc	
Euklid	Atg	1984	1,860	3,035	91.1	11.4	4.9	11	Cc	ex Sena-94, Maelo-92, Zuiderzee-88
Hemo	Atg	1968	872	1,400	59.7	10.0	4.6	11	Cc	ex Antje B-96, Claus-86
Hera	Deu	1975	1,202	1,300	75.0	10.2	3.3	10	C	ex Herm Kiepe-96
Ingelore	Deu	1960	524	500	54.5	8.7	3.3	9	C	ex Krautsand-97, Henriette II-78, Krautsand-76, Axel-76
Jan V †	Deu	1985	1,749	2,218	80.7	12.6	4.2	12	Cc	
Mary Ann	Pmd	1997	6,362	7,225	121.4	18.5	6.7	16	CC	ex CTE Valencia-98
Mistral	Atg	1966	1,064	1,196	68.4	10.6	4.0	11	C	ex Nadine-98, Ragna-90, Tillia-83, Suderelv-78, Frieda Graebe-73
Neuenbrok	Deu	1966	409	624	57.4	7.2	2.5	9	C	(len-85, len/deep-78)
RMS Duisburg	Atg	1983	1,281	1,572	74.9	10.6	3.4	10	C	ex Rhenus-97
RMS Ruhrort	Deu	1983	1,281	1,566	74.9	10.6	3.4	10	C	Amisia
Salona	Hnd	1973	939	1,443	60.9	9.6	4.3	11	C	ex Atlantic Fosna-90, Frei Mignon-90, Kimare-88, Arklow Dawn-87, I/a Annemor
Steen	Deu	1961	328	558	44.7	8.0	2.9	8	C	ex Ingrid I-82, Steenborg-81
Susann	Atg	1939	526	493	53.6	8.3	2.9	9	C	ex Ruth-89, Hans Georg-89, Morild-65, Sigborg-58, Reze-40
Tirador *	Deu	1997	1,596	2,220	88.2	11.4	3.7	12	C	
Tudor*	Deu	1984	1,296	1,420	79.6	10.0	3.1	10	Ccs	ex Kirsten-88
Widor *	Deu	1987	1,412	1,780	81.0	11.4	3.3	10	Cs	

* owned by Reederei Paul Hase KG or ** by Eicke Schiffahrts KG. † managed by Jan Vogelsang.

J. Poulsen Shipping A/S Dansus. *M. D. J. Lennon*

Rhein-Maas-und See-Schiffahrtskontor GmbH Einstein. *M. D. J. Lennon*

Rhein-Nord-Ostsee Befrachtungs GmbH

Germany

Funnel: Various.
Hull: Various.

Name	Flag	Year	GRT	DWT	Loa	Bm	Draft	Kts	Type	Former names
Albis	Atg	1984	1,781	2,550	83.2	11.5	4.3	10	Cc	ex Danubia-97
Elbia	Deu	1985	1,525	1,506	74.9	12.5	3.4	10	Cc	
Maria H *	Atg	1985	1,297	1,450	74.9	10.6	3.4	10	C	
Moldavia	Atg	1985	1,546	1,708	82.5	11.4	3.5	10	Cc	ex Dania Carina-96
RMS Walsum	Deu	1984	1,289	1,555	74.9	10.6	3.4	10	C	ex Mosa-98
Sea Tyne †	Deu	1984	1,289	1,536	74.9	10.6	3.4	9	C	
Simone	Deu	1982	1,710	2,319	80.3	11.4	4.3	11	C	
Thamesis	Deu	1997	2,848	4,168	89.7	13.6	5.7	13	Cc	
Visurgis	Deu	1997	2,853	4,167	90.0	13.6	5.7	13	C	

* managed for Janssen Ship's Service or † for Claus Nortemann.

J. R. Rix & Sons Ltd.

UK

Funnel: Red with deep blue top having 'J' over 'R' on red diamond.
Hull: Black with red boot-topping.

Name	Flag	Year	GRT	DWT	Loa	Bm	Draft	Kts	Type	Former names
Breydon Venture (2)	Gbr	1977	562	1,036	45.9	10.0	3.9	9	C	ex Wis-86
Harrix	Bhs	1977	1,992	2,750	79.1	12.4	5.4	10	Cc	ex Bettina-98, Barkenkoppel-86, Nordholm-79
Jonrix	Bhs	1977	999	2,210	79.0	12.5	4.8	11	Cc	ex Langeland II-94, Langeland-83
Lerrix	Bhs	1977	1,992	2,777	79.1	12.4	5.4	10	Cc	ex Stefan-98, Sanderskoppel-86
Lizrix	Bhs	1977	2,019	2,899	82.3	13.9	5.3	12	C	ex Yorksee-96, Katharina-90, Karlsvik-86, I/a Eriesee
Rix Falcon	Gbr	1960	172	250	43.3	5.4	2.1	-	T	ex Burtondale H-92
Rix Harrier (2)	Gbr	1979	572	1,046	45.7	9.5	3.9	8	T	ex Breydon Enterprise-97, Wib-87 (conv C-97)
Rix Kestrel	Gbr	1957	206	300	50.9	5.4	2.3	8	T	ex Burdale H-93
Rix Osprey	Gbr	1959	207	300	50.9	5.2	2.3	8	T	ex Beldale H-96 (rblt-79)
Timrix	Brb	1977	1,973	2,206	790	12.4	4.8	12	Cc	ex Kiri-99, Siggen II-97, Siggen-85

RMC Group plc

UK

South Coast Shipping Co. Ltd.

Funnel: Black with black 'RMC' on orange diamond on broad white band.
Hull: Black with red boot-topping.

Name	Flag	Year	GRT	DWT	Loa	Bm	Draft	Kts	Type	Former names
Bowcross	Gbr	1967	1,006	1,786	59.8	12.0	4.3	10	Dss	ex Chichester Cross-71
Sand Falcon	Gbr	1998	5,307	9,128	99.9	19.5	7.8	12	Dss	
Sand Fulmar	Gbr	1998	5,307	9,153	99.9	19.5	7.8	12	Dss	
Sand Harrier	Gbr	1990	3,751	5,916	99.0	16.5	6.6	11	Dss	
Sand Heron	Gbr	1990	3,751	5,916	99.0	16.5	6.4	11	Dss	
Sand Kestrel	Gbr	1974	3,110	4,722	98.7	18.2	5.1	13	Dss	ex Bowherald-94
Sand Kite	Gbr	1974	3,110	4,425	98.7	18.2	5.1	13	Dss	ex Bowknight-93
Sand Serin	Gbr	1974	1,219	2,120	66.6	12.2	4.8	10	Dss	
Sand Swan	Gbr	1970	1,164	1,944	66.6	12.5	4.4	10	Dss	
Sand Weaver	Gbr	1975	3,366	5,271	96.4	16.7	6.1	12	Dss	
Welsh Piper	Gbr	1987	1,251	1,923	69.0	12.5	4.4	11	Dss	

RMS Lubeck Schiffahrts. GmbH

Germany

Funnel: Various ownership or charter colours.
Hull: Various.

Name	Flag	Year	GRT	DWT	Loa	Bm	Draft	Kts	Type	Former names
Hannes D	Atg	1968	1,037	1,200	68.4	10.5	4.0	12	C	ex Windo-98, Mjovik-91, Windo-90, Nincop-88
Irlo	Deu	1969	1,208	1,964	74.0	10.8	5.1	12	Cc	ex Anta-94, Simone-89, Tina-76
Jessica	Deu	1965	530	584	47.8	8.8	3.1	10	C	ex Freiheit-91, Silja-78, Kahlenberg-77, Regina-71
Jolanda	Hnd	1956	499	964	57.8	9.0	3.5	10	C	ex Svend Dammann-89, Robox-69

Name	Flag	Year	GRT	DWT	Loa	Bm	Draft	Kts	Type	Former names
Largo II	Hnd	1973	531	680	49.7	8.3	3.5	11	C	ex Janine-89, Sterno-84, Saralil-79
Largona	Vct	1978	866	1,195	63.7	10.6	4.0	12	C	ex Biscay Spirit-95, Irimo-87
Tonja	Hnd	1957	399	864	53.7	7.8	3.9	10	C	ex Salona-86, Samstein-76, Felstein I-70, Tonja-69
Tonjo	Nor	1969	1,850	1,128	78.6	12.5	3.6	14	Rop	ex Haukeli-94, Canis-79
Ursula B	Atg	1964	1,011	1,185	66.2	10.6	4.0	11	C	ex Neuenfelde-95, Eduard Kahler-87, Heinrich Knuppel-71
Wiebke D	Atg	1980	1,441	1,795	81.0	11.3	3.3	10	Cs	ex Pandor-97

Rohden Bereederung GmbH & Co. KG   Germany

Funnel:	Colours not confirmed.
Hull:	Black with red boot-topping.

Name	Flag	Year	GRT	DWT	Loa	Bm	Draft	Kts	Type	Former names
Algol *	Atg	1995	1,864	2,489	82.4	11.5	4.8	12	Cc	ex RMS Algol-98, Algol-95
Antares *	Atg	1995	1,864	2,449	82.4	11.5	4.8	12	Cc	ex RMS Antares-99, Antares-96
Apus	DEn	1990	2,642	3,100	90.0	13.0	4.6	12	cc	ex Anke Ehler-98
Atair *	Atg	1995	1,864	2,489	82.4	11.5	4.8	12	Cc	ex RMS Atair-98, Atair-96
Canopus I	Cyp	1979	2,862	2,507	98.7	16.0	3.8	12	Cc	ex Canopus-94
Lys Clipper *	Atg	1995	2,456	3,706	87.5	12.9	5.5	12	Cc	ex Apollo-95
Lys Coronel	Atg	1978	2,089	2,461	86.6	12.8	4.9	13	Cc	ex Coronel-97, Christel-85 (len-86)
Pavo	Atg	1986	3,300	4,107	92.4	15.7	6.0	13	Cc	ex Seevetal-98
RMS Aldebaran *	Deu	1996	1,864	2,516	82.4	11.5	4.8	12	Cc	I/a Aldebaran
RMS Andromeda *	Deu	1997	1,864	2,516	82.5	11.5	4.8	12	cc	I/a Andromeda
RMS Arcturus *	Deu	1996	1,864	2,517	82.4	11.4	4.8	12	C	ex Arcturus-96
RMS Aries *	Deu	1997	2,456	3,703	88.0	12.9	5.5	11	Cc	I/a Aries
RMS Auriga *	Deu	1996	2,460	3,715	87.9	12.9	5.5	11	Cc	ex Auriga-96
RMS Lagune	Atg	1982	1,059	1,150	74.2	9.9	2.9	10	Cc	ex RMS Normandia-93, Lagune-93
Tucana	Atg	1985	2,732	3,825	90.4	14.0	6.3	14	Cc	ex Rangitikei-96, Lisa Heeren-92, Santa Paula-90, Lisa Heeren-89, Band Aid II-85, Lisa Heeren-85

* owned by subsidiary Elbe Trans Schiffahrts GmbH.

Reederei Rolf Rohwedder   Germany

Funnel:	Dark green.
Hull:	Dark green with black boot-topping.

Name	Flag	Year	GRT	DWT	Loa	Bm	Draft	Kts	Type	Former names
Alpha	Atg	1989	1,984	3,088	89.3	12.5	4.3	11	Cc	ex Barbel-93
Cliff	Atg	1983	1,518	1,760	82.5	11.4	3.5	10	Cc	ex Kiebitzberg-88
Jacqueline	Bhs	1986	1,790	2,800	82.5	12.6	4.5	11	Cc	ex Jutta R-90, Jacqueline-86
Jade	Atg	1985	1,948	3,051	89.3	12.5	4.7	10	Cc	ex Sea Jade-88
Jens R	Atg	1990	1,960	2,980	88.3	12.5	4.6	11	Cc	
Medway	Bhs	1977	1,475	2,271	69.0	13.5	4.5	9	C	ex Sea Medway-94
Mindful	Atg	1989	1,959	2,980	87.7	12.5	4.6	11	Cc	I/a Christian R
Sea Weser	Atg	1983	1,939	2,888	88.0	11.5	4.7	11	Cc	
Southern Amelia	Cyp	1991	3,186	4,185	93.0	15.0	5.8	12	Cc	ex Noumea Express-97, Nils R-97, I/a Kodaly

Royal Shipping BV   Netherlands

Funnel:	White or owners markings.
Hull:	Black or blue with red boot-topping.

Name	Flag	Year	GRT	DWT	Loa	Bm	Draft	Kts	Type	Former names
Beveland	Nld	1982	1,054	1,468	78.9	10.0	3.2	9	C	ex Elan-96, Vlieland-93
Elan	Nld	1997	2,377	3,471	89.0	12.4	4.9	11	Cc	
Harma	Nld	1979	999	1,450	65.0	10.7	4.0	10	C	
Jens	Nld	1984	1,171	1,586	79.1	10.1	3.4	11	C	ex Scorpio-96, Morgenstond-92
Lifana	Nld	1983	1,116	1,424	79.3	10.4	3.2	11	C	ex Thalassa-91
Osiris	Nld	1985	1,163	1,685	73.7	11.7	3.7	10	C	
Rachel	Nld	1984	1,162	1,685	73.7	11.7	3.7	10	C	ex Sunergon-94
Rein B	Vct	1958	492	710	48.8	9.0	3.5	9	C	ex Hendrik-B-93, Karina-90, Karin-89
Storm	Nld	1983	1,316	2,175	73.7	11.4	4.2	9	C	ex Maas-97, Stern-95, Maas-93 (len-88)

Name	Flag	Year	GRT	DWT	Loa	Bm	Draft	Kts	Type	Former names

Ernst Russ GmbH & Co.   Germany

Funnel: Black with red 'ER' bordered by narrow red bands.
Hull: Black or grey with red boot-topping.

Name	Flag	Year	GRT	DWT	Loa	Bm	Draft	Kts	Type	Former names
Antje	Deu	1998	5,056	6,858	117.9	18.2	7.1	17	CC	l/a Antje Russ
Caroline Russ (2)	Deu	1999	11,500	7,250	153.3	23.6	7.0	20	Rop	
Christian Russ	Ant	1994	7,167	8,858	134.1	19.7	8.0	16	CC	ex Ivaran Sexto-99, Christian Russ-98, Nedlloyd Crete-98, Christian Russ-96
Elisabeth Russ (2) *	Deu	1999	11,500	7,250	153.3	23.6	7.0	20	Rop	
Friedrich Russ (2) *	Deu	1999	11,500	7,250	153.3	23.6	7.0	20	Rop	
Martha Russ	Atg	1990	5,562	4,415	107.8	17.3	6.8	15	Rop	
Pauline Russ (2)	Deu	1999	11,500	7,250	153.3	23.6	7.0	20	Rop	

* on charter to Transfennica q.v.

Samskip H/F   Iceland

Funnel: Yellow with 'B&C' on diagonally quartered red/white flag, black top.
Hull: Grey with red boot-topping.

Name	Flag	Year	GRT	DWT	Loa	Bm	Draft	Kts	Type	Former names
Stapafell	Isl	1979	1,619	2,028	75.8	13.2	4.8	13	T	

Bruno Bischoff Reederei GmbH & Co., Germany

Name	Flag	Year	GRT	DWT	Loa	Bm	Draft	Kts	Type	Former names
Bremer Reeder	Atg	1984	2,191	1,492	77.7	13.2	3.5	11	Cp	
Bremer Roland	Nis	1985	1,322	1,230	71.2	11.6	3.2	10	Cp	
Bremer Zukunft	Deu	1998	2,985	4,852	98.4	16.9	5.9	15	CC	

Scanscot Shipping Services (Deutschland) GmbH   Germany

Funnel: Black, deep green top with white 'S' over two black bands.
Hull: green with white 'SCANSCOT', red boot-topping.

Name	Flag	Year	GRT	DWT	Loa	Bm	Draft	Kts	Type	Former names
Scan Arctic	Deu	1998	8,811	7,270	126.5	20.3	6.7	16	Ro	
Scan Botnia	Deu	1998	8,000	7,000	126.5	20.3	6.7	16	Ro	
Scan Oceanic	Gbr	1997	5,752	5,100	100.9	18.6	6.6	16	Ro	
Scan Polaris	Deu	1996	5,760	5,100	100.9	18.6	6.6	16	Ro	

Newbuildings: two further 8,000 grt 7,000 dwt roll-on, roll-off vessels due for 1999 delivery.

Wilhelm E.F. Schmid GmbH   Germany

Funnel: Various.
Hull: Various.

Name	Flag	Year	GRT	DWT	Loa	Bm	Draft	Kts	Type	Former names
Atlantik *	Atg	1993	4,193	5,401	111.1	16.2	6.6	16	Cc	ex Birgit Jurgens-97
Bjorn M	Deu	1955	328	480	47.6	8.5	2.7	9	C	ex Traute-86
Hanny	Deu	1960	319	477	45.3	8.5	2.7	10	C	ex Wiebke I-97, Mona Rosa-90
Helgoland	Deu	1955	492	632	54.1	8.0	2.9	8	C	ex Kaja H-98, Gauensiek-86, Witte Kliff-71, Marschenland-65 (len/deep-78)
Neuland	Deu	1966	494	500	53.2	8.4	3.1	9	C	ex Lilly K-96, Adele J-78 (len/deep-80)
Susanne M	Deu	1956	465	572	50.3	8.5	3.0	10	C	ex Gerda K-92, Gerhard Elfring-65 (len-79)
Ute	Deu	1984	1,520	1,837	76.5	11.5	3.9	10	C	(len-94)

* owned by Reinhold Fischer KG.

The Schulte Group   Germany

Funnel: Black with white 'S' on red disc on green band.
Hull: Dark grey with red boot-topping.

Name	Flag	Year	GRT	DWT	Loa	Bm	Draft	Kts	Type	Former names
Apollo Eagle	Atg	1972	4,225	6,341	101.2	16.1	7.2	12	Bc	ex Christiane Schulte-98, Christa-92, Christiane Schulte-87 (len/rblt-92)
Atrice	Lbr	1984	6,755							
Ben Flor	Lbr	1985	6,867	9,129	127.4	18.6	8.3	11	Lpg	
Derwent †	Pan	1990	3,494					-	Lpg	

Name	Flag	Year	GRT	DWT	Loa	Bm	Draft	Kts	Type	Former names
Dorothea Schulte **	Nis	1981	4,884	6,118	110.9	15.5	7.5	14	Lpg	
Funchalense †	Prt	1998	4,150	5,400	100.6	16.2	6.4	14	C	ex Caroline Schulte-98, Magdalena Schulte-98
Hajo ‡	Atg	1979	1,694	2,040	72.3	12.8	4.5	12	Cc	ex Nicholas-90, Osterheide-87
Happy Bee †	Pan	1997	5,420	7,246	113.6	16.5	7.6	15	Lpg	
Happy Eagle §	Phl	1993	3,733	4,512	98.6	15.0	6.5	15	Lpg	
Happy Fellow †	Phl	1992	3,703	4,444	99.4	15.0	6.5	15	Lpg	ex Sunny Fellow-95
Happy Girl †	Phl	1989	3,643	4,247	98.3	15.4	6.3	15	Lpg	ex Sunny Girl-95
Hermann Schulte **	Nis	1980	4,884	6,137	110.9	15.5	7.5	14	Lpg	
Jo Hassel	Vct	1986	5,359	8,122	108.5	17.8	8.0	13	Tch	ex Golden Sunshine-91, Golden Princess-87
Maria Schulte	Cyp	1997	4,150	4,895	100.6	16.2	6.4	15	Cc	
OPDR Porto	Cyp	1999	4,128	4,800	100.6	16.2	6.4	15	Cc	
OPDR Sevilla	Cyp	1999	4,128	4,800	100.6	16.2	6.4	15	Cc	
Torm Angola *	Cyp	1998	4,150	4,680	100.6	16.4	6.4	14	Cc	ex Lucie Schulte-99
Torm Congo	Cyp	1997	4,150	5,196	100.6	16.2	6.4	15	Cc	ex Angelica Schulte-99
Ullswater	Sgp	1996	5,945	7,678	121.0	19.3	6.8	14	Lpg	

italic * managed by subsidiaries Eurasia Shipping & Management Co. Ltd., Hong Kong, ** Dorchester Maritime Ltd., Isle of Man,
† Hanseatic Shipping Co. Ltd., Cyprus or ‡ Midocean Maritime Ltd., Isle of Man.
§ managed for Naess Shipping (Holland) BV.

Seatrade Groningen BV   Netherlands

Funnel: Blue with merged white 'S' and blue 'G' on orange square.
Hull: White with 'SEATRADE', red boot-topping.

Name	Flag	Year	GRT	DWT	Loa	Bm	Draft	Kts	Type	Former names
Adriatic *	Nld	1984	3,505	4,173	99.0	16.0	6.7	15	R	ex White Reefer-90
Antarctic	Bhs	1982	3,520	4,192	99.0	16.0	6.7	15	R	ex Ena Maru-89
Antigua	Ant	1991	4,190	4,468	105.4	16.0	6.8	15	Rc	ex Soria-96, Escambray-96
Antilla	Pan	1990	4,190	4,487	105.4	16.0	6.8	15	Rc	ex Salamanca-96, Yumuri-96
Arctic	Bhs	1983	3,526	4,156	99.0	16.0	6.7	15	R	ex Sapporo Maru-89
Aruba	Nld	1990	4,190	4,468	105.4	16.0	6.8	15	R	ex Segovia-96, Vinales-95
Asiatic	Bhs	1986	3,757	4,988	106.0	16.3	7.0	16	R	ex Sanuki Reefer-91
Atlantic Ice	Ant	1979	2,274	2,448	81.0	13.2	5.1	13	R	ex Atlantic-89 (len-82)
Baltic Ice	Ant	1979	1,198	2,468	81.7	13.2	5.1	13	R	ex Baltic-88 (len-81)
Cap Esterias ** (2)	Pan	1965	1,381	1,869	79.8	11.3	5.3	-	R	ex Satamaru-95, Ettore-91, Franca-90, Don Alberto-87, Dita Smits-76
Caribic	Nld	1993	4,683	6,697	113.8	16.3	8.3	-	R	
Casablanca	Nld	1980	2,989	3,536	101.9	14.5	5.3	14	R	(len-83)
Celtic Ice	Ant	1979	1,198	2,468	81.7	13.2	5.1	13	R	ex Celtic-89 (len-82)
Concorde Spirit (2)	Ant	1991	3,466	3,866	114.5	15.8	6.0	15	R	ex Trito-97, Kedon-96 (len-97)
Fenland **	Bhs	1979	2,004	1,815	90.8	12.1	5.2	13	R	ex Norbrit Vries-88, Boston Sea Lance-83 (len-85)
Joint Frost	Ant	1979	2,595	2,854	83.4	14.5	6.0	15	Rc	
La Bonita	Bhs	1981	2,798	4,700	90.3	15.2	6.4	11	C	ex Pearl King-90, Ichiban-84, Lotus King-84
La Minera	Bhs	1982	3,338	4,272	99.0	15.5	6.0	13	B	I/a La Bonita
Laura Christina	Ant	1978	2,980	3,800	101.9	14.5	5.3	14	R	ex Swalan-98, Laura Christina-90 (len-83)
Magdalena	Nld	1979	2,989	3,529	101.9	14.5	5.3	14	R	(len-83)
Maya	Nld	1978	2,989	3,547	101.9	14.5	5.3	14	R	(len-83)
Nickerie *	Nld	1985	4,202	4,278	108.0	18.0	6.2	16	R	I/a Americ
Normandic †	Bhs	1983	3,960	5,220	108.3	16.3	7.4	16	Rc	
Nova Cotta	Pan	1983	4,071	5,563	110.0	16.4	7.5	16	R	ex Isla Bonita-96, east Breeze-90
Nova Klipper	Ant	1992	5,225	6,454	(106.1)	17.8	6.7	16	R	
Nova Liguria	Bhs	1985	4,361	5,459	109.0	16.4	7.7	16	R	ex Ligurian Reefer-91, Ligurian Universal-90
Nova Terra	Bhs	1985	4,361	5,475	109.0	16.4	7.7	16	R	ex Adriatic Universal-90
Nova Zeelandia	Nld	1986	4,440	5,508	115.0	16.8	7.3	18	R	ex Mashu Reefer-92, Mashu Maru-88
Nyantic †	Bhs	1984	3,955	5,250	108.5	16.3	7.4	16	R	
Oceanic Ice **	Ant	1977	2,244	2,404	82.7	13.6	5.0	14	R	ex Oceanic-88
Tyro (2)	Ant	1990	3,466	3,600	114.5	15.8	6.0	15	R	ex Argut-96 (len-97)

italic * managed by Columbia Shipmanagement Ltd. or ** by H&G Transport BV, Netherlands or † owned by Hagenaes Management AS, Norway.

Name	Flag	Year	GRT	DWT	Loa	Bm	Draft	Kts	Type	Former names

Seatrans DA
Norway

Funnel: Orange with over lapping black 'ST' symbol inside black diamond outline,
or blue with white 'S' between two narrow white bands.
Hull: Orange with black 'SEATRANS'.

Name	Flag	Year	GRT	DWT	Loa	Bm	Draft	Kts	Type	Former names
Baltic News	Nis	1990	5,603	4,944	115.9	17.8	4.3	15	Cp	ex Nornews Supplier-98, Gold River-95
Nornews Express	Nor	1987	4,859	4,568	109.8	17.5	6.2	15	Cp	
Nornews Leader	Nor	1990	5,339	5,670	115.8	17.8	6.7	15	Cp	
Trans Arctic	Nis	1991	4,712	6,930	116.8	17.5	7.7	15	Tch	
Trans Baltic	Nis	1975	3,382	3,991	94.6	15.0	5.7	13	Cp	(len-85)
Trans Chemica	Bhs	1977	2,316	3,400	96.0	14.0	5.5	13	Tch	ex Castor Chemica-84, Corsica-81
Trans Dania	Nis	1989	5,167	5,353	113.4	17.8	6.7	15	Cp	
Trans Fennia	Nis	1982	7,307	5,500	115.6	19.0	6.1	15	Cp	
Trans Fjell	Nor	1978	2,195	1,900	77.0	14.0	5.4	12	Cp	
Trans Holm	Nis	1981	4,259	3,666	96.5	17.5	5.3	13	Tch	ex Estrella-93 (conv Cp-93)
Trans Nes	Nor	1980	2,065	1,478	76.7	14.0	4.9	12	Cp	
Trans Nordia	Nor	1986	4,876	4,585	110.5	17.6	6.3	15	Cp	
Trans Scandic	Nis	1992	4,716	6,927	116.8	17.8	7.7	15	Tch	
Trans Sea	Nor	1974	3,382	3,994	95.6	15.0	5.7	13	Cp	
Trans Sund	Bhs	1991	3,206	4,794	96.4	15.3	6.2	14	Tch	ex Lis Terkol-96, Stolt Lis Terkol-94
Trans Tind	Bhs	1980	1,635	2,250	87.2	12.8	4.8	14	Tch	(len-90)
Trans Vag	Nor	1979	2,065	1,487	76.7	14.0	4.9	12	Cp	
Trans Vik	Nis	1991	3,206	4,794	96.4	15.3	6.2	14	Tch	ex Bente Terkol-96, Stolt Bente Terkol-94

Seavoss Schiffahrt GmbH
Germany

Funnel and hull: Colours not confirmed.

Name	Flag	Year	GRT	DWT	Loa	Bm	Draft	Kts	Type	Former names
Angelburg	Atg	1981	1,939	2,890	88.0	11.3	4.7	11	Cc	ex Margaretha-96
Asseburg	Atg	1982	1,939	2,890	88.0	11.5	4.7	11	Cc	ex Catharina-96
Breitenburg	Atg	1982	1,939	2,890	88.0	11.3	4.7	11	Cc	ex Keitum-95, Jule-94, Balder-93, Jule-88
Kaaksburg	Atg	1981	1,939	2,889	88.0	11.3	4.7	11	Cc	ex Torex-95, Tini-95, Loke-93, Tini-88
Paaschburg	Atg	1980	3,228	3,996	93.3	15.5	5.8	14	Cc	ex Borstel-96, Jupiter-93, Iberian Bridge-93, Jupiter-92, ECL Cadet-92, Clipper-91, Manchester Clipper-80, I/a Clipper
Schulenburg	Cyp	1981	2,265	2,976	99.8	11.4	4.3	10	Cc	ex Ursula-96, Ursula Wessels-90
Steinburg	Atg	1982	1,939	2,885	88.0	11.3	4.7	11	Cc	ex Comet-95

Morten Seines Rederi
Norway

Funnel and hull: Colours not confirmed.

Name	Flag	Year	GRT	DWT	Loa	Bm	Draft	Kts	Type	Former names
Albenny	Nor	1973	689	904	49.6	10.1	3.9	11	Cc	ex Joika-73
Anntoro	Nor	1971	689	914	49.6	10.1	3.9	10	Cc	ex Cap Carrier-78, Nes Carrier-77, Gullsund-76, Joodur-73
Aquamarine	Nor	1975	538	815	49.7	8.3	3.9	10	C	
Heykur	Nor	1972	689	945	49.6	10.1	3.9	15	Cc	
Rossoy	Nor	1986	1,473	1,770	77.4	11.4	3.8	11	Cc	ex Borsfleth-98 (len-93)
Seines	Nor	1971	689	834	49.6	10.1	3.6	12	Cc	ex Brudanger-92, Cap Cargo-79, Nes Cargo-77, Gullhav-76

Shell-Royal Dutch Group
UK
Shell Tankers (UK) Ltd.

Funnel: Red with yellow shell.
Hull: Red with red boot-topping.

Name	Flag	Year	GRT	DWT	Loa	Bm	Draft	Kts	Type	Former names
Achatina	Gbr	1968	1,580	2,654	84.3	12.5	4.7	14	T	ex Shell Craftsman-93, Ardrossan-79 (len-91)

The Schulte Group Happy Girl. *Philip Kempsey*

Seatrans DA Trans Chemica. *J. Krayenbosch*

Name	Flag	Year	GRT	DWT	Loa	Bm	Draft	Kts	Type	Former names
Amoria	Gbr	1981	1,926	3,027	79.3	13.2	5.5	12	T	ex Shell Marketer-93
Arianta	Gbr	1982	1,926	3,027	79.3	13.2	5.5	12	T	ex Shell Technician-93
Asprella	Gbr	1981	1,926	3,027	79.2	13.2	5.5	12	T	ex Shell Seafarer-93
Magn *	Fro	1983	1,305	2,050	70.7	12.0	5.0	12	T	ex Hornisse-96

* owned by P/f Foroya Shell, Faeroes.

Rederiet M.H. Simonsen APS Denmark

Funnel: Light blue with white 'S', black top.
Hull: Red.

Name	Flag	Year	GRT	DWT	Loa	Bm	Draft	Kts	Type	Former names
Grindal	Dis	1956	397	668	53.8	7.4	2.8	-	T	ex Vestskjell-73 (len-80)
Oradana (2)	Dis	1971	1,639	2,495	76.0	11.5	4.8	10	Tch	ex Scarlino Primo-89
Oragreen	Bhs	1956	3,033	4,004	97.1	16.0	6.1	12	T	ex Vulcanus I-90, Vulcanus-83, Erich Schroder-72 (conv waste-91, widen-83, conv C-72)
Orakota	Dis	1981	1,727	2,578	85.0	13.0	4.7	12	T	ex Dakota I-94, Dakota-94, Doris-86
Orasund	Dis	1969	986	1,438	72.9	11.5	3.6	11	T	ex Capella-87, Tora Lupe-85, Torasund-76, Sinmar-71
Oratank	Dis	1968	986	1,438	72.9	11.5	3.6	11	T	ex Toratank-84, Bras-71
Orateca	Dis	1982	1,733	2,650	84.8	13.0	4.7	11	T	ex Tecumseh-95

I. M. Skaugen ASA Norway
Norwegian Gas Carriers AS

Funnel: Various.
Hull: Red with red boot-topping.

Name	Flag	Year	GRT	DWT	Loa	Bm	Draft	Kts	Type	Former names
Norgas Carine	Lbr	1989	7,260	9,259	132.2	18.0	8.6	17	Lpg	ex Norgas Teviot-98, Teviot-96
Norgas Challenger	Nis	1984	5,739	7,492	115.1	17.5	7.9	14	Lpg	ex San Francisco-89
Norgas Chief	Nis	1983	7,791	8,379	119.6	19.0	8.3	14	Lpg	ex Einar Tambarskjelve-88
Norgas Discoverer	Lbr	1971	7,173	8,738	125.4	19.1	8.6	17	Lpg	ex Bow Elm-88
Norgas Energy	Nis	1979	6,521	9,095	116.6	19.5	8.6	-	Lpg	ex Chem Energy-90, Helice-88
Norgas Navigator	Lbr	1977	5,889	7,155	112.7	18.6	7.5	15	Lpg	ex Norgas Wega-91, Chemtrans Wega-90, Bavaria Multina-78
Norgas Patricia	Nis	1991	7,095	9,470	126.2	17.9	8.6	16	Lpg	
Norgas Pilot	Nis	1977	5,196	6,035	112.1	16.8	7.6	15	Lpg	ex Magellan-87
Norgas Pioneer	Nis	1979	6,521	9,065	116.6	19.5	8.8	15	Lpg	ex Chem Pioneer-90, Admiral Cabral-87
Norgas Trader	Lbr	1981	7,000	8,493	118.7	18.5	8.8	16	Lpg	ex Coral Temse-87
Norgas Voyager	Lbr	1972	7,173	8,700	125.3	19.1	8.6	16	Lpg	ex Hardanger-88
Norgas Sailor	Nis	1976	5,696	6,325	112.4	16.8	7.6	15	Lpg	ex Vasco da Gama-87

Princess Carriers AS

Name	Flag	Year	GRT	DWT	Loa	Bm	Draft	Kts	Type	Former names
Princess of Penang	Pan	1979	5,463	9,033	115.7	18.3	8.1	13	Tch	ex Hegg-96, El Progreso-87, Hegg-84
Princess of Rotterdam	Pan	1977	5,036	8,322	111.5	17.5	8.0	13	Tch	ex Capella II-96, Stainless Commander-96, Golden Yon-89, Golden Star-83
Princess of Yosu	Mlt	1970	1,673	2,545	86.4	12.1	5.2	12	Tch	ex Stainless Lady-96, Ametist-89, Kimia Jaya-86, Chemical Distributor-83

Sloman Neptun Shiffahrts-Aktiengesellschaft Germany

Funnel: Black with blue over yellow bands or Unigas Pool colours.
Hull: Grey with red boot-topping or dark red with grey boot-topping.

Name	Flag	Year	GRT	DWT	Loa	Bm	Draft	Kts	Type	Former names
Alegre Feeder (2)	Deu	1982	4,291	3,641	92.4	18.1	4.6	12	Cc/Ro	ex Spirit of Progress-98, Mareika-93, Dorcas-93, Mareika-90, Sloman Royal-88
Alphagas	Atg	1996	4,924	6,360	114.6	15.7	7.3		Lpg	
Betagas	Atg	1997	4,924	6,375	114.6	15.8	7.3	16	Lpg	
Comma	Atg	1996	4,489	6,054	100.7	17.8	6.6	14	Cc	ex Sloman Commander-99
Deltagas	Lbr	1992	3,011	3,700	88.4	14.2	6.2	14	Lpg	
Epsilongas	Atg	2000	5,018	6,500	-	-	-	-	Lpg	

Shell-Royal Dutch Group Amoria. *J. Krayenbosch*

Rederiet M.H. Simonsen APS Orateca. *J. Krayenbosch*

Name	Flag	Year	GRT	DWT	Loa	Bm	Draft	Kts	Type	Former names
Etagas	Ant	1988	7,314	9,384	134.7	18.6	8.3	16	Lpg	
Gammagas	Lbr	1992	3,703	4,447	99.4	15.0	6.5	14	Lpg	
Lingegas	Ant	1981	2,700	3,403	82.6	14.1	6.5	13	Lpg	
Merwegas	Ant	1981	2,712	3,403	82.6	14.1	6.5	13	Lpg	
Omegagas	-	1999	-	-	-	-	-	-	Lpg	
Sloman Challenger	Atg	1995	4,489	6,016	100.7	18.0	6.7	14	Cc	ex Polar Challenger-98, Sloman Challenger-97
Sloman Regent (2)	Atg	1982	3,922	2,561	92.0	18.1	4.2	12	Cc/Ro	
Sloman Rider (2)	Atg	1979	3,887	2,570	92.0	18.1	4.2	12	Cc/Ro	
Sloman Rover (2)	Atg	1979	4,298	3,530	92.4	18.4	4.6	12	Cc/Ro	ex Buxsund-94, Heinrich S-94, Calypso I-85, Heinrich S-85, I/a Paoua
Sloman Runner (2)	Atg	1979	3,887	3,340	92.1	18.1	3.7	12	Cc/Ro	
Zetagas	Ant	1982	5,643	6,975	122.6	15.6	7.5	15	Lpg	

Soenderborg Rederiaktieselskab Denmark

Funnel and hull: Colours not confirmed.

Name	Flag	Year	GRT	DWT	Loa	Bm	Draft	Kts	Type	Former names
Adele	Dis	1967	2,471	2,419	89.3	11.8	5.8	14	Lv	ex Diana Clausen-84, Huelva-81 (len/conv C-81)
Alondra	Dis	1967	2,343	1,600	89.3	13.8	4.5	13	Lv	ex Dora Clausen-83, Algarve-80 (len-84, conv C-80)
Amelia	Dis	1972	2,629	2,080	77.3	13.8	5.1	13	Lv	ex Estetal-85 (conv C-84)
Caroline	Dis	1975	1,075	1,066	58.7	11.0	3.8	10	Lv	ex Trans Holm-89 (conv Cp-89, len-78)
Cimbria	Dis	1995	1,762	1,559	73.5	11.4	3.8	9	Lv	
Codan	Dis	1964	1,453	990	69.2	11.2	3.7	11	Lv	ex Athene-89, Susanne Clausen-84, Ardua-78, Padua-74 (conv C-78)
Felicia (2)	Dis	1987	3,183	1,748	85.4	14.0	3.5	13	Lv	ex Vanessa-96, Leeward Express-94, Vanessa-93 (conv Ro-96, len-90)
Finola (2)	Dis	1988	3,228	1,974	85.4	14.0	3.5	13	Lv	ex Christina C-97 (conv Cc/Ro-97, len-91)
Gerard Patrick Purcell	Pan	1970	2,978	2,568	88.5	13.9	5.5	13	Lv	ex Deichtor-83, Lubbecke-83, Ibesca Belgica-80, Ibesca Britannia-78, Lubbecke-77 (conv Cc-84)
Philomena Purcell	Dis	1973	3,013	2,650	88.3	13.0	5.0	13	Lv	ex Esteflut-82 (len/conv C-82)

Soetermeer, Fekkes' Cargadoorskantoor BV Netherlands

Funnel: Various.
Hull: Orange.

Name	Flag	Year	GRT	DWT	Loa	Bm	Draft	Kts	Type	Former names
Aletis	Nld	1996	2,055	3,234	90.0	12.5	4.6	11	Cc	
Coral	Nld	1988	851	1,260	64.3	10.6	3.4	11	C	ex Sirocco-98, Boeran-91
Hester	Nld	1981	1,511	1,766	82.5	11.3	3.6	10	Cc	ex Javazee-98, Anga-96, Vineta-94
Sprinter	Cyp	1993	1,983	3,204	90.4	12.5	4.6	11	Cc	
Tertius	Nld	1995	2,051	3,280	89.9	12.7	4.7	11	Cc	

Claus Speck GmbH Germany

Funnel: Various.
Hull: Various.

Name	Flag	Year	GRT	DWT	Loa	Bm	Draft	Kts	Type	Former names
Holstein *	Deu	1991	3,815	4,660	103.5	16.2	6.7	15	Cc	ex Gracechurch Planet-96, Nordic Bridge-94, ECL Commander-91, Schleswig Holstein-91
Odin	Atg	1994	2,997	4,530	97.3	16.2	5.9	14	Cc	
Frej	Atg	1994	2,997	4,470	97.3	16.2	5.9	14	Cc	

* managed for Land Schleswig-Holstein, Germany.

Sloman Neptun Shiffahrts-Aktiengesellschaft Alphagas. *J. Krayenbosch*

Soetermeer, Fekkes' Cargadoorskantoor BV Sprinter. *J. Krayenbosch*

Name	Flag	Year	GRT	DWT	Loa	Bm	Draft	Kts	Type	Former names

Spliethhoff's Bevrachtingskantoor BV

Netherlands

Funnel: Orange wiith black 'S' on diagonally quartered houseflag.
Hull: Brown with green boot-topping.

Name	Flag	Year	GRT	DWT	Loa	Bm	Draft	Kts	Type	Former names
Barentzgracht	Nld	1981	3,433	3,444	80.2	16.1	6.0	12	Cc	
Bataafgracht	Nld	1981	3,433	3,444	80.2	16.1	6.0	12	Cc	
Beursgracht	Nld	1981	3,433	3,448	80.2	16.1	6.0	11	Cc	
Bloemgracht	Nld	1980	3,433	3,444	80.2	16.1	6.0	12	Cc	
Bontegracht	Nld	1981	3,433	3,437	80.2	16.1	6.0	12	Cc	
Brouwersgracht	Nld	1980	3,343	3,445	80.2	16.1	6.0	12	Cc	
Heemskerkgracht	Nld	1982	4,430	7,554	97.2	16.1	8.1	12	Cc	
Heerengracht	Nld	1981	4,281	7,435	95.4	16.1	8.2	11	Cc	ex Carwood-82
Houtmangracht	Nld	1982	4,430	7,554	97.2	16.1	8.1	11	Cc	
Hudsongracht	Nld	1982	4,281	7,435	95.4	16.1	8.2	11	Cc	ex Carliner-89
Humbergracht	Nld	1981	4,281	7,435	95.4	16.0	5.9	11	Cc	ex Carpaper-89
Kaapgracht	Nld	1984	4,983	8,038	106.3	16.1	8.0	12	Cc	
Keizersgracht	Nld	1983	4,921	8,138	106.3	16.1	8.0	11	Cc	
Kielgracht	Nld	1984	4,983	8,038	106.3	16.1	8.0	12	Cc	
Klippergracht	Nld	1984	4,291	5,022	106.3	16.1	5.9	11	Cc	
Koggegracht	Nld	1983	4,921	8,138	106.3	16.6	8.0	11	Cc	
Koningsgracht	Nld	1983	4,291	8,138	106.3	16.6	8.0	11	Cc	
Lauriergracht	Nld	1988	5,994	9,467	113.1	19.4	8.5	14	Cc	
Leliegracht	Nld	1987	5,994	9,457	113.1	19.2	8.5	14	Cc	
Lemmergracht	Nld	1988	5,998	9,682	113.1	19.2	8.5	14	Cc	ex Kapitan Babiyevskiy-92, Woodca-88
Levantgracht	Nld	1988	6,037	9,595	113.2	19.2	8.5	14	Cc	ex Kapitan Medvetskiy-92, Palpca-88
Lijnbaansgracht	Nld	1988	5,994	9,462	113.1	19.4	8.5	14	Cc	
Lindengracht	Nld	1988	6,039	9,682	113.1	19.2	8.5	14	Cc	ex Kapitan Silin-92, Newca-88
Looiersgracht	Nld	1987	5,994	9,462	113.1	19.4	8.5	14	Cc	
Lootsgracht	Nld	1989	6,037	9,682	113.2	19.2	8.5	14	Cc	ex Mekhanik Volkosh-92, Tiger Speed-92, Mekhanik Volkosh-91, Poleca-89
Paleisgracht	Nld	1985	5,974	9,498	113.0	19.0	8.4	14	Cc	
Palmgracht	Nld	1985	5,974	9,536	113.0	19.0	8.4	14	Cc	
Parkgracht	Nld	1986	5,998	9,656	113.1	19.0	8.5	14	Cc	
Pauwgracht	Nld	1986	5,977	9,483	113.0	19.0	8.4	14	Cc	
Pietersgracht	Nld	1986	5,998	9,652	113.0	19.0	8.5	14	Cc	
Pijlgracht	Nld	1985	5,974	9,515	113.0	19.0	8.4	14	Cc	
Poolgracht	Nld	1986	5,998	9,672	113.1	19.0	8.5	14	Cc	
Prinsengracht	Nld	1985	5,974	9,490	113.0	19.0	8.4	14	Cc	
Valmin	Ant	1981	3,433	3,488	80.2	16.1	6.0	11	Cc	ex Bickersgracht-99

Stephenson Clarke Shipping Ltd.

UK

Funnel: Balck with silver band.
Hull: Black with red boot-topping.

Name	Flag	Year	GRT	DWT	Loa	Bm	Draft	Kts	Type	Former names
Aldrington *	Bhs	1978	4,297	6,570	103.6	16.1	7.0	14	C	
Ashington *	Bhs	1979	4,297	6,570	103.6	16.1	7.0	14	C	
Birling	Iom	1977	2,795	4,300	91.3	14.6	5.4	14	C	
Emerald	Iom	1978	2,795	4,300	91.3	14.6	5.4	14	C	
Harting	Iom	1981	2,813	4,300	91.3	14.6	5.8	12	Cc	
Steyning	Iom	1983	2,808	4,300	91.3	14.6	5.8	12	Cc	
Washington	Hrv	1977	6,400	9,008	127.0	18.7	7.6	14	C	

* on charter from A/S Ersco (Continental Ship Management AS).

Stolt-Nielsen Group

Norway

Stolt-Nielsens Rederi A/S

Funnel: White with white 'S' in red square, black top.
Hull: Black with red boot-topping.

Name	Flag	Year	GRT	DWT	Loa	Bm	Draft	Kts	Type	Former names
Stolt Avocet	Cym	1992	3,853	5,758	99.9	16.8	6.8	12	Tch	
Stolt Azalea *	Lbr	1988	4,740	7,582	108.0	18.2	7.1	12	Tch	

Spliethhoff's Bevrachtingskantoor BV Bontegracht. *J. M. Kakebeeke*

Stolt-Nielsens Rederi A/S Stolt Lily. *M. D. J. Lennon*

Name	Flag	Year	GRT	DWT	Loa	Bm	Draft	Kts	Type	Former names
Stolt Camellia *	Pan	1981	4,170	6,276	108.1	16.2	7.0	-	Tch	ex Universal Frontier-88
Stolt Dipper	Cym	1992	3,206	4,738	96.3	15.1	6.2	13	Tch	ex Margit Terkol-96, Stolt Margit Terkol-94
Stolt Egret	Lbr	1992	3,853	5,758	99.9	17.1	6.8	12	Tch	
Stolt Guillemot	Cym	1993	3,204	4,698	96.4	15.3	6.2	13	T	ex Sasi Terkol-96
Stolt Hikawa	Lbr	1992	4,529	8,080	108.0	18.2	7.2	13	Tch	
Stolt Hinyk	Lbr	1992	4,526	8,080	108.0	18.2	7.2	13	Tch	
Stolt Kestrel	Cym	1992	3,853	5,741	99.9	17.1	6.8	12	Tch	
Stolt Kite	Cym	1992	3,206	4,735	96.4	15.3	6.2	13	Tch	ex Randi Terkol-96
Stolt Kittiwake	Cym	1993	3,204	4,710	96.4	15.3	6.2	13	Tch	ex Astrid Terkol-96
Stolt Lily *	Lbr	1988	4,740	7,582	108.0	18.2	7.1	12	Tch	
Stolt Magnolia *	Pan	1985	4,461	7,133	107.0	18.2	6.8	12	Tch	ex Southern Eagle-89
Stolt Petrel	Cym	1992	3,206	4,761	96.4	15.3	2.5	11	Tch	ex Edny Terkol-96
Stolt Puffin	Lbr	1993	3,853	5,758	99.9	17.1	6.8	12	Tch	
Stolt Sunrise *	Lbr	1984	4,510	6,678	107.3	17.3	7.0	12	Tch	
Stolt Tern	Cym	1991	3,206	4,759	96.4	15.1	6.2	13	Tch	ex Jytte Terkol-96, Stolt Jytte Terkol-92

* owned jointly with NYK Line, Japan and managed by Far-East Transport Co. Ltd., Japan.

Lorentz Storesund & Sonner — Norway

Funnel and Hull: Colours not confirmed.

Name	Flag	Year	GRT	DWT	Loa	Bm	Draft	Kts	Type	Former names
Arunto	Fro	1966	1,316	2,439	78.6	11.5	5.1	11	C	ex Brunto-70
Astor S	Bhs	1976	1,854	3,090	80.1	14.2	5.4	12	C	ex Astor-96
Atlas S	Nis	1979	3,271	5,210	80.8	16.5	7.2	13	Cc	ex Atlas-98, Francois Villon-91, Germa Forest-84
Austvik	Cyp	1980	2,768	3,855	85.9	14.3	6.1	-	C	
Avant	Cyp	1979	3,340	5,210	80.8	16.5	7.2	13	Cc	ex Fondal-94, Germa Fondal-88
Forest Rover	Bhs	1981	4,227	7,433	95.4	16.1	6.0	12	C	ex Krasnogorsk-98, Angela Green-97, Krasnogorsk-96, Westafcarrier-88

Reederei Erwin Strahlmann — Germany

Funnel: Black with white 'B' on red diamond on broad white band.
Hull: Green with red boot-topping.

Name	Flag	Year	GRT	DWT	Loa	Bm	Draft	Kts	Type	Former names
Anjola	Atg	1977	1,519	2,143	74.0	12.0	4.0	9	Cc	ex RMS Polonia-94, Anjola-92
Azur	Atg	1981	1,829	3,080	81.9	11.4	5.0	11	Cc	ex Nordfahrt-95
Bounder	Cyp	1989	1,984	3,223	89.3	12.5	4.7	11	Cc	ex Borsteler Berg-97, Hetlo-94, Borsteler Berg-92
Christian	Cyp	1977	2,089	2,461	86.5	12.8	4.9	13	Cc	ex Alita-95 (len-87)
Falko	Atg	1980	1,512	2,332	82.5	11.4	4.2	10	Cc	ex Marne-95, Sea Elbe-94, I/a Christa Schutt
Gambler	Cyp	1979	2,319	2,850	99.7	11.4	4.2	11	Cc	ex Timor-98, Kathe-96, Kathe Wessels-90
Gard River	Atg	1976	2,128	2,505	93.8	12.9	4.2	10	Cc	ex Lys Carina-97, Hornbelt-95, Kuden-94, Carina-94 (len-79)
Helse	Atg	1992	1,582	1,900	81.2	11.4	3.6	10	Cc	I/a Hansa Carrier
Hunter	Cyp	1981	1,939	2,890	88.0	11.4	4.7	11	Cc	ex Deike-98
Jumper	Cyp	1990	1,960	2,999	89.0	12.5	4.4	11	Cc	ex Karibu-97, Petra-95
Koralle	Atg	1985	1,851	2,269	80.0	12.7	4.2	10	Cc	ex RMS Hollandia-94, Karalle-92
Marek	Atg	1983	1,999	3,345	88.0	11.4	4.5	11	Cc	ex Elly Bojen-95
Mike	Atg	1982	1,513	1,721	82.5	11.4	3.5	10	Cc	ex Patria-94
RMS Westfalia	Atg	1980	1,059	1,173	74.2	9.9	2.9	10	Cc	ex Karin E-92, Atoll-92
Roger	Atg	1984	1,520	2,183	82.5	11.4	4.0	10	Cc	ex Gudrun-92, Aros Anglia-92, Gudrun-90
Urte	Atg	1977	2,551	2,908	96.3	12.5	4.7	11	Cc	ex Kattrepel-90, Neuwulmstorf II-87, Neuwulmstorf-86 (len-77)
Walker	Cyp	1986	1,392	1,570	72.0	11.5	3.3	11	Cc	ex Petersberg-98, Echo Elke-91, Petersberg-89

Reederei Erwin Strahlmann Anjola. *J. Krayenbosch*

Svendborg Enterprise A/S Svendborg Gold. *M. D. J. Lennon*

Name	Flag	Year	GRT	DWT	Loa	Bm	Draft	Kts	Type	Former names

Svendborg Enterprise A/S

Denmark

Funnel and Hull: Colours not confirmed.

Name	Flag	Year	GRT	DWT	Loa	Bm	Draft	Kts	Type	Former names
Svendborg Gallant	Dis	1983	2,183	3,480	77.9	13.4	5.7	11	Cc	ex Tricolor Shan-93, Svendborg Gallant-92, Tricolor Star-91, Svendborg Gallant-89, Nuptse-86, Svendborg Gallant-85
Svendborg Gate	Dis	1983	2,034	1,686	77.6	13.4	3.7	10	Cc	ex Tricolor Gate-92, Saigon Gate-91, Svendborg Gate-90, Admiral Most-89, Agnete Dania-87
Svendborg Gold	Dis	1984	2,184	1,650	77.8	13.4	5.7	11	Cc	ex Forum Micronesia-93, Svendborg Gold-89, Pumori-86, Svendborg Gold-86
Svendborg Governor	Dis	1993	2,462	3,450	81.1	13.8	5.9	13	Cc	ex IAL Governor-94, Svendborg Governor-93
Svendborg Guardian	Dis	1987	2,161	1,720	77.9	13.5	3.7	11	Cc	

T&C (Thor Chartering) A/S

Denmark

Funnel: White.
Hull: Red with green boot-topping.

Name	Flag	Year	GRT	DWT	Loa	Bm	Draft	Kts	Type	Former names
Atlantic *	Ant	1975	2,679	4,020	87.1	13.1	5.9	-	C	ex Stella Atlantic-97, Alta Mar-91, Annika-84, Skogcell Forester-78
Cecilia	Vct	1977	552	710	49.7	8.3	3.5	10	C	ex Asta Wonsild-82
Jaguar	Dis	1985	1,044	1,294	65.5	10.1	3.8	10	Cc	
Leopard	Dis	1989	1,093	1,771	67.0	10.3	4.5	11	Cc	ex Skanlith-96
Lion	Dis	1985	1,044	1,294	65.5	10.0	3.4	10	Cc	
Lynx	Dis	1994	1,395	2,120	73.5	11.4	4.5	11	Cc	ex Southern Sanannah-98, Lynx-97, Thor Rikke-97
Maersk Basse Terre	Dis	1992	9,151	9,868	133.7	23.0	7.6	18	CC	ex Thor Susanne-98, Susanne Sif-98, Norasia Adria-96, Susanne Sif-92
Maersk Santo Tomas	Dis	1992	9,151	9,868	133.7	23.0	8.5	18	CC	ex Gitte Sif-98, Maersk Lima-96, I/a Gitte Sif
Maris	Ant	1984	1,043	1,056	65.5	10.1	3.9	10	Cc	ex Stella Maris-97, Johanne-95, Trueton-92, Jotun-90
Panther	Dis	1984	1,042	1,214	65.5	10.0	3.4	10	Cc	
Puma	Dis	1994	1,395	2,120	73.5	11.4	4.5	11	Cc	ex Thor Lisbeth-97
Thor Alice	Dis	1987	1,167	1,218	67.4	11.4	3.5	11	Cc	ex Southern Amedee-97, Thor Alice-96, Alice Riis-94
Thor Amalie	Dis	1984	3,120	4,274	88.6	15.9	6.0	13	Cc	ex Helga-98, Mulafoss-97, Helga-93, Calypso-92, Band Aid Hope-86, Calypso-85
Thor Eagle	Dis	1987	3,132	4,143	88.6	15.7	6.6	13	Cc	ex Steinkirchen-97
Thor Emilie	Dis	1975	1,655	2,130	75.7	11.9	4.7		Cc	ex Loften-97, Freja-96, Mosel-87
Thor Heidi	Dis	1976	1,858	2,480	83.6	11.8	4.7	12	Cc	ex Bolmen-97, Fenris-96, Marie Lehmann-86 (len-79)
Thor Inger	Dis	1988	1,187	1,210	67.4	11.5	3.5	11	Cc	ex Southern Havannah-97, Thor Inger-95, Inger Riis-94
Thor Kirsten	Dis	1987	1,086	1,720	67.4	11.4	4.3	11	Cc	ex Kirsten Riis-94
Thor Lone	Dis	1987	9,151	9,869	133.7	23.0	7.6	18	CC	ex Lone Sif-98, Norasia melita-96, Lone Sif-92
Thor Marie	Dis	1987	1,167	1,210	67.4	11.4	3.5	11	Cc	ex Marie Riis-94
Thor Mette	Dis	1986	1,167	1,200	67.4	11.4	3.5	11	Cc	ex Mette Riis-94
Thor Simba	Dis	1984	4,366	5,902	99.9	17.8	7.0	13	Cc	ex Helvetia-98, CPC Helvetia-96, Global Express No. 3-89, CPC Helvetia-88, Conti Helvetia-87
Thor Sofia	Dis	1984	3,120	4,281	88.6	15.7	6.0	12	Cc	ex Monika-98, Zim Saigon-97, Saigon Empress-93, Frauke-92, Scott Albatros-90, Frauke-89, Amonitas-88, Albatros I-87, Tequila Moonshine-86, Albatros-85
Tiger	Dis	1984	1,042	1,214	65.5	10.0	3.6	9	Cc	

* managed by Triton Shipping A/B, Sweden.

146

Name	Flag	Year	GRT	DWT	Loa	Bm	Draft	Kts	Type	Former names

Tarbit Shipping AB Sweden

Funnel: Various.
Hull: Various.

Name	Flag	Year	GRT	DWT	Loa	Bm	Draft	Kts	Type	Former names
Bitfjord	Swe	1971	1,573	1,986	85.2	12.3	3.5	12	Tch	ex Esso Valloy-95 (len-97)
Bitland	Swe	1995	4,025	4,450	105.0	15.8	5.8	14	Tb	ex Tasco 2-98
Bituma	Swe	1981	1,900	2,770	87.0	12.5	5.0	12	Tb	
Redo	Swe	1963	1,302	1,656	73.0	11.3	4.6	11	Tb	ex Nynas-76
Redonia	Swe	1981	1,838	2,950	76.9	12.7	5.8	12	Tch	ex Sletfjord-90

TSA Tanker Shipping AB

Name	Flag	Year	GRT	DWT	Loa	Bm	Draft	Kts	Type	Former names
Margaron	Swe	1970	1,003	1,392	66.0	11.0	4.1	11	T	ex Regine-84
Margita	Swe	1971	1,924	3,296	86.2	13.5	5.1	12	Tch	ex Deniz-A-90, Alchimist Flensburg-84, Chemathene-80, Alchimist Flensburg-79
Margot	Swe	1966	549	608	54.7	9.1	3.6	11	T	

Tarntank Rederi A/B Sweden

Funnel: Cream with white band on blue disc.
Hull: Light grey with red boot-topping.

Name	Flag	Year	GRT	DWT	Loa	Bm	Draft	Kts	Type	Former names
Tarnbris	Swe	1980	4,099	6,151	106.2	15.7	7.8	13	Tch	
Tarnland	Swe	1996	6,534	10,877	129.2	18.4	8.1	14	T	
Tarnsund	Swe	1989	4,465	8,828	113.4	18.0	8.3	13	T	
Tarnvind	Swe	1981	4,110	6,144	106.2	15.7	7.2	13	Tch	

Tesch Bereederungs Gmbh & Co. KG Germany

Funnel: White with blue top.
Hull: Blue.

Name	Flag	Year	GRT	DWT	Loa	Bm	Draft	Kts	Type	Former names
Katharina B	Deu	1997	3,999	5,865	100.0	18.2	6.6	16	CC	
Margareta B	Deu	1998	3,999	5,397	100.0	18.2	6.6	16	CC	
Thea B	Deu	1995	2,899	3,950	99.3	16.2	4.9	14	Cc	ex Bell Astron-97, I/a Thea B
Verena B	Deu	1992	3,958	5,356	108.0	16.5	6.0	16	Cc	ex Aquitaine Star-98, Verena B-97

Thien & Heyenga Bedreederungs-und Bed. GmbH Germany

Funnel: Various ownerships or charterers colours.
Hull: Various.

Name	Flag	Year	GRT	DWT	Loa	Bm	Draft	Kts	Type	Former names
Arcadian Faith	Cyp	1994	3,978	5,273	104.8	16.6	6.6	16	Cc	ex FLS Colombia-97, Arcadian Faith-94
Arcadian Sky	Cyp	1994	3,978	5,273	104.8	16.6	6.5	15	Cc	ex Frontier America-97, I/a Arcadian Sky
Calafia	Bhs	1978	2,989	3,550	101.9	14.5	5.4	14	R	ex Azteca-95, Calafia-92 (len-83)
Dakota	Cyp	1977	2,989	3,507	101.9	14.5	5.3	14	R	ex Jan Mayen-92, Jan Willem-90
Husum	Cyp	1983	5,966	8,035	127.7	20.4	6.6	15	Cc	ex Dragon Nias-96, Husum-96, Merkur America-92, AEL Europa-90, EA Progress-89, Husum-87, Husa-85, Contship Europe-84, Husum-83
Inca	Cyp	1978	2,989	3,536	101.9	14.5	4.8	14	R	(len-83)
Leerort	Atg	1982	5,967	8,020	127.7	20.4	6.6	15	Cc	ex Ville de Colombo-92, Leerort-89, Medipas Sea-88, Leerort-87, Convoy Runner-87, Leerort-86, Contship Beta-85, Leerort-85
Lima	Ant	1979	2,989	2,510	103.0	14.5	5.3	14	R	ex Mathilda-92 (len-83)
Melfi Atlantic	Atg	1993	4,766	5,649	99.9	18.2	6.0	14	Cc	ex St. Georg-98, HMS Portugal-96, St. Georg-95
Melfi Pacific	Atg	1992	4,766	5,874	99.9	18.2	6.0	14	Cc	ex St. Pauli-97, UB Leopard-96, St. Pauli-95, Portland Bay-94, Iberian Bridge-94, St. Pauli-93
Neerlandic	Atg	1985	3,955	5,386	108.8	16.3	7.3	16	Rc	
Stadt Cuxhaven	Deu	1996	4,004	5,125	104.8	16.4	6.6	16	Cc	ex Ivanan Segundo-97. Stadt Cuxhaven-97, Arcadian Star-96

Name	Flag	Year	GRT	DWT	Loa	Bm	Draft	Kts	Type	Former names
Stadt Essen	Deu	1997	4,000	5,125	104.8	16.4	6.6	16	Cc	
Stadt Kiel	Deu	1996	3,978	5,273	104.8	16.4	6.6	16	Cc	ex Eagle Caribe-97, Stadt Kiel-96
UAL Texas	Atg	1983	5,967	8,060	127.5	20.1	6.6	15	Cc	ex Ivaran Tercero-98, EWL Colombia-97, Heide-91, Merkur Portugal-91, Heide-90, Contship Egypt-90, AEL America-90, EA Prestige-89, Heide-88, Concorde Caribe-85, Heide-84

Johs. Thode GmbH & Co.   Germany

Funnel: Various.
Hull: Blue with red boot-topping.

Name	Flag	Year	GRT	DWT	Loa	Bm	Draft	Kts	Type	Former names
Altona *	Atg	1980	5,307	6,660	113.2	19.1	6.5	14	CC	ex Nedlloyd Lotus-95, Altona-93, Manchester Trader-91, Karyatein-89, I/a Altona
Charlotte	Atg	1969	1,440	1,477	77.3	11.8	4.0	11	Cc	ex hinrich Behrmann-89, tweed-70, I/a Hinrich Behrmann
Cuxhaven ***	Atg	1976	2,245	2,560	81.4	13.4	5.0	13	Cc	
Dania Suhr *	Atg	1979	4,126	5,672	104.8	16.1	6.6	14	Cc	ex Nedlloyd Antilles-98, ScanDutch Sicilia-92, Hansedamm-86, Ville du Zenith-85, Karaman-85, I/a Hansedamm
FAS Gemlik	Atg	1985	5,608	7,120	116.5	20.3	6.2	13	Cc/Ro	ex Cam Ayous Express-96, Nedlloyd Tulip-95, Ville d'Orient-92, Kathe Husmann-88, Bacol Vitoria-87, I/a Kathe Husmann
Hanseduo	Atg	1984	6,670	8,350	117.5	20.4	7.5	16	CC	ex Sea Mariner-98, Kent Explorer-96, Joanna Borchard-95, Emcol Carrier-89, Caravelle88, Holcan Elbe-86, Kahira-86, Caravelle-84
Hansewall *	Atg	1985	6,659	8,340	117.5	20.5	7.5	16	CC	ex Joanna Borchard-97, Levant Lesum-96, Levant Neva-96, Lucy Borchard-94, Miriam Borchard-92, Kalymnos-90, I/a Hansewall
Maersk Messina †	Deu	1997	3,995	5,865	100.0	18.2	6.6	16	CC	ex Uwe Kahrs-98
Navigia	Deu	1975	2,240	2,560	81.4	13.4	5.0	13	Cc	ex DFL Hamburg-94, Dana Navigia-90, Navigia-90, Donar-79
Nera II §	Atg	1985	2,472	3,050	90.0	13.7	4.4	11	Cc	ex Sylt -98
Peter Knuppel	Deu	1977	3,694	4,341	98.7	16.1	5.7	14	Cc	ex Maersk Tempo-91, Peter Knuppel-87, City of Salerno-86, Peter Knuppel-84, Katherine Borchard-83, Peter Knuppel-82, Eurobridge Link-80, Peter Knuppel-78
Priwall **	Cyp	1992	2,446	3,735	87.9	12.8	5.5	10	Cc	
Stadt Papenburg	Deu	1981	2,723	2,860	95.6	13.5	4.3	12	Cc	ex Odin-97, Vela-91
Susanne L ‡	Atg	1979	1,507	1,341	67.8	11.7	4.2	12	Cc	ex Bremer Mercur-95, Susanne L-89, Bremer Mercur-85, Susanne L-84

*owned by Dieter Behrens or **by Walter Meyer Schiffahrts KG.*
† owned by Johann Kahrs KG, ‡ by Reederei Gerhard Lange KG or § by Hans Bose GmbH.

Heinrich Thordsen KG   Germany

Funnel and Hull: Colours not confirmed.

Name	Flag	Year	GRT	DWT	Loa	Bm	Draft	Kts	Type	Former names
Elisabeth	Deu	1983	1,139	1,102	63.0	11.3	3.3	9	Cc	
Ilka	Deu	1985	1,366	1,300	71.8	11.3	3.2	-	C	
Irmgard	Deu	1981	1,139	1,113	63.0	11.3	3.3	10	Cc	
Maike	Deu	1989	1,599	1,908	82.0	11.5	3.7	10	C	

Name	Flag	Year	GRT	DWT	Loa	Bm	Draft	Kts	Type	Former names

Erik Thun A/B   Sweden

Funnel: White with yellow 'ETAB' on yellowedged blue swallowtail flag, black top.
Hull: Blue or green with red boot-topping.

Name	Flag	Year	GRT	DWT	Loa	Bm	Draft	Kts	Type	Former names
Altar ‡	Vct	1979	3,407	5,264	80.8	16.5	7.2	12	Ccp	ex Wind Ocean-98, Fredrik-92, Roberto Ivens-89, Gardenia-88, Germa Dolphin-83, Germa Team-81
Caramba	Vct	1966	1,441	1,860	74.7	11.3	5.0	12	C	Rania-93, Bergon-82, Palmon-80, Bergon-79, Barken-75
Ciboney **	Vct	1978	1,933	2,980	84.3	13.6	5.4	14	C	ex Lipsk N/Biebrza-94, I/a Nor
Eos (2)	Nis	1976	3,963	6,198	102.0	15.4	6.7	12	Bu	ex Eemsborg-84 (len-84)
Ice Star *	Nld	1997	2,904	5,390	89.0	13.4	7.0	13	C	
Lidan	Swe	1991	2,429	3,999	88.3	13.2	5.7	12	Ccu	
Malmnes †	Nis	1993	5,883	9,891	126.7	15.9	7.7	13	Bu	
Mornes	Nis	1991	5,385	9,125	116.6	15.8	7.9	-	Bu	
Naven	Nor	1991	2,497	4,175	88.3	13.2	5.5	-	C	ex Anna Buck-98
Nordanhav	Nld	1992	5,953	9,891	126.7	15.9	7.7	13	Bu	ex Moxnes-96
Nordic ‡	Ant	1978	2,877	4,958	88.0	13.1	6.8	12	C	ex Stella Nordic-97, Nordanhav-94
Nossan	Swe	1990	2,248	4,250	88.3	13.2	5.5	12	C	
Olivier	Nld	1986	1,999	3,960	88.0	13.2	5.3	12	C	
Ostanhav	Swe	1983	3,888	5,748	108.4	13.1	6.9	12	Cu	
POM Thule	Swe	1973	3,384	4,975	107.2	13.1	6.7	12	T	ex United Thule-95, Thuntank 1-92 (conv Tch-95, len-77)
Snow Star *	Nld	1996	2,904	5,398	89.0	13.4	7.0	12	C	
Tidan	Swe	1990	2,250	4,250	88.3	13.2	5.5	12	C	
Vestanhav	Cyp	1974	2,756	4,954	87.1	13.1	6.8	10	C	

* managed by Marin Ship Management BV, Netherlands or ** by Wind Shipping ApS, Denmark.
† owned by subsidiaries Thunbolaget AS, Norway or ‡ by Triton Shipping A/B, Sweden.

Wilhelm Tietjen Befrachtungsges.mbH   Germany

Funnel: Various owners or charteres colours.
Hull: light grey with red boot-topping.

Name	Flag	Year	GRT	DWT	Loa	Bm	Draft	Kts	Type	Former names
Andrea	Atg	1981	1,939	2,890	88.0	11.3	4.7	11	Cc	ex Lania-98, Carola-94,
Arctic Ocean *	Deu	1995	6,326	8,001	133.0	18.9	7.3	18	CC	ex Norasia Arabia-97, Arctic Ocean-96
Cervantes *	Atg	1994	5,026	6,449	117.0	18.2	6.9	16	Cc	ex Regia-97, Portland Bay-96, Regia-94
Georg Luhrs	Deu	1985	1,567	1,815	82.5	11.4	3.6	10	Cc	
Gracechurch Star *	Atg	1994	5,026	6,449	117.0	18.2	6.9	16	CC	ex Gerdia-96, Alum Bay-96, Gerdia-94
Kaban	Atg	1971	2,900	5,644	85.8	15.3	7.5	11	C	ex Kawan-97, Mirka-92, Mara-90, Mawan-87, Bohol-83, Saint Nazaire-81
Karina W	Deu	1965	658	719	55.1	9.3	3.2	10	C	ex Adele Hagenah-89
Medina	Atg	1971	2,863	5,656	85.8	15.3	7.4	10	C	ex Medi-97, Ania-92, Dina-90, Medina-87, Tarragona-85
Persia	Den	1957	556	745	51.0	8.9	3.7	9	C	ex grete-Gunda-85, Rebena-67
OOCL Nevskiy *	Deu	1995	6,326	8,002	133.0	18.9	7.3	18	CC	ex Arctic Fox-98
Urania	Deu	1978	1,486	1,626	70.8	12.8	3.9	11	Cc	ex Ulsnis-89

* owned by subsidiary Heinz Freese.

Torbulk Shipping (UK) Ltd.   UK

Funnel: Blue with raised diamond containing diagonal white 'TOR' above two red lines.
Hull: Black or green.

Name	Flag	Year	GRT	DWT	Loa	Bm	Draft	Kts	Type	Former names
Fosseland	Bhs	1979	1,059	1,559	66.9	10.8	4.1	11	Cc	ex Perelle-94
Pentland *	Brb	1980	909	1,315	60.0	11.3	3.9	12	C	ex Capacity-94, Lizzonia-89
Sea Humber	Bhs	1977	1,602	2,139	69.0	13.5	4.5	10	C	
Sea Trent	Bhs	1977	1,475	2,273	69.0	13.5	4.5	9	C	ex Sea Avon-96
Swanland	Brb	1977	1,978	3,150	81.0	13.9	5.4	12	C	ex Elsborg-96, Artemis-94, Elsborg-88, Carebeka IX-83

* managed for Onesimus Dorey (Shipowners) Ltd.

Name	Flag	Year	GRT	DWT	Loa	Bm	Draft	Kts	Type	Former names

Tordenskjord Rederi A/S   Norway

Funnel: Various, including blue with blue wavy line on broad white band.
Hull: Dark grey with red boot-topping.

Name	Flag	Year	GRT	DWT	Loa	Bm	Draft	Kts	Type	Former names
Cem Carrier (me)	Nis	1969	1,972	3,001	84.6	12.7	5.8	14	Ce	ex Portland Carrier-96, Fraguador-85
Cem Clipper	Mlt	1971	1,465	2,498	77.9	12.3	5.2	12	Ce	ex Seacement II-97, Suho Maru-95
Cem Crusher	Vct	1978	2,865	3,655	98.6	14.4	5.3	13	C	ex Kapall-97, Otter-85, Zurs-84, Agate-81, Solklint-80
Cem Feeder	Phl	1973	3,067	4,156	98.7	17.1	5.5	14	Ce	ex Terceirense-97, Cement King-89
Cem Freighter	Vct	1978	3,525	4,270	97.6	14.0	6.0	14	Ceu	ex Goliath II-96, Goliath-93
Cem River	Nis	1972	2,942	4,074	94.7	14.0	5.7	13	Ce	ex Arklow River-95, Milburn Carrier-89
Cemtrader † (2)	Atg	1968	3,762	3,957	123.5	15.0	4.5	11	Cc	ex Startrader-96, Popi-89, Kishinev-89 (conv.-89)
Fonnes	Vct	1978	3,971	5,753	105.7	15.4	6.9	13	B	ex General Romulo-89, Fonnes-88 (len-84)
Forest Carrier	Pan	1975	3,389	3,994	94.6	15.0	5.7		Cp	ex Paper Trader-97, Trans Trader-94, Paper Trader-91, Nornews Leader-91 (len-82)
Forest Link (2)	Pan	1973	7,107	5,924	127.3	17.7	6.4	17	Ro	ex Stellaria-80 (len-77)
Forest Ranger *	Nis	1982	7,140	5,600	130.4	18.5	6.0	11	Cp	ex Ferncroft-98
Forest Star	Pan	1974	2,592	2,794	76.6	15.0	5.7	13	Cp	ex Trans Star-95, Follum Supplier-90,
Garnes	Vct	1980	3,967	5,995	107.0	15.0	6.5	13	C	ex General Campos-92, Garnes-86 (len-83)
Rafnes	Cyp	1976	3,885	6,258	103.6	16.0	6.9	13	B	ex General Garcia-89, Rafnes-86
Rollnes	Cyp	1976	3,658	5,789	102.0	15.9	6.9	13	C	
Stenfjell	Nis	1976	2,818	1,724	87.0	14.5	4.5	13	Cp	ex Fjell-85 (len-89)
Risnes	Cyp	1976	3,890	5,699	103.6	16.1	7.0	13	B	ex General Luna-90, Ronnes-85
Vigsnes	Vct	1979	3,961	6,105	107.4	15.0	6.8	13	B	ex General Jacinto-92, Vigsnes-86 (len-80)

*all managed by Donnelly Shipmanagement Ltd., Cyprus, except * managed by F. H. Lorentzen, Norway or ** by Rederiet Stenersen A/S.*
† owned by subsidiary Fana Cement KS.

Hans Martin Torkelsen   Norway
A/S Aasen Shipping

Funnel: White with white 'A'on light blue panel, black top.
Hull: Black.

Name	Flag	Year	GRT	DWT	Loa	Bm	Draft	Kts	Type	Former names
Aasfjord	Nis	1978	3,086	3,960	94.2	15.4	5.8	13	Cc	ex Irafoss-97, Keflavik-89, Charm-82
Aasland	Nis	1969	1,285	1,298	75.7	11.0	3.5	11	Cc	ex Minitrans-86, Bell Cavalier-78, Valdes-75, Bell Cavalier-74, Valdes-73, I/a Geertien Bos
Aastind	Nor	1968	998	909	68.1	11.4	3.5	11	C	ex Vestbulk-91, Aasvaer-85, Torpo-83
Aastun	Nis	1975	3,136	4,240	94.4	15.4	5.7	13	C	ex Talisman-96
Aasvaer	Nis	1972	1,591	2,428	73.4	11.8	5.0	10	C	ex Muhlenburg-85

Transmarine Management ApS   Denmark

Funnel: Various.
Hull: Various.

Name	Flag	Year	GRT	DWT	Loa	Bm	Draft	Kts	Type	Former names
Amarant	Iom	1969	1,726	2,545	86.4	12.0	5.2	12	Tch	ex Kimia Maju-86, Chemical Sprinter-84
Amber	Iom	1997	2,893	4,999	99.9	15.4	6.3	12	Tch	ex Fortune Athena-98
Ametist **	Iom	1993	2,728	4,572	94.5	15.0	6.1	15	Tch	ex Han Chang No. 8-96
Falco	Pan	1969	1,637	2,885	82.1	11.5	5.4	12	T	ex Naven-89, Thuntank 4-81 (deep-70)

Torbulk Shipping (UK) Ltd. Sea Humber. *M. D. J. Lennon*

Tordenskjord Rederi A/S Rafnes. *J. Krayenbosch*

Name	Flag	Year	GRT	DWT	Loa	Bm	Draft	Kts	Type	Former names
Livia *	Pan	1973	1,831	3,195	82.8	13.0	6.1	13	Tch	ex Bimbo-81, Alecto-79, Bow Alecto-78

*managed for Rederi A/B Livia, Sweden or ** managed by Eaglehurst Ship Management Ltd., Isle of Man.*

Transonega Joint Stock Co.   Russia

Funnel: White with red over blue bands, black top.
Hull: Various.

Name	Flag	Year	GRT	DWT	Loa	Bm	Draft	Kts	Type	Former names
Amur-2511 (2)	Rus	1986	3,086	3,127	115.7	13.4	4.0	10	Cc	
Baltiyskiy-55 (2)	Rus	1966	1,865	2,121	95.6	13.2	3.3	10	C	
Carlo (2)	Blz	1969	2,478	2,925	114.2	13.2	3.4	10	C	ex Sormovskiy-14-97
Salmi (2)	Rus	1994	1,778	1,790	88.9	12.3	3.0	10	C	
Sampo (2)	Rus	1993	1,799	1,750	88.9	12.3	2.6	10	C	
Volgo-Balt 209 (2)	Rus	1978	2,473	2,893	114.0	13.2	3.6	10	C	
Volgo-Balt 210 (2)	Rus	1978	2,516	3,165	113.9	13.2	3.6	10	C	

Triton Bereederungs GmbH & Co. KG   Germany

Funnel: Blue.
Hull: Blue.

Name	Flag	Year	GRT	DWT	Loa	Bm	Draft	Kts	Type	Former names
Desiree *	Atg	1984	1,410	1,562	79.0	10.9	3.3	10	Cc	ex Mari Line-98, Sea Ems-96
Fiona **	Ant	1986	3,978	5,232	109.1	16.3	7.3	16	R	ex Cape Blanc-97, Nayadic-95
Lebasee	Nid	1997	2,528	3,526	88.6	12.8	5.5	12	Cc	ex Sao Vicemte-97, I/a Lebasee
Lys Crown	Pmd	1985	1,843	2,325	80.0	12.7	4.2	10	Cc	ex Ettina-97
Mareike	Pmd	1984	1,843	2,325	80.5	12.7	4.2	10	Cc	ex Lys Coast-98, Erkaburg-91, Lys-Coast-91, Erkaburg-91
Nadja *	Atg	1984	1,409	1,545	79.0	10.9	3.3	10	Cc	ex Mari Claire-98, Kirsten-94
Norder Till **	Atg	1986	1,416	1,550	79.0	11.6	3.3	10	Cc	ex Triton-98, Mari France-96, Simone-94
Triton Elbe	Atg	1988	910	1,083	69.1	9.5	3.0	10	Cc	ex Howden-98, Sea Danube-96
Triton Loga	Ant	1987	2,749	3,173	94.5	16.2	5.0	14	Cc	ex Jan Becker-99
Wester Till	Atg	1986	5,847	7,330	120.0	19.6	7.3	14	C/Ro	ex Cam Azobe Express-96, Ville de Lattakia-94, Ville de Smyrne-94, Med Leader-92, Thies-88, Bacol Brasilia-87, Thies-86

*owned by subsidiaries Novalines BV, Netherlands or ** by Reederei Triton Schiffahrts GmbH & Co. KG.*
Newbuildings: seven 3,215 grt 4,650 dwt dry cargo coasters due for 1999/2000 delivery.

Stefan Trybom AB   Sweden

Funnel: Blue.
Hull: Dark blue with red boot-topping,

Name	Flag	Year	GRT	DWT	Loa	Bm	Draft	Kts	Type	Former names
Gyle	Swe	1972	2,497	2,400	93.2	13.4	7.5	14	Cc	ex Rhein Merchant-95, Frisia 1-91, Duneck-86
Nord Transporter	Swe	1977	1,155	1,270	67.0	11.7	4.3	11	C	ex Safe Transporter-78
Nordcarrier	Swe	1977	1,689	1,600	71.4	12.9	3.8	10	Cc	ex Kiekeberg-89
Nordersand	Swe	1977	1,155	1,251	67.0	11.7	3.9	11	C	
Nordica	Swe	1976	499	1,271	67.0	11.7	3.9	11	C	
Nordking	Swe	1976	1,155	1,472	67.0	11.7	4.3	11	C	
Nordlandia	Swe	1977	1,155	1,251	67.0	11.7	3.9	11	C	
Nordtrader	Swe	1977	1,690	1,582	71.4	12.9	3.8	-	Cc	ex Tafelberg-89
Rauk	Swe	1969	1,141	1,270	74.0	10.8	5.1	12	C	ex Klinte-92, Larus-84, Bergvik-77, Larus-76, Actuaria-76, City of Dublin-71

James Tyrrell Ltd.   Eire
Arklow Shipping Ltd.

Funnel: White with coat of arms on white shield.
Hull: Light green with dark green or black boot-topping,

Name	Flag	Year	GRT	DWT	Loa	Bm	Draft	Kts	Type	Former names
Arklow Bay	Irl	1988	1,523	2,169	73.9	11.8	4.4	10	Cc	
Arklow Bridge	Irl	1996	4,783	7,184	99.9	17.1	6.8	12	C	
Arklow Brook	Irl	1995	4,783	7,184	100.0	17.1	6.8	12	C	
Arklow Castle	Irl	1996	5,006	6,807	116.4	19.5	7.1	16	CC	
Arklow Faith	Irl	1992	2,370	4,250	88.3	13.2	5.5	11	Cc	ex MB Thames-97

James Tyrrell Ltd. (Arklow Shipping Ltd.) Arklow Marsh. *M. D. J. Lennon*

Unifleet BV Anna Theresa. *J. Krayenbosch*

Name	Flag	Year	GRT	DWT	Loa	Bm	Draft	Kts	Type	Former names
Arklow Fame	Irl	1992	2,373	4,220	88.3	13.2	5.5	12	Cc	ex MB Avon-97
Arklow Fortune	Irl	1992	2,373	4,250	88.3	13.2	5.5	12	Cc	ex MB Humber-97
Arklow Freedom	Irl	1992	2,373	4,245	88.3	13.2	5.5	12	Cc	ex MB Clyde-97
Arklow Manor	Irl	1987	1,524	2,196	73.8	11.5	4.4	11	Cc	
Arklow Marsh	Irl	1988	1,524	2,171	73.8	11.5	4.4	11	Cc	
Arklow Meadow	Irl	1990	1,524	2,160	73.8	11.5	4.4	11	Cc	
Arklow Mill	Irl	1988	1,523	2,166	73.8	11.5	4.4	10	Cc	
Arklow Moor	Irl	1990	1,523	2,165	73.9	11.8	4.4	11	Cc	
Arklow Sand	Nld	1998	2,224	3,211	90.0	12.5	4.7	11	Cc	
Arklow Sea	Nld	1998	2,300	3,211	90.0	12.5	4.6	11	Cc	
Arklow Spirit	Irl	1995	2,271	3,211	90.0	12.7	4.7	11	Cc	
Arklow Spray	Irl	1996	2,300	3,211	90.0	12.5	4.7	12	Cc	
Arklow Vale	Irl	1989	2,867	4,289	88.2	13.6	5.8	11	Cc	
Arklow Valley	Irl	1992	2,827	4,254	88.2	13.7	5.8	11	Cc	
Arklow Valour *	Irl	1990	2,827	4,299	88.2	13.6	5.8	11	Cc	
Arklow Venture	Irl	1990	2,827	4,299	88.2	13.6	5.8	11	Cc	
Arklow View	Irl	1991	2,827	4,299	88.2	13.7	5.8	11	Cc	
Arklow Viking	Irl	1990	2,827	4,299	88.2	13.7	5.8	11	Cc	
Arklow Villa	Irl	1991	2,827	4,299	88.3	13.7	5.8	11	Cc	
Inisheer *	Irl	1985	1,839	2,167	78.0	12.7	4.3	-	Cc	ex Dunkerque Express-99, Inisheer-95, Lia Venture-88, Flagship 1-86, Elisa von Barssel-85
Inishfree *	Irl	1983	3,222	5,412	82.4	15.8	7.5	14	Cc	ex Lenneborg-97

* owned by subsidiary Coastal Shipping plc.
Newbuildings: two 2,300 grt 3,200 dwt dry cargo coasters due for 1999 delivery.

Unifleet BV   Netherlands

Funnel:	Red, some with white diagonally quartered flag.
Hull:	red or blue with red boot-topping.

Name	Flag	Year	GRT	DWT	Loa	Bm	Draft	Kts	Type	Former names
Anna Theresa	Cyp	1995	2,094	3,403	87.6	12.4	5.5	12	Tch	
Betty Theresa	Cyp	1981	4,269	6,570	106.7	16.5	7.3	12	Tch	ex Botany Troubadour-94
Charlotte Theresa	Cyp	1987	851	1,300	64.3	10.5	3.3	10	C	ex Tarja G-97, Tarja-87
Elka Theresa *	Cyp	1990	1,468	2,440	79.7	10.9	4.2	11	T	
Emilia Theresa	Iom	1998	3,356	5,529	103.5	16.0	5.8	-	Tch	
Gas Pioneer	Cyp	1992	1,173	1,400	76.1	11.4	3.3	10	Lpg	ex Kilgas Pioneer-97, Annagas-92
Ilona Theresa	Atg	1996	1,476	2,542	76.7	12.2	5.1	12	T	ex Densa Gundem-??
Sarah *	Atg	1982	1,988	2,857	88.0	11.4	4.5	11	Cc	ex Saga-95, Saimaasee-92
Thor Scan	Ant	1982	7,591	9,800	123.4	20.7	7.7	16	Ro/hl	
Titan Scan	Ant	1982	7,591	9,864	123.4	20.7	7.7	15	Ro/hl	

* owned by associated Seatrend Shipping NV Belgium.

Union Navale SA   France
Franco British Chartering Agency Ltd./UK

Funnel:	Blue with red band.
Hull:	Black with red boot-topping.

Name	Flag	Year	GRT	DWT	Loa	Bm	Draft	Kts	Type	Former names
Ardent (2)	Gbr	1983	700	1,180	50.0	9.5	3.6	9	C	
Cornet	Bhs	1976	892	1,255	64.0	10.5	3.8	11	Cc	ex Daunt Rock-88
Dowlais (2)	Gbr	1984	794	1,394	58.3	9.4	3.9	8	C	
Millac Star II	Bhs	1974	1,596	1,570	75.7	11.8	3.8	12	C	ex Emanaich-86, Caravelle-83
Roustel	Bhs	1978	892	1,240	64.0	10.5	3.7	11	Cc	ex Skellig Rock-88
Torrent (2)	Gbr	1991	999	1,733	63.6	11.0	4.1	9	C	

managed by Campbell Maritime Ltd., UK.

Union Transport Group plc   UK

Funnel:	Red with white 'UT'
Hull:	Light grey with red or black boot-topping.

Name	Flag	Year	GRT	DWT	Loa	Bm	Draft	Kts	Type	Former names
Douwe S **	Nld	1987	1,311	1,771	79.7	11.2	3.7	12	Cc	ex Torpe-93
Union Arbo	Bhs	1984	1,522	1,720	82.5	11.4	3.5	10	Cc	ex Birka-94
Union Elisabeth **	Nld	1997	1,905	2,665	88.6	12.6	4.0	10	Cc	ex Elisabeth S-97

Name	Flag	Year	GRT	DWT	Loa	Bm	Draft	Kts	Type	Former names
Union Jupiter	Brb	1990	2,230	3,274	99.7	12.6	4.3	11	Cc	
Union Mars	Brb	1981	986	1,448	69.9	11.3	3.4	11	C	
Union Moon *	Brb	1985	1,543	2,362	87.7	11.1	3.9	10	Cc	
Union Neptune *	Brb	1985	1,543	2,376	87.7	11.1	3.9	10	Cc	
Union Pearl	Brb	1990	2,230	3,222	99.7	12.5	4.3	11	Cc	ex Bromley Pearl-95
Union Pluto	Brb	1984	1,521	1,762	82.5	11.4	3.5	10	Cc	ex Phonix I-95, Phoenix-94, Osterberg-87
Union Robin	Nld	1983	1,525	2,320	78.6	12.1	4.1	11	C	ex Elisabeth S-95
Union Sun *	Brb	1985	1,543	2,376	87.7	11.0	3.9	10	Cc	
Union Titan	Brb	1986	1,543	2,376	87.7	11.0	3.9	10	Cc	
Union Topaz	Brb	1985	1,543	2,362	87.7	11.0	3.9	10	Cc	ex Bromley Topaz-92, Union Topaz-90
Union Venus	Brb	1984	1,522	1,890	82.5	11.4	3.5	10	Cc	ex Pinguin-95, Hansa-89

* owned and managed by A/S Ersco (Continental Ship Management AS), Norway or ** for Rederij H. Steenstra, Netherlands.

United European Car Carriers (Norway) A.S.   Norway
United European Car Carriers (UK) Ltd./UK
Funnel: Yellow with white 'UECC' on four small blue diamonds, blue top.
Hull: Light grey with blue or black 'UECC' on superstructure, pink boot-topping.

Name	Flag	Year	GRT	DWT	Loa	Bm	Draft	Kts	Type	Former names
Autocarrier	Nis	1982	6,421	1,472	89.5	18.3	4.3	13	V	ex Castorp-90
Autofreighter	Nis	1977	5,927	1,313	89.3	18.3	4.2	13	V	ex Fredenhagen-90
Autoline	Nis	1983	7,069	1,550	100.0	17.0	4.8	-	V	
Autopremier (2)	Nis	1997	11,591	4,443	126.9	18.8	6.2	20	V	
Autoprestige	Nis	1999	11,591	4,442	126.9	18.8	6.2	20	V	
Autopride (2)	Nis	1997	11,591	4,442	126.9	18.8	6.2	20	V	
Autoprogress	Nis	1997	11,591	4,442	126.9	18.8	6.2	20	V	
Autoracer (2)	Nis	1994	9,693	3,933	119.9	18.8	6.0	20	V	
Autoroute	Nis	1979	7,114	1,849	100.0	17.4	4.2	15	V	
Autorunner (2)	Swe	1994	9,693	3,933	119.9	18.8	6.0	20	V	
Autotransporter	Nis	1983	7,069	1,566	100.0	17.0	4.8	-	V	
Donington (2)	Nis	1976	5,351	1,400	105.5	15.9	4.2	15	V	ex Tertre Rouge-87
Estoril (2)	Atf	1974	1,592	1,200	100.5	16.0	4.0	15	V	ex Arnage-85
Goodwood (2)	Atf	1974	5,180	1,400	100.5	16.0	4.4	15	V	ex Mulsanne-85
Hockenheim (2)	Atf	1976	1,591	1,350	105.5	15.9	4.2	15	V	ex Hunaudieres-87
Indianapolis	Nis	1980	4,743	1,956	88.8	17.4	4.8	14	V	
Jarama	Nis	1980	4,743	1,956	88.8	17.4	4.8	14	V	
Le Castellet (2)	Atf	1982	7,930	2,437	116.5	18.3	5.2	15	V	
Montlhery (2)	Atf	1982	7,930	2,439	116.5	18.3	5.3	15	V	

Formed jointly by Nippon Yusen Kaisha, Japan and Walleniusrederierna AB, Sweden.

B.V. United Gas Carriers (Unigas International)   Norway
Funnel: Blue with blue 'U' on broad red band.
Hull: Red with black or pink boot-topping.
See under Anchor, Liquid Gas Shipping, Schulte Group, Sloman and Veder.

United Marine Dredging Ltd.   UK
Funnel: White with blue outlined 'UMD'
Hull: Light grey.

Name	Flag	Year	GRT	DWT	Loa	Bm	Draft	Kts	Type	Former names
City of Cardiff (2)	Gbr	1997	2,074	2,730	72.0	15.1	4.6	11	Dss	
City of Chichester (2)	Gbr	1997	2,074	2,730	72.0	15.1	4.6	11	Dss	
City of London (2)	Gbr	1989	3,660	5,989	99.8	17.5	6.3	12	Dss	
City of Westminster (2)	Gbr	1990	3,914	6,604	99.9	17.7	6.3	12	Dss	

Formed jointly by Tarmac Marine Ltd. and Pioneer Aggregates Ltd.

Anders Utkilens Rederi A/S   Norway
Funnel: White with blue 'AU' symbol between narrow blue bands.
Hull: Red with red boot-topping.

Name	Flag	Year	GRT	DWT	Loa	Bm	Draft	Kts	Type	Former names
Bergstraum	Nis	1996	6,045	9,494	123.6	19.2	7.2	14	Tch	
Christina	Nis	1996	6,045	9,494	123.0	19.2	7.2	-	Tch	
Fostraum	Nis	1991	2,470	2,910	85.0	13.0	5.5	14	Tch	
Havstraum	Nis	1991	4,931	7,975	115.1	18.3	7.0	-	Tch	

Name	Flag	Year	GRT	DWT	Loa	Bm	Draft	Kts	Type	Former names
Kilstraum	Nor	1988	2,894	4,618	85.7	15.4	6.2	12	Tch	
Listraum	Nis	1991	3,998	6,519	101.7	18.3	7.0	-	Tch	
Mostraum	Nis	1981	5,973	8,661	129.7	19.4	7.0	14	Tch	ex Alpine Rose-94, Alpine Finn-90, Aleksandr Kaverznev-88, Stena Phosphorus-85, OT-Phosphorus-83
Nordstraum	Nor	1985	2,898	4,165	85.7	15.2	6.2	12	Tch	
Rystraum	Nis	1977	4,070	6,433	110.6	16.6	6.9	14	Tch	ex Chimiste Sayid-88, Chimiste Louisiana-77
Saltstraum	Nor	1980	1,881	2,533	80.2	13.0	5.2	13	Tch	
Solstraum	Nis	1990	3,998	7,013	101.7	18.3	6.5	14	Tch	
Sundstraum	Nor	1993	3,206	4,794	96.4	15.3	6.2	13	Tch	ex Maj-Britt Terkol-96,
Sydstraum	Nor	1981	1,881	2,550	80.2	13.0	5.2	12	Tch	
Vikstraum	Nis	1981	5,985	6,693	129.6	19.4	7.0	14	Tch	
West Stream	Bhs	1979	1,834	2,550	80.2	13.0	5.2	13	Tch	ex Golfstraum-98

Van Ommeren Agencies Rotterdam BV   Netherlands

Funnel: Black with white 'V' inside white 'O'.
Hull: Black.

Name	Flag	Year	GRT	DWT	Loa	Bm	Draft	Kts	Type	Former names
Antwerpen **	Bel	1972	1,046	2,249	85.0	9.5	3.4	10	Tch	ex Lutjenbuttel-79
Chemgas Durian	Sgp	1997	3,607	3,942	96.0	16.2	5.5	12	Lpg	
Chemgas Mango	Sgp	1997	3,603	3,940	99.0	16.2	5.5	12	Lpg	
Gent **	Lux	1980	1,471	2,340	85.9	11.3	4.0	11	Tch	ex Jan-87
Pauillac *	Fra	1982	4,489	6,739	110.9	17.1	7.2	-	T	ex Port Racine-99, Nura-95

** owned by Van Ommeren Tankers (Soflumar), France or ** by Van Ommeren Tankvaart Belgie NV, Belgium.*

Van Uden's Scheepvaart en Agentuur Mij. BV   Netherlands

Funnel: Yellow with blue 'U' on white diamond on broad blue band.
Hull: Blue with red boot-topping or red with green boot-topping.

Name	Flag	Year	GRT	DWT	Loa	Bm	Draft	Kts	Type	Former names
Beatrixhaven	Mlt	1976	9,963	5,586	132.7	19.0	6.6	15	Ro	ex Marceline-98, Endeavour-97, Bassro Star-95, Marcel C-89, Inger Express-81, Seaspeed Dora-78
Klaas I	Hnd	1971	980	1,392	70.3	8.9	3.8	10	C	ex Willem B-90, Stephan J-80 (len-82)

Vlasov Group   Monaco
V. Ships

Funnel: Various ownerships or pool colours.
Hull: Various.

Name	Flag	Year	GRT	DWT	Loa	Bm	Draft	Kts	Type	Former names
Borthwick	Bhs	1977	1,596	2,104	79.2	12.8	5.3	14	Lpg	
Cheltenham	Bhs	1990	3,376	4,318	99.6	15.8	5.8	12	Lpg	
Coniston **	Bhs	1991	3,847	4,801	99.9	17.2	6.0	14	Lpg	
Cotswold **	Bhs	1989	3,368	4,143	99.1	14.4	5.1	12	Lpg	ex Diamante-91, Pennine-91
Everdina	Bhs	1981	2,698	3,043	93.4	14.4	5.3	13	Lpg	
Larvikstone	Bhs	1970	3,923	5,735	109.0	15.9	6.9	14	B	ex Tarnow-91
Malvern **	Bhs	1990	3,368	4,148	99.1	15.8	5.7	12	Lpg	
Melrose	Bhs	1971	1,999	2,713	87.0	13.2	6.1	14	Lpg	
Silver Dream *	Pan	1997	4,402	3,800	99.0	18.2	5.1	14	Lpg	
Silver Pride	Bhs	1990	2,856	3,595	95.6	14.8	5.8	-	Lpg	
Snowdon	Bhs	1989	3,219	3,814	99.1	16.0	5.3	12	Lpg	
Steuart	Bhs	1983	4,953	5,223	115.5	17.0	5.4	14	Cc	ex Maj Sif-96, Saigon Concorde-94, Maj Sif-93, Pegasus Pioneer-91, Maj Sif-89, Maj Sandved-88, Dagland-86, Maj Sandved-84
Sutter	Bhs	1983	4,953	5,223	115.5	17.6	5.4	14	Cc	ex Delmas Africa-97, Sutter-96, Tiger Force-96, Tiger Force-93, Mette Sif-92, OOCL Italia-88, Mette Sif-88

** owned by subsidiary Silver Line Ltd., UK or ** by 48% owned subsidiary MC Shipping Inc., Monaco.*

United European Car Carriers (Norway) A.S. Autoprogress. *J. Krayenbosch*

Anders Utkilens Rederi A/S Sundstraum. *J. Krayenbosch*

Van Uden's Scheepvaart en Agentuur Mij. BV Beatrixhaven. *J. Krayenbosch*

Name	Flag	Year	GRT	DWT	Loa	Bm	Draft	Kts	Type	Former names

Anthony Veder & Co. BV   Netherlands

Funnel: Blue with white 'A' and red 'V' on blue diamond on red band.
Hull: Orange-red with grey boot-topping.

Name	Flag	Year	GRT	DWT	Loa	Bm	Draft	Kts	Type	Former names
Coral Acropora	Nld	1993	3,096	2,417	101.4	14.0	5.1	12	Lpg	(len-96)
Coral Actinia	Nld	1993	2,274	2,446	101.4	14.0	7.2	12	Lpg	(len-95)
Coral Antillarum	Nld	1982	2,400	3,050	77.0	14.5	6.2	11	Lpg	ex Black Star-95, Ibiza Star-92, Quevedo-89
Coral Iris	Nld	1982	6,788	6,082	114.2	18.3	7.5	14	Lpg	ex Jean Alleaume-97
Coral Meandra	Nld	1996	4,054	5,000	92.4	15.3	6.6	14	Lpg	
Coral Millepora	Nld	1997	4,054	5,000	92.4	15.3	6.6	14	Lpg	
Coral Obelia	Nld	1996	3,853	4,150	92.4	15.3	6.6	14	Lpg	
Prins Alexander	Nld	1985	1,552	1,643	64.2	13.7	4.9	11	Lpg	
Prins Johan Willem Friso	Nld	1989	3,862	4,905	97.3	15.9	6.0	14	Lpg	
Prins Philips Willem	Nld	1985	1,552	1,648	64.2	13.7	4.9	11	Lpg	
Prins Willem II	Nld	1985	1,552	1,648	64.2	13.6	4.9	11	Lpg	
Sunny Clipper	Nis	1976	4,326	6,080	108.0	15.5	7.5	16	Lpg	ex Coral Isis-87

Vega-Reederei Friedrich Dauber KG   Germany

Funnel: Buff with white 'V' on broad black over red bands, black top.
Hull: Black, some with white 'BLACKBOXES', red or blue boot-topping.

Name	Flag	Year	GRT	DWT	Loa	Bm	Draft	Kts	Type	Former names
Heidberg	Deu	1985	1,957	2,892	88.0	11.5	4.7	11	Cc	
Kosterberg	Nld	1999	1,999	3,280	90.3	12.5	4.6	11	Cc	
Marlies Sabban	Deu	1986	2,120	3,028	92.1	11.5	4.7	10	Cc	ex Petra Gunda-95
Muhlenberg	Deu	1985	1,957	2,886	87.9	11.5	4.7	11	Cc	
Polterberg	Deu	1983	1,945	2,904	88.0	11.5	4.7	11	Cc	
Sullberg	Deu	1994	1,999	3,280	90.3	12.5	4.6	11	Cc	
Tafelberg	Deu	1981	1,939	2,890	88.0	11.3	4.7	11	Cc	ex Helga-92
Waseberg	Deu	1985	1,957	2,890	88.0	11.3	4.7	11	Cc	

Vertom Sheepvaart en Handelsmaatschappij B.V.   Netherlands

Funnel: Black, grey or blue with green 'V' on white disc, or white with green 'V'.
Hull: Grey, blue or black with red boot-topping.

Name	Flag	Year	GRT	DWT	Loa	Bm	Draft	Kts	Type	Former names
Explorer	Sgp	1984	3,949	6,120	106.6	18.1	6.6	14	Cc	ex Frisian Explorer-87, Samsun Express-85, I/a Carina Smits
Faith	Sgp	1985	3,949	6,025	106.6	18.1	6.6	14	Cc	ex Tiger Stream-96, Faith-95, Frisian Faith-87, Akak Faith-86, Frisian Faith-86, Esa I-85, Samsun Faith-85
Lady Anna	Cyp	1989	2,351	3,200	87.0	13.0	5.1	11	Cc	ex Amrum-95, Port Sado-93
Lady Clara	Cyp	1990	2,351	2,800	87.0	13.0	4.5	11	Cc	ex Baltrum-95, Port Faro-93
Lady Greta	Cyp	1989	2,351	3,200	87.0	13.0	5.1	11	Cc	ex Borkum-95, Port Vouga-93
Lady Linda	Cyp	1989	2,351	3,200	87.0	13.0	5.1	11	Cc	ex Mellum-94, Port Lima-93
Lady Lisa	Cyp	1990	2,351	3,200	87.0	13.2	5.1	11	Cc	ex Rottum-94, Port Foz-93
Lee Frances	Cyp	1985	3,307	3,980	92.2	15.9	6.6	14	Cc	
Lida	Vct	1974	992	1,448	62.8	10.8	4.1	10	C	ex Visserbank-90, Spray-86, Arina Holwerda-81
Saline	Nld	1993	1,990	3,604	89.9	13.0	5.0	12	C	I/a Salt Trader
Sunshine II	Cyp	1987	7,095	3,969	126.0	19.7	4.8	-	Ro	ex Franz-97
Sandy Cay	Cyp	1980	3,731	6,275	80.7	15.9	8.3	12	Cc	ex Trinity Square-98, Louise Green-96, Oostzee-94, Savonia-83, Oostzee-81
Wilma *	Nld	1985	4,365	6,317	106.0	16.6	6.7	12	Cc	ex Conex-90

* managed by Rialto Shipping BV.

Anthony Veder & Co. BV Prins Alexander. J. M. Kakebeeke

Vega-Reederei Friedrich Dauber KG Waseberg. *M. D. J. Lennon*

Name	Flag	Year	GRT	DWT	Loa	Bm	Draft	Kts	Type	Former names

Joint-Stock Volga Shipping Co.   Russia

Funnel: White with blue over red bands,black top.
Hull: Various.

Name	Flag	Year	GRT	DWT	Loa	Bm	Draft	Kts	Type	Former names
Aleksandr										
Marinesko *(2)	Rus	1984	1,785	1,776	86.7	12.3	3.0	10	C	ex ST-1303-94
Bakhtemir(2)	Rus	1978	1,522	1,755	82.0	11.9	3.3	8	Cc	
Boris Kornilov *(2)	Rus	1984	1,785	1,776	86.7	12.3	3.0	10	C	ex ST-1307-95
Bratislava	Rus	1994	2,446	3,718	87.9	12.8	5.2	12	Cc	
Druzhba Narodov(2)	Rus	1979	2,827	3,146	118.8	13.2	3.7	11	C	
Gidrostroitel										
A.P.Aleksandrov (2)	Rus	1981	2,491	3,100	114.1	13.9	3.7	10	C	ex Sormovskiy-3002-??
Ivan Shchepetov (2)	Rus	1994	3,376	3,186	102.3	16.4	4.2	13	Cc	
Kapitan										
Babushkin (2)	Rus	1984	1,785	1,777	86.7	12.3	3.0	10	C	ex ST-1306-??
Kapitan Ezovitov (2)	Rus	1984	3,070	3,377	107.4	16.7	3.5	10	C	
Kapitan Torsukov (2)	Rus	1984	1,649	1,223	88.9	12.3	2.5	10	C	ex ST-1305-??
Krasnovidovo (2)	Rus	1980	1,522	1,625	82.0	11.6	2.5	-	Cc	
Leninskiy										
Komsomol (2)	Rus	1978	2,827	3,146	118.8	13.2	3.7	11	C	
Nikolay Smelyakov	Rus	1997	2,914	3,837	96.3	13.6	5.2	11	Cc	
Professor										
Shanchurov (2)	Rus	1985	1,402	1,706	82.0	11.6	2.5	11	C	ex STK-1013-91
Professor Volskiy (2)	Rus	1982	2,491	3,100	114.1	13.5	3.7	10	C	ex Sormovskiy-3007-??
Sergey Losev (2)	Rus	1983	2,466	3,134	114.0	13.2	3.7	10	C	ex Sormovskiy 46-92
Sormovskiy-27 (2)	Rus	1973	2,478	3,134	114.0	13.2	3.7	10	C	
Sormovskiy-28 (2)	Rus	1973	2,478	3,134	114.0	13.2	3.7	10	C	
Sormovskiy-29 (2)	Rus	1973	2,484	3,134	114.0	13.2	3.7	10	C	
Sormovskiy-32 (2)	Rus	1974	2,484	3,134	114.0	13.2	3.7	10	C	ex XVII Syezd VLKSM-92, Sormovskiy-32-??
Sormovskiy-33 (2)	Rus	1974	2,484	3,134	114.0	13.2	3.7	10	C	
Sormovskiy-34 (2)	Rus	1974	2,484	3,134	114.0	13.2	3.7	10	C	
Sormovskiy-44 (2)	Rus	1981	2,484	3,134	114.2	13.2	3.4	10	C	
Sormovskiy-107 (2)	Rus	1973	2,478	3,135	114.0	13.2	3.7	10	C	ex 0050 Let SSSR-92
Sormovskiy-109 (2)	Rus	1974	2,484	3,134	114.0	13.2	3.7	10	C	
Sormovskiy-110 (2)	Rus	1974	2,484	3,134	114.0	13.2	3.7	10	C	
Sormovskiy-111 (2)	Rus	1975	2,484	3,134	114.0	13.2	3.7	10	C	
Sormovskiy-3048 (2)	Rus	1982	3,041	3,135	119.2	13.4	3.8	11	Cc	ex XVII Syezd Profsoyuzov-92
Sormovskiy-3049 (2)	Rus	1982	3,041	3,134	119.2	13.4	3.8	10	Cc	ex XI Pyatiletka-92
Sormovskiy-3051 (2)	Rus	1984	3,041	3,134	119.0	13.0	3.8	11	Cc	
Sormovskiy-3052 (2)	Rus	1984	3,041	3,134	119.2	13.4	3.8	10	Cc	
Sormovskiy-3053 (2)	Rus	1985	3,041	3,134	119.1	13.4	3.8	11	Cc	
Sormovskiy-3054 (2)	Rus	1985	3,041	3,134	119.1	13.4	3.7	10	Cc	
Sovietskaya										
Rodina (2)	Rus	1979	2,827	3,146	118.8	13.2	3.7	11	C	
ST-1304 * (2)	Rus	1984	1,719	1,652	86.7	12.3	3.0	10	C	ex Steamer-4-96, ST-1304-94
ST-1308 (2)	Rus	1984	1,766	1,777	86.7	12.3	3.0	10	Cc	
ST-1341 (2)	Rus	1989	1,766	1,694	86.0	12.0	3.0	10	Cc	
ST-1349 (2)	Rus	1990	1,639	1,135	89.6	12.3	2.5	10	C	
ST-1386 (2)	Rus	1984	1,628	1,140	86.2	12.3	2.5	10	C	
Starovolzhsk (2)	Rus	1979	1,522	1,260	82.0	11.9	2.8	-	Cc	
Steamer-1 * (2)	Rus	1983	1,719	1,652	86.7	12.3	3.0	10	Cc	ex ST-1301-94
STK-1002 (2)	Rus	1983	1,408	1,706	82.0	11.6	2.5	10	C	
Volga-35 (2)	Rus	1995	4,955	5,885	139.9	16.7	4.5	10	C	
Volzhskiy 10 (2)	Rus	1984	3,070	3,377	107.4	16.7	3.5	10	C	(short-95)
Znamya Oktyabrya (2)	Rus	1979	2,827	3,146	118.8	13.2	3.7	11	C	

* managed by Steamer Ltd., Russia.
About 36 other dry cargo vessels not currently involved in international trade.

Volga-Don Shipping Joint Stock Co.   Russia

Funnel: White with blue over red bands, black top.
Hull: Various.

Name	Flag	Year	GRT	DWT	Loa	Bm	Draft	Kts	Type	Former names
40 Let Pobedy (2)	Rus	1985	2,466	3,135	114.0	13.2	3.7		C	
Aksai	Rus	1996	3,796	4,400	100.6	16.2	4.8	11	Cc	

Vertom Sheepvaart en Handelsmaatschappij B.V. Faith. *J. Krayenbosch*

Joint-Stock Volga Shipping Co. Steamer-1. *M. D. J. Lennon*

Name	Flag	Year	GRT	DWT	Loa	Bm	Draft	Kts	Type	Former names
Amur-2502 (2)	Ukr	1984	3,086	3,159	115.1	13.4	4.0	10	Cc	ex Volgo-Balt 250-86
Amur-2503 (2)	Rus	1986	3,086	3,159	115.9	13.4	4.0	10	Cc	ex Volgo-Balt 251-86
Amur-2508 (2)	Ukr	1985	3,086	3,159	115.7	13.4	4.0	10	Cc	ex Volgo-Balt 256-85
Amur-2519 (2)	Rus	1987	3,086	3,148	115.7	13.4	4.0	10	Cc	
Amur-2523 (2)	Rus	1988	3,086	3,148	116.0	13.4	4.0	10	Cc	
Cosmos (2)	Rus	1987	1,640	1,273	86.7	12.3	2.5	10	Cc	ex Don 1-98, St-13215-94
Don *	Cyp	1996	3,796	4,400	100.6	16.2	4.8	11	Cc	
Don-2 (2)	Rus	1987	1,627	1,273	86.7	12.3	2.5	10	Cc	ex ST-1327-94
Don-3 (2)	Rus	1990	1,540	1,273	86.7	12.3	2.5	10	Cc	ex ST-1336-94
Don-4 (2)	Rus	1989	1,627	1,223	86.7	12.3	2.5	10	Cc	ex ST-1343-94
Ivan Kulibin (2)	Rus	1982	2,429	1,987	95.0	13.2	3.7	11	C	
Krasnyi Aksay (2)	Rus	1989	3,086	3,152	116.1	13.4	4.0	9	Cc	
Omskiy-138 (2)	Rus	1989	2,583	2,955	108.4	15.0	3.3	10	C	
Omskiy-139 (2)	Rus	1989	2,570	2,957	108.4	14.8	3.3	10	C	
Omskiy-144 (2)	Rus	1990	2,562	3,125	108.4	15.0	3.4	10	C	
Omskiy-145 (2)	Rus	1990	2,562	3,125	108.4	15.0	3.1	10	C	
Sormovskiy-10 (2)	Rus	1969	2,466	3,134	114.0	13.2	3.7	10	C	ex Velikly Pochin-92
Sormovskiy-17 (2)	Rus	1970	2,466	3,225	114.0	13.2	3.7	10	C	ex Aleksandr Tsyurupa-92
Sormovskiy-43 (2)	Rus	1981	2,466	3,134	114.0	13.2	3.4	10	C	
Sormovskiy-119 (2)	Rus	1982	2,466	3,134	114.0	13.2	3.7	10	C	
Sormovskiy-121 (2)	Cyp	1982	2,466	3,134	114.0	13.2	3.7	10	C	
Sormovskiy-122 (2)	Rus	1984	2,466	3,134	114.2	13.2	3.7	10	C	
Sormovskiy-123 (2)	Rus	1985	2,466	3,155	114.0	13.2	3.7	10	C	
Sormovskiy-3006 (2)	Rus	1982	2,491	3,100	114.1	13.5	3.7	10	C	
Sormovskiy-3050 (2)	Rus	1983	3,041	3,135	118.8	13.4	3.8	10	Cc	ex 0065 Let Sovetskoy Vlasti-93
Sormovskiy-3066 (2)	Rus	1990	3,048	3,391	118.7	13.4	4.1	10	Cc	
Temernik *	Rus	1997	3,796	4,400	100.7	16.2	4.8	11	Cc	
Volgo-Balt 234 (2)	Rus	1981	2,516	3,162	113.9	13.2	3.6	10	C	
Volgo-Balt 241 (2)	Rus	1982	2,516	3,150	113.9	13.2	3.6	10	C	
Volgo-Balt 247 (2)	Rus	1983	2,516	3,193	113.9	13.2	3.6	10	C	
Volgo-Balt 248 (2)	Rus	1984	2,516	3,193	113.9	13.2	3.6	10	C	
Voronezh *	Rus	1996	3,796	4,400	100.7	16.2	4.8	11	Cc	

* managed by Transchart Schiffahrts. GmbH, Germany.

Vroon BV   Netherlands

Funnel: Charterers colours or white with blue 'LE', blue top (Livestock Express).
Hull: Grey with red boot-topping.

Name	Flag	Year	GRT	DWT	Loa	Bm	Draft	Kts	Type	Former names
Angus Express	Phl	1967	991	957	80.8	10.8	3.4	14	Lv	ex Mediterranean Express-87, Amstelstroom-75 conv Ro-88, len-76)
Bison Express	Phl	1995	4,848	2,882	99.7	16.3	6.0	-	Lv	
Buffalo Express	Phl	1983	2,374	1,600	81.8	14.0	4.1	12	Lv	(len-84)
Cold Express *	Vut	1979	2,768	3,443	97.0	14.0	5.2	14	R	(len-83)
Devon Express	Phl	1997	6,159	3,656	116.6	15.9	5.3	16	Lv	
Holstein Express	Phl	1969	4,995	4,891	103.5	17.2	7.5	15	Lv	ex Al-Messilah-90, Cinderella-81, Nimos-77, Berkel-69 (conv C-82)
Ice Express *	Vut	1978	2,768	3,387	97.0	14.0	5.1	14	R	(len-83)
Iglo Express *	Phl	1979	4,239	4,880	118.2	15.8	6.6	14	R	ex Sunreef-84, Guadalupe-83 (len-85)
Irish Rose	Pan	1965	1,466	836	75.7	10.6	3.8	13	Lv	ex Leo-81, Tor Brabantia-71, Brabantia-71 (conv Cp-81)
Kerry Express (2)	Phl	1968	5,959	2,330	118.7	18.0	4.8	15	Lv	ex Caribbean Cloud-81, Federal Humber-80, Federal Tyne-78, Federal Byblos-77, Seaspeed Ferry-75, Speedway-73, Clearway-70, Sealord Challenger-69 (conv Ro-81, len-77)
Neptunic	Phl	1989	3,998	5,165	109.9	16.3	7.4	16	Rc	
Northern Explorer *	Nld	1991	3,999	5,129	109.9	16.3	7.3	16	Rc	
Northern Express *	Phl	1986	3,978	5,175	109.1	16.3	7.3	16	Rc	
Nova Zembla	Phl	1986	4,440	5,506	115.0	16.8	7.3	18	R	ex Aoshima Maru-88, l/a Sorachi Maru
Shorthorn Express	Phl	1998	6,872	4,422	116.6	15.9	6.0	16	Lv	
Zebu Express	Phl	1984	2,513	1,600	81.7	14.0	4.1	12	Lv	(len-84)

* operated by Seatrade Groningen BV.

Vroon BV Angus Express. *J. Krayenbosch*

Wagenborg Shipping BV Geulborg. *J. Krayenbosch*

Wagenborg Shipping BV

Netherlands

Funnel: Black with two narrow white bands.
Hull: Light grey with broad red band and white 'WAGENBORG', red or black boot-topping; managed vessels, various colours.

Name	Flag	Year	GRT	DWT	Loa	Bm	Draft	Kts	Type	Former names
Aaltje-Jacoba	Cyp	1995	1,682	2,503	81.7	11.1	4.5	10	C	
Adriana	Nld	1991	1,282	1,750	75.0	10.8	3.7	10	C	ex Flardinga-98
Ambassadeur	Nld	1997	2,224	3,132	88.0	12.5	4.6	11	Cc	
Amstelborg	Nld	1978	1,575	1,500	84.3	10.8	3.8	10	Cc	ex Rhein-90, Rheintal-88
Amy	Nld	1989	1,999	3,037	82.0	12.6	5.0	12	Cc	
Arion	Nld	1997	6,540	9,200	134.5	16.5	7.1	-	Cc	
ASSI Euro Link (2)	Nld	1972	5,018	9,470	163.5	21.2	7.1	16	Ro	ex Stora Korsnas Link II-92, Belgia-87, Jolly Argento-86, Belgia-80, Tor Belgia-79 (len-77)
ASSI Scan Link (2)	Nld	1974	13,436	9,640	163.5	21.1	7.1	16	Ro	ex Ocean Link-92, Baltic Wasa-85, Tor Finlandia-84 (len-77)
Aunborg	Bhs	1976	1,086	1,564	65.8	10.8	4.3	10	C	ex Jamie-98, Marico-95, Gina P-93, Kwintebank-92, Els Teekman-84
Baltic Link	Nld	1984	10,991	7,680	120.2	21.0	6.7	15	Rop	
Balticborg	Nld	1991	1,999	3,015	82.0	12.6	4.9	12	Cc	
Batavier	Cyp	1986	1,543	2,362	87.6	11.1	3.9	12	Cc	ex Venus-94, Bromley Sapphire-93, Union Sapphire-90
Bothniaborg	Nld	1991	1,999	3,015	82.0	12.5	4.9	12	Cc	
Cito	Cyp	1993	1,596	2,511	81.7	11.1	4.5	11	C	
Citox	Cyp	1975	1,183	1,652	75.0	10.2	3.9	10	C	ex Cito-94, Edina-89,
Delfborg	Nld	1978	3,699	5,595	83.1	16.7	7.8	12	Cc	
Denika **	Atg	1978	1,495	1,548	76.8	11.5	3.4	12	Cc	ex Sea Marlan-97, I/a Merlan
Deo Gratias	Nld	1974	916	1,401	79.9	9.0	3.0	10	C	ex Deo Volente-95, Maria-92, Pia-82, Cargoliner II-81
Deo Volente	Nld	1980	1,513	1,551	82.5	11.4	3.6	10	Cc	ex Elbstrand-95
Dependia	Nld	1997	1,849	2,521	81.9	12.5	4.3	11	Cc	
Dintelborg	Nld	1999	6,000	9,000	133.4	16.6	7.1	-	Cc	
Doggersbank	Nld	1996	2,774	4,180	89.8	13.6	-	-	C	
Donau	Nld	1993	2,058	3,250	81.1	12.4	5.2	-	Cc	
Dongeborg	Nld	1999	6,000	9,000	133.4	16.6	7.1	-	Cc	
Drechtborg	Nld	1999	6,000	9,000	133.4	16.6	7.1	-	Cc	
Eemsborg	Nld	1990	1,999	3,015	82.0	12.6	4.9	12	Cc	
Eendracht	Nld	1980	1,009	1,596	65.8	11.1	4.3	11	C	
Egbert Wagenborg	Nld	1998	6,540	9,150	134.6	16.5	7.1	16	Cc	
Elise	Nld	1996	1,682	2,503	81.9	11.1	4.5	10	C	ex Flevoborg-96
Elstar	Nld	1988	851	1,280	64.2	10.5	3.4	8	C	ex Varnebank-96
Fiona May	Cyp	1977	999	1,632	61.5	10.4	4.8	9	C	ex Serenell-95
Flinterborg †	Nld	1990	1,999	3,015	82.0	12.6	4.9	12	Cc	
Flinterdam †	Nld	1995	3,177	4,506	99.9	13.6	5.6	13	Cc	I/a Flinterzijl
Flintereems †	Nld	1999	4,360	6,250	111.8	14.6	6.3	13	Cc	
Flinterhaven †	Nld	1997	4,368	6,250	111.8	14.6	6.3	13	Cc	
Flinterland †	Nld	1994	2,818	4,216	91.5	13.6	5.8	12	Cc	
Flintermaas †	Nld	1999	4,360	6,250	111.8	14.6	6.3	13	Cc	
Flintermar †	Nld	1994	2,818	4,170	91.5	13.6	5.8	12	Cc	
Flinterzee †	Nld	1997	4,368	6,250	111.8	14.6	6.3	13	Cc	
Flinterzijl †	Nld	1995	3,117	4,512	99.4	13.6	5.2	13	Cc	
Gaastborg	Nld	1996	2,820	4,200	89.7	13.7	5.7	13	Cc	
Galatea	Nld	1985	998	1,490	78.0	10.6	3.2	10	C	ex Galaxa-92
Gelre	Nld	1992	1,576	2,168	81.7	11.0	4.1	12	C	
Geulborg	Nld	1994	2,769	4,200	90.2	13.6	5.7	12	Cc	
Giessenborg	Nld	1997	2,820	4,123	89.8	13.7	5.7	14	Cc	
Gooteborg	Nld	1998	2,835	4,128	89.7	13.7	5.7	14	Cc	
Gouweborg	Nld	1994	2,769	4,182	90.2	13.6	6.0	12	Cc	
Graneborg **	Deu	1997	2,863	4,113	85.0	13.6	5.7	13	Cc	
Grachtborg	Nld	1997	2,828	4,200	89.7	13.7	5.7	13	Cc	
Griffioen	Nld	1984	998	1,490	78.9	10.1	3.1	10	C	ex Ambassadeur-96, Michel-93
Griftborg	Nld	1995	2,771	4,149	87.7	13.7	5.7	13	Cc	
Hendrik B	Nld	1982	3,210	3,760	82.4	15.8	6.0	11	Cc	ex Polarborg-95
Heron	Nld	1986	851	1,276	64.3	10.6	3.4	11	C	ex Regina-98, Nes-95, Lingedijk-92

Wagenborg Shipping BV Reggeborg. *J. Krayenbosch*

Wagenborg Shipping BV Skagenbank. *J. Krayenbosch*

Name	Flag	Year	GRT	DWT	Loa	Bm	Draft	Kts	Type	Former names
Hydra	Cyp	1979	1,545	1,930	85.0	10.0	3.7	11	C	ex Waalborg-93, Vera Rambow-89
Ida Rambow	Deu	1996	2,863	4,112	85.0	13.3	5.7	13	Cc	
Ijsselborg	Nld	1985	3,913	6,446	96.8	15.5	7.1	12	Cc	ex Ijsselland-96
Itasca ‡	Nld	1989	1,994	3,015	83.3	12.6	5.0	11	Cc	ex Sambre-98
Jaguar	Nld	1991	1,559	1,800	79.7	11.1	3.7	10	Cc	ex Vera-96, Vera Rambow-96
Jason	Nld	1993	1,681	2,503	81.7	11.1	4.5		C	
Kasteelborg	Nld	1998	6,142	9,085	130.7	15.9	7.5	15	Cc	
Keizersborg	Nld	1996	6,142	9,085	130.7	15.9	7.5	15	Cc	
Koningsborg	Nld	1997	6,142	9,200	130.2	15.9	7.5		Cc	
Kroonborg	Nld	1995	6,142	9,100	130.7	15.9	7.5	14	Cc	
Ladon	Nld	1996	1,682	2,503	81.7	11.1	4.5		C	
Leonie	Nld	1996	1,682	2,500	81.7	11.1	4.5		C	ex Fivelborg-98
Maasborg	Nld	1974	2,905	3,658	81.8	15.3	6.0	13	C	
Maasvallei	Cyp	1984	998	1,498	78.9	10.0	3.1	11	C	
Magula **	Atg	1980	1,655	1,548	83.0	11.4	3.2	11	Cc	ex Sea Magula-98
Maria Smit	Cyp	1982	1,576	2,530	81.3	12.1	4.4	11	C	ex Biscay-96, Eems-94, Concord-94, Concordia-88
Marietje Andrea	Nld	1992	1,599	2,250	81.7	11.0	4.1	12	C	
Markborg	Nld	1997	6,540	9,400	134.6	16.5	7.1	16	Cc	
Marneborg	Nld	1997	6,410	9,200	134.5	16.5	7.1	16	Cc	
Merweborg	Nld	1997	6,540	9,400	134.6	16.5	7.1	16		
Michel	Nld	1993	1,576	2,246	81.7	11.1	4.1	12	Cc	
Moezelborg	Nld	1999	6,540	9,200	134.6	16.5	7.1	16	Cc	
Michiganborg	Nld	1998	6,540	9,200	134.5	16.6	7.1	16	Cc	
Morraborg	Nld	1999	6,540	9,200	134.6	16.5	7.1	16	Cc	
Musselborg	Nld	1999	6,540	9,200	134.6	16.5	7.1	16	Cc	
Namai	Nld	1998	4,446	6,250	111.8	15.0	6.4	13	Ccp	
Nes	Nld	1995	1,682	2,500	81.7	11.1	4.5	-	C	ex Boeran-95
Nescio	Nld	1993	1,596	2,510	82.0	11.1	3.3	11	Cc	
Nordic Link	Nld	1981	5,006	6,704	120.2	21.0	6.2	14	Rop	
Omega I	Nld	1974	777	1,191	70.0	9.5	2.9	11	C	ex Martini-97, Zodiac-92, Wandelaar-91
Orade (wj) **	Deu	1991	1,354	1,699	77.1	11.4	3.2	12	Cc	ex Sea Orade-98, I/a Orade
Panda	Nld	1989	852	1,300	64.2	10.6	3.4	11	C	ex Waran-93
Pioneer	Nld	1994	2,735	4,267	89.6	13.2	5.7	11	C	
Pionier	Nld	1985	1,486	2,261	79.8	11.1	4.1	10	Cc	
Reest	Nld	1987	920	1,496	64.2	10.5	3.7	11	C	ex Laura II-94
Reestborg (2)	Nld	1994	9,168	7,285	140.0	20.5	6.3	17	CC	
Reggeborg (2)	Nld	1994	9,168	7,285	139.8	20.5	6.3	17	CC	ex Levant Elbe-96, Reggeborg-95
Rijnborg	Nld	1991	1,999	2,952	82.1	12.5	4.9	11	Cc	
Sagitta	Nld	1988	851	1,280	64.3	10.5	3.4	11	C	ex Turan-93, Nescio-93
Sandettie	Nld	1989	852	1,279	64.3	10.5	3.4	10	C	ex Voran 93
Sayonara	Ant	1986	920	1,496	64.2	10.5	3.7	11	C	ex Laura-93
Scheldeborg	Nld	1991	1,999	3,005	82.0	15.4	5.8	12	Cc	
Schokland	Nld	1986	852	1,280	64.3	10.6	3.3	9	C	ex Buizerd-96
Schouwenbank	Nld	1998	2,774	4,140	89.9	13.6	-	13	Cc	
Sea Loire	Nld	1991	1,276	1,686	79.1	10.5	3.7	10	C	ex Skylge-97, I/a Terschelling
Sea Maas	Nld	1995	1,682	2,500	81.7	11.0	4.5	10	C	ex Futura-96
Sea Riss	Nld	1992	1,595	2,200	79.7	11.0	4.2	12	C	ex Solon-97
Sea Spider	Nld	1999	4,000	5,400	-	-	-	-	Cc	
Silmaril	Nld	1985	1,399	2,293	79.8	11.1	4.1	10	Cc	ex Jehan-98
Skagenbank	Nld	1991	1,999	3,015	82.2	12.5	4.9	11	Cc	
Steady *	Nld	1993	1,597	2,168	79.7	11.1	-	10	Cc	
Stern	Nld	1995	1,685	2,500	81.7	11.1	4.5	10	C	
Tim	Nld	1979	813	1,151	63.0	9.5	3.4	10	C	ex St. Michael-94, Jeanette B-90, St. Michael-89
Vechtborg	Nld	1998	6,939	8,737	132.2	15.9	7.1	15	Cc	
Veerseborg **	Deu	1998	6,170	8,700	132.0	15.9	7.1	15	Cc	
Vissorbank	Nld	1994	1,682	2,503	81.7	11.1	4.5	11	C	
Vlieborg	Nld	1999	6,540	9,200	134.6	16.5	7.1	16	Cc	
Vlistborg	Nld	1999	6,540	9,200	134.6	16.5	7.1	16	Cc	
Voorneborg	Nld	1999	6,170	8,700	132.0	15.9	7.1	15	Cc	
Waterman	Nld	1981	798	1,160	70.0	9.5	2.9	11	C	ex Marietje Andrea-92, I/a Grote Beer

166

Name	Flag	Year	GRT	DWT	Loa	Bm	Draft	Kts	Type	Former names
Willem Sr.	Nld	1983	999	1,474	79.9	10.1	3.2	11	C	ex Steady-92, Yvonne-89
Zeus	Nld	1992	1,999	3,030	82.0	12.5	4.9	12	Cc	
Zuiderzee	Nld	1988	851	1,278	64.3	10.6	3.4	11	C	ex Carolina-98, Feran-91
Zwartemeer	Nld	1991	1,999	3,030	81.5	12.4	5.0	12	Cc	

** managed for Rederij H. Steenstra, † for Flinter Groningen BV, Netherlands,
** for Frank Dahl, Germany, ‡ managed by Pohl Shipping GmBH, Germany.*

Warnholtz, Schmidt und Co.   Germany

Funnel: Grey with black 'WSCo' on white diamond on red/white diagonally quartered band.
Hull: Grey with red boot-topping.

Name	Flag	Year	GRT	DWT	Loa	Bm	Draft	Kts	Type	Former names
Aladin	Cyp	1982	1,499	1,768	82.5	11.4	3.5	10	Cc	
Ali Baba	Cyp	1983	1,518	1,768	82.5	11.4	3.6	10	Cc	
Sesam	Cyp	1981	1,499	1,768	82.5	11.3	3.5	10	Cc	
Sindbad	Cyp	1981	1,499	1,769	82.5	11.3	3.5	10	Cc	

Thomas Watson (Shipping) Ltd.   UK

Funnel: Yellow with narrow black band on broad red band.
Hull: Dark grey with red boot-topping.

Name	Flag	Year	GRT	DWT	Loa	Bm	Draft	Kts	Type	Former names
Lady Elsie	Cyp	1975	1,031	1,593	65.8	10.7	4.3	10	C	ex Canvey-92, Velox-88
Lady Rea	Cyp	1978	1,954	3,265	81.7	14.1	5.5	12	C	ex Ortrud-90, Carib Sun-88, Reggeland-87, Sylvia Delta-85
Lady Serena	Cyp	1995	2,394	3,697	87.4	12.3	5.4	11	Cc	ex Espero-96
Lady Sophia	Bhs	1977	2,208	4,083	82.1	13.3	6.4	10	Cc	ex Enns-95, Norned Thor-84, Holberg-79, Atlantic Progress-77 (len-79)
Lady Sylvia	Bhs	1979	1,707	2,703	73.4	13.2	5.1	11	C	ex Inishfree-94, Arklow Vale-88, Capricorn-85,

Hans Peter Wegener KG   Germany

Funnel: White with symbol on red square.
Hull: Red with red boot-topping.

Name	Flag	Year	GRT	DWT	Loa	Bm	Draft	Kts	Type	Former names
Atria	Deu	1986	2,673	2,973	88.0	13.0	4.4	11	Cc	
Containerships III	Deu	1990	5,796	6,350	122.0	19.0	6.9	16	CC	ex Carina-90
Containerships IV	Deu	1994	7,550	8,932	151.1	19.7	7.4	21	CC	
Containerships V	Deu	1996	7,550	8,912	151.1	19.7	7.4		CC	l/a Wega

Oskar Wehr KG   Germany

Funnel: Yellow with black 'OW' on disc interupting yellow over blue bands.
Hull: Black with red boot-topping.

Name	Flag	Year	GRT	DWT	Loa	Bm	Draft	Kts	Type	Former names
Birte Wehr	Tuv	1982	1,939	2,886	88.0	11.3	4.7	11	Cc	ex Humber Star-99, Birte Wehr-95, Katja-90
Thames Star	Tuv	1974	3,287	4,020	106.6	14.5	5.4	14	Cc	ex Janne Wehr-95, Containerships I-87, Janne Wehr-85, Roxane Kersten-83, Janne Wehr-81, Roxane Kersten-81, Janne Wehr-80 (len-81)

Andrew Weir & Co. Ltd.   UK

Funnel: Various, depending on service.
Hull: Grey

Name	Flag	Year	GRT	DWT	Loa	Bm	Draft	Kts	Type	Former names
Baltic Tern	Iom	1989	3,896	3,754	106.6	16.2	5.4	13	CC	
City of Manchester	Iom	1979	3,992	4,352	104.2	16.8	5.7	14	CC	ex Laxfoss-85, City of Hartlepool-84
Pacheco	Iom	1978	3,992	4,352	104.2	16.8	5.7	14	CC	ex City of Lisbon-98, Cervantes-96, City of Plymouth-93

Wesmar Shipping BV   Netherlands

Funnel: Cream with red top.
Hull: Grey with red boot-topping.

Name	Flag	Year	GRT	DWT	Loa	Bm	Draft	Kts	Type	Former names
Barentszzee	Nld	1973	1,045	1,536	71.2	9.8	3.8	10	C	ex Gersom-95, Realta-87

Name	Flag	Year	GRT	DWT	Loa	Bm	Draft	Kts	Type	Former names
Eembay	Atg	1984	2,882	4,200	99.8	14.6	5.2	11	Cc	ex Blankenese-99 (len-90)
Eembaltic	Atg	1985	2,881	4,190	99.8	14.6	5.2	11	Cc	ex Borgfeld-99 (len-90)
Eemeer	Nld	1999	2,539	3,380	-	-	-	-	Cc	
Eemhaven	Nld	2000	2,539	3,380	-	-	-	-	Cc	
Eemlagune	Nld	1985	2,800	2,980	85.6	15.3	4.4	11	Cc	ex Stadt Leer-99, Valiant-97, Stadt Leer-91
Eemland	Nld	1999	2,539	3,380	-	-	-	-	Cc	
Eemnes	Nld	1999	2,539	3,380	-	-	-	-	Cc	
Eemsea	Atg	1986	2,800	2,985	85.6	15.2	4.4	11	Cc	ex Stadt Norden-99, FLS America-97, Stadt Norden-97, Cafe Express-93, Stadt Norden-92, Delmas Zaire-90, Stadt Norden-89
Marjola	Nld	1981	2,061	3,085	82.4	12.8	5.1	12	Cc	ex Stella Baltic-96, Baske-93, Aldib-89, Britt-Mari-88, Brita Ragne-87, Pohjola-84
Markes	Nld	1980	2,061	2,730	82.5	12.8	5.4	12	Cc	ex Stella Arctic-96, Vik-93, Alkes-89, Miniland-88, Mustola-84

Gerhard Wessels
Germany

Funnel: Various.
Hull: Blue with red boot-topping.

Name	Flag	Year	GRT	DWT	Loa	Bm	Draft	Kts	Type	Former names
A. Wetzel *	Deu	1996	1,043	1,687	73.2	9.5	4.4	12	Cc	
Carrier	Cyp	1993	2,514	3,610	87.8	12.9	5.5	11	Cc	ex Seaprincess-99, Rugen-97
Clavigo *	Atg	1992	2,446	3,735	87.9	12.9	5.5	10	Cc	
Dutch Express	Nld	1998	2,999	4,450	99.9	12.8	5.7	13	Cc	
Dutch Navigator	Deu	1997	2,997	4,435	99.9	12.8	5.7	13	Cc	
Dutch Sky	Nld	1995	2,997	4,450	(95.3)	12.8	5.7	13	Cc	ex German Sky-97, Rhein Pilot-96, German Sky-96
Dutch Sun	Nld	1999	2,997	4,450	99.9	12.8	5.7	13	Cc	
Dutch Trader	Nld	1998	2,997	4,450	99.9	12.8	5.7	13	Cc	
Elisabeth-WE	Cyp	1985	1,950	2,871	85.5	12.5	4.4	10	Cc	ex Elisabeth W-86
Faust	Deu	1997	2,997	4,444	(95.3)	12.8	5.7	13	Cc	ex German Express-97
Fundo *	Cyp	1995	989	1,536	72.5	9.5	4.1	11	Cc	
German Bay	Atg	1997	2,997	4,450	99.9	12.8	5.7	13	Cc	
German Feeder	Deu	1997	2,997	4,444	(95.3)	12.8	5.7	13	Cc	
Julia Isabel †	Atg	1992	2,446	3,735	87.9	12.8	5.5	10	Cc	ex Saar Berlin-96, Julia Isabel-95
Komarno	Cyp	1993	2,446	3,701	87.9	12.8	5.5	10	Cc	
Lovosice *	Deu	1999	1,169	1,850	78.3	9.5	4.4	10	Cc	
Melanie Z *	Cyp	1984	1,289	1,555	74.9	10.6	3.4	9	C	ex RMS Francia-98, Oranje Rotterdam-92, Sea Tamar-91
Nordstern *	Atg	1994	2,446	3,702	87.9	12.9	5.5	11	Cc	
Pamir *	Cyp	1995	2,061	3,002	88.5	11.4	5.0	11	Cc	
Pardubice *	Deu	1997	1,169	1,800	78.3	9.5	4.4	-	Cc	
Parsival *	Cyp	1995	2,061	3,007	88.5	11.4	5.0	11	Cc	
Peary	Deu	1993	2,514	3,560	87.8	12.8	5.5	11	Cc	ex Larnaca Bay-99, Fischland-97
Pera *	Atg	1995	2,514	3,596	87.9	12.8	4.5	12	C	ex Botsman Vlasov-95
Peru *	Deu	1998	2,993	4,279	90.6	15.2	5.6	-	C	
Pilsen *	Deu	1997	1,169	1,831	78.3	9.5	4.4	12	Cc	
Plus	Deu	1998	3,500	4,250	-	-	-	-	Cc	
Podebrady *	Deu	1999	1,169	1,850	78.3	9.5	4.4	-	Cc	
Pola *	Deu	1990	1,690	1,857	82.5	11.4	4.5	10	Cc	ex Heinke-98
Pommern *	Cyp	1994	2,061	3,006	88.5	11.4	5.0	11	Cc	
Posen *	Atg	1993	2,514	3,560	87.7	12.8	5.5	11	Cc	ex Seaprogress-99, Usedom-97
Potosi *	Atg	1995	2,506	3,657	87.9	12.8	4.5	12	Cc	
Prasident *	Atg	1995	2,061	3,004	88.5	11.4	5.0	12	Cc	
Prompt	Deu	1998	3,500	4,250	-	-	-	-	Cc	
Rheinfels *	Atg	1991	2,381	3,700	88.8	12.8	5.5	11	Cc	
Wittenbergen *	Cyp	1992	2,381	3,700	87.9	12.8	5.5	10	Cc	

*owned by River-Liner Befrachtungs und Bereederungsges.mbH or † by Wolfgang Grimpe Schiffahrts KG.
Newbuildings: four 2,997 grt 4,450 dwt dry cargo coasters due for 1999 delivery.

Gerhard Wessels Melanie Z. *J. Krayenbosch*

John H. Whitaker (Holdings) Ltd. Whitank. *M. D. J. Lennon*

Name	Flag	Year	GRT	DWT	Loa	Bm	Draft	Kts	Type	Former names

Western Shipping Co.   Russia

Funnel: White with blue over red abnds, black top.
Hull: Various.

Name	Flag	Year	GRT	DWT	Loa	Bm	Draft	Kts	Type	Former names
Amur-2512 (2)	Rus	1986	3,086	3,159	115.7	13.4	4.0	10	Cc	
Amur-2513 (2)	Rus	1986	3,086	3,159	115.7	13.4	4.0	10	Cc	
Amur-2524 (2)	Rus	1988	3,086	3,148	116.0	13.4	4.0	10	Cc	
Amur-2532 (2)	Rus	1989	3,086	3,148	116.1	13.4	4.0	10	Cc	
Baltiyskiy-62 (2)	Rus	1967	1,865	2,140	95.9	13.2	3.4	10	C	
Kapitan Gusev (2)*	Cyp	1993	4,110	4,985	117.5	16.7	4.9	10	C	
Lava *	Rus	1995	2,794	3,897	96.3	13.6	5.3	11	Cc	
Neman *	Cyp	1996	2,914	4,237	96.3	13.6	5.5	11	Cc	
Parizhskaya Kommuna (2)	Rus	1971	2,478	2,925	114.0	13.2	3.4	10	C	
Sormovskiy-18 (2)	Rus	1970	2,478	2,925	114.2	13.2	3.4	10	C	
Sormovskiy-19 (2)	Vct	1970	2,484	2,925	114.2	13.2	3.4	10	C	
Sormovskiy-23 (2)	Rus	1971	2,478	3,134	114.0	13.2	3.7	10	C	ex 750-Letiye Goroda Gorkogo-91
Sormovskiy-3060 (2)	Rus	1988	3,048	3,391	118.7	13.2	3.9	10	Cc	
Sormovskiy-41 (2)	Rus	1980	2,478	3,134	114.0	13.2	3.7	10	C	
Sormovskiy-42 (2)	Rus	1980	2,478	3,134	114.0	13.2	3.7	10	C	
Sormovskiy-49 (2)	Rus	1984	2,478	3,135	114.0	13.2	3.7	10	C	
Sormovskiy-53 (2)	Rus	1986	2,466	3,135	114.0	13.2	3.7	10	C	
Volgo-Balt 192 (2)	Rus	1976	2,457	2,893	114.0	13.2	3.6	10	C	
Volgo-Balt 243 (2)	Rus	1983	2,554	2,893	114.0	13.2	3.6	10	C	
Volgo-Balt 244 (2)	Rus	1983	2,457	2,893	114.0	13.2	3.6	10	C	

* managed by Poseidon Schiffahrt. Germany.

John H. Whitaker (Holdings) Ltd.   UK

Funnel: Black with white 'W' on white-edged black disc on red and green flag beneath narrow red and green bands.
Hull: Black or dark blue with red boot-topping.

Name	Flag	Year	GRT	DWT	Loa	Bm	Draft	Kts	Type	Former names
Antonia B (2)	Gbr	1983	671	1,180	50.0	9.4	4.0	-	C	ex Whitonia-97
Betty-Jean (2)	Gbr	1989	794	1,360	58.3	9.5	3.9	8	C	
Borrowdale H	Gbr	1972	356	550	50.6	6.7	3.1	8	T	
Fast Ken (2)	Gbr	1992	1,382	2,220	77.8	11.1	4.0	9	C	ex Bowcliffe-94
Humber Endeavour	Gbr	1981	381	650	60.8	6.1	2.4	8	T	ex Fleet Endeavour-92
Humber Pride	Gbr	1979	380	650	60.8	6.1	2.4	9	T	
Humber Princess	Gbr	1979	380	650	60.8	6.1	2.4	9	T	
Humber Progress	Gbr	1980	380	650	60.8	6.1	2.4	9	T	
Humber Star	Gbr	1969	274	400	45.7	6.6	2.2	7	T	ex Wade Stone-77 (rblt-77)
Humber Transporter	Gbr	1967	645	960	58.9	10.7	2.9	9	T	ex Shell Transporter-84, Poilo-79 (len-69)
Jaynee W (2)	Gbr	1996	1,689	2,901	75.3	12.8	5.2	10	T	
Teesdale H (2)	Gbr	1976	499	1,050	43.9	10.0	3.9	7	T	ex Wilks-86 (conv C-86)
Whitank	Gbr	1976	686	1,030	61.0	9.3	3.7	11	T	ex Luban-87
Whitask	Gbr	1978	640	844	57.3	10.9	2.9	10	T	ex Bromley-93
Whitcrest	Gbr	1970	2,144	3,429	91.3	13.1	5.9	-	T	ex Esso Tenby-94
Whithaven	Gbr	1972	1,204	1,933	66.2	11.5	5.0	11	T	ex Frank C-94, Shell Director-93, Caernarvon-79
Whitide	Gbr	1970	1,148	2,083	74.5	10.2	4.9	11	T	ex Lindvag-90, Tarnvik-78
Whitkirk	Gbr	1969	730	1,219	64.6	9.2	3.7	10	T	ex Borman-89
Whitmariner (2)	Gbr	1979	1,363	2,562	88.8	11.4	4.4	12	Tch	ex Pallieter-98, Pierre Laffitte-90 (conv T-91)
Whitonia	Bhs	1977	2,002	3,153	83.0	14.3	5.9	13	Tch	ex Mare Aurum-98, Mare Novum-93
Whitsea	Gbr	1971	728	1,229	64.3	9.3	3.7	10	T	ex Bude-92
Whitspray	Gbr	1969	899	1,321	64.6	11.1	3.4	10	T	ex Bristolian 93 (len-71)
Whitstar	Gbr	1968	1,116	2,140	74.3	10.2	4.8	11	T	ex Furena-91, Furenas-90, Stardex-79, Lone Wonsild-?? (len-75)

Name	Flag	Year	GRT	DWT	Loa	Bm	Draft	Kts	Type	Former names

White Sea & Onega Shipping Co.

Russia

Funnel: White with blue over red bands, black top.
Hull: Various.

Name	Flag	Year	GRT	DWT	Loa	Bm	Draft	Kts	Type	Former names
Aleksandr Shotman (2)	Rus	1987	3,041	3,265	119.2	13.4	3.8	10	Cc	ex Sormovskiy 3059-89
Aleksey Afanasjev (2)	Rus	1981	2,491	3,111	114.1	13.5	3.7	10	C	ex Sormovskiy 3004-90
Amur-2501 (2)	Rus	1984	3,086	3,160	115.7	13.4	4.0	10	Cc	ex Volgo-Balt 249-84
Amur-2504 (2)	Rus	1984	3,086	3,152	115.7	13.4	4.0	10	Cc	ex Volgo-Balt 252-84
Amur-2505 (2)	Rus	1984	3,086	3,152	115.7	13.4	4.0	10	Cc	ex Volgo-Balt 253-84
Amur-2506 (2)	Rus	1986	3,086	3,152	115.7	13.4	4.0	10	Cc	ex Volgo-Balt 254-86
Amur-2509 (2)	Rus	1985	3,086	3,152	115.7	13.4	4.0	10	Cc	
Amur-2515 (2)	Rus	1986	3,086	3,152	113.9	13.4	4.0	10	Cc	
Amur-2517 (2)	Rus	1987	3,086	3,152	115.7	13.4	4.0	10	Cc	
Amur-2522 (2)	Rus	1987	3,086	3,152	116.0	13.4	4.0	10	Cc	
Amur-2528 (2) **	Rus	1989	3,086	3,148	116.0	13.4	4.0	10	Cc	
Amur-2531 (2)	Rus	1989	3,086	3,152	116.1	13.4	4.0	10	Cc	
Amur-2540 (2)	Rus	1991	3,086	3,152	116.0	13.4	4.0	10	C	
Andor (2)	Mlt	1974	2,516	3,180	114.0	13.2	3.6	10	C	ex Volgo-Balt 183-97
Arvin (2)	Mlt	1975	2,516	3,180	114.0	13.2	3.6	10	C	ex Volgo-Balt 189-97
Baltiyskiy-5 (2)	Rus	1962	1,865	2,121	95.6	13.2	3.3	10	C	
Baltiyskiy-6 (2)	Rus	1963	1,865	2,121	95.6	13.2	3.3	10	C	
Baltiyskiy-9 (2)	Rus	1963	1,865	2,121	95.6	13.2	3.3	10	C	
Baltiyskiy-56 (2)	Rus	1966	1,865	2,140	95.6	13.2	3.4	10	C	
Baltiyskiy-59 (2)	Rus	1966	1,865	2,140	95.9	13.2	3.4	10	C	
Baltiyskiy-66 (2)	Rus	1967	1,865	2,140	95.9	13.2	3.3	11	C	
Baltiyskiy-69 (2)	Rus	1967	1,948	2,140	95.9	13.2	3.4	10	C	
Baltiyskiy-101 (2)	Rus	1978	1,926	2,555	95.0	13.2	4.0	12	Cc	
Baltiyskiy-103 (2)	Rus	1978	1,926	2,600	95.0	13.2	4.0	12	Cc	
Baltiyskiy-105 (2)	Rus	1979	1,926	2,600	95.0	13.2	4.0	12	Cc	
Baltiyskiy-108 (2) **	Rus	1979	1,926	2,600	95.0	13.2	4.0	12	Cc	
Baltiyskiy-109 (2) *	Rus	1979	1,926	2,600	95.0	13.2	4.0	12	Cc	
Baltiyskiy-111 (2) *	Rus	1980	1,926	2,600	95.0	13.2	4.0	12	Cc	
Benenden (2)	Rus	1968	2,478	2,925	114.2	13.2	3.4	10	C	ex Sormovskiy-7-98
Berg (2) †	Mlt	1974	2,516	3,260	114.0	13.2	3.3	10	C	ex Volgo-Balt 185-96
Chalna (2)	Rus	1989	3,952	5,150	138.8	16.7	3.7	11	C	ex Volgo-Don 5102-94
Chupa (2)	Rus	1986	3,935	5,150	138.8	16.7	3.7	11	C	ex Volgo-Don 5096-94
Diva (2) †	Mlt	1974	2,572	3,260	114.0	13.2	3.6	10	C	ex Volgo-Balt 186-98
Girvas (2)	Rus	1981	2,776	3,292	105.9	16.7	3.4	10	C	ex Volgo-Don 5081-93
Grand (2) †	Mlt	1974	2,516	2,863	114.0	13.2	3.6	10	C	ex Volgo-Balt 180-97
Kalevala (2)	Rus	1986	2,829	3,220	105.3	16.7	3.4	10	C	ex Volgo-Don 5092-94 (short-94)
Kapitan Manaseyev (2)	Rus	1973	2,470	3,135	114.0	13.2	3.7	10	C	ex Sormovskiy-30-78
Kelarvi **	Rus	1995	1,596	2,300	81.4	11.3	4.2	11	Cc	
Kento *	Rus	1994	1,596	2,300	81.4	11.5	4.2	9	Cc	
Keret	Rus	1994	1,596	2,300	81.4	11.5	4.2	10	C	
Kivach (2)	Rus	1985	2,829	3,220	105.3	16.7	3.4	10	C	ex Volgo-Don 5090-95 (short-93)
Kizhi (2) **	Rus	1986	2,829	3,220	105.3	16.7	3.4	10	C	ex Volgo-Don 5093-?? (short-93)
Koriangi **	Rus	1993	1,596	2,300	81.4	11.5	4.2	9	Cc	
Kovera **	Rus	1995	1,596	2,300	81.4	11.5	4.2	11	C	
Ladva (2)	Rus	1988	3,952	5,150	138.8	16.7	3.7	10	C	ex Volgo-Don 5101-94
Lezhevo	Rus	1995	1,596	2,300	81.4	11.5	4.3	10	Cc	
Louhi	Rus	1988	3,952	5,150	138.8	16.7	3.7	10	C	ex Volgo-Don 5100-94
Meg	Rus	1993	1,596	2,300	81.4	11.5	4.2	10	Cc	
Morskoy-1 (2)	Rus	1966	1,595	2,226	88.0	12.4	3.7	11	C	
Nadvoitsy (2)	Rus	1988	2,829	3,220	105.3	16.7	3.4	10	C	ex Volgo-Don 5099-94 (short-94)
Onego *	Rus	1991	1,574	1,890	81.2	11.3	3.6	9	Cc	
Pavel Mochalov (2)	Rus	1979	2,478	3,135	114.0	13.2	3.7	10	C	
Petr (Pyotr) Anokhin (2)	Rus	1989	3,048	3,503	119.2	13.4	4.1	10	Cc	I/a Sormovskiy-3065
Pindushi (2)	Rus	1977	2,478	3,134	114.0	13.2	3.7	10	C	ex 60 let Velikogo Oktyabrya-94
Pryazha (2)	Rus	1989	3,952	5,150	138.8	16.7	3.7	11	C	ex Volgo-Don 5104-??
Pudozh (2)	Rus	1990	3,952	5,150	138.8	16.7	3.7	11	C	ex Volgo-Don 5106-94
Pyalma (2)	Rus	1988	2,829	3,220	105.3	16.7	3.4	10	C	ex Volgo-Don 5097-?? (short-94)
Roma *	Rus	1981	2,363	2,700	80.8	13.0	4.7	11	Cc	
Sandal	Rus	1993	1,596	2,300	81.2	11.4	4.3	11	Cc	
Seg	Rus	1993	1,596	2,300	81.4	11.5	4.2	9	Cc	
Shala (2)	Rus	1986	2,829	3,220	105.3	16.7	3.4	10	C	ex Volgo-Don 5094-94 (short-94)

Name	Flag	Year	GRT	DWT	Loa	Bm	Draft	Kts	Type	Former names
Shizhnya (2)	Rus	1987	2,829	3,220	105.3	16.7	3.5	10	C	ex Volgo-Don 5098-94 (short-94)
Shoksha (2)	Rus	1989	3,952	5,150	138.8	16.7	3.7	11	C	ex Volgo-Don 5103-94
Shuya *	Rus	1994	2,889	3,148	96.0	13.4	4.3	11	Cc	
Sogra (2)	Mlt	1991	4,966	5,985	139.8	16.6	4.5	10	C	ex Volga-4012-97
Sormovskiy-118 (2)	Rus	1981	2,478	3,147	114.0	13.2	3.7	10	C	
Sormovskiy-45 (2)	Rus	1982	2,478	3,135	114.0	13.2	3.7	10	C	
Sormovskiy-48 (2)	Rus	1983	2,466	3,134	114.0	13.2	3.7	10	C	
Sormovskiy-50 (2)	Rus	1983	2,466	3,135	114.0	13.2	3.7	10	C	
STK-1007 (2)	Rus	1984	1,408	1,347	82.0	11.6	2.9	10	C	
STK-1008 (2)	Rus	1984	1,408	1,347	82.0	11.6	2.9	10	C	
STK-1022 (2)	Rus	1984	1,408	1,706	82.0	11.6	2.9	10	C	
Suna *	Rus	1994	2,889	3,148	96.0	13.4	4.3	11	Cc	
Suoyarvi *	Rus	1994	1,596	2,300	81.4	11.5	4.2	10	Cc	
Syam *	Rus	1993	1,596	2,300	81.4	11.5	4.2	9	Cc	
Toyvo Vyakhya (2)	Rus	1985	2,466	3,135	114.0	13.2	3.7	10	C	
Tulos	Rus	1995	1,596	2,300	81.4	11.5	4.2	11	C	
Valdai (2)	Rus	1970	2,484	3,135	114.2	13.2	3.7	10	C	ex XVI Syend VLKSM-95
Volga (2)	Rus	1991	4,966	5,985	139.8	16.6	4.5	10	C	
Viditsa (2)	Rus	1970	2,478	3,135	114.2	13.2	3.7	10	C	ex 50-Let Sovietskoy Vlasti-95
Volga-4002 (2) §	Rus	1987	4,911	5,845	139.8	16.6	4.3	10	C	
Volga-4004 (2) ‡	Rus	1988	4,911	5,845	139.8	16.6	4.5	10	C	
Volga-4006 (2)	Rus	1988	4,911	5,845	139.8	16.6	4.5	10	C	
Volgo-Balt 177 (2)	Rus	1973	2,553	2,893	113.9	13.2	3.3	10	C	
Volgo-Balt 188 (2)	Rus	1975	2,516	3,180	114.0	13.2	3.6	10	C	
Volgo-Balt 191 (2)	Rus	1975	2,516	3,180	114.0	13.2	3.6	10	C	
Volgo-Balt 193 (2)	Rus	1976	2,516	3,180	114.0	13.2	3.6	10	C	
Volgo-Balt 194 (2)	Rus	1976	2,516	3,180	114.0	13.2	3.6	10	C	
Volgo-Balt 195 (2)	Rus	1976	2,516	3,180	114.0	13.2	3.6	10	C	
Volgo-Balt 196 (2)	Rus	1976	2,516	3,197	114.0	13.2	3.6	10	C	
Volgo-Balt 199 (2)	Rus	1976	2,516	3,180	114.0	13.2	3.6	10	C	
Volgo-Balt 200 (2)	Mlt	1977	2,516	3,180	114.0	13.2	3.6	10	C	
Volgo-Balt 202 (2)	Rus	1977	2,516	3,180	114.0	13.2	3.6	10	C	
Volgo-Balt 203 (2)	Rus	1977	2,516	3,180	114.0	13.2	3.6	10	C	
Volgo-Balt 205 (2)	Rus	1977	2,516	2,983	113.9	13.2	3.6	10	C	
Volgo-Balt 206 (2)	Rus	1977	2,516	3,180	114.0	13.2	3.6	10	C	
Volgo-Balt 208 (2)	Rus	1977	2,516	3,180	114.0	13.2	3.6	10	C	
Volgo-Balt 213 (2)	Rus	1978	2,516	3,180	114.0	13.2	3.6	10	C	
Volgo-Balt 214 (2)	Rus	1978	2,584	2,893	114.0	13.2	3.6	10	C	
Volgo-Balt 216 (2)	Rus	1979	2,516	3,180	114.0	13.2	3.6	10	C	
Volgo-Balt 219 (2)	Rus	1979	2,516	3,180	114.0	13.2	3.6	10	C	
Volgo-Balt 220 (2)	Rus	1979	2,516	2,893	114.0	13.2	3.6	10	C	
Volgo-Balt 223 (2)	Rus	1979	2,516	3,180	114.0	13.2	3.6	10	C	
Volgo-Balt 226 (2)	Rus	1980	2,516	2,893	114.0	13.2	3.6	10	C	
Volgo-Balt 227 (2)	Rus	1980	2,516	3,180	113.9	13.2	3.6	10	C	
Volgo-Balt 228 (2)	Rus	1980	2,516	3,180	114.0	13.2	3.6	10	C	
Volgo-Balt 229 (2)	Rus	1981	2,516	3,180	113.9	13.2	3.6	10	C	
Volgo-Balt 230 (2)	Rus	1981	2,516	3,180	114.0	13.2	3.6	10	C	
Volgo-Balt 231 (2)	Rus	1981	2,516	3,180	114.0	13.2	3.6	10	C	
Volgo-Balt 232 (2)	Rus	1981	2,516	3,180	114.0	13.2	3.6	10	C	
Volgo-Balt 235 (2)	Rus	1981	2,516	3,180	114.0	13.2	3.6	10	C	
Volgo-Balt 236 (2)	Rus	1982	2,516	3,180	114.0	13.3	3.6	10	C	
Volgo-Balt 237 (2)	Rus	1983	2,516	3,180	114.0	13.2	3.6	10	C	
Volgo-Balt 239 (2)	Rus	1982	2,516	3,180	114.0	13.2	3.6	10	Cc	
Volgo-Balt 240 (2)	Rus	1982	2,516	3,180	114.0	13.2	3.6	10	C	
Volgo-Balt 245 (2)	Rus	1983	2,516	3,180	114.0	13.2	3.6	10	C	
Vyg *	Rus	1992	1,598	2,300	81.2	11.3	3.7	9	Cc	
Windsor (2) †	Mlt	1973	2,457	3,288	114.0	13.2	3.6	10	C	ex Volgo-Balt 172-97

* managed by Transchart Schiffs. GmbH, ** by Poseidon Schiffs. GmbH, both Germany, † owned by subsidiary Maridan Shipmanagement co. Ltd., Cyprus, ‡ managed by Norchart BV, Netherlands or § by Lumar (Barcelona) SA, Spain.

Wijnne & Barends BV   Netherlands

Funnel: Black with black 'W&B' on white band or owners markings.
Hull: Red with black boot-topping.

Name	Flag	Year	GRT	DWT	Loa	Bm	Draft	Kts	Type	Former names
Aldebaren	Nld	1997	1,675	2,270	82.5	11.4	4.0	9	C	

Name	Flag	Year	GRT	DWT	Loa	Bm	Draft	Kts	Type	Former names
Andries	Nld	1972	648	841	70.0	8.2	-	10	C	ex Thalassa-83, Douwe-S-81, Trinitas-77
Bornrif	Nld	1996	1,842	2,600	81.6	12.5	4.3	-	Cc	
Claudia	Brb	1983	3,259	5,050	91.9	15.1	6.5	12	C	(len-92)
Constance	Nld	1985	3,259	5,105	91.9	15.1	6.5	12	C	
Dependent	Nld	1983	1,241	1,791	65.5	11.4	4.6	11	C	
Dioli	Ant	1983	1,513	1,761	82.5	11.4	3.6	10	Cc	ex Baltica-94
Erna	Nld	1979	1,772	2,822	75.1	12.6	5.4	12	C	ex Menna-95
Fiducia	Atg	1983	1,394	2,284	79.8	11.0	4.1	10	Cc	ex Fast Wil-96, Breehorn-93, Banjaard-92
Frisium	Nld	1992	1,786	2,355	87.0	12.4	3.7	10	C	ex Thalassa-98
Helene	Nld	1991	2,561	3,284	88.0	12.6	5.3	12	Cc	
Henderika Klein	Nld	1983	1,865	3,077	81.6	14.0	5.4	12	C	
Inger	Nld	1996	3,323	4,182	88.1	14.4	5.9	13	Cc	
Irina	Nld	1997	3,322	4,161	88.1	14.4	5.9	13	Cc	
Isabel	Nld	1997	3,225	4,250	88.1	14.5	5.9		Cc	
Kirsten	Nld	1995	2,561	3,290	88.0	12.6	5.3	12	Cc	ex Aros News-96, I/a Kirsten
Linda Marijke	Nld	1992	1,359	1,850	75.3	10.8	4.0	12	C	
Magda	Nld	1993	2,561	3,284	88.0	12.6	5.3	12	Cc	
Marie Christine	Nld	1991	2,561	3,284	88.0	12.6	5.3	-	Cc	
Mathilde	Nld	1995	2,561	3,332	88.0	12.6	5.3	11	Cc	
Menna	Nld	1996	2,561	3,332	88.0	12.5	5.3	12	C	
Morgenstond I	Nld	1993	2,650	4,250	89.0	13.2	5.7	12	Cc	
Morgenstond II	Nld	1997	3,782	5,425	100.9	14.5	6.3	14	Cc	
Nora	Nis	1982	1,999	2,954	83.3	12.6	5.4	13	C	(len-86)
Olga	Nld	1994	2,561	3,290	88.0	12.6	5.3	12	Cc	
Regulus	Nld	1997	2,375	3,471	89.1	12.5	4.9	11	Cc	
Verena	Nld	1977	1,769	2,728	75.1	12.6	5.4	13	C	ex Mathilde-94
Vios	Nld	1990	1,999	2,950	82.0	12.5	4.9	12	Cc	ex Morgenstond II-97

Newbuildings: four 4,240 grt 5,420 dwt dry cargo vessels due for 1999/2000 delivery.

Idwal Williams & Co. Ltd. UK
Graig Ship Management
Funnel: White with blue 'C' and diamond, narrow black top.
Hull: Blue with white 'Clipper', red boot-topping.

Name	Flag	Year	GRT	DWT	Loa	Bm	Draft	Kts	Type	Former names
Clipper Caldicot	Bhs	1999	6,714	8,874	100.5	20.4	-	16	Cc	
Clipper Cardiff	Bhs	1998	6,714	8,702	100.5	20.4	-	16	Cc	ex Maersk Brookly-99, Clipper Cardiff-98
Clipper Carmarthon	Bhs	1999	6,714	8,874	100.5	20.4	-	16	Cc	
Clipper Chepstow	Bhs	1999	6,714	8,874	100.5	20.4	-	16	Cc	
Clipper Conway	Bhs	1997	6,714	8,874	100.5	20.4	-	16	Cc	ex Maersk Takoradi-99, Clipper Conway-98
Clipper Cowbridge	Bhs	1998	6,714	8,874	100.5	20.4	-	16	Cc	

Charles M. Willie & Co. (Shipping) Ltd. UK
Funnel: Blue with Welsh flag (red dragon on white/green bands).
Hull: Dark blue with red boot-topping.

Name	Flag	Year	GRT	DWT	Loa	Bm	Draft	Kts	Type	Former names
Begona B	Esp	1992	3,779	5,861	92.8	17.1	6.6		C	ex Nenufar Uno-98, Celtic Crusader-95, Euro Trader-95, Celtic Crusader-93
Celtic Ambassador	Bhs	1994	3,739	5,788	92.8	17.1	6.5	13	Cc	ex Fairwind-96, Celtic Ambassador-94
Celtic Commander	Bhs	1993	3,840	5,833	92.8	17.2	6.5	13	Cc	ex Fairway-96, Celtic Commander-94
Celtic Endeavour	Bhs	1988	2,034	3,366	85.1	13.0	6.0	11	C	ex Iberian Sea-98, I/a Ahmet Madenci II
Celtic King	Bhs	1999	4,250	6,250	100.0	17.2	6.4	15	Cc	
Celtic Navigator	Bhs	1979	1,010	1,538	65.8	11.1	4.3	10	C	ex Wilant-89, Marant-88, Engel Klein-83
Emily Borchard	Bhs	1997	4,015	6,250	100.0	17.2	6.4	15	Cc	ex Gracechurch Meteor-97, I/a Celtic Monarch
Iberian Coast	Bhs	1979	1,029	1,391	72.2	11.3	3.3	11	C	ex Yulence-87, London Miller-81

Name	Flag	Year	GRT	DWT	Loa	Bm	Draft	Kts	Type	Former names
Iberian Ocean	Bhs	1979	1,029	1,391	72.2	11.3	3.3	11	C	ex Zealance-87, Birkenhead Miller-82
Judith Borchard	Bhs	1995	4,015	6,250	100.0	17.1	6.4	15	Cc	ex Gracechurch Sun-97, Celtic Prince-96
Louise Borchard	Bhs	1997	4,015	6,250	100.0	17.2	6.4	15	Cc	ex Celtic Princess-97
Ruth Borchard	Bhs	1996	4,015	6,250	100.8	17.2	6.4	15	Cc	ex Gracechurch Comet-97, Celtic Sovereign-96

Newbuildings: Three 3,840 grt 5,900 dwt dry cargo vessels due for 2000 delivery.

Wilson Management AS   Norway
Wilson Ship Management (Bergen) AS

Name	Flag	Year	GRT	DWT	Loa	Bm	Draft	Kts	Type	Former names
Alexis	Cyp	1975	3,658	5,790	102.0	15.9	6.8	13	B	ex Rocknes-93
Enterprise	Nis	1985	6,389	8,709	113.0	20.2	8.3	15	Bu	ex Torgnes-96
Fromnes	Phl	1978	3,949	5,800	105.7	15.4	6.9	13	B	ex Framnes-98 (len-84)
Hernes *	Cyp	1980	4,924	7,160	110.6	17.6	7.0	12	C	ex Rora Head-93
Hordnes	Pan	1980	4,913	7,107	110.6	17.6	7.0	12	C	ex Barra Head-96
Husnes	Mlt	1977	4,907	7,174	110.6	17.6	7.0	15	C	ex Hook Head-93, Sumburgh Head-90
Millennium Tiger	Phl	1995	7,249	7,150	134.3	19.9	7.1	14	Cc	ex Brinknes-97
Northern Langnes	Mlt	1996	2,246	3,695	87.9	12.9	5.5	10	Cc	
Northern Larsnes	Mlt	1996	2,446	3,694	88.0	12.8	5.5	11	C	
Northern Launes	Mlt	1997	2,446	3,695	88.0	12.8	-	11	Cc	
Northern Lesnes	Mlt	1995	2,446	3,712	88.0	12.9	5.5	11	Cc	
Northern Liftnes	Mlt	1996	2,446	3,680	87.9	12.9	5.5	10	Cc	
Northern Linanes	Mlt	1994	2,446	3,714	87.9	12.9	5.5	11	Cc	
Northern Lindnes	Mlt	1997	2,446	3,680	88.0	12.8	-	11	Cc	
Northern Loftnes	Mlt	1995	2,446	3,712	88.0	12.9	5.5	11	C	
Northern Loknes	Mlt	1996	2,446	3,670	88.0	12.8	5.5	11	Cc	
Northern Lurnes	Mlt	1997	2,446	3,695	88.0	12.8	-	11	Cc	
Reksnes	Pan	1977	3,885	6,258	103.6	16.0	6.9	13	B	ex General Valeriano-92, Reksnes-86
Radnes	Mlt	1976	3,885	6,258	103.6	16.0	7.0	13	B	ex Lugano-89, Radnes-84
Ramnes	Cyp	1981	3,937	6,186	103.6	16.0	7.0	12	B	ex General Peralta-90, Saint James-87, Ramnes-83
Rognes	Nld	1976	3,885	6,258	103.6	16.0	6.8	13	B	ex General Aquino-91, Rognes-87
Saint Brevin	Mlt	1975	3,842	6,258	103.5	16.1	7.0	12	B	ex Refsnes-83
Telnes	Pan	1982	6,944	10,110	117.7	20.6	8.5	14	Bu	
Tinnes	Pan	1983	6,944	10,110	117.7	20.6	8.5	14	Bu	ex General Bonifacio-88, Tinnes-86
Tornes *	Pan	1984	6,389	8,721	113.0	20.2	8.3	15	Bu	
Trollnes	Pan	1985	6,398	8,909	112.0	20.5	8.2	14	Bu	
Trones	Pan	1986	7,556	11,339	121.8	20.5	8.3	-	Bu	

* owned by subsidiary Jebsens Ship Management (London) Ltd., UK
Owned by Actinor Shipping ASA.

Paal Wilson & Co. AS   Norway

Funnel: Pale blue.
Hull: Pale blue or red with white 'Wilson', red boot-topping.

Name	Flag	Year	GRT	DWT	Loa	Bm	Draft	Kts	Type	Former names
Barco	Bhs	1972	1,923	3,240	91.3	13.3	5.1	12	C	ex Birona-89, Corona-88, Speed Bulk-86, Suavity-84
Bongo *	Bhs	1976	1,133	1,781	70.5	10.0	4.5	10	C	(len-80)
Botno *	Bhs	1971	1,097	1,595	74.8	10.0	3.7	9	C	(len-77)
Continental Beta	Mlt	1981	3,019	3,498	96.6	15.0	5.7	15	Ccw	ex MSC Beirut-98, Continental Beta-97, Sintra-95, Lux Baltic-89, Aranjuez-87, Isla de Tenerife-87, Lucia de Perez-85, Hvita-84, Lucia de Perez-83
Dalgo	Bhs	1971	1,977	2,630	77.1	12.9	6.4	13	C	ex Saby-90, Sassaby-83
Finno	Bhs	1970	1,097	1,384	74.8	10.0	3.7	11	C	(len-77)
Formo	Blz	1973	1,285	1,498	77.2	10.0	4.0	10	C	(len-80)

174

Charles M. Willie & Co. (Shipping) Ltd. Celtic Ambassador. *J. Krayenbosch*

Paal Wilson & Co. AS Kinso. *J. Krayenbosch*

Name	Flag	Year	GRT	DWT	Loa	Bm	Draft	Kts	Type	Former names
Grimo	Bhs	1983	1,998	3,126	77.0	13.0	5.5	-	C	ex Inishowen-95, Raimundo A-88
Haslo	Bhs	1976	1,895	3,049	84.1	13.6	5.3	-	Cc	ex Beito-87, Ask-82
Hedlo *	Bhs	1971	1,092	1,254	74.8	10.0	3.7	11	C	(len-79)
Hubro	Mlt	1971	2,092	3,203	87.0	12.7	5.0	12	C	ex Miramar-89, Anders-83
Justo *	Bhs	1970	1,090	1,365	74.3	10.0	3.7	11	C	(len-79)
Kambo *	Bhs	1971	1,097	1,240	74.8	10.0	3.7	11	C	(len-77)
Kinso *	Bhs	1972	1,106	1,225	74.9	10.0	3.7	10	C	(len-79)
Leiro	Nis	1981	2,468	3,053	97.9	13.7	4.5	11	C	(len-86)
Lindo	Nis	1982	2,468	3,053	98.1	13.7	5.2	11	C	(len-86)
Lutro *	Bhs	1975	1,259	1,395	76.5	10.6	3.6	11	C	(len-80)
Mango	Bhs	1981	2,693	3,550	89.0	14.2	6.2	13	Cc	ex Sota Arritokieta-87
Mingo	Bhs	1980	2,693	3,550	89.0	14.4	6.0	13	C	ex Sota Begona-87
Nicco	Bhs	1977	2,492	3,048	95.0	14.4	5.7	13	Ce	ex Fenris-87 (conv C-87, len-80)
Rinko	Nor	1972	2,627	3,200	90.2	14.8	4.7	14	Bu	ex Ringue-90, Atlantic Earl-87, Nad Monarch-75, Hainburg-72 (conv C-88)
Salmo	Bhs	1979	2,171	3,225	91.6	14.1	5.1	11	C	(len-83)
Stina	Atg	1976	2,279	2,560	81.4	13.4	5.2	13	Cc	ex Stefanie-96, Canopus-95
Trobo	Bhs	1976	1,202	1,325	74.8	10.6	3.6	11	C	(len-80)
Truro *	Bhs	1976	1,259	1,505	77.5	10.6	3.6	11	C	(len-79)
Tysso *	Bhs	1972	1,106	1,936	74.9	10.0	3.7	10	C	(len-79)
Victoria	Nis	1977	2,764	3,283	95.2	13.8	4.9	13	Cc	ex Continental Alpha-94, Commodore S-94, Scott Survivor-92, Commodore Enterprise-87

* owned by Frogner Finans AS.

Schiffahrtskontor Reederei Gebruder Winter Germany

Funnel: Various.
Hull: Black with red boot-topping.

Name	Flag	Year	GRT	DWT	Loa	Bm	Draft	Kts	Type	Former names
CMBT Corvette	Atg	1991	3,815	4,654	103.5	16.2	6.1	14	Cc	ex Corvette-94, Lloyd Scandinavia-92, Dana Corvette-91, I/a Corvette
Comet	Deu	1998	3,992	5,350	101.1	18.7	6.6	15	CC	
Corsar	Deu	1998	3,999	5,356	101.1	18.5	6.6	15	CC	
HMS Goodwill	Atg	1985	3,797	4,570	97.0	17.8	6.0	14	Cc	ex Commodore Goodwill-95, Akak Cedar-87
Rhein Carrier	Atg	1991	3,818	4,650	103.5	16.2	6.1	14	Cc	ex Churruca-98, Cimbria-93, Lloyd Iberia-92, Dana Sirena-91, I/a Cimbria

Wonsild & Son A/S Denmark

Funnel: Green with green 'W' on white rectangle or * green with black 'EM' on white edged light blue disc.
Hull: Green.

Name	Flag	Year	GRT	DWT	Loa	Bm	Draft	Kts	Type	Former names
Caroline Wonsild *	Ita	1994	2,349	2,693	89.6	14.0	5.2	13	Tch	
Costanza Wonsild *	Ita	1994	2,349	2,698	89.6	14.0	5.2	13	Tch	
Danchem East **	Dis	1992	1,666	2,774	79.0	13.0	5.2	12	Tch	
Danchem West **	Dis	1992	1,666	2,774	79.0	13.1	5.2	14	Tch	
Elena Lux	Dis	1969	884	1,256	65.0	10.6	3.7	11	Tch	ex Susanna-91, Peder Lysgaard-81
Ella Wonsild	Dis	1990	1,716	3,294	83.5	13.7	5.5	10	Tch	ex Ella Terkol-
Frances Wonsild *	Ita	1994	2,349	2,697	89.6	14.0	5.2	13	Tch	
Helle Wonsild	Dis	1991	1,716	3,294	83.5	13.7	5.5	11	Tch	ex Helle Terkol-95
Ida Wonsild †	Dis	1976	1,782	2,549	80.8	12.8	5.4	13	Tch	ex Merete Wonsild-96, Bencleuch-89
Irene Wonsild ‡	Dis	1976	1,782	2,567	80.8	12.8	5.4	13	Tch	ex Benmacdhui-89
Janne Wonsild *	Ita	1993	2,349	2,694	89.6	14.0	5.2	13	Tch	
Lady Camilla †	Iom	1973	1,999	3,310	93.3	14.0	5.4	12	Tch	ex Lubchem-98, Mobil Lubchem-91
Lone Wonsild *	Dis	1990	1,711	3,294	83.5	13.7	5.5	10	Tch	ex Lone Terkol-95
Mary Wonsild *	Ita	1994	2,349	2,698	89.6	14.0	5.2	13	Tch	

Wonsild & Son A/S Ida Wonsild. *J. Krayenbosch*

Schiffahrtskontor Tom Worden GmbH Angermanland. *M. D. J. Lennon*

Name	Flag	Year	GRT	DWT	Loa	Bm	Draft	Kts	Type	Former names
Mie Wonsild †	Dis	1974	1,780	2,581	80.8	12.8	5.4	12	Tch	ex Mopa Wonsild-97, Benvenue-89
Sarah Wonsild *	Ita	1993	2,349	2,702	89.6	14.0	5.2	13	Tch	

* managed for Marittima Etnea Srl, Italy.
** owned by Danchemical Tankers A/S, Denmark.
† managed by BR Shipmanagement A/S or ‡ Jens Jakonsen A/S.

Schiffahrtskontor Tom Worden GmbH Germany

Funnel: Various ownership or charterers colours.
Hull: Various.

Name	Flag	Year	GRT	DWT	Loa	Bm	Draft	Kts	Type	Former names
Angermanland	Atg	1989	3,845	4,334	104.9	16.0	5.4	14	Cc	
Dalarna	Deu	1997	3,796	4,400	100.7	16.2	4.8	11	Cc	ex Aurico 1-97
Dalsland	Deu	1999	4,150	5,450	-	-	-	-	Cc	
Gastrikland	Cyp	1992	4,090	4,450	111.1	16.1	6.0	14	Cc	ex Sea Voyager-98, Gastrikland-??
Gotland	Deu	1999	4,150	5,450	-	-	-	-	Cc	
Gracechurch Meteor	Deu	1997	3,999	5,865	100.0	18.2	6.6	17	CC	ex Merino-97
Halland	Deu	1999	4,150	5,580	-	-	-	-	Cc	
Halsingland	Deu	1990	3,845	3,936	104.9	16.3	5.9	14	Cc	
Lolland	Deu	1999	4,150	5,450	-	-	-	-	Cc	
Medelpad	Deu	1985	2,696	3,036	92.5	13.9	4.5	11	Cc	ex Merlin-97
MSC Mandala	Mlt	1985	2,691	3,036	92.5	13.9	4.4	11	Cc	ex Mandala-96
Oland *	Deu	1985	1,371	1,520	75.0	10.8	3.7	11	C	ex Drochtersen-98

* managed for Gunther Schulz Schulauer Schiffahrtskontor, Germany.

H.H. Wubbe Nachfolger Germany

Funnel: None.
Hull: Light blue with red boot-topping.

Name	Flag	Year	GRT	DWT	Loa	Bm	Draft	Kts	Type	Former names
Lass Mars (2)	Deu	1992	1,515	2,386	74.9	11.4	4.4	11	C	l/a Mars
Lass Moon (2)	Deu	1992	1,515	2,386	74.9	11.4	4.4	10	C	ex Moon-92
Lass Neptun (2)	Deu	1993	1,512	2,366	74.9	11.4	4.4	11	C	ex Wolgast-94, Lass Neptun-93, l/a Neptun
Lass Saturn (2)	Deu	1993	1,513	2,366	74.9	11.4	4.4	10	C	ex Greifswald-94, Lass Saturn-93
Lass Uranus (2)	Deu	1992	1,515	2,386	74.9	11.4	4.3	11	C	l/a Uranus

Zadeko Shipping NV Belgium

Funnel: Blue with grey over white over grey bands.
Hull: Light grey with red boot-topping.

Name	Flag	Year	GRT	DWT	Loa	Bm	Draft	Kts	Type	Former names
Apody (2)	Atg	1984	4,759	3,502	95.5	18.2	4.6	12	Ro	ex Nour-90, Mai Rickmers-90, Mercantil Vassouras-90, Apody-88
Askania (2)	Atg	1983	4,291	3,619	92.5	18.2	4.6	12	Ro	ex Seacrest Askania-92, Askania-91
Cindya (2)	Ant	1984	4,566	3,502	93.5	18.2	4.6	12	Ro	ex Mercantil Mage-89, Araguary-88
Jessica (2)	Ant	1984	4,566	3,502	93.5	18.2	4.6	12	Ro	ex Mercantil Valencia-89, Amambahy-88
Nordica (2)	Atg	1984	4,999	4,250	104.8	18.2	4.5	12	Cc/Ro	ex Berulan-91, ScanDutch Liguria-91, Berulan-89, Hans Behrens-88
Norlandia (2)	Ant	1983	4,998	4,250	104.9	18.0	4.6	12	Cc/Ro	ex Barber Norlandia-85, Norlandia-84
Ostara (2)	Ant	1983	6,950	4,403	106.3	19.9	3.7	13	Cc/Ro	ex Callisto-94, Jumbo Callisto-94, Tiger Creek-90, Callisto-90, Jumbo Callisto-89, Callisto-88

Wubbe Nachfoige Laas Mars. *J. Krayenbosch*

Zadeko Shipping NV Askania. *J. M. Kakebeeke*

Other owners or managers

A. K. Aagesen & Partners A/S, Norway

Name	Flag	Year	GRT	DWT	Loa	Bm	Draft	Kts	Type	Former names
Balbao	Atg	1971	3,534	3,852	108.9	16.1	5.0	15	Cc	ex Bilbao-94, Pinguin-89, Manchester Faith-85, Nahost Kurier-85, Pinguin-74 (len-77)
Elvita	Pan	1971	1,097	1,295	76.2	12.3	3.2	12	Ta	ex Sunrana-90, Stavskjell-88
Tarco Sea	Nis	1971	1,300	1,280	75.7	11.1	3.8	12	Tch	ex Esdorp-86, Ostediek-82, Catriona-72, I/a Ostediek (conv C-86)
Viscaria	Nis	1973	1,859	2,437	82.8	11.8	4.7	12	Ta	ex Jurgen-93, Jurgen Wehr-93, Jurgen W-78, Jurgen Wehr-77 (conv C-94, len-81)

Aalborg Portland, Denmark

Name	Flag	Year	GRT	DWT	Loa	Bm	Draft	Kts	Type	Former names
Kongsdal (2)	Dis	1980	5,257	7,465	118.6	17.1	7.1	13	Ce	
Portland	Dnk	1976	2,861	4,477	98.3	15.9	6.3	15	Ce	

Joachim J Actun, Germany

Name	Flag	Year	GRT	DWT	Loa	Bm	Draft	Kts	Type	Former names
Connie	Atg	1965	658	749	54.9	9.2	3.2	9	C	ex Jade-94, Franz Held-82, Mignon-70

Admiral Ltd., Russia

Name	Flag	Year	GRT	DWT	Loa	Bm	Draft	Kts	Type	Former names
Mekhanik Tormasov (2)	Rus	1972	3,469	4,553	132.6	16.9	3.3	-	T	ex Volgoneft-232-94
Volgo-Balt 217 (2)	Rus	1979	2,516	3,191	113.9	13.2	3.6	10	C	

Gebruder Ahrens KG, Germany

Name	Flag	Year	GRT	DWT	Loa	Bm	Draft	Kts	Type	Former names
Hanna	Deu	1996	3,999	5,215	101.1	18.5	6.6	15	Cc	
Rija	Deu	1998	3,999	5,215	101.1	18.5	6.5	15	Cc	

Alderney Shipping, UK

Name	Flag	Year	GRT	DWT	Loa	Bm	Draft	Kts	Type	Former names
Burhou I	Gbr	1978	674	953	57.5	10.1	3.4	11	C	ex Lancresse-97, Bressay Sound-94, Edgar Dorman-89
Isis	Iom	1978	674	953	57.5	10.1	3.4	11	C	ex Deer Sound-94, David Dorman-89
Ortac	Vct	1974	891	1,400	60.9	9.8	4.2	11	C	ex Teal 1-97, Hoxa Sound-94, Murell-88

Alexanders Partners (Shipbroking) Ltd., UK

Name	Flag	Year	GRT	DWT	Loa	Bm	Draft	Kts	Type	Former names
Kish	Brb	1978	1,961	2,973	84.2	13.6	5.4	14	C	ex Niewiadow-93, I/a Ran

Skips A/S Alexandra, Norway

Name	Flag	Year	GRT	DWT	Loa	Bm	Draft	Kts	Type	Former names
Alexandra S	Nis	1972	1,432	1,440	76.9	11.9	3.6	12	Cc	ex Alexandra-97, Alexandra S-85
Anita	Bhs	1975	2,627	3,739	93.2	13.6	5.6	13	C	ex Junior-95, Larissa Star-93, Pafic-92, Nova-90, Junior Lotte-84

Allantone Supplies Ltd., UK

Name	Flag	Year	GRT	DWT	Loa	Bm	Draft	Kts	Type	Former names
Conveyor (2)	Gbr	1980	198	307	33.5	6.6	2.4	7	T	
Onward Mariner	Gbr	1970	239	339	40.2	6.7	2.5	8	T	

Alpex Schiffsverwaltung-Seetransport Agentur & Warenhandel GmbH, Germany

Name	Flag	Year	GRT	DWT	Loa	Bm	Draft	Kts	Type	Former names
Dora	Hrv	1970	1,811	3,196	84.1	13.5	5.5	12	Tch	ex Rowena-96, Narcelle-96, Tuna-90, Rubisea-77

Alpha Ship, Netherlands

Name	Flag	Year	GRT	DWT	Loa	Bm	Draft	Kts	Type	Former names
Jamtland	Nld	1992	4,071	5,697	104.4	16.2	6.4	14	Cc	ex Chopin-97, Ville d'Autan-93, Chopin-92, Stella Adriatic-92, I/a Christina

Altex Shipping Co. Ltd., Russia

Name	Flag	Year	GRT	DWT	Loa	Bm	Draft	Kts	Type	Former names
Alexandre	Khm	1965	2,726	3,579	102.3	14.0	6.0	13	C	ex Yanales-95
Dibson 1	Khm	1964	2,756	3,434						
Helena 1	Khm	1970	2,736	3,950	102.3	14.0	6.2	13	C	ex Gus-Khrustalny-95

Name	Flag	Year	GRT	DWT	Loa	Bm	Draft	Kts	Type	Former names
Ivan Derbenev	Rus	1978	3,987	4,600	139.6	19.2	6.6	16	Ro	
Leja	Khm	1970	2,736	3,950	102.3	14.1	6.0	13	C	ex Krasnoborsk-95
Lidiya	Khm	1967	2,736	3,930	102.3	14.0	6.0	13	C	ex Turku-95

Carl E L Andersen, Denmark
Name	Flag	Year	GRT	DWT	Loa	Bm	Draft	Kts	Type	Former names
Monsunen	Dis	1965	383	564	48.1	8.7	3.0	10	C	ex Ota Riis-72

Janus Andersen & Co., Denmark
Name	Flag	Year	GRT	DWT	Loa	Bm	Draft	Kts	Type	Former names
Danfeeder	Dis	1975	1,987	1,970	82.1	12.8	4.8	13	Cc	ex Barbara-Britt-90
Danstar	Dis	1976	1,440	1,389	72.0	13.1	3.9	12	C	ex Satelith-8
Fykan	Dis	1970	1,395	1,016	71.2	13.2	3.0	12	Cp	ex Palo-96, Trans Sun-90, Fykan-87
Klevstrand	Dis	1970	1,194	996	71.2	13.2	3.0	12	Cp	
Livarden	Dis	1973	1,449	1,626	78.5	11.5	4.4	10	Cp	(len-75)
Lorelei	Dis	1956	294	437	45.6	8.1	2.6	8	C	ex Ellen Peter-75, Claudia-73, Elbstrand-73, Heinz Helmut-65
Opnor	Dis	1962	412	593	50.8	8.3	3.1	10	C	ex Gerda Vesta-64
Saturn	Dnk	1966	627	772	53.6	9.4	3.4	10	C	ex Dorca-89, Douro Star-79, Wilma Frank-72

Leif Andorsen, Norway
Name	Flag	Year	GRT	DWT	Loa	Bm	Draft	Kts	Type	Former names
Kongstind	Nor	1972	689	599	49.6	10.1	2.9	11	Cc	ex Ringhav-90, Stjernhav-80, Ravnur-79

Fritz Andreassen, Norway
Name	Flag	Year	GRT	DWT	Loa	Bm	Draft	Kts	Type	Former names
Nordbulk	Nis	1970	1,937	2,524	77.3	12.8	5.8	12	Cc	ex Running Bear-93, Euro Partner-87, Helene Graebe-83, Seeberg-78, Strombron-73, I/a Seeberg
Nordfrakt	Nis	1969	1,900	2,519	77.3	12.8	6.5	12	Cc	ex Gardway-94, Euro Tramper-87, Jorn Graebe-83, Falkenberg-78, Velazquez-73, I/a Falkenberg
Nordkyst	Nor	1970	688	920	47.2	9.5	3.2	12	C	(len-85)

Anglo Dutch Management Services Ltd., UK
Name	Flag	Year	GRT	DWT	Loa	Bm	Draft	Kts	Type	Former names
Elm	Vct	1975	959	1,511	65.0	10.8	4.1	11	C	ex Wilhelmina V-97
Ivy	Cyp	1975	1,483	2,320	76.4	12.0	4.8	11	C	ex Daniel D-98, Daniella-94, Daniel-87
Oak	Brb	1972	1,507	2,256	76.5	12.1	4.6	12	C	ex Lady Sandra-97, Hendrik B-95, Ventura-94

Antilia Joint Stock Shipping Co., Russia
Name	Flag	Year	GRT	DWT	Loa	Bm	Draft	Kts	Type	Former names
Riga Trader	Rus	1973	4,814	6,780	130.3	17.3	7.3	15	C	ex Pioner Moskvy-97
Volgo-Balt 102 (2)	Rus	1969	2,457	2,907	114.1	13.2	3.5	10	C	
Volgo-Balt 107 (2)	Rus	1969	2,457	2,907	114.1	13.2	3.6	10	C	
Volgo-Balt 121 (2)	Rus	1970	2,554	2,907	114.0	13.2	3.5	10	C	

Oy Arctic Chartering Ltd., Finland
Name	Flag	Year	GRT	DWT	Loa	Bm	Draft	Kts	Type	Former names
Mari	Fin	1978	1,925	2,265	79.8	12.8	4.4	12	Cc	ex Anne-98, Pentland-95, Mara-93, Trabant-91

Argo Shipping, Latvia
Name	Flag	Year	GRT	DWT	Loa	Bm	Draft	Kts	Type	Former names
Refrizherator-606 (2)	Rus	1982	1,531	1,080	82.0	11.6	2.8	10	R	

operated by Argo Shipping Ltd., Channel Isles.

P/O Arktikmorneftegazrazvedka, Russia
Name	Flag	Year	GRT	DWT	Loa	Bm	Draft	Kts	Type	Former names
Pioner Koly	Rus	1981	4,814	6,070	130.3	17.4	6.9	15	C	
Shuya	Rus	1983	5,082	5,834	115.8	17.1	7.0	14	T	

Arktisk Marin A/S, Norway
Name	Flag	Year	GRT	DWT	Loa	Bm	Draft	Kts	Type	Former names
Norbjorn	Nis	1973	1,924	1,264	77.5	13.0	3.9	13	Cp	ex Bremer Handel-95, Birte Ritscher-82, Bell Voyager-79 (conv C-??)
Norsel	Nis	1972	499	1,250	71.3	11.6	3.6	12	T	ex Rose-Marie S-94 (conv Tch-95)

Name	Flag	Year	GRT	DWT	Loa	Bm	Draft	Kts	Type	Former names

Roger Arnesens Rederi, Norway

Name	Flag	Year	GRT	DWT	Loa	Bm	Draft	Kts	Type	Former names
Grethe	Nis	1972	1,879	1,260	76.7	13.1	4.3	13	Cc	ex Grunnvaag-91, Fallow Deer-81, Federal Bermuda-77, Fallow Deer-76 (conv CC-81)

Kjell Arnesen Shipping A/S, Norway

Name	Flag	Year	GRT	DWT	Loa	Bm	Draft	Kts	Type	Former names
Ana Safi	Pan	1975	3,004	4,106	93.5	14.5	6.2	15	Cc	ex OPDR Safi-98, Safi-96, Liberta-88, Zim Jamaica-80, Liberta-76
Forum Samoa (2)	Pan	1979	6,861	5,536	118.7	19.3	6.7	14	Ro	
Gerlin	Nis	1977	2,282	2,560	81.4	13.4	5.0	13	Cc	ex Susan Borchard-91, Orion-90
Koningshaven	Pan	1975	3,004	4,106	93.5	14.5	6.3	14	Cc	ex OPDR Rabat-98, Rabat-97, Diana II-88, Diana-83
Tirador	Deu	1997	1,596	2,214	88.2	11.4	3.7	12	Cs	

Association Setos-Service, Russia

Name	Flag	Year	GRT	DWT	Loa	Bm	Draft	Kts	Type	Former names
Piligrim (2)	Rus	1965	720	870	55.0	10.4	3.6	8	C	ex Svirskaya-94

Aston Enterprise Ltd., Russia

Name	Flag	Year	GRT	DWT	Loa	Bm	Draft	Kts	Type	Former names
Aston Prelude * (2)	Rus	1992	4,966	5,885	139.8	16.6	4.5	10	Cc	ex Yalta-92
Lidia V (2)	Rus	1972	2,753	3,056	114.0	13.2	3.6	-	C	ex Aston Trader-98, Volgo-Balt 155-96

*managed or * owned by subsidiary Aston Trading GmbH, Germany.*

Astramar Shipping Agency, Latvia

Name	Flag	Year	GRT	DWT	Loa	Bm	Draft	Kts	Type	Former names
Anton (2)	Vct	1972	2,580	3,143	114.0	13.8	3.6	10	C	ex Enely-98, Central-97, Volgo-Balt 156-93
Baltiyskiy-38 (2)	Vct	1966	1,865	2,121	95.9	13.2	3.4	11	C	

Auklandshamn Management A/S, Norway

Name	Flag	Year	GRT	DWT	Loa	Bm	Draft	Kts	Type	Former names
Akershus	Nis	1977	2,362	1,650	79.1	12.8	4.5	12	Ccp	
Ania B	Bhs	1972	3,720	6,200	96.9	16.1	7.2	13	Cc	ex Ania-90, Reliance-90, Philemon-88, Carlota Bolten-73
Apollo	Bhs	1979	3,416	5,228	81.0	16.5	7.2	13	Ccp	ex Kapos-98, Keplion-86, Germa Lionel-84
Orion	Bhs	1979	3,416	5,228	81.0	16.5	7.2	13	Ccp	ex Sio-98, Kepwealth-86, Germa Karma-84

Ture A. Axelsson, Sweden

Name	Flag	Year	GRT	DWT	Loa	Bm	Draft	Kts	Type	Former names
Baltic Press	Swe	1979	6,413	4,623	135.9	16.8	4.6	13	Ro	(len-82)
Baltic Print	Swe	1979	6,415	4,623	135.4	16.8	4.6	13	Ro	(len-82)

Bunther P W Bahr, Germany

Name	Flag	Year	GRT	DWT	Loa	Bm	Draft	Kts	Type	Former names
Mignon	Atg	1966	1,069	1,220	68.4	10.6	3.9	12	C	ex Jana-96, Jan Suhr-81, Sieegerland-74

Baltcom Shipping Co. Ltd., Russia

Name	Flag	Year	GRT	DWT	Loa	Bm	Draft	Kts	Type	Former names
Elizaveta (2)	Rus	1990	3,390	4,540	107.4	16.7	3.2		C	ex Volzhskiy-34-??
Mary 2 (2)	Rus	1990	1,719	1,750	88.9	12.3	3.0		Cc	ex Nasezhda-97, ST-1334-92

Oy Baltic Commerce International Ltd., Finland

Name	Flag	Year	GRT	DWT	Loa	Bm	Draft	Kts	Type	Former names
Jessica	Fin	1976	703	1,180	60.1	9.6	3.2	10	C	ex Tiger-97, Aurora-H-96, Cawi-93, Skimmer-92, Union Emerald-89, Elan-82

Baltic Shipping GmbH, Germany

Name	Flag	Year	GRT	DWT	Loa	Bm	Draft	Kts	Type	Former names
Franko	Deu	1965	342	480	48.0	7.2	2.5	11	C	(len/deep-78)

Baltic Tramping Co., Germany

Name	Flag	Year	GRT	DWT	Loa	Bm	Draft	Kts	Type	Former names
Claudia A	Vct	1977	721	1,010	60.0	9.5	3.2	10	C	ex Marlin I-98, Skua-92, Union Gem-89
Elvi Kull	Atg	1955	474	730	57.9	8.1	2.9	8	C	ex Jens Peter-84, Reinhold Krusemark-62 (len-58 & 78)

Name	Flag	Year	GRT	DWT	Loa	Bm	Draft	Kts	Type	Former names

Baltramp Shipping Ltd., Poland
Ruciane	Pol	1972	807	1,057	59.6	10.2	4.2	11	C	

Barents Management AS, Norway
Barenso (2)	Nis	1969	1,630	1,020	71.6	11.5	3.6	12	Cc	ex Morejarl-96
Lynx	Nor	1975	1,954	1,200	76.0	13.5	3.4	13	Ccp	ex Askja-92, Lynx-82

Bernd Bartels   Germany
Gracechurch Crown	Atg	1991	3,815	4,665	103.6	16.2	6.1	14	Cc	ex Zenit-91

Bas Shipping KS, Norway
Bas	Nor	1966	299	912	54.3	9.6	3.3	11	C	ex Soren Fridolf-84

BD Shipsnavo GmbH, Germany
Maria D	Deu	1986	2,370	2,760	87.8	12.9	4.5	11	Cc	

Owned by Bernard Dopp Schiffahrts KG.

Beaudeau International, Netherlands
Rim	Mlt	1973	3,493	4,800	106.1	14.8	7.1	14	C	ex Rimnicu Vilcea-98
Save	Mlt	1978	3,493	4,795	106.1	14.8	7.1	14	C	ex Saveni-98

Bernd Becker KG, Germany
Jacob Becker	Deu	1995	3,999	5,315	101.1	18.5	6.6	15	Cc	ex UB Tiger-97, Jacob Becker-95
Otto Becker	Deu	1989	2,749	3,144	94.5	16.1	5.0	14	Cc	

Heino Behmann, Germany
Heinrich Behrmann	Deu	1975	2,240	2,560	81.4	13.8	5.0	13	C	ex Bourgogne-89, Komet I-78, Saracen Prince-76, I/a Komet

J. Bekkers Co. BV, Netherlands
Falcon Chemist	Lbr	1977	4,486	6,810	115.2	16.5	7.1	13	Tch	ex Allied Chemist-95

F. H. Bertling Reederei GmbH, Germany
KML Carus	Bhs	1969	948	1,147	71.2	9.3	3.5	11	C	ex Rafto-98 (len-76)

Friedrich Beutelrock GmbH & Co. KG, Germany
Carolin	Cyp	1981	3,593	4,153	99.9	15.8	5.1	12	Cc	ex Njord-92, Manchester Prince-89, Njord-86, City of Oporto-85, Njord-81

Heinrich Beutler KG, Germany
Cementina	Hnd	1960	900	1,205	64.1	10.9	4.2	12	Ceu	ex Cemking-99, Kabedi-91, Curlew-90, Halliburton 602-88, Cementine-78

Bibutank SA, Belgium
Inno	Lux	1973	1,811	3,150	110.0	11.4	2.8	12	T	ex Inez-89

Bjal A/S, Denmark
Bjal Senior	Dis	1977	1,275	2,140	72.2	10.4	4.8	11	C	ex Eva Bres-98 (len-81)

Bjare Shipping HB, Sweden
Meonia	Cyp	1972	2,756	4,954	87.0	13.1	6.8	11	Cc	ex Eos-82

Bjerrum & Jensen ApS, Denmark
Lars Bagger	Dis	1957	326	469	44.9	8.3	2.9	9	C	ex Ulsnaes-89, Welf-??
Taladi	Dis	1971	1,106	1,250	64.6	11.0	3.6	12	C	ex Sonja Hove-93, Stevnsland-83, Mor-Sines-76, Ruth Klint-72

Klaus & Willem Blanck, Germany
Beta	Deu	1967	1,064	1,190	68.4	10.6	4.0	11	C	ex Betty-97, Rolf-85
Hela	Deu	1966	861	1,065	61.8	10.0	4.0	10	C	ex Lore-93, Wotan-91

Dieter Blanke, Germany

Warfleth	Atg	1980	1,022	1,092	74.0	9.5	2.9	10	C	

John Henry Bollhorst, Germany

Stadt Wangen	Atg	1964	934	1,470	61.6	10.8	4.5	11	C	ex Sebastian-87, Steinburg-85, Nordlicht II-76

Egon Blohm KG, Germany

Atula	Tuv	1986	2,006	2,723	81.9	12.7	4.5	11	Cc	ex RMS Mercator-96, Atula-94

BM Shipping Co., Russia

Volgo-Balt 171 (2)	Rus	1973	2,457	3,288	114.0	13.2	3.6	11	C	

Aug. Bolten Wm. Miller's Nachfolger GmbH & Co., Germany

Artemis I	Cyp	1972	4,255	6,341	101.4	16.0	7.2	13	Bc	ex Artemis-82, Susan Miller-78 (len/rblt-91)
Condock V * (2)	Deu	1984	6,763	4,762	106.0	19.6	5.0	13	Cc/bg	ex Submerger I-93, Este Submerger I-92

Brandaris Bedeederungs. GmbH, Germany

Brandaris	Deu	1985	2,007	2,460	78.4	13.0	4.5	10	Cc	

Brattli Shipping, Norway

Gevostar	Nor	1969	1,088	1,458	72.7	11.5	3.5	12	T	
Glennstar	Nor	1968	872	1,516	64.5	10.4	4.4	11	Tch	ex Fjordtank-97, Bitank-94, Titan-93
Havtank	Nor	1969	1,083	1,341	69.5	10.8	3.7	11	T	ex Havstraum-90, Amalienborg-74
Polartank	Bhs	1969	1,084	1,774	69.5	11.6	5.0	11	Tch	ex Bergen Faith-97, Dutch Faith-96

Henry Breuer KG, Germany

Alk *	Deu	1998	6,362	7,223	121.4	18.5	6.7	16	CC	
Paula	Deu	1985	2,590	3,053	88.0	12.8	5.3	11	Cc	

* owned by Jan Breuer.

Horst Brey, Germany

Jutta-B	Deu	1965	637	580	55.9	8.8	3.1	9	C	ex Hendrik-87, Doris-78, Gebina-70 (len-74)
Uwe Ursula	Deu	1935	198	335	37.9	7.0	2.7	8	C	

Briggs Marine Environmental Services Ltd., UK

British Shield	Gbr	1979	2,804	3,659	97.9	13.7	5.8	13	Tpr	ex Oscona-97, Seneca-95 (conv Tch-97)

Brinkman Marine Services BV, Netherlands

Alliance	Cyp	1979	1,094	1,551	65.8	10.8	4.3	11	C	ex Galliard-94, Alliance-87
Hugo	Cyp	1978	1,094	1,577	65.8	10.8	4.3	11	C	ex Hugo Brinkman-87
Paulina B	Cyp	1975	1,096	1,589	65.8	10.8	4.3	-	C	ex Paulina Brinkman-87

Britannia Aggregates Ltd., UK

Britannia Beaver	Gbr	1991	3,610	5,786	100.0	17.7	6.2	12	Dss	

Brovigs Rederi AS, Norway

Ketty Brovig	Nis	1984	3,329	4,115	98.7	15.5	5.4	14	C	ex Rockabill-98, Hasselwerder-94, Gracechurch Crown-90, Hasselwerder-94, City of Mancherster-85, Hasselwerder-84 (len-89)
Cis Brovig	Nis	1985	3,329	4,496	98.7	15.7	5.7	14	Cc	ex Gisela Bartels-96, Gracechurch Harp-89, I/a Gisela Bartels (len-86)

Name	Flag	Year	GRT	DWT	Loa	Bm	Draft	Kts	Type	Former names
P&O Nedlloyd Pemba	Nis	1984	5,998	7,950	127.5	20.4	6.6	15	CC	ex Emirate Star-99, Dea Brovig-98, Uwa Bhum-97, Eagle Star-95, Vanellus-89, Seas Plata-88, Vanellus-87, EA Challenge-87, Vanellus-85

Christian Hinrich Brunckhorst, Germany

Name	Flag	Year	GRT	DWT	Loa	Bm	Draft	Kts	Type	Former names
Schulau	Atg	1978	1,678	1,964	72.3	12.8	4.5	12	Cc	

Reedereiverwaltung Wilfried Buck, Germany

Name	Flag	Year	GRT	DWT	Loa	Bm	Draft	Kts	Type	Former names
Laila	Atg	1983	2,837	2,352	91.0	13.5	4.5	10	Ro	
Linda Buck	Cyp	1985	2,295	2,584	95.9	14.2	4.1	10	Ro	ex Britannia-96, RMS Britannia-93, Linda Buck-93
Rolf Buck	Cyp	1985	2,295	2,591	95.9	14.2	4.1	10	Cc/Ro	

Bulk Ships Ltd., Channel Islands (UK)

Name	Flag	Year	GRT	DWT	Loa	Bm	Draft	Kts	Type	Former names
Meteor	Blz	1969	3,077	4,313	103.0	14.6	5.8	12	C	ex Ikaria-95, Nubia-94, Meteor-91, Bengate-77, Jenka-74

Bulkfrakt AS, Norway

Name	Flag	Year	GRT	DWT	Loa	Bm	Draft	Kts	Type	Former names
Ringfjell	Vct	1971	872	1,340	60.8	9.5	4.3	8	C	ex Ringhav-96, Wilko-95, Clasina-89, Ramsland-87, Bebko-85

Bullas Tankcraft Co. Ltd., UK

Name	Flag	Year	GRT	DWT	Loa	Bm	Draft	Kts	Type	Former names
Medway Trader (2)	Gbr	1977	496	1,000	42.5	9.9	4.1	10	C	ex Mersey Trader-89
Rapid II	Gbr	1971	801	1,392	69.4	9.0	3.0	11	T	ex Celtic 4-94, Oiltrans 31-81
Thames Rapid	Gbr	1974	589	670	58.9	10.3	2.6	-	T	ex Rapid-86, BP Rapid-86, Sheppey-76
Tidal Trader (2)	Gbr	1977	492	800	42.5	10.0	3.6	9	C	ex Irwell Trader-89

Hendrik Buma, Netherlands

Name	Flag	Year	GRT	DWT	Loa	Bm	Draft	Kts	Type	Former names
Robeta	Nld	1985	1,372	1,570	75.1	10.8	3.8	11	C	ex Beta-98

Carl Buttner Gmbh & Co., Germany

Name	Flag	Year	GRT	DWT	Loa	Bm	Draft	Kts	Type	Former names
Hai *	Deu	1981	2,025	3,150	86.7	12.5	5.8	12	T	
Stor	Deu	1982	2,510	4,040	89.1	15.0	5.6	11	Tch	

* managed by German Tanker Shipping GmbH & Co. KG.

Capelle Chartereing en Trading BV, Netherlands

Name	Flag	Year	GRT	DWT	Loa	Bm	Draft	Kts	Type	Former names
Blue Moon	Cyp	1975	1,010	1,559	65.8	10.8	4.3	11	C	ex Elina-97, Elina B-90, Elisabeth Holwerda-87
Irene	Cyp	1978	1,010	1,548	65.8	11.1	4.3	12	C	ex Pien Tulip-93, Azolla-93
Wijmers	Cyp	1984	3,259	5,050	91.9	15.1	6.5	14	C	ex Alecto-97, Clarissa-94 (len-92)

Cebo Marine BV, Netherlands

Name	Flag	Year	GRT	DWT	Loa	Bm	Draft	Kts	Type	Former names
Caravelle	Nld	1972	999	1,270	70.6	10.4	3.5	12	Ce	ex Geeststroom-76 (conv C-??)
Carine	Nld	1969	999	1,280	70.6	10.4	4.0	12	Ce	ex Bart-83, Garza-82, Geestduin-76 (conv C-??)
Noblesse C	Nld	1980	1,095	1,637	66.1	11.4	4.4	12	C	ex Noblesse-98

Cementa A/B, Sweden

Name	Flag	Year	GRT	DWT	Loa	Bm	Draft	Kts	Type	Former names
Ostanvik	Swe	1974	4,013	4,940	107.1	16.1	6.0	14	Ce	
Sunnanvik	Swe	1978	7,454	9,060	124.0	18.0	7.7	14	Ce	
Vastanvik	Swe	1966	2,256	3,282	90.5	13.0	5.8	-	Ce	

Charterfrakt, Sweden

Name	Flag	Year	GRT	DWT	Loa	Bm	Draft	Kts	Type	Former names
Baltic Bright	Swe	1996	9,708	6,300	134.4	20.5	5.7	15	Ro	

Jorgen Christensen, Denmark

Name	Flag	Year	GRT	DWT	Loa	Bm	Draft	Kts	Type	Former names
Gert Hansen	Dis	1955	300	483	41.8	8.2	3.1	9	C	ex Trabant-71, Nanna-64
Susanna	Mlt	1977	1,982	3,050	80.7	14.3	5.1	12	C	ex Christina-93, Hubert-89, Gardazee-86, Susanna-83

Owned by subsidiary O. K. Shipping I/S

Name	Flag	Year	GRT	DWT	Loa	Bm	Draft	Kts	Type	Former names

P. F. Cleemann Shipping ApS, Denmark
| Lille-Tanja | Dis | 1963 | 363 | 470 | 45.3 | 8.3 | 3.3 | 10 | C | ex Mimi Hansen-81, Anne Vesta-64 |

Cross Shipping A/S, Norway
| Cross Coast | Nor | 1983 | 818 | 930 | 54.9 | 9.6 | 3.4 | - | C | ex Maria-98 |

Colchester Dock Transit Co. Ltd., UK
| Hein | Bhs | 1971 | 1,241 | 1,049 | 72.9 | 11.0 | 3.1 | 11 | Cc | ex Inge Meyn-95, Gerda Freese-83, Magula-79 |

Colstar Ltd., UK
| Humber Dawn (2) | Gbr | 1967 | 291 | 400 | 45.7 | 7.5 | 2.1 | 7 | T | ex Druid Stone-77 (len-77) |

Compagnie Nationale de Navigation, France
| Ariana (2) | Atf | 1988 | 7,876 | 7,190 | 115.2 | 19.4 | 7.3 | 15 | Ro | |
| Beaulieu | Fra | 1983 | 3,081 | 4,800 | 89.9 | 15.8 | 6.6 | 13 | Cn | ex EWL Paramaribo-90, Uilenspiegel-88 (conv Cc-96) |

Consolidated Pool Carriers GmbH, Germany
| Love Letter | Atg | 1987 | 6,500 | 8,914 | 114.9 | 20.5 | 8.1 | 15 | Cc | ex Gallia-97, CPC Gallia-95, Conti Gallia-87 |
| Love Song | Atg | 1986 | 5,400 | 8,914 | 114.9 | 20.5 | 8.1 | 14 | Cc | ex Nippon-97, CPC Nippon-96, Conti Nippon-87 |

D. Cook Ltd., UK
| Daystream | Gbr | 1965 | 422 | 691 | 55.6 | 8.4 | 3.1 | 10 | T | ex Whitonia-82, Axel-70 |
| Onward Pioneer | Gbr | 1955 | 164 | 250 | 37.1 | 5.8 | 2.0 | 8 | T | |

Also operates hopper/dredgers.

Cuxhavener Mineralot GmbH und Co. Bedeiligungs KG, Germany
| Heide | Deu | 1986 | 672 | 1,100 | 58.0 | 10.0 | 3.1 | 10 | Tch | |

D.L.S. Shipping AB, Sweden
Tri Box	Cyp	1973	2,669	3,786	84.3	14.4	6.3	13	C	ex Louise-92, Louise Smits-84, Tobias Lonborg-77
Caytrans Dolphin	Cyp	1992	2,598	3,114	86.0	14.5	5.6	13	Cc	ex Caytrans Dolphin-98, Asaka-97, Tashkent-95
Daisy	Cyp	1992	2,598	3,114	86.0	14.5	5.6	13	Cc	ex Caytrans Gator-98, Leoni-97, Ashkhabad-95

Dalmulder & Van Dijk BV, Netherlands
Avon 1	Vct	1971	2,643	4,471	90.1	15.5	5.7	13	Tch	ex Orion-97, Massira-95, Olanda-76, Kristian Ravn-71
Tamar	Vct	1973	4,315	6,720	113.1	16.7	7.4	14	Tch	ex Arctic Star-97, Arctic Tar-95, Al Khlood-90, Silverpelerin-80
Trent	Vct	1970	604	1,142	62.5	9.5	3.6	11	T	ex Anne H-97, Biene-90

Dalriada Shipping Ltd., UK
| Bure | Pan | 1969 | 347 | 610 | 44.4 | 7.9 | 3.2 | 9 | C | ex Cadence-85 |

Dannebrog Rederi AS, Denmark
Dansborg	Dis	1990	4,173	7,580	109.5	16.4	8.1	14	Tch	ex Ist-91 (launched 1977)
Schackenborg	Dis	1979	12,076	8,002	135.0	24.3	6.7	15	Ro	ex Dana Cariba-84
Skanderborg	Dis	1979	12,076	8,002	135.0	24.3	6.7	15	Ro	ex Dana Arabia-84
Skodsborg	Dis	1979	12,076	8,002	135.0	24.3	6.7	15	Ro	ex Dana Africa-84

H. H. Danship A/S, Denmark
Kis Sobye	Dis	1982	1,760	1,650	80.6	12.0	3.6	10	C	ex Poul Sobye-88, Kis Sobye-87, Kirsten Sobye-85 (len-85)
Pax	Dis	1981	1,499	1,773	82.5	11.4	3.5	10	Cc	
Pernille W	Dis	1982	1,499	1,721	82.5	11.4	3.5	10	Cc	ex Pionier-89

F Dede KG, Germany
| Gracechurch Harp | Atg | 1991 | 3,815 | 4,659 | 103.5 | 16.0 | 6.1 | 14 | Cc | ex Sven Dede-91 |
| Inka Dede | Atg | 1992 | 5,006 | 6,580 | 116.7 | 18.2 | 6.9 | 16 | Cc | ex Armada Sprinter-96, Inka Dede-?? |

186

Name	Flag	Year	GRT	DWT	Loa	Bm	Draft	Kts	Type	Former names

A. O. Delac Shipping Co., Russia

Name	Flag	Year	GRT	DWT	Loa	Bm	Draft	Kts	Type	Former names
Laura I	Hnd	1972	1,160	1,120	71.1	10.3	3.7	11	C	ex Solar Bay-97, Purtse-94, Gleb Sedin-91

Delom SA, France

| Cap Afrique | Atf | 1978 | 1,583 | 2,401 | 108.6 | 16.0 | 5.0 | 17 | Ro | ex Saint Charles-90, Catherine Schiaffino-89 |
| Cap Canaille (2) | Atf | 1977 | 1,576 | 2,743 | 109.8 | 17.5 | 5.2 | 16 | Ro | ex Libeccio-92, Seafowl-92, Gyptis-87, Cap Lardier-83 |

Delta Shipping & Trading BV BA, Belgium

| Ulla | Cyp | 1981 | 2,704 | 2,700 | 77.3 | 15.0 | 5.9 | 13 | C | ex Magnus S-92, Ringvoll-88, Namdalingen-84 |

Denval Marine Consultants Ltd., UK

| Roseanne (2) | Cyp | 1982 | 7,744 | 4,106 | 112.8 | 18.7 | 6.4 | 14 | Ro | ex Faroy-89, Reina del Cantabrico-87, Salah Labiad-85, Reina del Cantabrico-83 |

Halfdan Ditlev-Simonsen & Co Management A/S, Norway

| Annamaria (2) | Nis | 1975 | 4,280 | 6,599 | 111.5 | 16.7 | 7.0 | 14 | Tch | ex Tol Sailer-97, Lucor Wickliffe-91, Delchim Cevennes-78 |
| Tol Runner | Pan | 1976 | 5,054 | 8,041 | 125.2 | 17.0 | 7.3 | 15 | Tch | ex Chemtrans Sirius-86 (len-87) |

Donauexpress Schiffahrt GmbH, Germany

| Donau Express | Khm | 1966 | 795 | 840 | 63.7 | 9.5 | 2.9 | 11 | C | ex Este-92, Claus Jurgens-80, Realta-73 (len-67) |

Rainer Fred August Drevin, Germany

| OOCL Neva | Deu | 1995 | 6,326 | 7,946 | 129.8 | 20.0 | 7.3 | 17 | CC | ex Nova-99, Norasia Adria-97, Nova-96 |

Hans-Peter Eckhoff, Germany

Kamilla	Atg	1985	2,740	2,785	98.3	13.6	4.3	11	Cc	
Lever (gt)	Atg	1971	2,488	3,598	90.8	13.9	6.2	15	Cc	ex Dever-98, Karat II-97, Europe-94, Naftilos-93, Ville d'Aurore-92, Baracuda-91, Deichland-87, Bomberg-83, Roxane Kersten-80, Bomberg-77
Lys Carrier	Atg	1994	2,446	3,726	87.9	12.9	5.2	12	Cc	ex Nunki-94

Ecomar Schiffahrts GmbH, Germany

| Lys-Chris * | Atg | 1993 | 2,416 | 3,582 | 85.0 | 13.0 | 4.5 | 12 | Cc | ex Marie Chris-93 |
| Southern Queen | Atg | 1979 | 2,481 | 3,932 | 86.2 | 14.0 | 4.9 | 13 | Cc | ex Rangikura-97, Northern Transporter-93, Tim Thielemann-91, Universal Carrier-90, Tim Thielemann-89, Christa Thielemann-85 |

* Owned by Johann Schepers, Germany.

Heinz Ehler KG, Germany

| Katharina Ehler | Deu | 1993 | 3,992 | 5,335 | 100.0 | 18.4 | 6.6 | 15 | Cc | |
| Monika Ehler | Deu | 1996 | 6,362 | 6,750 | 121.4 | 18.5 | 6.7 | 16 | CC | |

Bernt Eide, Norway

| Rignator | Nor | 1968 | 769 | 839 | 55.3 | 10.5 | 3.1 | 11 | C | ex Askita-86, Bjerkosund-78, Grete Sleire-74, Hamlet-74 |

Oddvar & Einar Eidshaug Rederi A/S, Norway

Sveanord	Nor	1976	783	1,068	59.7	10.3	3.9	12	C	ex Nordnes-96, Finnport I-94, Andramari-93
Sveafjord	Nor	1972	1,599	1,584	76.0	11.8	3.9	11	Cc	ex Edith Sabban-88
Sveatind	Nor	1975	707	847	57.6	9.3	3.4	11	C	ex Kalve-85, Sundstad-83

Name	Flag	Year	GRT	DWT	Loa	Bm	Draft	Kts	Type	Former names

Einarsen Shipping AS, Norway
Mercator	Nis	1971	1,359	1,370	76.3	11.9	3.9	13	Cc	ex Lautonia-89, Heinrich Knuppel-85

Ektank AB, Sweden
Ek-Cloud	Swe	1976	5,788	9,722	134.6	17.2	7.9	14	Tch	ex Lotos-83, Joaker-77
Ekfors	Iom	1974	5,529	9,927	126.8	17.2	7.9	13	Tch	(len-81)

Eilbrecht & Janssen KG, Germany
Jan-Willem	Atg	1986	1,525	1,505	74.3	12.5	3.3	10	Cc	
Elke	Atg	1984	1,299	1,537	74.9	10.6	3.2	10	C	ex Mareike B-94, Sea Tagus-91, Webo-Carrier-88, Mareike B-86

Elmar A/S, Norway
Storfosna	Bhs	1966	818	864	58.5	10.0	4.5	11	C	ex Lovima-77, Lysholmen-73
Tanto	Bhs	1960	1,003	1,021	64.9	10.5	3.9	12	C	

Kjell N Engen, Norway
Gelo	Nis	1972	932	918	57.9	10.4	4.1	12	C	ex Torgelow-92

Dag Engstrom Rederi A/B, Sweden
Rodona (2)	Swe	1980	6,568	3,085	136.1	16.5	4.7	14	Ro	ex Balder Dona-84 (len-82)
Sapphire (2)	Swe	1980	6,568	4,538	136.1	16.5	4.7	14	Ro	ex Azua-87, Rovinga-84, Balder Vinga-84 (len-82)

AS Enkounet, Estonia
Ontika (2)	Est	1965	1,995	2,121	96.0	13.2	3.3	10	C	ex Baltiyskiy-42-98

E. P. Shipping & Trading BV, Netherlands
Germa	Cyp	1978	906	1,485	63.0	10.0	3.8	11	C	ex Edgerma-94
Ilse	Nld	1975	1,547	2,723	73.4	11.8	5.5	14	C	ex Sian-97, Irina-91, Coenraad Kuhlman-86
Paphos	Nld	1992	1,999	3,186	81.2	12.4	5.2	-	Cc	

Erka Shipping GmbH, Germany
Sinar Bandung	Cyp	1979	4,012	4,352	104.2	16.8	5.7	14	CC	ex Erka Sun-98, City of Lisbon-88, City of Perth-85
MCC Vantage (2)	Cyp	1976	5,400	7,169	120.0	20.4	6.0	16	CC	ex Dragon Nias-96, Erka Oriental-95, Tiger Star-94, Dilos-92, Prince-89, BCR Prince-86, Black Prince-85, Imstar-83

Eugesta Co. Ltd., Lithuania
Allora	Hnd	1964	517	549	47.9	8.3	3.3	10	C	ex Brufjord-95, Arctic Trader-92, Seco-92, Tove Kristin-89, Sun West-87, Elsa F-84

Euro-Baltic Shipping Services, Estonia
Baltic (2)	Est	1963	1,865	2,121	95.6	13.2	3.3	11	C	ex Baltiyskiy-13-97

Euroship A/S, Norway
Euro Bulk	Nis	1979	1,016	1,452	72.3	11.3	3.3	10	C	ex Quiescence-98
Eurotrans	Nis	1979	1,016	1,452	72.5	11.3	3.3	10	C	ex Piquence-98

F & R Shipping A/S, Norway
Saturn	Nis	1970	782	864	55.3	10.5	3.3	11	C	ex Fjordhav-88, Anders Kjonno-84, Grethe Steen-75, Gulf Navigator-72, Grethe Steen-71

Falmouth Oil Services Ltd., UK
Falmouth Endeavour	Gbr	1972	754	1,276	62.7	9.8	4.2	11	T	ex Marwah II-87
Falmouth Enterprise	Gbr	1972	1,287	2,189	76.0	11.2	5.1	11	T	ex Brady Maria-87, Hama Maru No.5-84

Name	Flag	Year	GRT	DWT	Loa	Bm	Draft	Kts	Type	Former names

Farsund Bulk Line AS, Norway
Tri-Sky	Nis	1965	931	1,068	61.2	10.6	3.9	11	C	ex Tranevaag-91, Tjaerevaag-91, Mathilde-85

Faversham Ships Ltd., UK
Celebrity	Gbr	1976	633	946	57.6	10.0	3.3	10	C	
Conformity	Gbr	1975	599	880	56.1	9.9	3.2	11	C	

Fenix Schiffahrts. GmbH, Germany
Fenix	Atg	1965	1,039	1,145	66.2	10.6	3.3	11	C	ex Stadt Bremen-98, Schonau-94, Paul-85

Fern Trading Ltd., Eire
Eastfern	Irl	1981	1,171	1,644	70.6	10.8	4.2	11	C	ex Arklow Abbey-96

F-G Shipping Oy Ab, Finland
Bore Sea **	Fin	1990	5,873	4,234	108.4	17.5	5.8	15	Rop	
Finnbeaver **	Fin	1991	5,972	4,690	114.4	18.0	6.2	16	Rop	ex Ann-Mari-97
Finnoak	Fin	1991	6,620	5,399	122.0	19.0	6.2	16	Rop	ex Ahtela-97
Finnpine	Fin	1984	8,996	7,669	120.2	21.0	6.7	-	Rop	ex Solano-94
Kemira	Fin	1981	5,582	8,250	112.7	17.5	8.2	14	C/Tch	
Pamela * (2)	Fin	1978	585	1,056	45.9	10.0	3.9	9	C	ex Pamela C-95, Alice PG-91

*owned by subsidiary VG-Shipping Oy, Finland or ** owned by Oy Rettig AB Bore, Finland.

Field Shipping & Chartering BV, Netherlands
Rulewave Warrior	Bhs	1978	1,473	1,426	84.9	9.5	3.3	10	Cc	ex Topaz-95, Aramon-94, Markab-86

Managed by Field Ship Management Services Ltd., UK.

Uwe Fischer K.G., Germany
Andrina F	Atg	1990	1,568	1,890	81.2	11.3	3.7	9	Cc	ex Simone-92
Petra F	Atg	1985	1,567	1,976	81.2	11.5	3.7	9	Cc	

Fisker & Bom, Denmark
Poseidon	Dis	1970	1,083	1,042	65.1	11.0	3.7	11	C	ex Santoni-87, Ida Bres-79, Nore-74, Ida Bres-72

Fjordglimt Invest AS, Norway
Vestland	Nor	1984	1,023	1,330	67.2	10.8	3.8	11	C	ex Sevald-95, Barbanza-94

John Fleming Construction Ltd., Eire
Romeo	Cyp	1983	1,908	3,152	81.6	14.1	5.4	12	C	ex Andromeda-93

Foka-Gas N.V., Belgium
Brigitte Gas	Nld	1998	1,200	-	-	-	-	-	Lpg	

Flensburger Schiffsparten-Vereinigung AG, Germany
Saturn	Lbr	1980	5,938	7,958	126.3	20.1	6.6	15	CC	ex Monagas-99, Saturn-98, FAS Trieste-96, EWL Rotterdam-96, Saturn-95, Zim Caribe III-94, Gothia-91, Medipas Sky-88, Nicolo Gazzolo-88, Gothia-87, Jumna Pioneer-86, Gothia-85, Concorde Antilles-85, CCNI Andino-84, Gothia-82, European Eagle-80, Gothia-80

Owned by subsidiary Baltic Bereederung GmbH & Co. KG.

Svend Flyvbjerg, Denmark
Anne Sofie	Dis	1972	823	941	60.7	9.5	3.8	11	C	ex Bremer Roland-84
Saxo *	Dis	1984	1,566	1,717	82.5	11.4	3.7	10	Cc	ex Poseidon-98
Spica	Dis	1988	1,167	1,210	67.4	11.4	3.5	11	Cc	ex Fortuna Coast-95

*managed bu O.K. Shipping.

Name	Flag	Year	GRT	DWT	Loa	Bm	Draft	Kts	Type	Former names

Fonnship A/S, Norway
Sava Star	Pan	1992	2,026	3,080	74.7	12.7	6.0	12	Cc	

Foroohari Schiffahrts KG, Germany
Melfi Panama	Atg	1985	3,120	3,635	88.6	15.7	6.0	13	Cc	ex Manzur-98, Frontier Colombia-97, Esperanza-97, Manafoss-92, Esperanza-88

P/F Skipafelagia Foroyar, Faeroes
Blikur	Fro	1979	2,854	1,460	88.8	14.5	4.5	12	Ccp	
Lomur	Fro	1978	2,854	1,450	88.8	14.5	4.5	14	Ccp	

A/S Frakt, Norway
Myraas	Nor	1985	1,208	1,119	63.0	11.5	3.4	10	Cc	ex Alko-96
Myrtind	Nor	1971	1,323	1,808	70.8	11.1	4.5	11	C	ex Ina-93, Sanna-93, Inger-88, Sanna-87, Teka-85

France Euro Tramp SA, France
Fret Aquitaine	Atf	1984	4,292	4,515	102.5	17.6	5.5	13	Cc	ex Cygne-97, Arklow Rose-90, Faroe Trader-87
Fret Languedoc	Atf	1987	5,755	7,443	107.5	19.3	7.9	14	Cchl	ex Sea Tiger-97, Svenja-96, Jumbo Britania-92, Conti Britania-92, Elbstrom-89, Kestrel-88, Elbestrom-87
Fret Sologne	Atf	1987	5,476	7,765	107.5	19.3	7.9	13	Cc	ex Sea Lion-97, Regine-95

Asmund Rune Fredheim, Norway
Heimglimt	Nor	1966	933	1,228	70.4	9.3	3.5	10	C	ex Bergstraum-93, Reitan-74 (len-79)

Reederei Eugen Friederich Bereederungs-und-Befrachtungs GmbH, Germany
Mercs Kirinda	Lka	1966	1,932	2,501	82.5	13.0	5.3	13	C	ex Latania-98, Litania-85

Friis & Frederiksen Shipping APS, Denmark
New Wave	Hnd	1966	829	1,050	66.5	9.4	3.3	10	C	ex Greif-96, Katinka-92, Liv-Kristin-92, Nixe-91, Nadir I-89, Christa Thielemann-79 (len-73)

Peter & Gretel Funk, Germany
Anja Funk	Atg	1964	530	560	47.8	8.8	3.1	9	C	ex Theresia M-80, Ilona-73

Gallic Shipping Ltd., UK
Leszek G *	Pol	1977	1,991	3,285	91.5	13.3	5.2	12	Cc	ex Leslie Gault-92

* managed by Seascot Shipmanagement Ltd.

Hans Otto Gadermann, Germany
Mika	Cyp	1971	1,895	2,366	78.0	12.8	5.5	12	C	ex Luna-92, Lona-88, Janica-88, Euro Freighter-87, Maria Graebe-83, Kungsbron-73, I/a Maria Graebe

Garant Ship Repairing Co., Lithuania
Volgo-Balt 118 (2)	Rus	1970	2,457	2,907	114.0	13.2	3.5	10	C	

Gdanskie Przedsiebiorstwo Obrotu Produktami Naftowymi, Poland
Palica	Pol	1977	999	1,345					T	
Romanka	Pol	1982	997	1,430	64.9	10.4	4.7	12	T	

Gearbulk Shipping Ltd., Norway
Rathboyne	Nis	1997	4,406	6,649	113.4	15.8	6.7	14	Ta	
Rathrowan	Irl	1991	2,920	4,059	96.0	14.5	5.9	12	Tab	

Managed by Kristian Gerhard Jebsen Skipsrederi A/S, Norway.

Gefonzo BV, Netherlands
Pride of Braila (2)	Nld	1998	2,077	3,200	110.0	11.4	3.6	13	Cc	
Pride of Veere (2)	Nld	1998	2,034	3,200	110.0	11.4	3.6	13	Cc	

Name	Flag	Year	GRT	DWT	Loa	Bm	Draft	Kts	Type	Former names
Genchem Marine Ltd., UK										
Brendonian	Gbr	1966	587	837	54.0	9.1	3.6	10	C	ex Brendonia-84
Ellen W	Vct	1974	459	645	47.8	8.8	3.1	9	C	ex Guy Chipperfield-82
Nautic W	Vct	1971	470	646	49.4	8.8	3.1	9	C	ex Roy Clemo-86, Commodore Trader-81
Tia	Blz	1964	486	750	50.3	8.8	3.5	-	C	ex Elmham-92, Pekari-89, Trostan-81, Northgate-79
Tora	Vct	1969	478	713	53.1	8.8	3.3	10	C	ex Domba-88, Hoomoss-87, Kosmos-79, Apollo II-70
Henry Gerdau KG GmbH & Co., Germany										
Komet III	Deu	1991	4,169	4,752	111.1	16.1	6.0	15	Cc	ex Portugal Bridge-97, Komet III-96, Gracechurch Comet-96, Komet III-91
Ole	Deu	1977	3,694	4,418	98.7	16.1	5.7	14	Cc	ex Maersk Euro Decimo-94, Maersk Turbo-91, Pegasus-88, Planet I-85, Ville du Levant-83, Planet-79
Planet V	Deu	1994	4,984	7,014	116.4	19.5	7.1	16	Cc	ex Gracechurch Planet-97, Planet V-96
Gerdes Schiffahrts. GmbH & Co. KG, Germany										
Ajos G	Deu	1996	2,061	3,000	88.5	11.4	5.0	10	Cc	
Gerhein	Atg	1988	910	1,085	69.1	9.5	3.0	9	Cc	ex Karina G-98, Sea Douro-96, l/a Leda
Pia	Deu	1987	2,236	2,850	82.3	12.6	4.9	11	Cc	
Joint Stock Co. Gertron, Estonia										
Kagu	Est	1977	1,596	2,824	63.7	12.5	6.6	12	C	ex Anna Kern-98, Anna Drent-93, Frendo Dansea-77, l/a Frendo North
H Geurts, Netherlands										
Elfenmeer	Nld	1962	345	550	52.5	7.2	2.5	8	C	ex Bonheur-83, Jans-80, Christian-73
Hans-Peter Gewandt, Germany										
Ingrid	Cyp	1990	1,960	2,803	89.3	12.5	4.3	10	Cc	
Gillie & Blair Ltd., UK										
River Dart	Gbr	1981	536	825	50.0	9.3	3.4	10	C	
Sverre Gjerde, Norway										
Berghav	Mlt	1971	1,432	1,610	76.9	11.9	3.6	11	Cc	ex Christina-85
Glusing Transport GmbH, Germany										
Merle	Deu	1980	510	593	49.8	9.2	2.9	10	T	
D. J. Goubert Shipping Ltd., UK										
Candourity	Gbr	1975	559	880	56.1	9.9	3.2	10	C	
Horst Gunter Gobel, Germany										
Scotland	Atg	1974	1,888	2,340	76.7	13.2	5.2	13	Cc	ex Hornburg-95, Husum-85
Virgo	Atg	1978	2,361	2,369	86.5	13.0	4.9	13	Cc	ex Lys-Bris-98, Virgo-89
Granstrom Identek Rederi AB, Sweden										
Seinehaven	Atg	1970	2,445	2,510	88.5	13.9	5.3	14	Cc	ex Oued Ziz-92, Taurus II-90, Traveway Express-89, Nattco Carara-85, Taurus II-84, Taurus-84, Widukind-83, Zim Constanza-82, Widukind-81

Name	Flag	Year	GRT	DWT	Loa	Bm	Draft	Kts	Type	Former names

Gravvik Sjotransport A/S, Norway

Name	Flag	Year	GRT	DWT	Loa	Bm	Draft	Kts	Type	Former names
Gullhav	Nor	1973	853	1,120	60.7	9.5	3.5	10	C	ex Unlis-96, Uniwind-90, Thunbox 1-85, Viking Ole-79
Gullholm	Nor	1973	907	950	55.6	11.0	3.8	10	C	ex Lena-95, Vestland-89, Trans Oy-89 (len-79)

Greill Reederei und Befrachtung GmbH, Germany

Name	Flag	Year	GRT	DWT	Loa	Bm	Draft	Kts	Type	Former names
Anna-Lina	Deu	1997	5,730	6,870	121.9	19.0	6.9	17	CC	ex Lauritzen Peru-99, Anna-Lina-98, I/a Greil

Rederi AB Gronqvist, Finland

Name	Flag	Year	GRT	DWT	Loa	Bm	Draft	Kts	Type	Former names
Casandra	Fin	1970	1,197	1,900	74.0	10.9	5.-58	12	Cc	ex Anne-94, Frank-92, Frank Nibbe-85, Ostestern-77, Owen Kersten-73, I/a Ostestern
Tower Julie	Fin	1972	572	900	55.8	9.9	3.3	10	C	

Gropa A/S, Denmark

Name	Flag	Year	GRT	DWT	Loa	Bm	Draft	Kts	Type	Former names
Martina	Lbr	1968	696	862	55.0	9.3	3.5	10	Tch	ex Julie A-90, Lilian A-89, Julie A-88, Jytte Dania-86 (conv C-89)

Johann Grossmann, Germany

Name	Flag	Year	GRT	DWT	Loa	Bm	Draft	Kts	Type	Former names
Kai	Atg	1968	1,152	1,719	73.4	11.8	4.3	11	C	ex George Junior-90, Leonardo-83, Dorrit Lea-79
Nord Star	Atg	1973	1,799	2,815	86.4	12.0	5.5	12	C	ex Bona Fe-97, Norrstal-77

Gard Gullaksen, Norway

Name	Flag	Year	GRT	DWT	Loa	Bm	Draft	Kts	Type	Former names
Fonntind	Nor	1965	731	829	55.0	9.3	3.5	11	C	ex Oksoy-79, Austri-78, Alfsnes-76, Berg0-75, Frendo Simby-75, Lutro-75

Kapitan Heinz Haack, Germany

Name	Flag	Year	GRT	DWT	Loa	Bm	Draft	Kts	Type	Former names
Marjesco	Deu	1988	2,184	2,735	82.0	12.7	4.7	11	Cc	ex Unitas H-96

Johann Franz Hallhuber, Sweden

Name	Flag	Year	GRT	DWT	Loa	Bm	Draft	Kts	Type	Former names
Bella I	Hnd	1957	492	660	52.6	8.7	3.4	10	C	ex Bella-96, Randi Stevns-87, Flora S-76

Halsvik Cementstoperi AS, Norway

Name	Flag	Year	GRT	DWT	Loa	Bm	Draft	Kts	Type	Former names
Halsvik	Nor	1979	639	965	59.5	9.9	3.2	10	C	ex Hester-97, Gersom-94, Sprinter-93, Gersom-86

Uwe Hamdorf, Germany

Name	Flag	Year	GRT	DWT	Loa	Bm	Draft	Kts	Type	Former names
Talea	Atg	1977	1,801	2,623	81.2	11.8	5.1	11	Cc	ex Anna H-94, Parnass-88

Reederei Reinhard Hamm KG, Germany

Name	Flag	Year	GRT	DWT	Loa	Bm	Draft	Kts	Type	Former names
Annegret	Deu	1995	3,998	5,218	101.1	18.5	6.6	-	Cc	
Mediterraneo	Deu	1993	3,992	5,350	100.0	18.4	6.6	15	Cc	ex Margret-99

Roald Hamnes, Norway

Name	Flag	Year	GRT	DWT	Loa	Bm	Draft	Kts	Type	Former names
Lena	Nor	1974	1,926	1,118	76.0	13.5	3.5	13	Ccp	ex Nour Han-95, Katia-93, Burfell-93, Hekla-92, Vela-84, I/a Polstraum

Hansatee Ltd., Estonia

Name	Flag	Year	GRT	DWT	Loa	Bm	Draft	Kts	Type	Former names
Kapella (2)	Bhs	1974	7,564	1,856	110.1	17.5	5.8	18	Ro	ex Marine Evangeline-98, Spirit of Boulogne-95, Marine Evangeline-93, Duke of Yorkshire-78

Reederei Peter Hansel, Germany

Name	Flag	Year	GRT	DWT	Loa	Bm	Draft	Kts	Type	Former names
Laura	Atg	1982	1,939	2,890	88.0	11.3	4.7	11	Cc	ex Ilka-98

Hansel Schiffahrts und Bereederungs GmbH & Co., KG, Germany

Name	Flag	Year	GRT	DWT	Loa	Bm	Draft	Kts	Type	Former names
Jupiter	Cyp	1985	1,839	2,167	78.6	12.6	4.3	12	Cc	I/a Dirk

Name	Flag	Year	GRT	DWT	Loa	Bm	Draft	Kts	Type	Former names

H.E. Hansen-Tangen, Norway

Name	Flag	Year	GRT	DWT	Loa	Bm	Draft	Kts	Type	Former names
Sunrana	Nis	1976	3,663	5,482	102.3	15.8	6.9	13	C	ex Arklow Beach-95, Atlantic Fisher-88, Sandgate-82

Jorgen Robot Hansen, Denmark

| Atlas | Dis | 1961 | 524 | 723 | 52.6 | 9.0 | 3.5 | 9 | C | ex Dina-87 |

Nils Conrad Hojlund Hansen, Denmark

| Ardua | Dis | 1978 | 952 | 1,050 | 60.2 | 10.4 | 3.6 | 10 | Cc | |

Ejv. Hansens, Denmark

| Ostersoen | Dis | 1967 | 778 | 857 | 58.4 | 10.0 | 3.5 | 12 | Cp | ex Energi-95, Condor-89, Brimar-87, Haico Holwerda-81, Roelof Holwerda-76, Tor Parisia-73, Parisia-71 |

Harris & Dixon (Shipbrokers) Ltd., UK

| Ilona G | Gbr | 1990 | 999 | 1,700 | 69.1 | 10.8 | 3.9 | - | C | |

Harstad Shipping AS, Norway

| Lolita | Nor | 1967 | 674 | 834 | 55.0 | 9.3 | 3.5 | 10 | C | ex Myster-82, Lolita-80, Myster-79, Lolita-76, Rikke Lonborg-74, Marag Moon-72, Birgit Dania-71 |

Rederi AB Hasting, Sweden

| Caroline | Bhs | 1984 | 4,274 | 7,010 | 107.0 | 18.2 | 6.6 | 12 | Tch | ex Hoko Hero-93 |

Hartel Shipping & Chartering BV, Netherlands

| Carima | Vct | 1972 | 1,537 | 2,627 | 76.4 | 12.3 | 3.5 | 12 | Cc | ex Coulant-94, Arushi-91, Asmaa-89, Merc Phoenecia-77 |

Olav Haugland, Norway

| Bergen Star | Nor | 1981 | 2,538 | 2,467 | 80.9 | 13.0 | 5.2 | 12 | Tch | ex Crestar-96, Keke-90, Torasund-85 |

Albert Hauschild GmbH, Germany

| Unika | Atg | 1971 | 1,773 | 1,426 | 76.6 | 12.8 | 4.1 | 12 | Cc | ex Arnis-85 |

Hay & Co., UK

| Shetland Trader | Gbr | 1980 | 909 | 1,315 | 60.0 | 11.3 | 3.9 | 11 | C | ex Portland-97, Comity-93, Angelonia-88 |

Reederei Hans Heinrich KG, Germany

| Lappland | Deu | 1998 | 5,058 | 6,650 | 118.5 | 18.2 | 7.1 | 17 | CC | |

A.F. Harmstorf & Co. GmbH, Germany

| Industrial Beacon | Atg | 1991 | 3,113 | 3,487 | 92.7 | 15.1 | 5.3 | 12 | Cc | ex Bremer Makler-96, Gordon Reid-95 |

Kapt. Laurenz Held, Germany

| Isartal | Atg | 1989 | 2,369 | 3,750 | 87.9 | 12.9 | 4.5 | 11 | Cc | |

Helgis Verwaltungs. GmbH & Co. KG, Germany

| Andra | Atg | 1983 | 2,605 | 3,235 | 90.0 | 14.0 | 5.6 | 13 | Cc | ex Arnarfell-94, Sandra M-89, Sandra-87, Band Aid III-85, Sandra-85 |
| FAS Istanbul | Ant | 1986 | 6,638 | 9,730 | 126.1 | 18.6 | 8.3 | 15 | Cc | ex Helgis-94, Carib-Explorer-93, Merkur Europe-92, Helgis-91, Khyber-91, Helgis-90, Norasia Alexandria-90, Helgis-89, Nordsk Express-87, George H. Scales-87, Helgis-86 |

Name	Flag	Year	GRT	DWT	Loa	Bm	Draft	Kts	Type	Former names

Helmship GmbH, Germany

Name	Flag	Year	GRT	DWT	Loa	Bm	Draft	Kts	Type	Former names
Rangitane	Atg	1984	3,120	4,134	88.5	15.7	6.5	13	Cc	ex Antje B-93, Osprey-88, Antje B-87, Band Aid Carrier-86, Antje B-85
Janna	Atg	1983	4,455	6,154	106.0	17.5	7.0	13	Cc	ex Auckland Express-96, Scol Trader-85, Iceland-84, l/a Karthago

Reederei Alfred Hinsch KG, Germany

Name	Flag	Year	GRT	DWT	Loa	Bm	Draft	Kts	Type	Former names
Geestborg	Deu	1997	2,863	4,140	90.5	13.6	5.7	13	Cc	l/a Unitas-H
Veritas H	Atg	1995	2,899	3,950	97.8	16.4	4.9	15	CC	ex Regulus-97, Veritas H-96

Hollming Oy Shipping (Crystal Pool Ltd.) Finland

Name	Flag	Year	GRT	DWT	Loa	Bm	Draft	Kts	Type	Former names
Crystal Amethyst	Lux	1993	5,677	8,143	112.0	18.2	7.5	14	Tch	
Crystal Emerald	Lux	1993	5,677	8,143	112.0	18.2	7.5	14	Tch	
Crystal Pearl	Lux	1994	5,677	8,143	112.0	18.2	7.5	14	Tch	

Holthe Shipping AS, Norway

Name	Flag	Year	GRT	DWT	Loa	Bm	Draft	Kts	Type	Former names
Risvaer	Nor	1974	882	914	55.6	11.0	3.8	10	C	ex Heggholmen-95, Trans Sund-93

Holyhead Towing Co. Ltd., UK

Name	Flag	Year	GRT	DWT	Loa	Bm	Draft	Kts	Type	Former names
Yeoman Rose (2)	Blz	1975	507	965	42.5	10.0	3.6	9	C	ex Island Swift-90, Seaborne Trader-87

Hordafor Shipping AS, Norway

Name	Flag	Year	GRT	DWT	Loa	Bm	Draft	Kts	Type	Former names
Hordafor Pilot	Nor	1974	1,662	2,200	77.1	12.6	4.8	12	Tch	ex Essberger Pilot-97, Tom Lima-92, Solvent Explorer-87, Essberger Pilot-77

Schiffahrtskontor Horn-Linie OHG, Germany

Name	Flag	Year	GRT	DWT	Loa	Bm	Draft	Kts	Type	Former names
Hornbaltic	Esp	1980	3,080	3,152	92.2	15.5	5.0	14	C	ex Hornbelt-80
Hornfels	Esp	1985	4,453	6,131	106.0	17.5	7.0	14	Cc	ex CGM Tchekhov-93, Hornfels-90, ScanDutch Sandinia-90, Hornfels-86

Subsidiary of Del Monte Fresh Fruit International Inc.

Huelin-Renouf Shipping Services, Channel Islands (UK)

Name	Flag	Year	GRT	DWT	Loa	Bm	Draft	Kts	Type	Former names
Huelin Dispatch	Bhs	1978	1,892	2,360	79.8	12.8	4.5	12	Cc	ex Stenholm-96, Visbur-92, Stenholm-91, Suderelv-91

Hvistendahls Rederi A/S, Norway

Name	Flag	Year	GRT	DWT	Loa	Bm	Draft	Kts	Type	Former names
Liftmar	Nis	1974	2,021	2,896	79.7	15.2	5.3	13	Chl	ex Marsteinen-90, Stril Lyon-88, Stokksund-85 (conv C-83)

Interorient Navigation Hamburg GmbH, Germany

Name	Flag	Year	GRT	DWT	Loa	Bm	Draft	Kts	Type	Former names
Aristaios *	Cyp	1975	8,301	6,128	124.2	19.6	7.0	16	Ro	ex Inzhener Bashkirov-96
Arneb	Deu	1986	3,640	2,515	88.6	14.3	5.1	13	Ro	ex Alster Rapid-95
Avaloni *	Cyp	1975	8,301	6,128	124.2	19.6	7.0	16	Ro	ex Maritime Lee-96, Mekhanik Konovalov-95
Condock I * (2)	Ant	1979	4,939	3,603	92.4	19.6	4.8	12	Cc/bg	ex Ondo-97, Condock I-97

* owned by Interorient Navigation Co. Ltd., Cyprus.

Intraboot Shipping, Netherlands

Name	Flag	Year	GRT	DWT	Loa	Bm	Draft	Kts	Type	Former names
Admiral (2)	Cyp	1980	2,426	3,225	105.0	15.0	2.8	10	Cc	ex Omskiy-17-94

Intrada Chartering Ltd., UK

Name	Flag	Year	GRT	DWT	Loa	Bm	Draft	Kts	Type	Former names
Highland Carrier (2)	Bhs	1981	1,150	1,266	64.0	14.5	3.7	11	Ro	ex Trinity Bay-98, Leichardt-90
Scot Pioneer	Bhs	1984	1,587	1,901	82.0	11.5	3.5	11	C	ex Silvia-98
Scot Ranger	Bhs	1997	2,260	3,418	84.9	12.7	5.1	11	C	
Scot Trader	Bhs	1986	1,585	1,900	82.0	11.5	3.7	10	C	ex Wotan-93, Scot Trader-91, Wotan-86

Name	Flag	Year	GRT	DWT	Loa	Bm	Draft	Kts	Type	Former names
Irtysh Shipping Co., Russia										
Irtysh 1 *	Rus	1996	2,086	2,913	88.4	12.3	4.5	10	Cc	I/a Ataman Golovatiy
Irtysh 2 *	Rus	1996	2,086	2,913	88.4	12.3	4.4	11	C	
Omskiy-125 (2)	Rus	1985	2,441	2,957	108.4	14.8	3.3	10	C	
Omskiy-105 (2)	Rus	1980	2,441	2,905	108.4	15.0	3.1	10	C	
Omskiy-107 (2)	Rus	1981	2,441	2,905	108.4	15.0	3.1	10	C	
Omskiy-108 (2)	Rus	1981	2,452	2,185	108.4	15.0	2.5	10	C	

* managed by Poseidon Schiffahrt GmbH, Germany.

Name	Flag	Year	GRT	DWT	Loa	Bm	Draft	Kts	Type	Former names
Bertil Ivarsson, Sweden										
Vinga	Swe	1971	1,097	1,042	64.6	11.0	3.7	10	C	ex Acamar-84, I.W.Winck-80, Jytte Bres-80, Wrath-74, Jytte Bres-72
Gerhard Jacobs Jnr., Germany										
Hammelwarden	Deu	1960	388	608	55.3	7.3	2.6	9	C	(len-82, len/deep-78, len-68)
Heinz-Gerog Jacobs, Germany										
Ria	Deu	1960	337	443	46.5	8.5	2.7	9	C	ex Thea K-89, Castor-70, Moni-65
Kapt. Erich Jagemann, Germany										
Stella Maris	Deu	1967	824	788	62.0	9.9	3.3	10	C	
JAIF Shipping Co. Ltd., Russia										
Olenegorsk	Rus	1965	3,544	4,302	105.9	14.6	6.6	14	Cc	
Sasha Borodulin	Rus	1970	3,703	4,646	105.6	15.6	6.8	14	Cc	
Jens Jakobsen A/S, Denmark										
Tina Jakobsen	Dis	1980	2,401	3,345	93.0	13.9	5.7	14	Tch	ex Multitank Antares-96, Blue Bird-89, Bird Island-87, Chemtrans Antares-85 (len-83)
Containerschiffsreederei H.-W. Janssen GmbH, Germany										
Curacao	Lbr	1996	3,335	4,994	97.0	16.0		12	Tch	ex Capella-96
Multitank Iberia	Lbr	1995	3,716	5,797	100.0	16.5	6.7	15	Tch	

Vessels owned by subsidiary Martime-Gesellschaft fur Maritime Dienstleistungen.mbH.

Name	Flag	Year	GRT	DWT	Loa	Bm	Draft	Kts	Type	Former names
Sjoetransporter Janssen AS, Sweden										
Nordgard	Swe	1969	1,428	1,464	77.0	11.8	4.0	12	Cc	ex Heimvik-89, Gerd-86, Klaus Block-83
Janssonfrakt - E.G.Jansson AB, Sweden										
San Remo	Mlt	1965	1,283	1,225	72.1	11.3	3.7	12	C	ex Saxen-89
Jens & Waller, Germany										
Nyland	Deu	1995	2,996	4,622	100.0	16.7	6.0		Cc	I/a Helene
Varmland	Deu	1995	2,997	4,624	100.0	16.7	6.0	15	Cc	I/a Wilhelm
Jenset Rederi AS,Norway										
Hanne Christine	Nis	1984	2,969	2,876	89.8	16.0	4.9	13	Cc	ex Caribbean Breeze-97, Grimsnis-93, Blue Caribe Carrier-93, Grimsnis-91, Ville du Mistral-85, Grimsnis-84
Reederei Walter Jess, Germany										
Nordfeld	Cyp	1977	1,896	2,944	84.2	11.8	4.7	11	Cc	(len-84)
Nordsee	Atg	1978	2,579	2,954	88.7	15.5	4.9	14	Cc	ex Seaboard Clipper-99, Nordsee-96
Nordwind	Cyp	1976	2,161	1,800	86.8	12.8	4.7	13	Cc	
Karl Runar Johansson, Sweden										
Thalassa	Swe	1971	1,834	3,038	80.0	14.3	5.3	12	C	ex Rondane-78

Name	Flag	Year	GRT	DWT	Loa	Bm	Draft	Kts	Type	Former names

Joint Stock Alekseevskaya Reb, Russia

Name	Flag	Year	GRT	DWT	Loa	Bm	Draft	Kts	Type	Former names
Magadan (2)	Rus	1977	2,360	2,923	108.4	15.0	3.0	10	C	
Minsk (2)	Rus	1982	2,360	2,923	108.4	15.0	3.0	10	C	
Minusinsk (2)	Rus	1978	2,360	2,923	108.4	15.0	3.0	10	C	ex Omskiy-104-81
Refrizherator-604 (2)	Rus	1982	1,597	1,400	82.0	11.6	2.5	10	R	
Refrizherator-605 (2)	Rus	1982	1,597	1,400	82.0	11.6	2.5	10	R	
Refrizherator-609 (2)	Rus	1983	1,597	1,130	82.0	11.6	2.9	10	R	
Tiksi (2)	Rus	1980	2,360	2,217	108.4	15.0	2.5	10	C	
Ust-Kut (2)	Rus	1985	2,446	2,760	108.4	14.8	3.0	10	C	ex Omskiy-127-85

Various others.

Juhl & Ehrhorn, Denmark

Name	Flag	Year	GRT	DWT	Loa	Bm	Draft	Kts	Type	Former names
Elisabeth Clipper	Dis	1983	1,560	2,610	67.7	12.2	3.4	10	Cc	
Karen Clipper	Dis	1978	1,105	1,285	62.9	11.2	3.9	11	Cc	
Mette Clipper	Dis	1977	1,105	1,281	62.9	11.2	3.9	11	C	

Juhlke Schiffahrts KG, Germany

Name	Flag	Year	GRT	DWT	Loa	Bm	Draft	Kts	Type	Former names
Ems Star	Cyp	1995	5,887	7,800	121.9	19.6	6.3	-	CC	

Kapt. Klaus Juls (Golo Shipping), Germany

Name	Flag	Year	GRT	DWT	Loa	Bm	Draft	Kts	Type	Former names
Kormoran	Atg	1966	658	743	55.1	9.3	3.3	10	C	ex Dorte Star-89, Millac Star-84, Dorte Star-81, Harle Riff-72

C. V. Joriston Scheepvaart Onderneming, Netherlands

Name	Flag	Year	GRT	DWT	Loa	Bm	Draft	Kts	Type	Former names
Sea Shannon	Nld	1996	1,670	2,268	82.5	11.3	4.1	10	C	l/a Joriston

Heinz-Alfred Jungclaus, Germany

Name	Flag	Year	GRT	DWT	Loa	Bm	Draft	Kts	Type	Former names
Grauerort	Deu	1965	449	690	56.7	7.2	2.8	9	C	

Klaus Jurgens, Germany

Name	Flag	Year	GRT	DWT	Loa	Bm	Draft	Kts	Type	Former names
Portugal Bridge	Deu	1996	4,986	6,506	116.4	19.5	7.1	17	CC	ex Antje Jurgens-97

Kendall Bros., UK

Name	Flag	Year	GRT	DWT	Loa	Bm	Draft	Kts	Type	Former names
KB II	Gbr	1960	552	605	51.7	9.2	3.7	10	Dss	ex Glen Hafod-85

Heinrich Kiepe, Germany

Name	Flag	Year	GRT	DWT	Loa	Bm	Draft	Kts	Type	Former names
Heljo	Atg	1993	2,416	3,574	85.0	13.0	5.4	11	Cc	ex Hornsund-97, Heljo-96

Kiepe-Schepers KG, Germany

Name	Flag	Year	GRT	DWT	Loa	Bm	Draft	Kts	Type	Former names
Rhein Trader	Deu	1991	3,815	4,155	103.5	16.2	6.1	14	Cc	

Trond A. Kittilsen Shipping AS, Norway

Name	Flag	Year	GRT	DWT	Loa	Bm	Draft	Kts	Type	Former names
Ulsund	Nor	1971	1,572	2,106	76.6	12.3	4.6	12	C	ex Eva-95, Mina-93, Eva-91, Eikvaag-91, Golden Bay-91, Scan Voyager-86, Islands Star-84, Alafoss-80, Merc America-74

Gunnar Kjonnoy Rederi AS, Norway

Name	Flag	Year	GRT	DWT	Loa	Bm	Draft	Kts	Type	Former names
Thelita	Nor	1971	1,448	1,397	70.8	13.0	3.6	11	Cc	ex Elin Christine-97, Peter Alba-80, Peter Staerke-77
Thurso	Nor	1972	806	884	60.1	10.0	3.4	12	C	

Klingenberg Bereederungs und Befrachtungs OHG, Germany

Name	Flag	Year	GRT	DWT	Loa	Bm	Draft	Kts	Type	Former names
Nicola	Deu	1999	6,000	9,500	-	-	-	-	CC	
Vanessa	Atg	1994	5,684	7,300	120.0	19.6	6.2	14	Cc	
Ville de Mijo	Atg	1993	5,684	7,416	120.0	19.6	6.2	14	Cc	

Herbertus Klose, Germany

Name	Flag	Year	GRT	DWT	Loa	Bm	Draft	Kts	Type	Former names
Iris-Jorg	Deu	1956	281	435	45.3	8.0	2.6	9	C	ex Seestern-65, Eilenburg-64

Brodrene Klovning Shipping AS, Norway

Name	Flag	Year	GRT	DWT	Loa	Bm	Draft	Kts	Type	Former names
Norsk Drott *	Nor	1982	1,891	2,666	80.2	13.4	5.3	14	T	
Norsk Viking *	Nor	1980	1,891	2,596	80.2	13.4	5.3	14	T	
Trans Borg	Nis	1980	3,541	5,280	101.4	15.9	6.7	12	Tch	ex Kongstraum-87, Brage Baltic-85

* owned by Ofotens og Vesteraalens Damps. ASA.

Name	Flag	Year	GRT	DWT	Loa	Bm	Draft	Kts	Type	Former names

Knohr & Burchard Nfl. GmbH & Co., Germany
Name	Flag	Year	GRT	DWT	Loa	Bm	Draft	Kts	Type	Former names
Isebek	Lbr	1996	3,711	5,700	99.9	16.5	6.7	15	Tch	ex Multitank Saxonia-97
Jersbek	Lbr	1982	2,690	3,872	91.7	13.7	6.2	12	Tch	ex Cape Island-87
Lasbek	Lbr	1984	2,699	4,029	91.7	13.6	6.4	12	Tch	ex Sandy Island-87

Koehn & Bohlmann Reederei KG, Germany
Name	Flag	Year	GRT	DWT	Loa	Bm	Draft	Kts	Type	Former names
Poetenitz	Cyp	1982	1,934	2,890	88.0	11.5	4.7	11	Cc	ex Diogo do Couto-95, Svenja-86
Stepenitz	Cyp	1977	1,768	2,416	81.4	11.9	4.8	11	Cc	ex Noordland-89

Kommercial Transport Ltd., Estonia
Name	Flag	Year	GRT	DWT	Loa	Bm	Draft	Kts	Type	Former names
City of Liverpool (2)	Khm	1967	1,595	2,157	88.0	12.4	3.3		C	ex Nevel-98, Vasiliy Nazarov-97, Morskoy 4-92
Konda (2)	Rus	1978	1,380	1,268	82.0	11.6	2.5	-	C	
Vagay (2)	Est	1980	1,380	1,032	82.0	11.6	2.5	-	C	
Vorotynsk (2)	Khm	1968	1,595	2,157	87.9	12.4	3.3	11	C	ex Elisey Drokin-97, Morskoy-9-92.

Koole Tanktransport BV, Netherlands
Name	Flag	Year	GRT	DWT	Loa	Bm	Draft	Kts	Type	Former names
Star Aruba	Nld	1972	1,151	1,531	71.0	10.4	3.7	12	T	
Star Bonaire	Nld	1997	2,257	3,420	90.1	12.0	5.1	12	T	

Gerd Koppelmann, Germany
Name	Flag	Year	GRT	DWT	Loa	Bm	Draft	Kts	Type	Former names
Alteland	Deu	1995	2,996	4,602	100.0	16.7	6.0	15	Cc	l/a Patria
Katherine Borchard	Atg	1979	5,378	7,283	126.3	18.1	6.5	15	Cc	ex Concordia-86, Katherine Borchard-86, Concordia-85, Zim Australia-82, l/a Concordia

Jorg Kopping Shipping Co., Germany
Name	Flag	Year	GRT	DWT	Loa	Bm	Draft	Kts	Type	Former names
Geest Merchant	Atg	1995	2,899	3,916	99.3	16.2	4.9	16	CC	ex Marburg-97
Geest Trader	Atg	1995	2,899	3,950	99.2	16.4	4.9	14	CC	ex Limburg-95
Hamburg	Deu	1991	3,466	4,707	96.7	15.8	6.0	13	Cc	ex Judith Borchard-97, Hamburg-91
Rendsburg	Atg	1991	3,469	4,706	96.7	15.8	6.0	13	Cc	ex Ruth Borchard-97, Rendsburg-91

Gerhard Krawinkel, Germany
Name	Flag	Year	GRT	DWT	Loa	Bm	Draft	Kts	Type	Former names
Gerhard K	Deu	1967	418	645	55.0	7.2	2.9	9	C	ex Gerhard-K-81 (len/deep-83)

Kris Consult A/S, Norway (Kristen O. Johnsens Rederi AS)
Name	Flag	Year	GRT	DWT	Loa	Bm	Draft	Kts	Type	Former names
Antares	Nis	1969	1,373	1,370	76.3	11.9	3.9	13	Cc	ex Gardwill-91, Amazone-86, Bele-75, Tor Ireland-75, Bele-73
Mathilde	Nis	1971	2,526	2,410	92.8	13.4	4.9	14	Cc	ex Anden-88, Traveway Spirit-86, Masa-86, Tainio-84, Anna Knuppel-81
Northern Reefer	Nis	1973	4,193	4,597	118.2	16.1	6.6	-	R	ex Studlafoss-98, Hofsjokull-97, Maco Viking-78, Satsu Maru No.58-??
Sokna	Nis	1970	1,371	1,370	76.3	12.0	4.0	13	Cc	ex Birte-89, Arktis-82, Tor Timber-75, Arktis-72

Karl Heinz Kruse, Germany
Name	Flag	Year	GRT	DWT	Loa	Bm	Draft	Kts	Type	Former names
Tina	Deu	1960	328	518	47.2	7.3	2.6	8	C	ex Timo-94, Freiheit-78 Shipping(len/deep-82, len-69)

Agence Maritime Lalemant, Belgium
Name	Flag	Year	GRT	DWT	Loa	Bm	Draft	Kts	Type	Former names
Craziest Dream	Pan	1982	4,316	7,160	104.1	16.5	7.6	12	Cc	ex Diamante X-92, Diamante-91, Duro Diez-82
Jose Maria	Bhs	1977	4,014	6,234	108.2	15.9	6.6	13	Cc	ex Fer Caribe-87
Misty	Vut	1983	5,868	8,522	119.5	18.6	7.4	13	Cc	ex Lex Naranjo-96, Ebano-89
Dreamy	Pmd	1983	2,692	3,103	91.3	14.4	6.4	12	C	ex Uralar Sexto-95

Herbert Lamprecht, Germany
Name	Flag	Year	GRT	DWT	Loa	Bm	Draft	Kts	Type	Former names
Nautica	Blz	1963	1,196	1,265	74.7	10.8	3.9	11	C	ex Nautila-93, Nautica-85

Name	Flag	Year	GRT	DWT	Loa	Bm	Draft	Kts	Type	Former names

P. Rudbeck Larsen's Eftf. ApS, Denmark

Name	Flag	Year	GRT	DWT	Loa	Bm	Draft	Kts	Type	Former names
Deneb	Dis	1981	1,175	2,099	70.2	10.4	4.9	10	Cc	ex Kines-94, Elsebeth Vesta-86
Markab	Dis	1971	1,083	1,073	64.6	11.0	3.6	11	C	ex Lone Stevns-90, Mor Aveiro-77, Nelly Klint-72

Torsten Larsson, Sweden

| Ekland | Swe | 1974 | 2,406 | 2,946 | 83.5 | 14.1 | 5.1 | 12 | C | ex Bettie Lil-97, Kaela-96, Scotfield-96, Michaela-93, Virgo-92, Fairmead-86, Hyde Park-82, Syon Park-74 |

Rederiet Sverre Leiren A/S, Norway

| Frima Star | Nld | 1978 | 1,094 | 1,180 | 62.7 | 11.2 | 3.6 | 10 | Ce | ex Avebe Star-97, Star-85 |

Managed by Wagenborg Shipping BV, Netherlands, q.v.

K/S Leonard A/S, Norway

| Leonard | Nis | 1973 | 974 | 1,097 | 59.3 | 10.8 | 4.6 | 10 | C | ex Dream Three-86, Frendo Trader-79, Eger Trader-76, Nenny Trader-74, I/a Nenny Conveyer |

Leonhardt & Blumberg, Germany

| Karl Leonhardt | Sgp | 1974 | 4,382 | 6,874 | 105.6 | 17.4 | 6.8 | 15 | C | ex Cavalla River-89, Karl Leonhardt-87, Makiy-82, Pasania-76 |
| Ursula Leonhardt | Sgp | 1974 | 4,382 | 6,874 | 105.6 | 16.4 | 6.8 | 12 | C | ex Satsuky-82, Juno I-76 |

Leth & Co., Germany

Eberhard	Atg	1983	3,075	5,238	105.8	15.1	5.6	12	Tch	(len-85)
Paul	Cyp	1980	3,003	5,166	104.0	15.0	5.7	12	Tch	(len-84)
Willy	Cyp	1981	3,070	5,238	105.8	15.1	5.7	12	T	ex Gerhard-88 (len-85)

Managed by Carl F. Peters GmbH & Co.

Libra Shipping BV, Netherlands

Blackbird	Vct	1967	1,197	1,735	75.8	11.2	4.4	12	C	ex Hawthorn-92, Francinaplein-77, Hunnau-73, Ortrud Muller-69
Bluebird	Bhs	1982	1,115	1,688	67.4	11.3	4.1	10	Cc	ex Alice-95, Alila-92, Peacock Venture-88
Egret	Vct	1967	633	738	57.4	9.1	2.8	9	C	ex Cormorant-86, Moon Trader-86, A. Held-79 (len-73)

Wilfried Liesenberg, Germany

| Jan-Dirk | Deu | 1950 | 285 | 438 | 42.6 | 7.5 | 3.0 | 8 | C | ex Heinrich Nagel-75, Jurgen-66 |

Liman Joint Stock Co., Russia

| Komandor (2) | Rus | 1979 | 3,151 | 4,000 | 104.2 | 14.4 | 6.6 | 14 | C | ex MT-995-96 |

Limarko UAB, Lithuania

| Sonata | Ltu | 1977 | 1,995 | 2,467 | 79.0 | 12.4 | 5.1 | 11 | Cc | ex Grouse-97, Groden-94, Oeland II-87, Oeland-83 |

Heinz Litmeyer Schiffahrts KG, Germany

| Emsland | Atg | 1984 | 1,857 | 2,200 | 80.2 | 12.7 | 4.2 | 10 | Cc | |
| Reint | Nld | 1966 | 628 | 738 | 57.5 | 9.1 | 2.9 | 10 | C | (len-73) |

Hermann Lohmann, Germany

| Santa Maria | Deu | 1985 | 3,062 | 3,670 | 99.4 | 14.0 | 5.1 | 12 | Cc | |

Compagnie des Long-Liners, France

| Clipper Carthage (2) | Vct | 1976 | 4,307 | 2,499 | 117.9 | 15.8 | 4.7 | 16 | Ro | ex Nebhana-98 |
| Clipper Cayenne (2) | Vct | 1977 | 5,080 | 2,797 | 101.0 | 17.8 | 5.6 | 16 | Ro | ex Mejerda-98 |

Losinyy Ostrov Joint Stock Co., Russia

| ST-1340 (2) | Rus | 1992 | 1,768 | 1,761 | 88.9 | 12.0 | 3.0 | 10 | Cc | |

Name	Flag	Year	GRT	DWT	Loa	Bm	Draft	Kts	Type	Former names

Ivar Lothe, Norway
Name	Flag	Year	GRT	DWT	Loa	Bm	Draft	Kts	Type	Former names
Fosenbulk	Nis	1973	863	945	60.8	9.5	3.9	11	C	ex Ingrid Maria-97, Gravel Bulk-91, Leca Bulk-80, Ull Gard-77

Lundqvist Rederierna, Finland
| Camilla | Fin | 1982 | 10,085 | 7,600 | 133.4 | 20.9 | 6.9 | 14 | Rop | |

Gido Luhrs, Germany
| Apollo Hawk | Atg | 1972 | 4,255 | 6,329 | 101.5 | 16.1 | 7.2 | 13 | Cc | ex Esther-98, Esther Bolten-74 (len/rblt-91) |
| Lagik | Atg | 1976 | 1,721 | 2,554 | 92.4 | 11.3 | 4.0 | 11 | Cc | ex Mari Galante-96, Lai Da Toma-94, Ostermaat-86 |

Helmut Luhrs Schiffahrts KG, Germany
| Beate | Atg | 1969 | 1,223 | 1,998 | 74.0 | 10.8 | 5.1 | 12 | Cc | ex Stefanie-94, Cosmea-90, Elke Kahrs-84, Baltic Concord-74, I/a Elke Kahrs |
| Syrena | Atg | 1972 | 1,777 | 2,999 | 80.0 | 13.8 | 5.3 | 13 | C | ex Maik Primo-95, Rudolf Kurz-81 |

Ivar Lundh & Co. A/B, Sweden
| Breant | Swe | 1979 | 5,197 | 3,328 | 110.0 | 16.8 | 4.6 | 13 | Ro | |

Managed by Brax Shipholding Rederi AB, Sweden.

Lupin Shipping Ltd., Denmark
Lamaro	Vct	1972	1,282	1,769	70.9	11.1	4.5	12	C	ex Lamar-97, Antares-94, Sandrea-93, Lamaro-92, Tamara-85
Larita	Vct	1970	1,055	1,046	64.6	11.0	3.6	11	C	ex Engenes-90, Bergmann-89, Frengen-86, Egin-84
Lovinda	Vct	1966	734	1,240	59.3	9.7	3.1	10	C	ex Dorinda-89, Ramsjo-82, Herm Kiepe-74

Schiffahrtskontor Waltraut Maciej GmbH, Germany
| Weisa | Atg | 1971 | 1,217 | 1,972 | 74.5 | 10.9 | 5.1 | 12 | C | ex Eurotrader-86, Kini Kersten-80, Relay-74, Osterland-73 |

O. E. Maeland Shipping, Norway
Hako	Nor	1971	1,409	1,380	76.3	12.1	4.0	13	Cc	ex Sea Girl-94, I/a Fortuna
Hava	Bhs	1979	2,023	2,359	79.7	13.0	5.1	13	Cc	ex Baltic Amber-97, Nora Heeren-96
Korni	Nor	1970	1,395	1,370	76.3	11.9	3.9	13	Cc	ex Bremer Uranus-91, Argus-89, Tor Humber-73, Ronan-73

Manx Car Carriers Ltd.,UK
City of Amsterdam *	Lbr	1999	9,990	2,200	-	-	-	15	V	
City of Barcelona	Iom	1993	9,576	2,402	99.9	20.6	5.0	15	V	
City of Paris *	Lbr	1999	9,990	2,200	-	-	-	15	V	
City of Rome *	Lbr	1999	9,990	2,200	-	-	-	15	V	
City of Sunderland	Iom	1993	9,576	2,417	99.9	20.6	5.0	16	V	

Subsidiary of Nissan Motor Car Carrier Co. Ltd., managed by Denholm Ship Management (IOM) Ltd.
* owned by Euro Marine Ships Inc., formed jointly by Nissan, Leif Hoegh & Co. ASA and Mitsui OSK Lines Ltd.

Marconsult Gesellschaft fur Reedereiberatung mbH, Germany
| Elbe Star | Cyp | 1984 | 3,777 | 4,596 | 97.1 | 17.2 | 5.2 | 12 | Cc | ex Pul Sejahtera-92, Rex Star-90 |

Mariship Co. NV, Netherlands Antilles
| Zwanet | Ant | 1977 | 2,029 | 3,100 | 82.3 | 13.9 | 5.3 | 12 | C | ex Arpa Sun-92, Bottenviken-88, Regulus-86, Bottenviken-83, I/a Deltasee |

Name	Flag	Year	GRT	DWT	Loa	Bm	Draft	Kts	Type	Former names

Marstal Shipping, Denmark

Name	Flag	Year	GRT	DWT	Loa	Bm	Draft	Kts	Type	Former names
Anto	Dis	1967	781	802	56.0	10.4	3.5	11	C	ex Finlandia-91
Conto	Dis	1969	1,055	1,170	64.6	11.0	3.8	12	C	ex Stina-92, Sabine-91, Linhav-87, Cimbria-86, Wingsea-83, Merc Pacific-74
Juto	Dis	1968	969	1,223	68.0	10.0	3.8	11	C	ex Start-98, Thunpall 1-86, Tor Francia-73, Francia-71 (len/deep-73)

Mathies Reederei GmbH, Germany

Name	Flag	Year	GRT	DWT	Loa	Bm	Draft	Kts	Type	Former names
Gotaland	Deu	1978	2,578	2,937	88.7	15.5	4.9	14	Cc	ex Helene Waller-94, Rachel Borchard-87, Helene Waller-86, Thiassi-79, Helene Waller-78
Marianne *	Deu	1978	1,934	2,415	84.6	13.5	4.0	12	Cc	ex Detlef Schmidt-94 (len-94)
Svealand	Deu	1975	2,240	2,380	81.5	13.4	5.0	13	Cc	ex Ulla-89, Osteclipper-86, Nic-Clipper-79, Osteclipper-78

* owned by subsidiary Jonannes Ick.

Mats A. Mattsson, Sweden

Name	Flag	Year	GRT	DWT	Loa	Bm	Draft	Kts	Type	Former names
Hellevik	Swe	1975	1,957	1,537	82.1	12.8	4.2	13	Cc	ex Schwaneck-91
Listerland	Swe	1977	2,068	2,189	81.1	12.8	4.8	13	B	ex Aros Force-97, Norrland-90
Sterno	Swe	1970	1,300	1,350	75.7	11.1	3.6	12	C	ex Seto-84, Ostestrom-83, Mariona-72, I/a Ostestrom

O.H. Meling & Co., Norway

Name	Flag	Year	GRT	DWT	Loa	Bm	Draft	Kts	Type	Former names
Stavtank	Nis	1995	4,268	8,491	115.1	18.3	7.5	14	T	

Nils Olav Melingen, Norway

Name	Flag	Year	GRT	DWT	Loa	Bm	Draft	Kts	Type	Former names
Sava Lake	Pan	1990	2,030	3,080	74.7	12.7	6.0	12	Cu	

A.E. Mengwall, Sweden

Name	Flag	Year	GRT	DWT	Loa	Bm	Draft	Kts	Type	Former names
Bellona	Swe	1965	2,050	2,996	87.0	12.5	5.4	13	T	ex Stella Atlantic-78

Mermaid Marine Management Ltd., UK

Name	Flag	Year	GRT	DWT	Loa	Bm	Draft	Kts	Type	Former names
Alpine Girl	Bhs	1975	3,984	6,418	110.0	16.6	6.9	14	Tch	ex Dintel-86, Quimico Lisboa-86, I/a Chemist Lisbon
Alpine Lady	Bhs	1977	4,009	6,433	110.5	16.6	6.9	13	Tch	ex Multitank Antares-88, Dommel-87, Quimico Leixoes-86

Herbert Meyer, Germany

Name	Flag	Year	GRT	DWT	Loa	Bm	Draft	Kts	Type	Former names
Karin	Deu	1988	1,986	2,618	82.5	12.5	4.6	11	Cc	

Peter Meyer, Germany

Name	Flag	Year	GRT	DWT	Loa	Bm	Draft	Kts	Type	Former names
Arosia	Atg	1977	1,678	2,800	72.0	12.8	5.5	12	Cc	ex Corvette-90, Eco Dao-83, Corvette-81, Else Beth-78, I/a Corvette

Bernd Meyering, Germany

Name	Flag	Year	GRT	DWT	Loa	Bm	Draft	Kts	Type	Former names
Aura	Cyp	1992	2,416	3,601	85.0	13.0	5.4	12	Cc	ex Lume Bay-98, Jens-93

Mezeron Ltd., Isle of Man (UK)

Name	Flag	Year	GRT	DWT	Loa	Bm	Draft	Kts	Type	Former names
Auldyn River	Iom	1961	417	585	54.2	7.6	2.3	8	C	ex Claudia W-98, Eberstein-79 (len/deep-75 & 83)
Silver River	Iom	1968	277	373	44.7	7.4	2.7	10	C	ex Nathurn-86, Sea Trent-82, Seacon-71

Mirfak Scheepvaart BV, Netherlands

Name	Flag	Year	GRT	DWT	Loa	Bm	Draft	Kts	Type	Former names
Aruba	Ant	1980	4,904	7,550	117.8	18.5	6.0	14	Cc	ex Maashaven-94, Jomsborg-89, Maashaven-88, Breslau-87, Togo Brewer-83, I/a Breslau
Herman Bodewes	Vct	1978	2,697	3,636	82.2	15.1	6.1	13	Cc	ex Herman Danielsen-86, Herman Bodewes-84

Name	Flag	Year	GRT	DWT	Loa	Bm	Draft	Kts	Type	Former names

Kare Misje & Co. Rederi A/S, Norway

Name	Flag	Year	GRT	DWT	Loa	Bm	Draft	Kts	Type	Former names
Dogger	Nis	1976	1,092	1,585	65.8	10.8	4.3	10	C	ex Dollard-96, Doggersbank-95
Fortuna	Nis	1979	1,094	1,519	65.8	10.8	4.3	10	C	ex Arklow Glen-94, Tromp-84
Natacha	Bhs	1982	1,636	2,380	70.1	13.1	5.0	10	Bc	ex Natacha C-98, Natacha Caldas-91, Natacha-90, Norbrit Maas-87, Norbrit Faith-85
Nautilus	Nis	1978	1,094	1,519	65.8	10.8	4.3	10	C	ex Arklow Dew-94, Arklow View-91, Terona-84

Heinz Moje KG, Germany

Name	Flag	Year	GRT	DWT	Loa	Bm	Draft	Kts	Type	Former names
Deneb	Deu	1994	3,992	5,350	101.1	18.4	6.5	15	Cc	ex OOCL Neva-99, Deneb-98, Rhein Partner-98, Rhein Liffey-95, I/a Deneb
Maris	Deu	1995	3,999	5,325	100.6	18.5	6.6	15	Cc	

Jorn Moller Skibsagentur ApS, Denmark

Name	Flag	Year	GRT	DWT	Loa	Bm	Draft	Kts	Type	Former names
Supidana	Dis	1969	1,109	1,036	64.6	11.0	3.5	11	C	ex Finla-97, Dinah-85, Stefanie-76

A/S Morerutene, Norway

Name	Flag	Year	GRT	DWT	Loa	Bm	Draft	Kts	Type	Former names
Jotunheim	Nor	1983	1,962	1,700	77.6	13.0	4.4	14	Rop	ex Viking-96, Star Viking-92
Sunnmore	Nor	1985	2,706	2,000	79.9	15.0	5.0		Cp	

Mundo Schiffahrts GmbH & Co. KG, Germany

Name	Flag	Year	GRT	DWT	Loa	Bm	Draft	Kts	Type	Former names
Mundo 1	Cyp	1984	1,860	3,035	91.1	11.4	4.9	10	Cc	ex Seawisp-96, Senara-95, Seawisp-92, Umeazee-88,

Murmansk Shipping Co., Russia

Name	Flag	Year	GRT	DWT	Loa	Bm	Draft	Kts	Type	Former names
Pavlik Larishkin	Rus	1971	3,693	4,642	105.7	15.6	6.8	14	Cc	
Tonya Bondarchuk	Rus	1972	3,708	4,687	105.6	15.7	6.8	14	Cc	

Nautilus Chartering NV, Netherlands

Name	Flag	Year	GRT	DWT	Loa	Bm	Draft	Kts	Type	Former names
Celine	Bhs	1996	821	1,020	67.4	10.6	3.0	-	Tch	ex C-Bitez-96
Dennis Danielsen	Cyp	1978	1,946	2,537	79.8	13.1	5.2	12	C	ex Otto Danielsen-96, Atlantic Cape-95, Flex Fortuna-85, Amigo Fortuna-79

Navimer SA, Switzerland

Name	Flag	Year	GRT	DWT	Loa	Bm	Draft	Kts	Type	Former names
Prince Henri	Lux	1990	2,522	4,686	110.0	12.5	5.5	12	Tch	
Regina	Lux	1987	1,731	2,680	110.0	11.4	2.2	11	T	
Vomero	Pan	1973	8,557	7,268	149.2	18.9	6.4	17	Ro	ex Aquila-90, Sea Road-89, Aquila-89, Nahost Pionier-79, Ehrenfels-77, Ipswich Pioneer II-76, I/a Aquila (len-76)

N. C. Schiffahrtsburo GmbH & Co. KG, Germany

Name	Flag	Year	GRT	DWT	Loa	Bm	Draft	Kts	Type	Former names
Baltica	Hnd	1971	2,397	2,445	88.5	13.9	5.3	14	Cc	ex San Pancracio I-94, Baltica-85, Scol Hunter-77, Baltica-76

Nedjan Shipping AS, Norway

Name	Flag	Year	GRT	DWT	Loa	Bm	Draft	Kts	Type	Former names
Borre	Nis	1980	2,061	3,085	82.4	12.8	5.1	12	Cc	ex Borne af Simrishamn-97, Svarte-91, Ann-Mari-90, Ann Ragne-86, Repola-84
Debora	Nis	1965	2,331	2,390	94.0	13.3	4.7	13	C	ex Porrino-90, Lill-Nina-88, Conti Liban-83, Cremon-75

Nes H/F, Iceland

Name	Flag	Year	GRT	DWT	Loa	Bm	Draft	Kts	Type	Former names
Haukur	Nis	1966	1,133	1,397	65.0	12.1	4.0	12	Ce	ex Freyfaxi-83
Lomur	Nis	1983	1,516	1,570	72.5	11.3	3.6	10	Cc	ex Ocelot-94, Captain Most-90, Karen Dania-87

Name	Flag	Year	GRT	DWT	Loa	Bm	Draft	Kts	Type	Former names
Svanur	Nis	1983	1,516	2,600	72.5	11.7	3.6	10	Cc	ex Svanur II-95, Louise-95, Lynx-94, Jette Dania-92, Skipper Most-92, Jette Dania-87

Managed by A/S Shipmanagement Ltd., Norway.

Neva-Stream Joint Stock Co., Russia

Symphony	Vct	1975	2,856	3,336	99.3	13.5	4.9	14	Cc	ex Bokelnburg-97, Kini Kersten-89, Bokelnburg-88, Isle of Man-83, Bokelnburg-81, Bourgogne-78, Bokelnburg-75 (len-78)
Tigra (2)	Rus	1970	2,484	2,925	114.2	13.2	3.4	10	C	ex Shushenskoye-98

Nevel Joint Stock Co., Russia

Baltiyskiy-40 (2)	Rus	1965	1,865	2,121	95.6	13.2	3.3	10	C	
Volgo-Don 5035 (2)	Rus	1972	3,946	3,822	138.8	16.7	3.8	10	C	

Kim Ulnits Nielsen, Denmark

Adriane	Dis	1970	1,371	1,280	69.8	11.6	3.6	12	Cc	ex Cito-97, Adria-90, Adriana-86

William Nielsen & Co., Denmark

Caroline Samso	Dnk	1959	159	249	33.5	6.5	3.0	10	C	ex Jane-94, Janto-65

Kjell Nilsen, Norway

Polarbulk	Nor	1972	1,547	1,289	76.6	12.3	3.5	12	C	ex Dyna Bulk-96, Frakt-89, Slot Scandinavia-84, Merc Scandinavia-80

Nina ApS, Denmark

Thyra Moller (2)	Dis	1990	2,762	3,020	91.5	16.8	4.3	14	Cc/Ro	ex Sysette-97, Mekong Harmony-96, Sysette-94, Maersk Deccan-94, Sysette-93
Tokai (2)	Dis	1987	1,814	1,976	85.4	14.0	3.5	13	Rop	ex Katrine-96, Cari Bridge-94, Katrine-93 (len-90)

Kjellrun Noesten, Norway

Renate	Nor	1965	557	615	50.6	8.7	3.2	11	C	exSylvia-92, Eksor-88, Bulkfart-86, Eldaroy-85, Pokal-80, Svennor-74, Bios-74, Ferro-70

Noordwest Shipmanagement BV, Netherlands

Lenie	Nid	1979	848	1,3	64.8	10.0	3.4	10	C	ex Willem-97, Lenie-95

Nora Reederei und Verwaltungesellschaft m.b.H., Germany

MF Malta	Atg	1991	2,481	3,232	87.5	13.0	5.1	12	Cc	ex Intermodal Malta-96, Wannsee-94, Medeur Terzo-92, Wannsee-92

Norbal Schiffahrtskontor Lange & Luhr, Germany

Whestgate	Khm	1965	1,315	1,691	72.9	11.6	4.6	12	C	ex Helena Husmann-77
Truco	Blz	1958	496	825	60.4	9.0	3.4	10	C	ex Alfa-96, Charlette-86, Wera Bohrnsen-85, Kai-65

Norbroker Shipping & Trading AS, Norway

Ingrid Maria	Nis	1985	1,211	1,117	63.0	11.5	3.4	10	Cc	ex Gesche-97
Stina	Bhs	1971	1,318	1,380	76.4	11.9	3.7		Cc	ex Garden-95, Mistresse-85, Lucia-80, Tor Forest-74, Lucia Bos-71

Owned by subsidiary Bines Shipping A.S K/S.

Nord-Ost Ltd., Russia

Sormovskiy-5 (2)	Rus	1968	2,478	2,925	114.2	13.2	3.4	10	C	
Volgo-Balt 116 (2)	Rus	1970	2,584	2,907	114.0	13.2	3.5	10	C	
Volgo-Balt 150 (2)	Rus	1971	2,457	3,180	113.8	13.2	3.6	10	C	

Name	Flag	Year	GRT	DWT	Loa	Bm	Draft	Kts	Type	Former names

Nord Ship Management Ltd., UK

Name	Flag	Year	GRT	DWT	Loa	Bm	Draft	Kts	Type	Former names
Commodity	Gbr	1975	633	946	57.6	10.0	3.3	10	C	
Nord Star	Gbr	1978	460	727	49.3	9.0	3.2	10	C	ex Kava Sound-94, Ordinence-89

Nordgrens Rederi AB, Sweden

Name	Flag	Year	GRT	DWT	Loa	Bm	Draft	Kts	Type	Former names
Tinto	Swe	1977	1,191	1,550	74.8	10.6	3.3	11	C	ex Frakto-89, Tinto-83 (len-80)
Wani Logger	Nis	1976	2,602	3,092	87.9	14.6	5.4	14	Cc	ex Logger-96, Norrbotten-92, Well Martin-89, Westerdiek-86, Gastrikland-80, Westerdiek-77

Nordschweden Frachtienst Verwaltungs GmbH, Germany

Name	Flag	Year	GRT	DWT	Loa	Bm	Draft	Kts	Type	Former names
Alegra	Cyp	1997	2,805	4,241	89.9	13.2	5.7	-	Cc	
Eleonore	Cyp	1982	1,988	2,864	87.6	11.4	4.5	11	Cc	ex Altamira-95, Bottensee-95
Esmeralda	Deu	1998	2,834	4,620	89.9	13.2	6.1	-	C	
Isabella 1	Cyp	1998	2,844	4,230	89.9	13.2	5.7	-	Cc	l/a Isabella

Normannes AS, Norway

Name	Flag	Year	GRT	DWT	Loa	Bm	Draft	Kts	Type	Former names
Normannes	Nis	1976	4,576	7,020	110.8	19.0	7.2	13	C	ex La Briantais-98, Sophie B-89, Havstril-83, Kings River-79

Norminol AS, Norway

Name	Flag	Year	GRT	DWT	Loa	Bm	Draft	Kts	Type	Former names
Havnor	Nis	1968	902	1,188	60.6	10.2	4.2	11	T	ex Magn I-97, Magn-96, Helle Wonsild-81

Norship A/S, Norway

Name	Flag	Year	GRT	DWT	Loa	Bm	Draft	Kts	Type	Former names
Cemcon	Bhs	1981	3,875	6,174	106.8	15.8	6.8	-	Ce	ex Galizano-96

Nortech (Scotland) Ltd., UK

Name	Flag	Year	GRT	DWT	Loa	Bm	Draft	Kts	Type	Former names
Fulford	Gbr	1960	477	522	49.8	10.2	2.6	-	T	ex Charmo-91
Perfecto	Gbr	1967	652	1,008	59.2	10.7	3.5	9	T	ex Shell Driver-89, Perfecto-79 (len-69)

North Africa Middle East Shipping & Engineering Co. Holland BV, Netherlands

Name	Flag	Year	GRT	DWT	Loa	Bm	Draft	Kts	Type	Former names
SW Runner	Gbr	1965	575	762	62.3	9.5	3.1	10	Tch	ex Goldcrest-98, Silverkestrel-94, Goldcrest-92, Carrick Kestrel-87, Silverkestrel-75 (len-69)
SW Trader	Gbr	1966	688	952	57.0	9.8	4.4	11	Tch	ex Sandlark-98, Silverlark-94, Sandlark-92, Ice Lark-87, Finnlark-76
Viking Sky	Pan	1971	1,940	2,837	79.9	12.8	5.6	13	CC	ex polianni Due-98, Vento-96, Marco Polo-90, Esther del Mar-89, Manchester Rapido-77, l/a Esther del Mar-??

Nygard Shipping A/S, Norway

Name	Flag	Year	GRT	DWT	Loa	Bm	Draft	Kts	Type	Former names
Dura Bulk	Dis	1973	1,952	2,398	87.8	13.2	5.0	15	C	ex Brunborg-85
Trader Bulk	Nor	1978	1,730	3,055	80.0	14.0	5.3	14	C	ex Celtic Challenger-95, Argo Valour-86

Partr. Nyholm DA, Denmark

Name	Flag	Year	GRT	DWT	Loa	Bm	Draft	Kts	Type	Former names
Nyholm (2)	Dnk	1992	1,515	2,376	74.9	11.4	4.4	10	C	ex Lass Sun-98, Sun-92

A/B Nynas Petroleum, Sweden

Name	Flag	Year	GRT	DWT	Loa	Bm	Draft	Kts	Type	Former names
Engelsberg	Swe	1969	4,248	5,030	123.2	15.7	5.7	14	Tb	
Framnas	Swe	1973	4,230	5,061	122.8	15.6	5.5	-	Tb	(len-73)

O & S Shipping GmbH (Nobis Shipping GmbH), Germany

Name	Flag	Year	GRT	DWT	Loa	Bm	Draft	Kts	Type	Former names
Med Record (2)	Atg	1979	3,922	2,570	91.9	18.1	3.7	12	Ro	ex Sloman Record-97, Med Record-96, Sloman Record-95

Newbuildings: eight 4,000 grt 6,000 dwt dry cargo vessels ordered for 1999/2000 delivery .

Name	Flag	Year	GRT	DWT	Loa	Bm	Draft	Kts	Type	Former names

J.O. Odfjell A/S, Norway

Name	Flag	Year	GRT	DWT	Loa	Bm	Draft	Kts	Type	Former names
Jo Hegg	Lbr	1985	5,357	7,918	108.5	17.9	8.0	13	Tch	ex Golden Queen-89
Jo Spirit	Lbr	1998	4,425	6,285	107.4	15.9	7.0	13	Tch	I/a Proof Spirit
Jo Maple	Nld	1991	4,988	8,236	115.2	18.1	7.7	12	Tch	
Jo Palm	Nld	1991	4,988	8,236	115.2	18.1	7.7	12	Tch	

Klaus Dieter Oelze Schiffahrts KG, Germany

Name	Flag	Year	GRT	DWT	Loa	Bm	Draft	Kts	Type	Former names
Anke-Angela	Atg	1984	1,547	1,735	82.5	11.4	3.5	10	Cc	ex Claudia-Isabell-97

Fred. Olsen & Co., Norway

Name	Flag	Year	GRT	DWT	Loa	Bm	Draft	Kts	Type	Former names
Bencomo	Pan	1983	6,182	4,200	128.1	18.0	5.6	20	Rc	

Odvar Olsen (Goliat Shipping A/S), Norway

Name	Flag	Year	GRT	DWT	Loa	Bm	Draft	Kts	Type	Former names
Clare (2)	Nis	1972	5,617	2,850	114.9	17.4	5.3	17	Ro	ex Dana Baltica-96, Vinzia E-94, Norcrest-93, Wesertal-92, Meyer Express-73, Wesertal-72
Seaboard Venture (2)	Nis	1978	6,991	3,506	113.4	19.5	5.5	14	Ro	ex Motupe-93, Railro-92, Panama City-89, Railro-87, Costa Rica-84
Seahawk (2)	Nis	1975	10,171	7,597	137.6	20.6	7.2	18	Ro	ex Dana Minerva-97, Fichtelberg-95, Norcliff-93, Fichtelberg-92, Spirit of Dublin-92, Fichtelberg-91, I/a Tor Caledonia

See other chartered out vessels in freight ferry section.

Ohlsson & Lnde Shipping A/S, Denmark

Name	Flag	Year	GRT	DWT	Loa	Bm	Draft	Kts	Type	Former names
Thuro	Dis	1963	451	670	51.8	8.7	3.3	10	C	ex Uno-91, Stevnsklint-81

Oljola AB, Sweden

Name	Flag	Year	GRT	DWT	Loa	Bm	Draft	Kts	Type	Former names
Vastsjo	Swe	1970	903	1,435	69.8	10.0	4.2	11	Tch	ex Doverian-96, Whitdale-94, Danae-88, Pass of Chisholm-84, Cordene-75 (len-72)

Orimi Group, Russia

Name	Flag	Year	GRT	DWT	Loa	Bm	Draft	Kts	Type	Former names
Sormovskiy-2 (2)	Rus	1968	2,478	2,925	114.2	13.2	3.4	10	C	

Louis Ormestad A/S, Norway

Name	Flag	Year	GRT	DWT	Loa	Bm	Draft	Kts	Type	Former names
Anglia	Nis	1971	1,220	2,039	74.0	10.8	5.1	12	Cc	
Lobo	Nis	1972	1,741	2,850	86.6	12.9	5.1	12	C	ex Alva-88, Superiority-86
Loyal Partner	Nis	1979	2,610	4,449	86.5	14.4	6.8	13	Cc	ex Cotalba-98, Bulko-90, Parayas-90, Bulko-89, Parayas-86, Cabauno-85, Duro Siete-81
Loyal Trader	Nis	1972	1,861	2,958	84.2	13.6	5.3	12	C	ex Bulk Master-95, Soknatun-93

Osterstroms Rederi AB, Sweden

Name	Flag	Year	GRT	DWT	Loa	Bm	Draft	Kts	Type	Former names
Louise	Vct	1971	1,227	1,845	71.4	11.9	4.5	12	Cc	ex Irmelin-95, Weststream-89, Osteturm-83
Mets	Vct	1971	2,397	3,720	88.5	13.9	6.5	12	Cc	ex Aquila-94, Nautic-94, Elmwood-90, Nautic-87, Pepilo-82, nautic-82

O.T. Tonnevold AS, Norway

Name	Flag	Year	GRT	DWT	Loa	Bm	Draft	Kts	Type	Former names
Thornburg	Lbr	1981	4,238	4,447	101.3	17.1	5.4	13	Cc	ex Joan Sif-97, FAS Redsea-96, Joan Sif-96, Kamsar Trader-94, Anne Sif-93, Nedlloyd Shuttle-92, Asifi-91, Anne Sif-86, Frellsen Birgitte-82
Thorndale	Lbr	1981	4,238	4,380	101.3	17.1	5.5	13	Cc	ex Kathe Sif-97, Azzahra-96, Kathe Sif-96, Kathrine Sif-90, Frellsen Annette-82, Jugo Carrier-82, Frellsen Annette-81

Parkside Warehousing & Transport Co. Ltd., UK

Name	Flag	Year	GRT	DWT	Loa	Bm	Draft	Kts	Type	Former names
Borelly	Gbr	1971	571	905	55.7	9.9	3.3	10	C	ex Jana Weston-84

Name	Flag	Year	GRT	DWT	Loa	Bm	Draft	Kts	Type	Former names

Passat Joint Stock Co., Lithuania
Stropus (2)	Ltu	1966	1,865	2,121	96.0	13.2	3.3	10	C	ex Baltiyskiy-52-97
Sumanus (2)	Ltu	1988	4,911	5,845	139.8	16.6	4.5	10	C	ex Volga-4005-98

Wilhelm Pekholtz GmbH & Co., Germany
Kaja-H	Atg	1969	1,251	1,408	74.1	10.9	3.7	10	C	ex Castor-98 (len/widen-74)

Reederei Gebruder Person KG, Germany
Faros	Deu	1978	2,038	2,411	86.4	12.8	4.9	13	Cc	ex Lubeca-88
Sparos	Deu	1979	2,047	2,515	86.7	12.8	4.9	13	Cc	I/a Inka

Carl F. Peters GmbH & Co., Germany
Ebony	Atg	1967	1,914	3,290	91.3	12.6	5.1	12	T	ex Navichem Sirius-91, Jan-89 (len-78)

Newbuildings: two 4,000 grt 6,780 dwt tankers on order for 1999 delivery.

Jonny Petersen, Germany
Kerstin	Atg	1984	2,683	3,040	92.5	13.9	4.5	11	Cc	

Reederei Georg Peterson, Germany
Anne Catharina	Atg	1986	3,147	3,324	90.0	15.5	4.7	12	Cc	ex Georgetown-87, Anne Catharina-86
Christopher Meeder	Atg	1976	2,154	2,200	86.9	13.0	4.8	13	Cc	

Owned by subsidiary Reederei Johanna Claussen.

S. P. Pettersson, Sweden
West Sky	Swe	1968	2,544	2,523	90.1	15.2	4.6	14	Cc	ex Solway-93, Dixie-92, Solway Firth-90, Solway Fisher-85

Phenix Shipping, France
Clipper Cherokee	Fra	1975	4,020	5,288	105.4	17.4	6.3	11	Cc/hl	ex Huali-93, Stellaprima-89, Internavis I-81

Oy Pipping & Co. AB, Finland
Helen	Fin	1979	1,826	2,213	79.8	12.8	4.4	12	Cc	ex Norden-93, Holger-86
Maria VG	Fin	1972	1,854	2,946	80.0	13.8	5.3	13	C	ex Marika-97, Pingo-86, Pingvin-79

Pistoor Schiffahrtsgesellschaft KG, Germany
Freya	Deu	1991	1,548	2,412	79.6	11.3	4.4	10	Cc	

Polar Shipping A/S, Norway
Fjord	Pan	1976	2,062	1,560	69.6	14.5	4.9	12	Ccp	ex Sfinx-97, Ice Bird-95, Studlafoss-92, Isberg-90, Fjord-86

Point Shipping Co., Eire
Dunany	Brb	1983	1,785	2,535	77.1	13.2	5.0	12	C	ex Cowdray-94, Ballygrainey-90
Hope	Brb	1982	1,785	2,535	77.1	13.2	5.0	12	C	ex Shoreham-93, Ballygarvey-90

Pontus Navigation Joint Stock Co., Russia
Sormovskiy-36 (2)	Rus	1976	2,466	3,136	114.0	13.2	3.6	10	C	ex Fyodor Podtelkov-94, Sormovskiy-36-??, Fyodor Podtelkov-92
Sormovskiy-54 (2)	Rus	1978	2,466	3,134	114.0	13.2	3.7	10	C	ex 0060 Let VLKSM-92
Sormovskiy-116 (2)	Rus	1978	2,466	3,134	114.0	13.2	3.7	10	C	ex Mikhail Krivoshiykov-92

Pooja Shipping & Trading Co. Ltd., Netherlands
Shyamlee	Vct	1972	1,160	1,614	71.1	10.4	3.7	12	C	ex Star Bonaire-95, Rechlin-92

Alan Pratt and others, UK
Severn Side	Gbr	1952	244	406	41.0	6.5	2.5	7	C	

Name	Flag	Year	GRT	DWT	Loa	Bm	Draft	Kts	Type	Former names

Pride Shipping & Management A/S, Norway
Ocean Pride	Nis	1974	2,592	2,750	87.9	14.4	4.8	14	Cc	ex Landwind-96, Mer Eagle-91, Annika-89, Rio Star-87, Annika-86

Wilhelm Raap Schiffahrts KG, Germany
Niederelbe	Deu	1982	1,939	2,890	88.0	11.4	4.7	11	Cc	

Raatgever OA
Vitoria Nova	Nld	1959	499	745	56.6	9.6	3.0	9	C	ex Vitoria Novas-89, Anita-87, Roelina-85, Michel-84, Sea Vigor-79, Heinrich Hauschildt-76

Wilfried Rambow KG, Germany
Gerda	Deu	1995	3,999	5,300	100.6	18.5	6.6		Cc	
Lucy Borchard	Deu	1996	6,362	7,223	121.4	18.5		16	CC	ex Solid-97, Sven-96
Vera	Deu	1996	3,999	5,207	101.1	18.5	15.0	15	Cc	

Heinz & Bernd Rambow, Germany
Bernd	Deu	1966	453	683	52.4	8.5	3.0	10	C	ex Brake-88, Rewi-78, Reind-75 (len-80)

Ramsey Steam Ship Co. Ltd., Isle of Man (UK)
Ben Ellan	Iom	1981	538	824	50.0	9.3	3.4	9	C	ex River Tamar-90
Ben Maye	Iom	1979	548	805	48.8	9.1	3.6	10	C	ex Vendome-95, Peroto-94
Ben Vane	Iom	1978	541	772	50.2	9.0	3.4	9	C	ex Bulk Moon-88, Julia S-81

Rana Ship Managers AS, Norway
Vistafjord	Mlt	1966	1,437	1,630	75.3	11.8	5.6	13	C	ex Salini-97, Tunstein-87, Kehdingen-85

Rass Schiffahrt GmbH & Co., Germany
Hohebank	Bhs	1978	1,687	1,851	79.7	12.8	3.7	11	Cc	
Canarias	Deu	1993	3,992	5,335	100.0	18.4	6.6	15	Cc	ex Hoheweg-99, OOCL Nevskiy-98, Hoheweg-98, Armada Reliance-95, Hoheweg-95
Susan Borchard	Deu	1996	6,362	7,223	121.4	18.5	6.7	16	CC	ex Pentland-97, Hohebank-96

Rechdan Joint Venture Co., Russia
Mologa	Rus	1996	2,914	3,837	96.3	13.6	5.2	11	Cc	

Haram Regnskap, Norway
Starvik	Nor	1972	973	1,097	59.3	10.8	4.6	10	C	ex Leopold-95, Dream One-86, Frendo Cargo-79, Eger Cargo-76, Nenny Cargo-74

Carsten Rehder, Germany
Almania	Atg	1983	4,366	5,900	99.9	17.8	6.9	13	Cc	ex CPC America-92, Conti Almania-92
Arosette	Atg	1971	1,205	1,968	74.5	10.8	5.1	12	Cc	
Cabot Strait	Atg	1984	7,335	9,300	127.1	19.9	8.1	15	Cc	ex Vento del Golfo-98, Mile One-96, Sea Venture-95, Norasia Arabia-94, John M-93, Norasia Adria-92, Holcan Rijn-89, John M-88

Rejo Shipping A/S, Norway
Korsnes	Pan	1979	3,967	6,156	107.0	15.0	6.5	13	C	ex General Ricarte-92, Korsnes-86 (len-83)

Oddmar Rekstad, Norway
Kyst	Nor	1982	403	475	48.4	8.5	3.0	10	C	ex Glenfyne-96, Lille-Birgit-89

Name	Flag	Year	GRT	DWT	Loa	Bm	Draft	Kts	Type	Former names

Remi Charter AB, Sweden

Name	Flag	Year	GRT	DWT	Loa	Bm	Draft	Kts	Type	Former names
Arena	Swe	1960	530	721	52.5	8.8	3.8	10	C	ex Underas Sandtag VI-95, Carina-65, Norskint-65

Renck & Hessenmuller, Germany

Ahrenshoop	Deu	1970	1,641	1,350	75.7	11.3	3.6	12	Cc	ex Frankto-78, Stokkfrakt-77, Frakto-75, Anglo Unit-74, Karen Oltmann-72
Ortrud	Atg	1978	1,922	2,965	95.0	11.4	4.7	12	Cc	ex Solveig-91, Pirat-87, Hip Pancevo-83, Pirat-81

Scheepvaartbedrijf Rensen BV, Netherlands

Sterrenburg	Nld	1997	1,200	1,770	86.0	11.4	-	-	C	

Reederei Bertram Rickmers G.m.b.H., Germany

Berulan	Atg	1995	8,633	9,200	133.0	22.9	7.7	17	CC	ex Magdalena-98, Berulan—97, Louise Borchard-96, I/a Berulan

Rederiet Carsten Rousing ApS, Denmark

Anders Rousing	Dis	1979	1,324	1,565	69.0	11.4	3.5	10	C	ex Norbox-95, Heljo-89
Sarah Rousing	Dis	1979	1,456	1,578	81.9	10.0	3.5	10	C	ex Alexander-94

Rialto Shipping BV, Netherlands

Katharina	Nld	1978	1,863	2,955	80.2	12.5	5.5	12	C	ex Flinterdijk-98, Maritta Johanna-91

Rigel Schiffahrts GmbH, Germany

Oderstern	Iom	1992	5,480	9,028	109.7	17.7	8.5	12	Tch	
Weserstern	Iom	1992	5,480	9,028	110.0	17.7	8.5	12	Tch	

Rosali Shipping GmbH & Co. KG, Germany

Rosali	Cyp	1972	4,255	6,341	96.9	16.1	7.2	13	Cc	ex Linde II-93, Endurance-89, Baucis-88, Alice Bolten-73

Royal Arctic Line A/S, Denmark

Arina Arctica	Dis	1984	6,759	4,330	110.0	21.9	6.2	16	CC	ex Nuka Ittuk-93 (conv Cp-94)
Irena Arctica	Dis	1995	8,939	5,817	108.7	21.5	6.5	-	CC	
Kista Arctica	Dis	1973	4,209	4,990	93.9	17.3	7.4	14	C	ex Nungu Ittuk-93, Gronland-83

Owned by Government of The Kingdom of Denmark.

Rudolf & Runge Bereederrungsgesellschaft, Germany

Montania	Cyp	1981	2,265	2,970	99.8	11.4	4.3	10	Cc	ex Thekla-96, Clovis-88, Thekla Wessels-86,
Normannia	Cyp	1983	1,946	2,904	88.0	11.5	4.7	11	Cc	ex Baursberg-97

Rubert Shipping, Denmark

Dania	Dis	1971	642	880	58.7	10.3	3.6	10	C	
Elfi	Dis	1961	407	584	46.9	8.3	3.2	8	C	ex Jupiter-88, Atlantic Sky-87, Joal-86, Hoan-77, Peder Most-73
Lake Pejo	Dis	1961	407	584	50.8	8.3	3.1	10	C	ex Rita L-88, Marie Th.-84, Louis S-74

Reederei Hans August Sabban, Germany

Birgit Sabban	Deu	1984	2,119	3,042	92.1	11.5	4.7	11	Cc	

Ou RVA, Estonia

Kirre	Khm	1970	1,798	2,483	82.0	12.5	5.4	12	C	ex Sovietskiy Pogranichnik-97

Knut Saetre og Sonner, Norway

Karmsund	Nor	1979	2,728	1,250	89.4	14.5	4.6	13	Ccp	(len-87)
Ranafrakt	Nor	1987	1,156	1,323	58.0	11.7	3.5	10	Cc	ex Heyo Prahm-97
Tananger	Nor	1980	4,636	4,380	102.5	16.5	6.1	14	Ro	ex Forest Swan-95, Jerome B-93, Canis-91
Tri Frakt	Nor	1973	2,677	3,777	84.3	14.4	6.3	14	C	ex Frakt-94, Kiri-94, Makiri-92, Makiri Smits-84

Name	Flag	Year	GRT	DWT	Loa	Bm	Draft	Kts	Type	Former names
Sandfrakt A/S, Norway										
Faktor	Nor	1971	793	823	55.3	10.5	3.3	11	C	ex Rytind-87, Scanblue-77, Bente Steen-77
Nor Viking	Nor	1977	1,992	3,048	80.1	14.4	5.6	13	C	ex Norro-92, Norrviken-88
Vikanes	Nis	1967	2,659	4,475	99.9	14.7	6.1	13	C	ex Tofton-95, Rugia-76
Sandhammaren Shipping AB, Sweden										
Linden	Mlt	1982	3,222	5,327	82.4	15.8	7.5	14	Cc	ex Lindeborg-96
Salama	Mlt	1970	2,092	3,251	87.0	12.7	5.0	-	C	ex Lekna-93, Demi-89, Ranie-85, Kristina-84, Alice-73

Owned by subsidiary Pelmar Shipping AB.

Name	Flag	Year	GRT	DWT	Loa	Bm	Draft	Kts	Type	Former names
Sauda Bulk AS, Norway										
Gardsea	Nis	1971	1,937	2,452	77.0	12.9	4.1	12	Cc	ex Ilse L-89, Hella-87, Gazelle-82
Gardwind	Nis	1970	1,900	1,522	77.3	12.8	4.1	12	Cc	ex Kiefernberg-87
Rudolf Schepers, Germany										
Batavier VI	Nld	1997	2,599	3,600	92.8	15.9	4.9	-	CC	l/a Ijsseldijk
Borussia Dortmund	Deu	1996	6,378	7,147	121.4	18.5	6.7	16	CC	
Christopher	Deu	1990	2,292	2,690	84.9	12.9	4.4	11	Cc	
Reederei Wilhelm Schepers KG, Germany										
Lena S	Deu	1982	1,692	2,318	80.3	11.4	4.3	10	C	
Klaus Schneider Schiffahrts KG, Germany										
Coastal Sound	Deu	1983	2,046	1,876	78.0	13.9	5.0	13	Cc	ex Kirsten-98, Christopher Caribe-93, Saturnus-92, Craigavad-88
Schoning Befrachtungskontor GmbH & Co. KG, Germany										
Thule	Deu	1996	2,771	4,140	90.5	13.6	5.7	-	Cc	
Sea River Chartering BV, Netherlands										
Diamond	Nld	1985	1,487	2,284	79.5	11.3	4.4	10	C	
Ruby	Nld	1986	1,512	2,475	79.6	11.3	4.4	9	C	
Sea Truck Shipping A/S, Norway										
Baltic Sea	Nis	1977	2,282	2,566	81.4	13.7	5.0	13	Cc	ex Carina-89
Seaway SAM, Monaco										
Natissa	Vct	1995	1,554	2,030	81.6	11.4	3.7	10	C	ex Sea Rhone-99
Sea Ruhr	Vct	1995	1,554	2,044	81.6	11.4	3.7	10	Cp	
See-Transit Schiffahrts-und Speditions. GmbH, Germany										
Conro Trader (2)	Atg	1978	6,051	3,000	110.0	18.1	4.2	12	Ro	ex Helena Husmann-86, Areucon Caroline-78
Petersburg	Atg	1985	1,838	2,285	80.6	12.7	4.2	11	Cc	ex Peter S-93
Rhine-Liner	Atg	1978	2,319	2,851	99.7	11.4	4.1	10	Cc	ex Rhone Liner-92, Smederevo-82, Rhone Liner-81
Shipping Co. Sibnec, Russia										
Sibnec (2)	Rus	1965	1,948	2,624	96.0	13.2	3.8	10	C	ex Baltiyskiy-27-96
Ships-Cont Ltd. Oy, Finland										
Petsamo	Fin	1976	2,356	2,650	84.3	13.5	5.0	14	Cc	ex DFL Helsinki-92, Cimbria-89, Aros Freighter-85, Frat I-83, Voline-82
Sibum GmbH & Co. KG, Germany										
Maria Sibum	Deu	1986	8,108	9,393	132.7	22.7	7.5	17	Cc	ex Kent Trader-97, Independent Concept-98, Karaman-93, ACT 10-88, Ya Maira Sibum-??
Stefan Sibum	Deu	1996	5,712	6,850	121.9	19.0	6.7	17	Cc	

Name	Flag	Year	GRT	DWT	Loa	Bm	Draft	Kts	Type	Former names

Kurt Alwin Otto Siemer, Germany

Name	Flag	Year	GRT	DWT	Loa	Bm	Draft	Kts	Type	Former names
Katharina Siemer	Cyp	1985	2,061	3,357	88.0	11.5	5.2	11	Cc	ex Katharina S-99, RMS Hispania-95, Katharina Siemer-93
Stephanie S	Cyp	1980	1,751	2,422	85.9	11.4	4.0	10	Cc	ex RMS Lettia-96, Stephanie Siemer-93

Sinbad Shipping A/B, Sweden

Name	Flag	Year	GRT	DWT	Loa	Bm	Draft	Kts	Type	Former names
Chemical Exporter	Mlt	1975	4,292	6,493	111.5	16.7	7.0	16	Tch	ex Isola Azzurra-92 Ashfield-88, pinta-84, La Cumbre-83, Delchim Dauphine-76

Rederij Sirenia, Netherlands

Name	Flag	Year	GRT	DWT	Loa	Bm	Draft	Kts	Type	Former names
Dolfijn	Nld	1989	1,987	2,450	81.2	12.4	5.0	-	C	

Rederi AB Sirius, Sweden

Name	Flag	Year	GRT	DWT	Loa	Bm	Draft	Kts	Type	Former names
Sirius	Swe	1970	1,660	2,541	85.9	12.0	4.6		T	ex Picasso-97, Sivona-93, Ekfjord-76, l/aTankfjord (len-71)

Rederi AB Situla, Sweden

Name	Flag	Year	GRT	DWT	Loa	Bm	Draft	Kts	Type	Former names
Situla	Iom	1965	1,049	2,000	69.8	10.4	5.1	11	T	ex Neptun-68 (len-92)

Petter Arnt Slotvik, Norway

Name	Flag	Year	GRT	DWT	Loa	Bm	Draft	Kts	Type	Former names
Seresa	Nor	1969	1,127	818	61.3	11.0	3.9	13	Cp	ex Bronnay-99, Baroy-86 (len-73)

A/S Sol Shipping Co., Latvia

Name	Flag	Year	GRT	DWT	Loa	Bm	Draft	Kts	Type	Former names
Alexandra S	Mlt	1974	2,527	4,040	102.5	13.6	5.6	12	Tch	ex Lucy PG-97, Corrie Broere-88 (len-83)
Elena S	Mlt	1976	2,841	4,443	92.8	14.5	6.8	13	Tch	ex Bras-97, Weelek No.5-95, Ulf-90, Oliver-88, Bras-83
Vadim S	Mlt	1978	4,060	6,863	108.8	11.4	4.0	11	Tch	ex Leticia-97

Johannes Skaten Rederi, Norway

Name	Flag	Year	GRT	DWT	Loa	Bm	Draft	Kts	Type	Former names
Alrita	Nor	1976	559	880	56.1	9.9	3.2	10	C	ex Arnhild-96, Bay Fisher-96, City-95

Skibsaksjelskapet Solvang, Norway

Name	Flag	Year	GRT	DWT	Loa	Bm	Draft	Kts	Type	Former names
New Providence	Lbr	1978	2,313	3,092	75.7	14.0	6.8	13	Lpg	ex Clipper Lady-92, Hestia-88

Solar Schiffahrtsges. & Co. KG, Germany

Name	Flag	Year	GRT	DWT	Loa	Bm	Draft	Kts	Type	Former names
Argonaut	Atg	1978	2,361	2,384	86.5	13.0	4.9	14	Cc	ex Randi-97, Hamilton Trader-92, Alex-89, Lys Calypso-89, Aros Calypso-88, Fjordtrader-86, Aros Calypso-86, Aros Trader-85, Argonaut-83

Rederij Guy Somers, Belgium

Name	Flag	Year	GRT	DWT	Loa	Bm	Draft	Kts	Type	Former names
Manuella	Lux	1988	1,853	3,200	109.7	11.4	3.9	11	Tch	
Equinox	Cyp	1993	5,050	9,431	122.8	16.7	6.8		Tch	
Sam	Cyp	1985	2,054	3,720	110.0	11.4	4.0	11	Tch	ex Inez III-95

C. H. Sorensen Management AS, Norway

Name	Flag	Year	GRT	DWT	Loa	Bm	Draft	Kts	Type	Former names
Viator	Nis	1976	4,845	6,033	106.7	17.0	7.4	14	Lpg	ex Island Gas-96, Boral Gas-82, Hebe-80
Aino	Nis	1977	6,726	6,830	116.5	19.5	7.8	14	Lpg	ex Nestefox-95

Evald Kare Sortland, Norway

Name	Flag	Year	GRT	DWT	Loa	Bm	Draft	Kts	Type	Former names
Eva Merethe	Nor	1971	682	589	54.5	9.5	3.1	11	C	ex With Junior-88, Snertholm-77 (len-83)

Name	Flag	Year	GRT	DWT	Loa	Bm	Draft	Kts	Type	Former names

Sovboptrans Joint Venture, Russia

Name	Flag	Year	GRT	DWT	Loa	Bm	Draft	Kts	Type	Former names
Baltiyskiy-21 (2)	Rus	1964	1,865	2,121	95.6	13.2	3.3	10	C	
Baltiyskiy-68 (2)	Rus	1967	1,865	2,140	95.9	13.2	3.4	10	C	
Burevestnik Revolyutsii (2)	Rus	1968	2,484	3,135	114.2	13.2	3.4	10	C	

Sprante Schiffahrts GmbH & Co. KG, Germany

Name	Flag	Year	GRT	DWT	Loa	Bm	Draft	Kts	Type	Former names
Topaz	Atg	1975	2,999	4,760	88.0	13.0	6.7	12	C	ex Aspen-92

SRAB Shipping AB, Sweden

Name	Flag	Year	GRT	DWT	Loa	Bm	Draft	Kts	Type	Former names
Arctica	Ant	1969	2,518	4,232	98.9	12.5	6.4	12	Ta	ex Arctic 1-94, Otelia-88
Barbara	Mlt	1969	1,611	1,479	77.9	13.0	4.0	12	Cc	ex Barbara-Ann-84
Ara	Mlt	1970	1,939	1,420	76.9	12.9	4.1	13	Cc	ex Janor-95, Ara-93, Sara-86, Ara-85, l/a Schwarzenberg

St. Helier Port Services Ltd., Channel Islands (UK)

Name	Flag	Year	GRT	DWT	Loa	Bm	Draft	Kts	Type	Former names
Ronez	Gbr	1982	870	1,117	64.7	10.1	3.5	10	Ce	

Stabben Junior A/S, Norway

Name	Flag	Year	GRT	DWT	Loa	Bm	Draft	Kts	Type	Former names
Stabben Junior	Nor	1977	1,114	1,570	65.8	10.7	4.3	12	C	ex Margriet-97, Alecto-89, Marjan-86

Stavangerske Linjefart AS, Norway

Name	Flag	Year	GRT	DWT	Loa	Bm	Draft	Kts	Type	Former names
Tungenes (2)	Nis	1979	4,234	3,041	109.0	16.5	4.8	15	Ro	ex Astrea-92, l/a Erik Jarl

A/S Stein Line, Norway

Name	Flag	Year	GRT	DWT	Loa	Bm	Draft	Kts	Type	Former names
Stein Fighter	Nis	1978	2,811	1,640	85.7	13.9	3.9	16	Ro	ex Giovanna Eleonora-94
Steinbjorn	Nis	1973	1,047	1,109	63.6	10.0	3.8	11	Cp	ex Jylland-89 (len-80)

Rederiet Stenersen A/S, Norway

Name	Flag	Year	GRT	DWT	Loa	Bm	Draft	Kts	Type	Former names
Dicksi	Nis	1998	5,685	8,629	115.1	18.3	7.2	15	Tch	
Green Arctic	Nis	1980	2,526	2,725	90.1	15.0	4.5	12	Rc	ex Stenstraum-93, San Carlos-91, Stenstraum-90, Kilstraum-85
Green Frio	Nis	1979	2,249	2,432	81.8	14.2	5.1	14	R	ex Norcan-94

Stjordal Sjotransport AS, Norway

Name	Flag	Year	GRT	DWT	Loa	Bm	Draft	Kts	Type	Former names
Tanja	Nor	1971	689	589	49.6	10.1	2.8	11	Cc	ex Ringhav-95, Tanja-94, Frekoy-93, Tanja-86, Linhav-81, Nesland-74

F. Stolzenberger, Germany

Name	Flag	Year	GRT	DWT	Loa	Bm	Draft	Kts	Type	Former names
Arngast	Deu	1958	833	1,030	61.1	10.1	3.8	10	C	ex Beta-97, Drochtersen-91, Baltica-75, Weser-64

Storfjord Shipping A/S, Norway

Name	Flag	Year	GRT	DWT	Loa	Bm	Draft	Kts	Type	Former names
Faste Jarl	Nor	1967	1,541	1,245	75.9	12.3	3.6	13	C	

Strand Shipping A/S, Norway

Name	Flag	Year	GRT	DWT	Loa	Bm	Draft	Kts	Type	Former names
Lotta	Mlt	1973	1,519	2,178	76.2	11.9	4.8	13	Cc	ex Chiemsea-85, Chiemsee-82
Ranafjord	Mlt	1975	1,656	2,130	75.8	11.9	4.7	11	Cc	ex Hilros-93, Ume-85
Ranosen	Mlt	1975	2,791	3,357	-	-	-	-	Cc	ex Ouezzane-99
Salina *	Mlt	1982	1,895	3,033	83.8	12.6	5.2	11	C	ex Inishark-97, Darell-89 (len-86)

* managed by Rune Jakobsens Rederi A/S, Norway.

Birgir Strom, Denmark

Name	Flag	Year	GRT	DWT	Loa	Bm	Draft	Kts	Type	Former names
Kajama	Dis	1930	263	447	(39.25)	9.7	3.6	7	C	ex Wilfried-64 (deep-53, len-35 & 51)

J. P. Strom, Norway

Name	Flag	Year	GRT	DWT	Loa	Bm	Draft	Kts	Type	Former names
Tello	Nor	1974	1,739	1,175	67.5	12.7	3.7	12	C	ex Nornanborg-85, Lysholmen-80
Tinto	Nor	1975	1,739	1,664	82.5	12.7	3.7	12	C	ex Lysfoss-83 (len-87)
Torello	Nor	1970	1,944	1,402	85.5	12.6	3.6	14	Cp	ex Paper Express-95, Nornews Express-86, Sirius-74 (len-74)

Name	Flag	Year	GRT	DWT	Loa	Bm	Draft	Kts	Type	Former names

Stuwe & Co. Schiffahrts GmbH, Germany
La Rochelle Express	Deu	1975	2,240	2,560	81.4	13.4	5.0	13	Cc	ex Lappland-97, Yankee Clipper-93, Lappland-79, Manchester Falcon-76, I/a Lappland

Sudremex Joint Stock Co., Russia
Yana Komarova (2)	Rus	1966	1,865	2,059	96.0	13.2	3.3	10	C	ex Baltiyskiy-48-98, Wren-94, Baltiyskiy-48-92

Suisse-Outremer Reederei AG, Switzerland
Martin P	Che	1985	4,294	6,328	106.0	16.6	6.9	13	Cc	ex Yunus II-90
Sea Rhine	Bhs	1978	1,475	2,269	69.0	13.5	3.6	9	C	

Sunntrans Holding A/S, Norway
Calypso	Nis	1977	1,104	1,580	65.7	10.8	4.3	-	C	ex Alice-96, Calypso-95
Sea Wave	Nis	1970	1,223	2,020	74.0	10.8	5.1	11	C	ex Alidia-90, Alicia-85, Alicia D-75, Alicia-72

Edvin Svenson Skeppsmakleri AB, Sweden
Ala	Est	1968	1,064	1,203	68.4	10.6	4.0	12	Cc	ex Gala-95, Tor Normandia-77, Gala-76
Dalhem	Pan	1977	2,581	2,937	88.4	15.8	4.9	13	Cc	ex Sabine D-96, Gustav Behrmann-89, Contship Two-79, Gustav Behrmann-77
Wallona	Pan	1967	1,614	2,235	86.8	11.6	5.2		C	(len-74)

Swan Shipping A/S, Norway
Norcliff *	Nis	1995	8,407	5,866	125.3	19.7	6.2	14	Rop	I/a Crown Link
Trans Carrier **	Nis	1994	8,407	6,266	125.0	19.7	6.2	14	Rop	ex Swan Hunter-99, Korsnas Link-94

* managed by Acomarit Services Maritimes SA, Switzerland or ** by Seatrans DA, Norway q.v.

Rederi Swedia AB, Sweden
Vinga Helena	Swe	1985	4,320	6,400	115.0	15.8	7.2	14	Tch	

Swedish Nuclear Fuel & Waste Management AB, Sweden
Sigyn (2)	Swe	1982	4,166	2,044	90.3	18.0	4.0	11	Ron	

Managed by Rederi AB Gotland.

Holger und Herbert Szidat KG, Germany
Holger	Atg	1995	3,999	5,207	101.2	18.5	6.6	15	Cc	ex UB Lion-97, Holger-95
Jana	Atg	1990	3,125	3,070	89.1	16.2	4.8	14	Cc	

Tankafrica SA, France
Tour Margaux	Atf	1992	5,499	9,063	112.0	17.7	8.0	13	Tch	
Tour Prignac	Vct	1981	3,602	6,585	99.9	16.1	7.9	14	Tw	ex Full Cry-84

Rederi AB Tanker Line, Sweden
Alvtank	Swe	1969	1,390	2,456	87.0	12.5	4.3	13	T	ex Neptun-93 (len-75)

Taubatkompaniet Management AS, Norway
Boa Rhino	Nis	1979	2,171	2,700	91.6	14.1	3.5	11	C	ex Rhino-93 (len-83)

Reederei Rainer Tegtmeier, Germany
Henning S	Atg	1989	1,307	1,739	74.9	10.6	3.7	10	C	
Werder Bremen	Atg	1985	1,297	1,529	74.9	10.6	3.4	10	C	

Thibu Shipping Ltd., Netherlands
Kibu	Mlt	1974	2,187	2,180	88.8	12.8	5.2	12	Cc	ex Pootsman Kibus-95, Yunyy Partizan-92

Toostuspanga Liisinguas AS, Estonia
Erne	Est	1965	2,828	3,659	102.3	14.0	5.9	13	C	ex Kaberneeme-96, Nevales-93

Name	Flag	Year	GRT	DWT	Loa	Bm	Draft	Kts	Type	Former names
Odd. H. Torjusen A/S, Sweden										
Nordic Frost	Nis	1973	2,317	1,458	80.4	12.8	4.2	13	Ro	ex Suurlaid-98, Donar-75
Trio	Vct	1965	858	1,006	59.9	9.5	3.9	11	C	ex Arold-95, Horsa-76
Torso Rederi AB, Sweden										
Windia	Swe	1969	1,303	2,226	76.3	11.9	3.9	13	Cc	ex Flensia-95, Eystein-95, Iris I-94, Iris-93, Tor Baltic-76, Iris-75
Trans Marine Bureau Ltd., Estonia										
Fighter	Blz	1971	1,560	1,847	77.9	11.5	4.9	12	C	ex Mohni-97
Kunder	Blz	1970	1,800	2,230	82.0	12.5	5.1	12	C	ex Yakob Kunder-98
Transtor St. Petersburg Agency, Russia										
Cygna (2)	Cyp	1988	1,785	1,776	86.6	12.3	3.0		C	ex Galina-97, Kapitan Palkin-96, ST-1333-??
Tresvik AS, Norway										
Vestvang	Vct	1968	729	1,063	56.7	9.3	3.5	11	C	ex Tevla-91
Trinitas BV, Netherlands										
Trinket	Cyp	1991	1,574	1,890	81.2	11.3	3.6	10	Cc	ex Nessand-94, Hanse Controller-91
Trio's Shipping & Trading AS, Norway										
Ulriken	Nor	1972	1,470	1,626	78.5	11.5	4.4	11	C	(len-75)
Troms Fylkes Dampskibsselskap A/S, Norway										
Bjarkoy	Nis	1997	1,627	2,490	85.3	12.1	4.5	12	T	
Senja	Nor	1997	1,400	1,870	75.6	12.1	4.5	-	T	
Trollskald	Nor	1990	1,280	1,900	65.7	12.0	5.1	11	T	ex Trollshell-92
Egil Ulvan Rederi A/S, Norway										
Mikal With	Nor	1980	1,155	1,183	64.2	11.0	3.8	11	Cp	ex Tresnes-94, Paletten-94
Unicom										
Gornozavodsk	Mlt	1991	3,936	4,168	97.8	17.3	5.6	12	Cc	ex Orient Vigour-97, Gornozavodsk-96, Pudong Express-96, Gornozavodsk-94
Uglegorsk *	Bhs	1990	3,936	4,200	97.8	17.3	5.6	13	C	ex Cam Bubinga Med-96, Uglegorsk-95
Unitas Schiffahrts. GmbH & Co. KG, Germany										
Ady	Atg	1995	2,899	3,950	99.3	16.2	4.9	14	Cc	ex Bell Ady-97
German	Deu	1993	3,585	4,150	99.9	16.3	5.4	15	Cc	ex CMBT Challenge-97, Aquitaine Challenge-96, German-96, Gracechurch Star-95, German-94, Jork-93
Iduna	Deu	1991	3,585	4,150	98.8	16.3	5.4	15	Cc	
A. J. Van der Koog, Netherlands										
Bernice	Nld	1978	1,252	1,623	73.1	11.3	3.4	11	Cs	ex Condor-98
Varm-Dal Marine AB, Sweden										
Mineva	Hnd	1968	1,672	2,658	82.2	13.1	4.9	-	C	ex Nieuwmoer-91, Domino-87, Kortenaer-87, Kortina-85, Kortenaer-84, Hovin-71 (len-73)
Verona	Mlt	1972	1,508	2,315						
Rigina	Vct	1957	792	1,070	59.6	9.6	3.9	10	C	ex Regina-76, Westbris-76, Vedette-76
Rederi AB Veritas Tankers, Sweden										
Astral	Swe	1980	5,127	7,700	114.0	18.3	7.5	-	Tch	ex Eken-96
Avior	Swe	1970	3,264	6,000	98.3	14.4	7.4	12	Tch	ex Ekfjord-88, Amity-77, Pointe du Toulinguet-76, Amity-75, Thuntank 5-72 (deep-77)

212

Name	Flag	Year	GRT	DWT	Loa	Bm	Draft	Kts	Type	Former names

Victor & Family Ltd., Latvia

Name	Flag	Year	GRT	DWT	Loa	Bm	Draft	Kts	Type	Former names
Julia	Blz	1967	2,740	3,930	102.2	14.0	6.2	15	C	ex Lazdijai-98, Lyuban-92
Victor	Lva	1968	2,740	3,930	102.3	14.0	6.0	13	C	ex Birzai-97, Bereznik-91

Voge & Maguire Ltd, UK

Name	Flag	Year	GRT	DWT	Loa	Bm	Draft	Kts	Type	Former names
Geest Atlas	Bmu	1996	2,906	3,950	99.5	16.4	5.0	15	CC	ex Bell Atlas-97

Ernst-August Von Allworden, Germany

Name	Flag	Year	GRT	DWT	Loa	Bm	Draft	Kts	Type	Former names
Joanna Borchard	Deu	1997	6,362	7,200	121.4	18.2	6.7	16	CC	I/a Petuja
Magda	Deu	1995	3,999	5,216	100.6	18.5	6.6	15	Cc	
Rhein Partner	Atg	1994	3,992	5,350	100.0	18.4	6.5	15	C	ex Berolin-98, UB Jaguar-97, Iberian Bridge-96, Berolin-94

Uwe Von Allworden K.G., Germany

Name	Flag	Year	GRT	DWT	Loa	Bm	Draft	Kts	Type	Former names
Andorra	Atg	1984	2,119	3,042	92.1	11.5	4.7	11	Cc	ex Halina-97, Idun-89, Halina-88
Hera	Dnk	1990	2,660	3,240	90.0	13.0	4.6	11	Cc	

Hans-Hinrich Von Ronn, Germany

Name	Flag	Year	GRT	DWT	Loa	Bm	Draft	Kts	Type	Former names
Navigator	Atg	1981	1,811	2,668	78.6	12.8	4.6	10	Cc	

Vortika Shipping Co., Lithuania

Name	Flag	Year	GRT	DWT	Loa	Bm	Draft	Kts	Type	Former names
Sea Walker (2)	Ltu	1968	1,583	2,155	85.1	12.4	3.5	10	C	ex Julius-99, Tuapse-94 (short-94)
Martynas (2)	Ltu	1967	1,583	2,190	85.1	12.4	3.5	10	C	ex Gagra-94 (short-95)

Hans Matthaus Voss, Germany

Name	Flag	Year	GRT	DWT	Loa	Bm	Draft	Kts	Type	Former names
Uppland	Deu	1984	3,093	3,175	95.5	15.2	4.4	12	Cc	ex Karin-92

Rolf Wagle A/S, Norway

Name	Flag	Year	GRT	DWT	Loa	Bm	Draft	Kts	Type	Former names
Carolina	Nis	1972	1,564	1,535	74.9	11.8	3.9	11	C	ex Bellatrix-89, Thies-84
Heidi	Nis	1972	1,391	1,678	76.5	12.0	3.9	12	C	ex Clipper II-86, Silke Riedner-85, Bottensee-81
Henriette	Nis	1971	2,464	2,510	88.5	13.9	6.5	13	Cc	ex Denise-90, Frauden-85, Frauke-81, Comar II-74, Frauke-72
Norunn	Nis	1972	2,586	3,263	90.4	14.8	5.2	14	Cc	Marine Trader-94, Gimo Trader-92, Gimo Celtica-90, Sandnes-90, Ringen-88, Laxfoss-87, Hofsa-86, Bonaventure II-84, Atlantic King-81, Shaikah Al Quraichi-79, Atlantic King-78, Nad King-75, Korneuburg-72
Tone	Nor	1970	1,331	1,430	76.4	11.9	3.6	10	C	ex Conny T-85, Traffic-81, Dynacontainer III-72, I/a Wally Bos

Gisela Waller Bereederung, Germany

Name	Flag	Year	GRT	DWT	Loa	Bm	Draft	Kts	Type	Former names
Martrader	Atg	1982	5,938	7,754	126.5	20.3	6.6	15	CC	ex EWL Venezuela-97, Merzario Francia-91, Premier-91, Woermann Sankura-90, City of Rotterdam-89, Noble-86, sanna-86, Premier-85, Singapore Eagle-85, Premier-82

Thomas Wang A/S, Denmark

Name	Flag	Year	GRT	DWT	Loa	Bm	Draft	Kts	Type	Former names
Trader Bulk	Nor	1978	2,181	3,055	92.0	14.0	5.3	14	C	ex Celtic Challenger-95, Argo Valour-86 (len-97)

Gerhard Warnk GmbH & Co., Germany

Name	Flag	Year	GRT	DWT	Loa	Bm	Draft	Kts	Type	Former names
Alizee	Atg	1982	1,499	1,900	82.5	11.4	3.5	10	Cc	ex Bingum-95, Echo Carrier-90, Bungsberg-90
Suntis	Deu	1985	1,564	1,815	82.5	11.3	3.6	10	Cc	

Name	Flag	Year	GRT	DWT	Loa	Bm	Draft	Kts	Type	Former names

Reederei Weser-Schiffahrts-Agentur GmbH & Co. KG, Germany

Abitibi Claiborne	Deu	1986	7,580	7,879	123.0	20.0	7.4	14	Ccp	ex Weser-Importer-88, Scol Enterprise-87, Weser-Importer-86
Abitibi Orinoco	Deu	1986	7,580	7,875	123.4	20.1	7.4	14	Ccp	ex Weser-Harbour-88, Scol Venture-87, Weser-Harbour-86

AB Westco, Sweden

Lady Bos	Swe	1979	2,141	3,300	80.3	13.9	6.6	13	Cc	

Wenkat Marine BV, Netherlands

West Master	Nis	1972	1,174	1,900	77.3	12.2	4.8	12	Tch	ex Vest Master-99, Fjord Master-97, Fjord Master 1-97, Etilico-95

Seeschiffahrt Andre Wieczorek, Germany

Clara	Atg	1975	1,672	2,130	75.8	11.8	4.7	11	Cc	ex Anita-95, Heide-Catrin-91

Wind Shipping ApS, Denmark

Afrodite *	Vct	1973	2,760	4,954	87.0	13.1	6.8	12	C	ex Alice-93
Conti Blue *	Vct	1972	2,229	3,510	80.5	13.6	6.1	12	C	ex Kutina-90, Super Scan-79
Iris 1	Mlt	1980	1,532	1,478	81.9	10.0	3.6	10	C	ex Fast Sim-97, Opal-92, Larissasee-88

* managed for Overseas Maritimes Services SA, Switzerland.

Rederiet Erik Winther, Denmark

Karen Winther	Dis	1977	3,437	4,100	96.5	16.0	5.6	12	Cc	

Bernd Wittowski, Germany

Sea Elbe	Atg	1986	1,636	1,910	82.5	11.3	3.8	10	Cc	ex Silke-95
Sea Thames	Atg	1985	1,616	1,922	82.5	11.4	3.8	10	Cc	ex Kurt Jensen-94
Sea Weser	Atg	1986	1,616	1,920	82.5	11.3	3.8	10	Cc	ex Jan Meeder-97

Reederei Hermann Wulff, Germany

Tugela	Lbr	1985	8,643	9,327	133.4	21.8	7.6	17	CC	ex Guatemala-99, Ridge-93, Kalkara-93, John Wulff-87, Maersk Jakarta-87, Maersk Pinto-87, John Wulff-86, Ville de Nadir-86, I/a John Wulff

Yenisei River Shipping Co., Russia

Igarka (2)	Rus	1986	2,426	2,500	108.4	15.0	2.8	10	Cc	ex Omskiy-36-92
Ivan Yarygin (2)	Rus	1975	2,463	2,834	108.4	14.8	3.0	10	C	ex Omskiy 6-98
Krasnoyarsk (2)	Rus	1971	2,457	3,190	114.0	13.2	3.6	10	C	ex 350 Let Gorodo Krasnoyarskogo-??, Volgo Balt-143-71
Mekhanik Vakutin (2)	Rus	1975	3,994	3,775	136.8	16.7	2.8	11	C	ex Volgo-Don 5062-??
Neva (2)	Rus	1987	1,497	1,669	82.0	11.6	3.3	11	Cc	ex STK-1030-92
Nikolay Psomiadiy (2)	Rus	1986	2,426	2,500	108.4	15.0	2.8	-	C	ex Omskiy-35-91
Okhta (2)	Rus	1977	3,463	5,217	132.6	16.9	3.1	10	T	ex Volgoeft-133-??
Pushkino (2)	Rus	1963	1,652	2,064	103.6	12.4	2.8	10	C	
Yenisey (2)	Rus	1988	1,497	1,669	82.0	11.6	3.3	11	Cc	ex STK-1032-92

Other vessels - 15 dry cargo and 1 tanker not listed.

John Ytreland, Norway

Rytind	Nor	1971	1,732	2,088	76.5	12.0	4.2	-	Cc	ex Pike-87, Alandsea-85, Alandzee-83, Alandsee-82 (len-94)

Karl-Heinz Zalewski, Germany

Bianca	Atg	1972	1,934	1,531	77.0	13.0	3.9	13	Cc	ex Atria-86

Zegluga Gdanska, Poland

Laila	Pol	1977	681	1,067	62.2	9.5	3.0	10	C	ex Stera-98, Stern-92, Marco-84

214

Name	Flag	Year	GRT	DWT	Loa	Bm	Draft	Kts	Type	Former names

Reederei Horst Zeppenfeld G.m.b.H. & Co. K.G., Germany

Name	Flag	Year	GRT	DWT	Loa	Bm	Draft	Kts	Type	Former names
Asia Feeder	Lbr	1999	6,246	7,233	121.9	18.6	7.3	-	CC	
Lauritzen Chile	Lbr	1997	6,246	7,233	121.9	18.6	7.3	-	CC	
Sea Racer	Lbr	1993	5,999	6,886	121.0	18.6	6.6	10	CC	

Managed by Reederei Navylloyd A.G., Switzerland.

Zirkel Verwaltungs GmbH, Germany

Name	Flag	Year	GRT	DWT	Loa	Bm	Draft	Kts	Type	Former names
Hunte	Atg	1980	1,710	1,644	71.4	12.8	3.9	11	Cc	ex Frey-90
Tainui	Atg	1993	2,410	3,300	85.4	12.6	5.2	13	Cc	

INDEX

Ferries

Coastal Vessels

Name	Page
40 Let Pobedy	160
A. Wetzel	168
A.B.Amsterdam	64
A.B.Bilbao	64
A.B.Dublin	64
A.B.Liverpool	64
A.B.Lubeck	64
A.B.Valencia	64
Aaltje-Jacoba	164
Aasfjord	150
Aasland	150
Aastind	150
Aastun	150
Aasvaer	150
Ability	85
Abitibi Claiborne	214
Abitibi Orinoco	214
Abruka	84
Achatina	136
Addi L	108
Adelaide	98
Adele	140
Admiral	194
Adra	104
Adriana	164
Adriane	202
Adriatic	135
Ady	212
Afrodite	214
Agatha	80
Agila	113
Agility	85
Agnes	102
Ahlers Belgica	50
Ahrenshoop	207
Aida	80
Aila	81
Aino	209
Ajos G	194
Akershus	182
Aksai	160
Akvile	113
Ala	211
Alacrity	85
Aladin	167
Albenny	136
Albis	132
Alblas	127
Alcoa Chemist	82
Aldebaren	172
Aldeboorn	52
Aldrington	142
Alegra	203
Alegre Feeder	138
Aleksandr Grin	120
Aleksandr Marinesko	160
Aleksandr Shotman	171
Aleksey Afanasjev	171
Alert	62
Aletis	140
Alexander Kuprin	120
Alexander Tvardovskiy	120
Alexandra S	180
Alexandra S	209
Alexandre	180
Alexandria	80
Alexis	174
Algirdas	113
Algol	133
Ali Baba	167
Alice PG	74
Alina	80
Alissa	116
Alizee	213
Alk	184
Alka II	100
Alliance	184
Allora	188
Almania	206
Almenum	128
Alondra	140
Alpha	133
Alphagas	138
Alpine Girl	200
Alpine Lady	200
Alrek	113
Alrita	209
Alstergas	50
Alstern	50
Alta Mar	68
Altar	149
Alteland	127
Alteland	197
Altona	148
Alvina M.	58
Alvtank	211
Amarant	150
Ambassadeur	164
Amber I	84
Amber II	84
Amber	150
Ambience	75
Amelia	140
Amenity	85
Ametist	150
Amisia J	106
Amity	85
Amoria	138
Amrum Trader	72
Amstelborg	164
Amsteldiep	98
Amur-2501	171
Amur-2502	162
Amur-2503	162
Amur-2504	171
Amur-2505	171
Amur-2506	171
Amur-2507	120
Amur-2508	162
Amur-2509	171
Amur-2510	120
Amur-2511	152
Amur-2512	170
Amur-2513	170
Amur-2514	120
Amur-2515	171
Amur-2517	171
Amur-2518	121
Amur-2519	162
Amur-2520	120
Amur-2521	120
Amur-2522	171
Amur-2523	162
Amur-2524	170
Amur-2525	120
Amur-2526	121
Amur-2527	120
Amur-2528	171
Amur-2531	171
Amur-2532	170
Amur-2537	121
Amur-2540	171
Amy	164
Ana Safi	182
Anchorman	86
Anders Rousing	207
Andor	171
Andorra	213
Andra	193
Andrea	149
Andreas Boye	66
Andries	173
Andrina F	189
Anette Theresa	100
Anette	102
Angela J	106
Angelburg	136
Angermanland	178
Anglia	204
Anglia	78
Anglia	80
Angus Express	162
Angus	88
Ania B	182
Anita B	61
Anita	180
Anja	114
Anja C	74
Anja Funk	190
Anja II	62
Anjola	144
Anke Bettina	66
Anke-Angela	204
Anna Meryl	110
Anna Theresa	154
Anna-Lina	192
Annamaria	187
Anne Boye	66
Anne Catharina	205
Anne Sif	107
Anne Sofie	189
Anne Timber	58
Anne	80
Annegret	192
Annegret	98
Annette-J	130
Annika-M	130
Annlen-G	68
Anntoro	136
Annuity	85
Antarctic	135
Antares	133
Antares	197
Antares	52
Antigua	88
Antigua	135
Antilla	135
Antina	80
Antje	134
Anto	200
Anton	182
Antonia B	170
Antonina II	61
Antwerpen	156
Apache	56
Apody	178
Apollo Eagle	134
Apollo Hawk	199
Apollo	182
Apuole	113
Apus	133
Aquamarine	136
Aquarius	128
Aquatic	76
Aqueduct	76
Ara	210
Arabella C	126
Arcadian Faith	147
Arcadian Sky	147
Arco Adur	94
Arco Arun	94
Arco Avon	94
Arco Axe	94
Arco Beck	94
Arco Bourne	94
Arco Dart	94
Arco Dee	94
Arco Dijk	94
Arco Humber	94
Arco Severn	94
Arco Thames	94
Arco Trent	94
Arco Tyne	94
Arctic Ocean	149
Arctic Swan	118
Arctic	135
Arctica	210
Ardent	154
Ardua	193
Arena	207
Argonaut	100
Argonaut	209
Ariana	186
Arianta	138
Arina Arctica	207
Arion	112
Arion	164
Aristaios	194
Arklow Bay	152
Arklow Bridge	152
Arklow Brook	152
Arklow Castle	152
Arklow Faith	152
Arklow Fame	154
Arklow Fortune	154
Arklow Freedom	154
Arklow Manor	154
Arklow Marsh	154
Arklow Meadow	154
Arklow Mill	154
Arklow Moor	154
Arklow Sand	154
Arklow Sea	154
Arklow Spirit	154
Arklow Spray	154
Arklow Vale	154
Arklow Valley	154
Arklow Valour	154
Arklow Venture	154
Arklow View	154
Arklow Viking	154
Arklow Villa	154
Arktis Atlantic	80
Arktis Blue	80
Arktis Breeze	80
Arktis Carrier	80
Arktis Crystal	81
Arktis Dream	81
Arktis Faith	81
Arktis Fantasy	81
Arktis Fighter	81
Arktis Force	81
Arktis Future	81
Arktis Grace	81
Arktis Hope	81
Arktis Hunter	81
Arktis Light	81
Arktis Mariner	81
Arktis Mayflower	81
Arktis Meadow	81
Arktis Meridian	81
Arktis Mermaid	81
Arktis Mirage	81
Arktis Morning	81
Arktis Ocean	81
Arktis Pearl	81
Arktis Pride	81
Arktis Princess	81
Arktis Queen	81
Arktis River	81
Arktis Sea	81
Arktis Sirius	81
Arktis Sky	81
Arktis Spring	81
Arktis Trader	81
Arktis Venture	81
Arktis Vision	81
Arnarfell	126
Arneb	194
Arngast	210
Arnold Ikkonen	122
Aros News	66
Arosette	206
Arosia	200
Arrow	62
Artemis I	184
Artemis	92
Aruba	135
Aruba	200
Arula	84
Arunto	144
Arvin	171
Ashington	142
Asia Feeder	215
Asiatic	135
Askania	178
Askholm	75
Asperity	85
Aspia	82
Asprella	138
Asseburg	136
ASSI Euro Link	164
ASSI Scan Link	164
Assiduus	80
Asta	113
Aston Prelude	182
Astor S	144
Astra	52
Astral	212
Astrid Bres	117
Atair	133
Athens	62
Atlantic	146
Atlantic Bay	124
Atlantic Coast	124
Atlantic Comet	124
Atlantic Ice	135
Atlantic Island	124
Atlantic Moon	124
Atlantic River	124
Atlantik	134
Atlantis	76
Atlas S	144
Atlas	193
Atria	167
Atrice	134
Atula	184
Audacity	85
Audre	113
Aukse	113
Auldyn River	200
Aunborg	164
Aura	200
Aurelia	80
Auriga	54
Aurora	124
Austvik	144
Authenticity	85
Autocarrier	155
Autofreighter	155
Autoline	155
Autopremier	155
Autoprestige	155
Autopride	155
Autoprogress	155
Autoracer	155
Autoroute	155
Autorunner	155
Autotransporter	155
Avaloni	194
Avant	144
Averity	85
Avior	212
Avon 1	186
Aztek	56
Azur	144
Baccara	66
Bakhtemir	160
Bakkafoss	102
Balbao	180
Balina	102
Baltic	188
Baltic Breeze	52
Baltic Bright	185
Baltic Carrier	127
Baltic Champ	90
Baltic Courier	90
Baltic Horizon	110
Baltic Ice	135
Baltic Link	164
Baltic Merchant	127
Baltic Meteor	90
Baltic News	136
Baltic Press	182
Baltic Print	182
Baltic Sailor	127
Baltic Sea	208
Baltic Sif	107
Baltic Skipper	127
Baltic Sprinter	90
Baltic Swan	120
Baltic Tern	167
Baltica	201
Balticborg	164
Baltimar Boreas	60
Baltimar Neptune	60
Baltimar Nereus	60
Baltimar Notos	60
Baltimar Okeanos	60
Baltimar Orion	60
Baltimar Saturn	60
Baltimar Sirus	60
Baltimar Venus	60
Baltiyskiy-5	171
Baltiyskiy-6	171
Baltiyskiy-9	171
Baltiyskiy-21	210
Baltiyskiy-38	182
Baltiyskiy-40	202
Baltiyskiy-55	152
Baltiyskiy-56	171
Baltiyskiy-59	171
Baltiyskiy-62	170
Baltiyskiy-66	171
Baltiyskiy-68	210
Baltiyskiy-69	171
Baltiyskiy-101	171
Baltiyskiy-102	120
Baltiyskiy-103	171
Baltiyskiy-105	171
Baltiyskiy-106	54
Baltiyskiy-107	120
Baltiyskiy-108	171
Baltiyskiy-109	171
Baltiyskiy-110	120
Baltiyskiy-111	171
Baltiyskiy-201	120
Baltiyskiy-202	120
Banjaard	128
Banwell	76
Barbara	210
Barbara	70
Bardsey	75
Barenso	183
Barentsee	167
Barentzgracht	142
Barmouth	76
Barten	72
Bas	183
Bassma	56
Bataafgracht	142
Batavier VI	208
Batavier VII	128
Batavier	164
Baumwall	123
Baumwall	127
Bavaria	68
Beate	199
Beatrixhaven	156
Beaulieu	186
Becquer	112
Begona B	173
Bella I	192
Bellini	90
Bellona	200
Beluga Spirit	112
Ben Ellan	206
Ben Flor	134

Name	No.
Hoocrest	110
Hoopride	110
Hope	205
Hordafor Pilot	194
Hordnes	174
Horizon	122
Hornbaltic	194
Hornestrand	128
Hornfels	194
Houtmangracht	142
Hubro	176
Hudsongracht	142
Huelin Dispatch	194
Huemmling	74
Hugo	184
Humber Arm	56
Humber Dawn	186
Humber Endeavour	170
Humber Fisher	86
Humber Pride	170
Humber Princess	170
Humber Progress	170
Humber Star	170
Humber Transporter	170
Humbergracht	142
Hunte	215
Hunter	144
Husnes	174
Husum	147
Hvitanes	126
Hydra J.	106
Hydra	166
Hydrobulk	102
Hydrogas	102
Hydrogas II	102
Hydrogas III	102
Iberian Coast	173
Iberian Ocean	174
Ibiza	66
Ice Bird	55
Ice Crystal	55
Ice Express	162
Ice Field	55
Ice Star	149
Ice Star	55
Ida Rambow	166
Ida Wonsild	176
Iduna	212
Igarka	214
Iglo Express	162
Igor Grabar	122
Iida	58
Ijsseldiep	98
Ijssellborg	166
Ikiena	94
Ilka	148
Ilona G	193
Ilona Theresa	154
Ilse	188
Ina Lehmann	113
Inca	147
Indian	114
Indianapolis	155
Industrial Ace	81
Industrial Alliance	68
Industrial Beacon	193
Industrial Caribe	81
Industrial Carrier	60
Industrial Explorer	68
Industrial Frontier	81
Industrial Harmony	68
Industrial Leader	66
Industrial Millenium	104
Industrial Pioneer	81
Inga	70
Ingelore	130
Inger	173
Ingrid Maria	202
Ingrid	191
Inka Dede	186
Inna	60
Innes	88
Inno	183
Innsbruck	126
Irena Arctica	207
Irene Wonsild	176
Irene	185
Irina Trader	60
Irina	173
Irish Rose	162
Irishgate	86
Iris-Jorg	196
Irlo	132
Irmgard	148
Irtysh 1	195
Irtysh 2	195
Isabel	173
Isabella 1	203
Isargas	96
Isartal	193
Isebek	197
Ishim	123
Isis	180
Isnes	64
Itasca	166
Ivan Derbenev	181
Ivan Gorthon	56
Ivan Kulibin	162
Ivan Ryabov	122
Ivan Shadr	122
Ivan Shchepetov	160
Ivan Yarygin	214
Ivy	181
Izhora	123
Jacaranda	66
Jacob Becker	183
Jacobus Broere	72
Jacqueline	133
Jade	133
Jadegas	96
Jaguar	146
Jaguar	166
Jakarta Star	124
Jakob Kosan	112
Jamtland	180
Jan Fabian	61
Jan V	130
Jana	211
Jan-Dirk	198
Janet C	74
Janna	194
Janne Wonsild	176
Janra	123
Jan-Rasmus	62
Jan-Willem	188
Jarama	155
Jarikaba	86
Jason	166
Jaynee W	170
Jenbo	92
Jenclipper	92
Jenka	92
Jenlil	92
Jenna Catherine	70
Jens Munk	128
Jens R	133
Jens	133
Jerome H	112
Jersbek	197
Jessica	178
Jessica	132
Jessica	182
Jo Hassel	135
Jo Hegg	204
Jo Maple	204
Jo Palm	204
Jo Spirit	204
Joanna Borchard	213
Johann	66
Johanna C	74
Johanna Trader	56
Johanna	116
John C. Helmsing	98
Joint Frost	135
Jolanda	132
Jonas	74
Jonrix	132
Jose Maria	197
Jotunheim	201
Judith Borchard	174
Julia Isabel	168
Julia	213
Julie	104
Jumbo	58
Jumbo Challenger	107
Jumbo Spirit	107
Jummegas	96
Jumper	144
Jupiter	127
Jupiter	112
Jupiter	192
Juris Avots	110
Justo	176
Juto	200
Jutta-B	184
Kaaksburg	136
Kaapgracht	142
Kaban	149
Kagu	191
Kai	192
Kaja-H	205
Kajama	210
Kajen	127
Kalana	84
Kalevala	171
Kambo	176
Kamilla	187
Kapella	192
Kapitan Babushkin	160
Kapitan Drobinin	122
Kapitan Ezovitov	160
Kapitan Glotov	122
Kapitan Gusev	170
Kapitan Kuroptev	122
Kapitan Lus	122
Kapitan Manaseyev	171
Kapitan Mironov	122
Kapitan Ponomarev	122
Kapitan Torsukov	160
Kapitan Yakovlev	122
Kapten	84
Kapten Konga	84
Kapten Voolens	84
Karen Clipper	196
Karen Winther	214
Karin B	126
Karin Cat	128
Karin	114
Karin	200
Karina Danica	88
Karina W	149
Karl Leonhardt	198
Karmsund	207
Kasira	110
Kasla	52
Kassari	84
Kasteelborg	166
Katharina B	147
Katharina Ehler	187
Katharina Siemer	209
Katharina	207
Katherine Borchard	197
Katholm	75
Kati K	60
Katja	94
Katrin	127
Kay L	112
KB II	196
Keizersborg	166
Keizersgracht	142
Kelarvi	171
Kells	88
Kemira	189
Kenmare	88
Kento	171
Keret	171
Kernave	113
Kerry Express	162
Kerstin	205
Kessma	56
Ketty Brovig	184
Key	100
Kibu	211
Kiefernwald	58
Kielgracht	142
Kilchem Mediterranean	107
Kilchem Acid	107
Kilchem Adriatic	107
Kilchem Baltic	107
Kilchem Biscay	107
Kilchem Bothnia	107
Kilchem Caribbean	107
Kilchem Labrador	107
Kilchem Navigator	107
Kilchem Oceania	107
Kilgas Champion	107
Kilgas Commander	107
Kilgas Crusader	107
Kilgas Discovery	107
Killarney	88
Kilstraum	156
Kim	128
Kim	92
Kindrence	76
Kinsale	88
Kinso	176
Kirre	207
Kirsten	173
Kirsten	62
Kirsten	80
Kis Sobye	186
Kish	180
Kista Arctica	207
Kivach	171
Kizhi	171
Klaas I	156
Klazina C	74
Klenoden	82
Klevstrand	181
Klintholm	75
Klippergracht	142
Klostertal	126
KML Carus	183
Knud Kosan	112
Koerier	54
Koggegracht	142
Koida	122
Kolguev	121
Komandor	198
Komarno	168
Komet	116
Komet III	191
Komet	60
Komponists Caikovskis	110
Konda	197
Kongsdal	180
Kongsholm	75
Kongstind	181
Koningsborg	166
Koningsgracht	142
Koningshaven	182
Konstantin Paustovskiy	120
Konstantin Yuon	122
Kopenhagen	66
Kopersand	68
Koralia	84
Koralle	144
Koriangi	171
Kormoran	196
Korni	199
Korsholm	75
Korsika	66
Korsnes	206
Koscierzyna	127
Kosterberg	158
Kotlas	122
Kovera	171
Krasnovidovo	160
Krasnoyarsk	214
Krasnyi Aksay	162
Kreva	113
Kronholm	75
Kronoborg	88
Kroonborg	166
K-Toulson	76
Kunder	212
Kurkse	84
Kylemore	88
Kyst	206
La Bonita	135
La Minera	135
La Rochelle Express	211
Ladoga-1	120
Ladoga-2	120
Ladoga-3	60
Ladoga-5	60
Ladoga-6	120
Ladoga-8	60
Ladoga-11	120
Ladoga-12	120
Ladoga-13	120
Ladoga-14	120
Ladoga-15	120
Ladoga-16	120
Ladoga-17	120
Ladoga-18	120
Ladoga-19	120
Ladoga-101	120
Ladoga-102	120
Ladoga-103	120
Ladoga-104	120
Ladoga-105	120
Ladoga-106	120
Ladoga-107	120
Ladoga-108	120
Ladon	166
Ladva	171
Lady Anna	158
Lady Bos	214
Lady Camilla	176
Lady Clara	158
Lady Elena	76
Lady Elsie	167
Lady Greta	158
Lady Hilde	76
Lady Kathleen	76
Lady Linda	158
Lady Lisa	158
Lady Martine	76
Lady Rea	167
Lady Serena	167
Lady Sophia	167
Lady Stephanie	76
Lady Sylvia	167
Lagarfoss	104
Lagik	199
Laguna	76
Laila	185
Laila	214
Lake Pejo	207
Lamaro	199
Langefoss	117
Langeland	117
Langesund	117
Lani	84
Lanrick	55
Laola	85
Lappland	193
Largo	58
Largo II	133
Largona	133
Larita	199
Lark	70
Lars Bagger	183
Larvikstone	156
Lasbek	197
Lass Mars	178
Lass Moon	178
Lass Neptun	178
Lass Saturn	178
Lass Uranus	178
Lauenburg	76
Laura	82
Laura Christina	135
Laura I	187
Laura Kosan	112
Laura	192
Lauriergracht	142
Laurina-Neeltje	54
Laurits Kosan	112
Lauritzen Chile	215
Lava	170
Le Castellet	155
Lea	100
Lebasee	152
Lech	126
Ledagas	96
Lee Frances	158
Leerort	147
Leeswig	116
Lehola	84
Leiro	176
Leja	181
Leliegracht	142
Leman IV	82
Lemmergracht	142
Lena S	208
Lena	192
Lena	98
Lengai	98
Lenie	202
Leninskiy Komsomol	160
Leo	110
Leona	70
Leonard	198
Leonid Bykov	116
Leonid Leonov	120
Leonie	166
Leopard	146
Lerrix	132
Lesley PG	74
Leszek G	190
Lette Lill	66
Levantgracht	142
Lever	187
Leysand	68
Lezhevo	171
Liban Car	56
Libra	58
Lida	158
Lidan	149
Lidia V	182
Lidiya	181
Lifana	133
Liftmar	194
Ligo	120
Lijnbaansgracht	142
Lille-Tanja	186
Lillgard	82
Lima Chemist	84
Lima	147
Linda	82
Linda Buck	185
Linda Kosan	112
Linda Marijke	173
Linden	208
Lindengracht	142
Lindholm	66
Lindo	176
Lingegas	140
Linito	64
Link Star	92
Linz	126
Lion	146
Lis Weber	66
Lisa Lehmann	113
Lisa	128
Lisa	52
Lisbeth C	126
Lissa	100
Listerland	200
Listraum	156
Livarden	181

Name	Page
Torrent	154
Tour Margaux	211
Tour Prignac	211
Toyvo Vyakhya	172
Trader Bulk	203
Trader Bulk	213
Tramp	60
Trans Arctic	136
Trans Baltic	136
Trans Borg	196
Trans Carrier	211
Trans Chemica	136
Trans Dania	136
Trans Fennia	136
Trans Fjell	136
Trans Holm	136
Trans Nes	136
Trans Nordia	136
Trans Scandic	136
Trans Sea	136
Trans Sund	136
Trans Tind	136
Trans Vag	136
Trans Vik	136
Transgard	102
Transmar	96
Transmare	128
Transportor	74
Traquair	55
Traveberg	58
Trenden	82
Trent	186
Tri Box	186
Tri Frakt	207
Trina	98
Trinket	212
Trio	212
Tri-Sky	189
Triton Elbe	152
Triton Loga	152
Triton	62
Triumph	62
Trobo	176
Trollnes	174
Trollskald	212
Trones	174
Troubadour	128
Trout	75
Truco	202
Truro	176
Tucana	133
Tudor	130
Tugela	214
Tulos	172
Tungenes	210
Turbulence	76
Turi	100
Twaite	75
Tyne Fisher	86
Tyr	98
Tyro	135
Tysso	176
UAL Africa	98
UAL Angola	98
UAL Texas	148
Uglegorsk	212
Ulla	187
Ullswater	135
Ulriken	212
Ulsund	196
Ultramar	96
Umba	122
Unden	50
Unicom Gornozavodsk	212
Unika	193
Union Arbo	154
Union Elisabeth	154
Union Jupiter	155
Union Mars	155
Union Moon	155
Union Neptune	155
Union Pearl	155
Union Pluto	155
Union Robin	155
Union Sun	155
Union Titan	155
Union Topaz	155
Union Venus	155
United Nadja	72
United Nelly	72
United Nora	72
United Tony	72
Universal 1	121
Unkas	56
Uno	100
Uphusen	64
Uppland	213
Urania	149
Uranus	112
Uranus	75
Urgence	76
Ursula B	133
Ursula C	126
Ursula Leonhardt	198
Urte	144
Ust-Kut	196
Ute Johanna	70
Ute	134
Utturn	64
Uwe Ursula	184
Vadim S	209
Vagay	197
Vahalis	54
Vaida	84
Vaindlo	54
VAL Rooach	106
Valdai	172
Valentin Pikul	121
Valga	84
Valiant	62
Valkla	85
Valmin	142
Van Lang	108
Vanerland	70
Vanessa C	74
Vanessa	196
Vanguard	106
Varmland	195
Vasiliy Malov	121
Vasiliy Shukshin	121
Vastanvik	185
Vastsjo	204
Vechtborg	166
Vectis Falcon	74
Vectis Isle	74
Vedette	62
Veerseborg	166
Vega	54
Veliuona	113
Velox	62
Vento di Ponente	74
Vento di Tramontana	108
Ventspils	110
Vera Mukhina	122
Vera	206
Verdi	90
Verena B	147
Verena	173
Veritas	116
Veritas H	194
Veritas	54
Verona	212
Verona	64
Vest	75
Vestanhav	149
Vesting	54
Vestland	189
Vestvang	212
Viator	209
Vibrence	76
Victor	213
Victoria	176
Victress	64
Viditsa	172
Vigsnes	150
Vikanes	208
Viking Sky	203
Vikingbank	54
Vikla	117
Vikstraum	156
Viktor Koryakin	122
Viljandi	85
Villach	126
Ville de Damiette	108
Ville de Mijo	196
Vilsandi	85
Vinga Helena	211
Vinga	195
Vinland Saga	85
Vios	173
Virgo Gas 1	112
Virgo	191
Virtsu	85
Viscaria	180
Viscount	64
Vissorbank	166
Vistafjord	206
Visten	50
Visurgis	132
Vita	126
Vitoria Nova	206
Vitorino Nemesio	76
Vitta Theresa	100
Vivaldi	104
Vladimir Filkov	116
Vlieborg	166
Vlieland	128
Vlistborg	166
Voke	113
Volga	172
Volga-35	160
Volga-4002	172
Volga-4003	121
Volga-4004	172
Volga-4006	172
Volga-4007	55
Volga-4008	121
Volga-4009	55
Volga-4011	55
Volgo-Balt 102	181
Volgo-Balt 107	181
Volgo-Balt 116	202
Volgo-Balt 118	190
Volgo-Balt 121	181
Volgo-Balt 126	121
Volgo-Balt 131	121
Volgo-Balt 150	202
Volgo-Balt 153	122
Volgo-Balt 171	184
Volgo-Balt 177	172
Volgo-Balt 188	172
Volgo-Balt 190	121
Volgo-Balt 191	172
Volgo-Balt 192	170
Volgo-Balt 193	172
Volgo-Balt 194	172
Volgo-Balt 195	172
Volgo-Balt 196	172
Volgo-Balt 199	172
Volgo-Balt 200	172
Volgo-Balt 202	172
Volgo-Balt 203	172
Volgo-Balt 204	121
Volgo-Balt 205	172
Volgo-Balt 206	172
Volgo-Balt 208	172
Volgo-Balt 209	152
Volgo-Balt 210	152
Volgo-Balt 213	172
Volgo-Balt 214	172
Volgo-Balt 215	121
Volgo-Balt 216	172
Volgo-Balt 217	180
Volgo-Balt 219	172
Volgo-Balt 220	172
Volgo-Balt 223	172
Volgo-Balt 226	172
Volgo-Balt 227	172
Volgo-Balt 228	172
Volgo-Balt 229	172
Volgo-Balt 230	172
Volgo-Balt 231	172
Volgo-Balt 232	172
Volgo-Balt 234	162
Volgo-Balt 235	172
Volgo-Balt 236	172
Volgo-Balt 237	172
Volgo-Balt 238	121
Volgo-Balt 239	172
Volgo-Balt 240	172
Volgo-Balt 241	162
Volgo-Balt 243	170
Volgo-Balt 244	170
Volgo-Balt 245	172
Volgo-Balt 246	122
Volgo-Balt 247	162
Volgo-Balt 248	162
Volgo-Don 5035	202
Volzhskiy 10	160
Volzhskiy-32	116
Volzhskiy-35	116
Volzhskiy-37	116
Volzhskiy-38	116
Vomero	201
Voorneborg	166
Voronezh	162
Vorotynsk	197
Voyager	54
Vuoksa	123
Vyborgskaya Storona	123
Vyg	172
Vytautas	113
Wachau	126
Waddens	62
Waddenzee	128
Wahlstedt	116
Waldtraut B	64
Walker	144
Waliona	211
Walsertal	126
Walter Hammann	94
Wangeroege	70
Wani Logger	203
Warber	54
Warfleth	184
Warfsum	128
Warka	128
Wasaborg	88
Waseberg	158
Washington	142
Waterman	166
Waterway	78
Wear Fisher	86
Weisa	199
Wejherowo	128
Welsh Piper	132
Werder Bremen	211
Werfen	127
Weser	70
Wesergas	50
Weserstern	207
West Master	214
West Sky	205
West Stream	156
West Trader	52
Wester Till	152
Western Trader	74
Westgate	86
Westwind	58
Whestgate	202
Whitank	170
Whitask	170
Whitcrest	170
White Sea	114
Whitesnow	123
Whithaven	170
Whitide	170
Whitkirk	170
Whitmariner	170
Whitonia	170
Whitsea	170
Whitspray	170
Whitstar	170
Widor	130
Wiebke D	133
Wiebke K	110
Wiebke	98
Wielun	128
Wightstone	123
Wijmers	185
Wilhelmine Steffens	94
Wilke	70
Willem Sr.	167
Willy II	116
Willy	116
Willy	198
Wilma	158
Wilma	98
Winden	82
Windfjord	114
Windia	212
Windsor	172
Winsum	128
Wirdum	64
Wisida Arctic	82
Wittenbergen	168
Wolthusen	64
Wotan	70
Wyszkow	128
Xandrina	80
Yana Komarova	211
Yarrow	55
Yekaterina Belashova	122
Yenisey	214
Yeoman Rose	194
Yvette	61
Zamoscvorechye	123
Zebu Express	162
Zephyr	75
Zetagas	140
Zeus	112
Zeus	167
Zgorzelec	128
Zillertal	127
Zim Caribe 1	80
Zim Espana	130
Znamya Oktyabrya	160
Zug	127
Zuiderzee	167
Zuppert	127
Zurs	127
Zwanet	199
Zwartemeer	167
Zwartewater	128